Look for these Other Craftmaster books by McGraw-Hill

Ammen ■ *Metalcasting*
Geary ■ *Welding*

LOCKSMITHING

Bill Phillips

McGraw-Hill

New York   San Francisco   Washington, D.C.   Auckland   Bogotá
Caracas   Lisbon   London   Madrid   Mexico City   Milan
Montreal   New Delhi   San Juan   Singapore
Sydney   Tokyo   Toronto

Library of Congress Cataloging-in-Publication Data

Phillips, Bill, 1960-
  Locksmithing / Bill Phillips.
    p. cm.
  Rev. ed of: Professional locksmithing techniques, 2nd., ©1996.
  ISBN 0-07-134436-5
    1. Locksmithing. I. Phillips, Bill, 1960– Professional
locksmithing techniques. II. Title.
  TS520. P545 1999
  683'.3—dc21   99-34586
                                                      CIP

McGraw-Hill

A Division of The McGraw·Hill Companies

This book was published previously under the title *Professional Locksmithing Techniques*, Second Edition.

1 2 3 4 5 6 7 8 9 0 AGM/AGM 9 0 4 3 2 1 0 9

ISBN 0-07-134436-5

The sponsoring editor for this book was Zoe G. Foundatos, the editing supervisor was Frank Kotowski, Jr., and the production supervisor was Pamela A. Pelton. It was set in Melior per the CMS design by Joanne Morbit and Paul Scozzari of McGraw-Hill's Professional Book Group composition unit in Hightstown, N.J.

Printed and bound by Quebecor/Martinsburg.

 This book is printed on recycled, acid-free paper containing a minimum of 50% recycled de-inked fiber.

McGraw-Hill books are available at special quantity discounts to use as premiums and sales promotions, or for use in corporate training programs. For more information, please write to the Director of Special Sales, McGraw-Hill, 11 West 19th Street, New York, NY 10011. Or contact your local bookstore.

For Merlin and Ondra (HAH, HMB)

CONTENTS

Acknowledgments   xiii

Introduction   xv

Chapter 1   **The Business of Locksmithing**   1

Recent Changes to the Business   2

Learning the Business   3

Employment Options   5

Chapter 2   **Basic Types of Locks and Keys**   9

Terminology   9

Types of Keys   14

Chapter 3   **Key Blanks and Key Blank Directories**   23

Choosing the Right Blank   23

Key Blank Directories   28

Cutting Keys by Hand   37

Chapter 4   **Warded, Lever Tumbler, Disc Tumbler, and Side Bar Wafer Locks**   43

Warded Locks   43

Lever Tumbler Locks   47

Disc Tumbler Locks   49

Side Bar Wafer Locks   52

Chapter 5	**Pin Tumbler Locks**	**53**
	Parts	55
	Operation	55
	Repairs	55
	Tubular Key Locks	59
Chapter 6	**Locksmithing Tools**	**61**
	Electric Drill	62
	Cordless Drill	65
	Broken-Key Extractor	65
	Plug Follower	65
	Plug Holder	66
	Tool Lists	66
Chapter 7	**Key-In-Knob, Deadbolt, and Cylinder Key Mortise Locks**	**83**
	Handing of Doors	83
	Key-In-Knob Locks	84
	Deadbolt Locks	86
	Cylinder Key Mortise Locks	86
Chapter 8	**High-Security Cylinders**	**113**
	The CorKey System	113
	DOM IX KG System Cylinder	119
	Kaba Gemini	121
	Medeco Cylinders	126
	Schlage Primus Cylinders	129
Chapter 9	**Pushbutton Combination Locks**	**137**
	1000 Series Locks	138
	Series 3000	146

Chapter 10 **Lock Picking, Impressioning,**
and Forced Entry   **151**

    Lock Picking   152

    Key Impressioning   158

    Forced Entry Techniques   162

Chapter 11 **Masterkeying**   **165**

    Warded Locks   166

    Lever Tumbler Locks   168

    Disc Tumbler Locks   168

    Pin Tumbler Locks   168

Chatper 12 **Nonlocking Door Hardware**   **171**

    Butts and Hinges   171

    High-Security Strike Plates   177

    Install-A-Lock Door Reinforcers   179

    Miscellaneous Products   182

Chapter 13 **Emergency Exit Door Devices**   **187**

    Distinctive Exit Devices Also Provide Safety   188

    Pilfergard Model PG-10   195

    Pilfergard Model PG-20   198

    Exitgard Models 35 and 70   200

    Alarm Lock Models 250, 250L, 260, and 260L   202

    Electronic Exit Lock Model 265   204

    Alarm Lock Models 700, 700L, 710, and 710L   209

    Alarm Lock Model 715   213

Chapter 14 **Electricity for Locksmiths**   **219**

    Basic Principles   220

    Running Wires   224

    Safety   224

Chapter 15	**Electromagnetic Locks**	**225**
	Installing a Model 62 Magnalock	226
	Troubleshooting a Magnalock	245
	Other Magnalocks	249
Chapter 16	**Electric Strikes**	**251**
	Strike Selection	251
	Electrical Considerations	253
	Troubleshooting	256
Chapter 17	**Key Duplicating Machines**	**273**
	Half-Time Key Machine	273
	Borkey 986	276
	Borkey 954 Rexa 3/CD	280
	Framon DBM-1 Flat Key Machine	283
	Ilco Unican Model .023 Key Machine	285
	Ilco Unican 018 Lever-Operated Key Machine	293
Chapter 18	**Key Coding Machines**	**303**
	Theory of Code Key Cutting	303
	KD80 Code Cutting Key Machine	306
	Exacta Code Key Cutter	314
	Framon DC-300 Duplicating Code Machine	317
	Borkey 989 Top-Cut	322
Chapter 19	**Automotive Lock Servicing**	**329**
	Basics	329
	Automotive Lock Differences	330
	Vehicle Identification Numbers	331
	American Motors Corporation	331
	Audi	334
	BMW	334

Chrysler   334

Datsun   337

Honda   338

Ford   339

General Motors   343

Opening Locked Vehicles   353

Chapter 20   Closed Circuit Television Systems   359

Basics   359

Pan-and-Tilt Technology   361

Consider the Big Picture before Installing
a CCTV System   370

**Chapter 21   Access Control, Alarms, and
System Integration   375**

Plan Component Design Prior to Installing System   375

A New Breed of Standalone Readers:
The High-Security Alternative   378

Design and Integration of Alarm Systems
into Access Control Systems   384

Integrated Fire Alarm and Security Systems   388

The Art of Integrating Fire and Security Systems   394

Systems Integration: More than the Sum
of Its Parts   398

Integrated Systems: The Whole-Building Approach   404

Chapter 22   Working as a Locksmith   411

Locksmithing Associations   411

Certifications   412

Licensing   413

Planning Your Job Search   414

Starting Your Own Business   422

Laws about Duplicating Keys   425

Sue Yourself . . . Before Someone Else Does   426

Ethics of Locksmithing   432

Chapter 23   Test Your Knowledge   435

Answers to the Test   447

Frequently Asked Questions   449

Appendices

A Security Training Programs   459

B Security Trade and Professional Journals   463

C Lockset Function Charts   465

D Comparative Key Blank List   471

E Depth and Space Charts   481

F ANSI/BHMA Finish Numbers   489

G Locksmith Suppliers Profiles/Addresses   495

H Security Organizations   499

I Other Locksmithing-Related Sites   501

Glossary   503

Index   537

ACKNOWLEDGMENTS

While writing this book, I received help from many companies and individuals. Much of it was in the form of technical information, photographs, drawings, advice, and encouragement. Without such assistance, this book could not have been written.

I'd like to thank all the readers of my locksmithing books and articles who took the time to write to me. I was happy to read every letter, even the most critical ones. Those comments and questions helped make this book what it is.

Special thanks to McGraw-Hill Senior Editor Zoe G. Foundotos for her patience and helpful ideas.

I'd also like to thank the following for their technical assistance: A-1 Security Manufacturing Corp.; Alarm Lock Systems, Inc.; Arrow Mfg. Co.; Associated Locksmiths of America; CCTV Corp.; Control Systems International; Dom Security Locks; ESP Corporation; Folger Adam Company; Framon Manufacturing Co. Inc.; Anthony "A. J." Hoffman, CML; Ilco Unican Corporation; the International Association of Home Safety and Security Professionals; Jerry L. Jacobson, Ph.D. of Vicon Industries, Inc.; Keedex Mfg.; Kustom Key, Inc.; Kwikset Corporation/A Safer America; Lori Corporation; Master Lock Company; MBS Fire Technology Inc.; Medeco Security Locks; Bert Michaels; Monarch Tool & Mfg. Co., Inc.; Wayne D. Moore of MBS Fire Technology; Stephen F. Nelson of Honeywell, Inc.; Charlie Pierce of L.R.C. Electronics Company; Ashley R. Rolfe of Newman Tonks, Inc.; Schlage Lock Company; Charles A. Sennewald, CMC, CPP; Lionel Silverman; Simplex Access Controls Corporation; Slide Lock Tool Company; Lars R. Suneborn of Hirsch Electronics; Michael Swiecicki of Simplex Time Recorder Company; and Frederick D. "Bud" Toye of Toye Corporation.

Finally, I'm especially grateful to the following: Gloria Glenn, for challenging me to write; Michael and Danny, for making me want to write; and to Janet Griffin and Patricia Bruce, for their encouragement, inspiration, and willingness to listen.

INTRODUCTION

While writing this book, I kept three goals in mind: to make it simple to understand; to provide everything someone needs to know to begin a lucrative career in locksmithing; and to make it an indispensable reference source for the security professional.

Throughout this book, I include step-by-step instructions, helpful illustrations, charts, and checklists. I explain in detail how to quickly pick open locks, impression keys, open any car door, and install and service electric strikes, electromagnetic locks, and emergency exit door devices. This is the only locksmithing book that comprehensively covers state-of-the-art physical and electronic security matters, such as closed circuit television systems, access control systems, and systems integration concerns.

Among the topics here that are especially useful for someone planning a career in locksmithing are: how to get hired as a locksmith; how to start a successful locksmithing business; the pros and cons of joining a locksmithing association; legal and ethical issues; and licensing and certifications.

I often get questions from readers of my articles and books, which include locksmiths, students, and apprentices. For this book, I compiled a list of the most frequently asked questions and include my answers. (See the FAQ in this book.) I give direct "no-nonsense" answers in which I share my trade secrets and personal experiences. I also give my opinions when appropriate.

The book's appendices are a handy reference source. They include listings of trade journals, suppliers, trade associations, locksmithing schools, locksmithing-related information on the Internet, and a lot of technical information. In addition to names and addresses, many listings include company profiles, phone numbers, fax numbers, email addresses and website addresses.

I've written nine security books, including *The Complete Book of Locks and Locksmithing*, 4th Edition (McGraw-Hill)—which is the world's best-selling locksmithing book. I know of no locksmithing book anywhere that gives more useful information than the one you're reading now. I hope you enjoy reading it, as much as I enjoyed writing it.

After you've read *Locksmithing*, let me know what you think. And tell me what you'd like to see in the next edition. Send your comments and questions to:

Bill Phillips
c/o Box 2044
Erie, PA 16512-2044

Or send email to: billphillips@iahssp.org

LOCKSMITHING

The Business of Locksmithing

"Locksmith Wanted for New Orleans Area . . . Plenty of work." "Bondable locksmith needed for outside work in Northern Illinois area." "California Is Having a Recession But We're Not!! Join the team of one of the most progressive locksmith shops in the country."

These are excerpts from advertisements that appeared in one issue of a locksmithing trade journal while I was writing this book. That journal and others regularly include "help wanted" ads from locksmith shops throughout the United States. Similar ads appear in local newspapers every day. As is pointed out by the *Encyclopedia of Careers and Vocational Guidance,* Tenth Edition (1997), "The locksmith trade itself has remained stable, with few economic fluctuations, and locksmiths with an extensive knowledge of their trade are rarely unemployed."

In 1995, there were an estimated 80,000 locksmiths and 14,000 locksmith shops in the United States. According to *The Hallcrest Report II: Private Security Trends,* there will be about 90,000 locksmiths by the year 2000. The average locksmith shop grossed over $242,000 annually during the late 1990s. Entry-level locksmiths earned $10–$12 per hour, and experienced locksmiths earned an average of $48,000 annually. How much you can earn will depend on your business and technical skills and on your creativity.

QUICK》》TIP Because of the speed at which they can be posted, more and more locksmithing jobs are appearing on the Internet before or instead of being printed in newspapers and trade journals. To find current listings, check the websites of locksmithing-related trade associations, or do an online search. Try the keywords "locksmith" and "locksmithing" with "jobs" and "employment."

Recent Changes to the Business

In the past, a locksmith was basically a hybrid of carpenter and mechanic. The locksmith's work was limited mainly to installing mechanical locksets, opening locked car doors, rekeying mechanical locks, and duplicating keys (Figure 1.1). As more automobile clubs and department stores began competing for those jobs, locksmiths responded by offering more services.

In addition to the usual services, locksmiths now sell, and maintain, a wide array of sophisticated security devices (Figure 1.2). The changing role of locksmiths can be seen as increasing numbers of col-

FIGURE 1.1

Although today's locksmith offers a wide variety of services, lock installation is still a major part of locksmithing.

leges and institutions combine their physical and electronic security departments, making one department responsible for establishing key control, maintaining physical locking devices, and installing and servicing electronic access control systems. (See Chapter 21 for information on access control systems.)

A person planning to become a locksmith should be able to use the most common hand and power tools, be mechanically inclined, be a good reader, and have no serious criminal record. Because many locksmithing jobs require the locksmith to drive, a good driving record can also be helpful.

FIGURE 1.2

In addition to locks, today's locksmith installs sophisticated security devices. *(Courtesy of MRL Inc.)*

Learning the Business

Most locksmiths get their initial training either by working as an apprentice or by completing a correspondence course. Some people use books and videotapes to teach themselves locksmithing. Others learn the trade by completing a residential program at a college or trade school.

I learned through each of those methods. I first began studying locksmithing by reading and practicing on my own. Next I completed several correspondence courses. Then I began working as an apprentice. Eventually I attended the now defunct National School of Locksmithing & Alarms in New York City.

As a rule, the most comprehensive training comes from a good residential program. Such a program exposes a person to a wide variety of locking devices and tools and combines hands-on training with lectures and reading material. However, few people live close enough to a residential program to become a student, and many residential programs are expensive and time consuming. Because there was no locksmithing school close to me, I had to move hundreds of miles away and live there for about nine months. The tuition was nearly $5000. (Some residential programs today last over a year and cost more than $8000.) See Appendix A for a list of residential and correspondence security training programs.

Correspondence courses typically cost from a few hundred dollars to about $1000. The most popular ones come with various locksmithing tools (including a key duplicating machine), and allow you to consult with an instructor by telephone while you're taking the course.

Certainly there are advantages to hands-on, in-person instruction, and in working with an instructor by mail and over the phone. But books and videos can be a great low-cost alternative. You can probably find locksmithing books in your public library. Locking device manufacturers often make informative service/installation manuals and videos, and provide them to locksmiths for free or at little cost.

The least expensive way to learn the trade is through on-the-job training. How much you can learn working as an apprentice depends on who you're working under and how much your mentor wants to teach you. Some locksmiths see employees as potential competition and are leery of sharing knowledge. Such a locksmith is likely to teach only a few basic tasks, such as key cutting and floor sweeping. Another problem with learning as an apprentice is that teaching is a special skill, and few people can do it well. The fact that a locksmith has a lot of knowledge and experience doesn't mean he or she can properly teach another person.

Regardless of how a person learns the basics, every locksmith needs to continue learning throughout his or her career.

QUICK»TIP "If you wait for about a month before responding to enrollment literature from a correspondence school, you'll probably get a letter offering reduced tuition. If you continue to wait another month or so, the tuition will likely drop even more and you'll probably be offered other incentives (such as tools or supplies at no extra charge)."

Continuing education comes from reading books, taking residential or correspondence classes, reading trade and professional journals, and talking with more experienced locksmiths and other security professionals. See Appendix B for a list of security trade and professional journals.

Employment Options

Some of the work opportunities for locksmiths include owning or working in a locksmithing shop, working as an in-house locksmith for a private or public organization, working for a manufacturer or distributor, teaching, and designing security-related products. Most people begin their locksmithing career by working for a locksmithing shop. This allows a person to gain a great deal of experience while being paid. Other people prefer to begin their own locksmithing business without first working for another locksmithing shop.

Owning a Shop

Successful owners of locksmithing shops usually have business acumen and a broad base of locksmithing skills. Many small shops are one-man or family operations, with the owner wearing all the hats. Other locksmithing shops have 30 or more full-time employees, and the owners rarely have to go out on calls. The number of employees a shop has isn't as important to its success as the range and quality of work the shop performs.

There are two basic types of locksmithing shops: store-front and mobile. A store-front shop is operated from a building customers walk into. A mobile shop is operated from a vehicle, usually a van or truck. Mobile shops always go to the customer to perform services. Most store-front shops use vehicles to allow them to offer both in-store and mobile services (Figure 1.3).

This flexibility gives the store-front more money-making opportunities than the mobile shop. A building gives a business a more professional and stable image, which helps in obtaining work. A building also provides a place to display a variety of merchandise. However, a store-front shop is more expensive to start and operate than a mobile shop. Rent, utility bills, merchandise, and additional equipment are a few of the extra expenses a store-front shop has.

FIGURE 1.3

Using both a store-front and a service vehicle allows a locksmith to sell merchandise and offer out-of-shop services. *(Courtesy of Roy's Lock Shop)*

Low start-up and operating costs are two reasons many locksmiths prefer operating a mobile shop. Another is that a mobile shop owner doesn't need a broad range of locksmithing skills because mobile shops generally offer only a few services.

Working in a Shop

Although there are a few notable exceptions, most mobile shops don't hire employees. When mobile shop owners need help, they usually subcontract work to other locksmiths. This allows mobile shop owners to avoid the cost of employee compensation insurance, employee benefits, extra record keeping, etc.

A locksmith who works for a small to mid-size shop has varied tasks daily. On any given day he or she may go out to install several locksets, open a car door, and change a safe combination, then go back to the shop to rekey some locks and wait on customers.

Some large shops assign specific duties to their locksmiths. For example, one may be assigned to only wait on customers, another to just service locking devices in the shop, and another to go out on calls. Sometimes the jobs are even more specific—such as only servicing safes.

> **TRADE SECRET**
>
> A locksmith can earn extra money by being on call to open locked cars and homes on Sundays, holidays, and at night.

Locksmiths who work in a shop usually earn an hourly wage plus extra pay for night and weekend work. Some hard-working locksmiths earn more money working overtime than they make as their base pay. A few also earn commissions for selling merchandise.

In-House Locksmiths

Universities, school systems, hotels, and cities are major employers of in-house locksmiths. Competition is fierce for in-house jobs because they usually offer good pay, job security, and a controlled work environment.

Most locksmiths who work in-house once worked for a locksmithing shop. In-house locksmiths often have a broad range of locksmithing skills, but rarely have to use most of those skills. Their work is usually limited to installing and servicing a few types and brands of security devices and hardware. In-house locksmiths don't ordinarily have to sell merchandise.

Working for a Manufacturer or Distributor

Manufacturers and distributors of security products and supplies are good sources of employment for many locksmiths (Figure 1.4). They hire locksmiths to stock products, sell merchandise, help develop new products, and conduct seminars. Sometimes they hire apprentice locksmiths to sell merchandise or stock products.

Instructors

Locksmithing instructors usually have at least five years of locksmithing experience. Some schools require their instructors to also have at least 120 hours of teacher training.

Manufacturers of locking devices frequently use instructors to conduct seminars. However, few locksmiths make their living solely by teaching; most also work in a shop.

FIGURE 1.4

Manufacturers and distributors of locksmithing products are good sources of employment for locksmiths. *(Courtesy of Accredited Lock Supply Co.)*

Designing Security-Related Products

Some locksmiths have made money designing new locking devices and products to make locksmithing easier. Many of them are employed by manufacturers, but it isn't unusual for locksmiths to invent new tools or to creatively modify locking devices while working for a locksmithing shop. Some locksmiths have formed their own companies to manufacture their inventions. Others have sold their ideas.

To learn more about finding a job as a locksmith or starting a locksmithing business, see Chapter 22. That chapter also tells how to get certified and licensed.

Basic Types of Locks and Keys

Terms such as "mortise bit-key lock" and "Medeco key-in-knob lock" mean little to most people, but provide useful information to locksmiths. Like other trades, locksmithing has its own vocabulary to meet its special needs.

Terminology

Laypersons frequently use a generic name like padlock, automobile lock, or cabinet lock when referring to a lock. Such a name has limited value to locksmiths because it is very general. It simply refers to a broad category of locks that are used for a similar purpose, share a similar feature, or look similar to one another.

Locksmiths identify a lock in ways that convey information needed to purchase, install, and service it. The name they use is based not only on the purpose and appearance of the lock, but also on the lock's manufacturer, key type, method of installation, type of internal construction, and function.

The names used by a locksmith are typically formed by combining several words. Each word in the name provides important information about a lock. The number of words a locksmith uses for a name depends on how much information he or she needs to convey.

When ordering a lock, for instance, the locksmith needs to use a name that identifies the lock's purpose, manufacturer, key type, appearance, etc. However, a name that simply identifies the lock's internal construction may be adequate for describing a servicing technique to another locksmith.

Generic Names

Some of the most commonly used generic lock names include automobile lock, bike lock, ski lock, cabinet lock, deadbolt lock, gun lock, key-in-knob lock, luggage lock, lever lock, padlock, combination lock, and patio door lock. Sometimes generic terms have overlapping meanings. A padlock, for instance, can also be a combination lock. Figure 2.1 shows a variety of padlocks.

The *key-in-knob lock* refers to a style of lock that is operated by inserting a key into its knob (Figures 2.2a and 2.2b). A *lever lock* has a lever as a handle (Figures 2.3a and 2.3b). A handleset has a built-in grip handle (Figure 2.3c). A *deadbolt lock* projects a deadbolt (Figure 2.4a and 2.4b). As the names imply, the automobile lock, bike lock (Figure 2.5), ski lock (Figure 2.6), patio door lock, etc., are based on the purposes for which the locks are used. Sometimes locks that share a common purpose look very different from one another. Figure 2.7 shows several styles of patio door locks.

Manufacturer's Names

Locksmiths often refer to a lock by the name of its manufacturer, especially when all or most of the company's locks share a common characteristic. Locks manufactured by Medeco Security Locks, Inc., for example, all have similar internal constructions. Simply by knowing a lock is a Medeco lock, a locksmith can consider the options for servicing it.

Several lock manufacturers are so popular in the locksmithing industry that every locksmith is expected to be familiar with their names and the common characteristics of each manufacturer's locks. Those manufacturers include Arrow, Best, Corbin, Dexter, Ilco Unican, Kwikset, Master, Medeco, Russwin, Sargent, Schlage, Weiser, and Yale.

Key Types

Many times a lock is identified by the type of key used to operate it. Bit key locks and tubular key locks are two common examples. Tubular

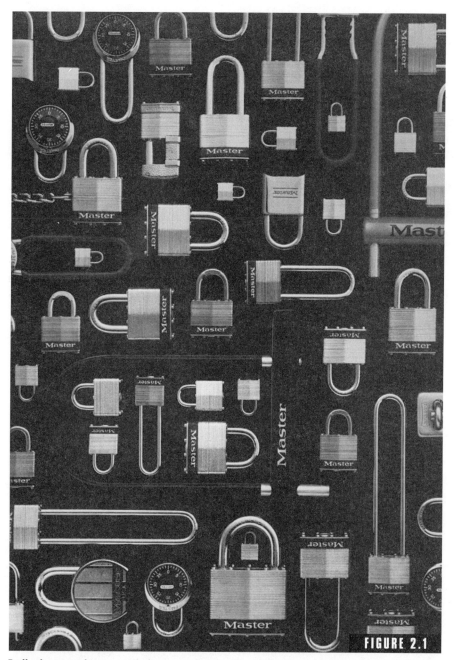

Padlocks come in assorted shapes and styles for different purposes. *(Courtesy of Master Lock Company)*

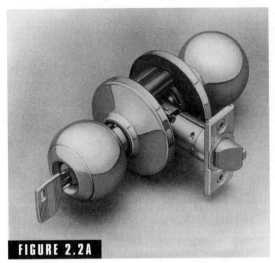

FIGURE 2.2A

A popular key-in-knob lock. *(Courtesy of Master Lock Company)*

key locks, sometimes called Ace locks, are primarily used on vending machines and coin-operated washing machines (Figure 2.8). Bit key locks are used on many closet and bedroom doors. When speaking about a bit key lock, locksmiths usually use a name that reveals how it is installed.

Installation Method

The terms "rim lock" and "mortise lock" identify locks based on installation method. A *rim lock,* or surface-mounted lock, is designed to be installed on the surface, or rim, of a door (Figures 2.9, 2.10, and 2.11).

A *mortise lock* is designed to be installed in a mortise, or recess, in a door. Figure 2.12 shows a mortise bit key lock installed. Not all mortise locks are operated with a bit key; the lock in Figure 2.13 uses a cylinder key.

Internal Construction

For servicing locks, names based on their internal constructions are usually most helpful to a locksmith. Examples include warded lock, pin tumbler lock, disc tumbler lock, wafer tumbler lock, lever tumbler lock, and side bar lock.

Lock names based solely on internal construction don't indicate the lock's purpose, installation method, function, or appearance, but only refer to its type of cylinder or parts inside its lock case. A lock that uses a pin tumbler cylinder, for example, is called a *pin tumbler lock* or a *pin tumbler cylinder lock.* A lock with wards inside its case is called a *warded lock.*

Note: Some people use the terms "lever lock" and "lever tumbler lock" synonymously. However, the latter refers to a type of internal construction, whereas the former refers to a type of handle used (refer back to Figure 2.3).

Most types of cylinders can be used with a wide variety of locks. A key-in-knob lock, for example, can use a disc tumbler cylinder or a pin tumbler cylinder. Both cylinder types can also be used with many other types of locks. Which type of cylinder is best to use depends on the level of security needed, how much money someone is willing to spend, and whether or not the cylinder needs to fit into an existing keying system. (Later chapters provide more information about the internal constructions of locks.)

Lock Functions

Entrance lock, classroom lock, and vestibule lock are names based on how a lock functions. A *classroom lock*, for example, is one whose inside knob is always in the unlocked position for easy exiting and whose outside knob can be locked or unlocked with a key. An *institution lock*, however, has both knobs always in the locked position to prevent easy exiting; a key must be used on either knob to operate the lock. (Lock functions are listed in Appendix C.)

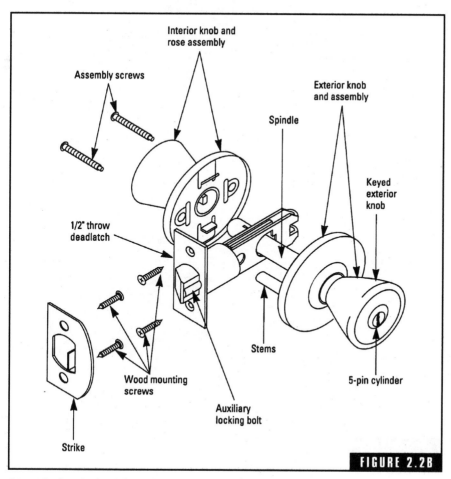

FIGURE 2.2B

A popular key-in-knob lock. *(Courtesy of Arrow Lock Company)*

Lever locks come in many different handle sizes. *(Courtesy of Kwikset Corporation)*

At this point, you should have a good idea of how locksmiths identify locks. They simply combine several applicable terms that provide the necessary specificity. Now when you hear a name like mortise bit key lock, you should better understand what it means. Don't worry if you don't remember all the names used for locks. The purpose of this chapter is to help you understand the logic behind some of the most commonly used names.

Types of Keys

A *key* is the device that operates locks. Keys come in a wide variety of shapes and sizes.

The most common keys, those typically used on homes and cars, share many common features. Usually such keys are made of metal, are 1- to 2-inches long, and have

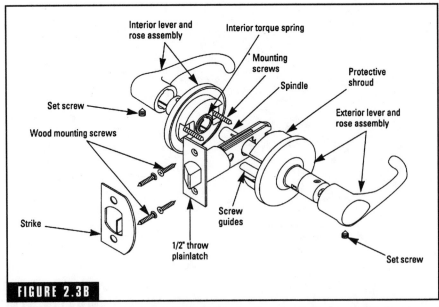

Lever locks are frequently used in facilities for the physically impaired. *(Courtesy of Kwikset Corporation)*

the following parts: a gripping area for turning the key; a thin blade with grooves or "millings" along the blade's length on one or both sides; and jagged U- or V-shaped cuts of varying depths spaced along one or both edges of the blade. If you look at your keys, you'll probably find that most fit that description.

QUICK»TIP

Look at your key bows and try to identify which lock keyways they fit. There are several distinctive bows that you probably encounter regularly. THe more keys you can identify by bow, the faster you'll be able to find the right blank to duplicate keys.

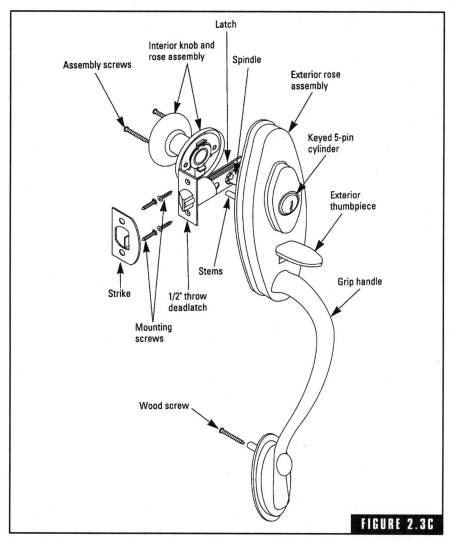

FIGURE 2.3C

Lever locks are frequently used in facilities for the physically impaired. *(Courtesy of Kwikset Corporation)*

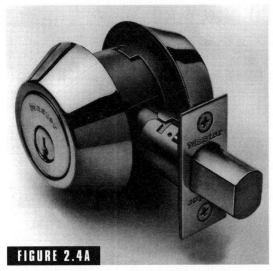

FIGURE 2.4A

A deadbolt is a popular lock for homes and businesses.

Keys come in many other shapes and sizes for operating a wide variety of locks. Some keys for low-cost magnetic padlocks, for instance, are thin rectangular bars about 2-inches long. Keys for some electric locks are roughly the size and shape of a dime. Electronic door locks at many hotels use thin plastic keys that are roughly the size and shape of a playing card.

A locksmith doesn't need to know everything about all the different kinds of keys, but it is a good idea to become familiar with the basic types. There are eight basic types of keys locksmiths commonly sell and work with: bit key, barrel key, flat key, corrugated key, cylinder key, tubular

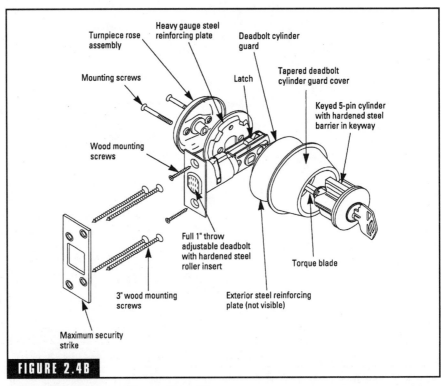

FIGURE 2.4B

A deadbolt lock can provide good security.

key, angularly bitted key, and dimple key. Virtually all other mechanical keys are variations of these types.

Keys usually have all or most of the following features: a bow; a blade or bit; ward cuts or throat cuts; a stop; and tumbler cuts.

The *bow* (rhymes with "toe") is the handle of the key; it's the part you grip when using the key to operate a lock. The *blade* is the part that's inserted into a lock's keyway.

Ward cuts and *throat cuts* on a key's blade permit it to bypass obstructions on or within a lock; these cuts are needed to allow a key to enter or be rotated in a lock.

The *stop* of a key, usually the key's shoulder or tip, makes the key stop within a lock at the position the key needs to be in to operate the lock. Without a stop, you would need to slide a key in and out of a lock and guess when it's in the correct position to operate the lock.

The *tumbler cuts*, or bitting, on a blade manipulate tumblers within a lock into position for the lock to operate. To operate a lock, each tumbler cut on a key must correspond in spacing (position) and depth to a tumbler within the lock.

Bit Keys

A bit key is used for operating bit key locks. It is usually made of iron, brass, steel, or aluminum (Figure 2.14). This key is sometimes erroneously called a skeleton key. The main parts of a bit key are the bow, shank, shoulder, throat, post, bit, tumbler cuts, and ward cuts.

FIGURE 2.5

A bike lock secures bikes to racks, posts, and other anchor points. *(Courtesy of Master Lock Company)*

FIGURE 2.6

A ski lock safeguards both skis and poles by securing them to a rack, tree, or post. *(Courtesy of Master Lock Company)*

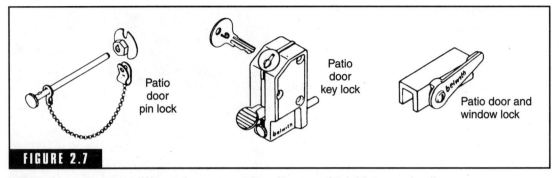

FIGURE 2.7

Patio locks can look very different from one another. *(Courtesy of Belwith International)*

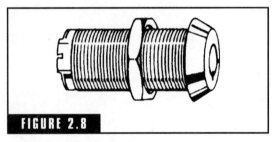

FIGURE 2.8

A typical tubular key lock.

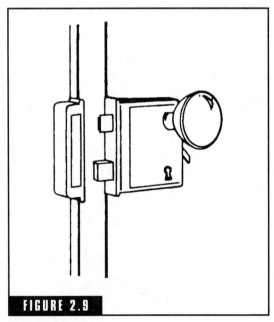

FIGURE 2.9

A rim bit key lock installed on a door. *(Courtesy of Ilco Unican Corp.)*

Barrel Keys

The barrel key comes in a variety of sizes and styles. Some barrel keys look similar to bit keys and have most of the same parts. The major difference between the two types is that the barrel key has a hollow shank. Another difference is that many barrel keys don't have a shoulder, post, or blade.

Flat Keys

As the name implies, a flat key, or flat steel key, is flat on both sides. Most are made of steel or nickel silver (Figure 2.15). Such keys are often used for operating a lever tumbler lock, a type of lock used on luggage and safe deposit boxes.

The parts of a flat key are the bow, blade, tip, stop, throat cut, and tumbler cut. The *throat cut* allows a key to bypass an obstruction found on most lever tumbler locks.

Corrugated Keys

Many corrugated keys look similar to flat keys. Both types usually have the same parts. Corrugated keys have corrugations, or ripples, along the length of their blades. They are designed to allow the key to fit into correspondingly shaped keyways. Unlike most flat keys, corrugated keys have cuts on both sides of their blades.

Corrugated keys are often used with warded padlocks. Some corrugated keys are designed to operate other types of locks. For example, Schlage Lock Company used to manufacture a key-in-knob lock that used special types of corrugated keys. Those keys look more like cylinder keys than flat keys (Figure 2.16).

Cylinder Keys

The most popular key today is the cylinder key. It is used to operate pin tumbler locks and disc tumbler locks. You probably have several cylinder keys to unlock the front door of your home or the doors of your car (Figure 2.17).

The parts of a cylinder key are the bow, shoulder, blade, tumbler cuts, keyway grooves, and tip. The *shoulder* acts as a stop; it determines how far the key will enter the keyway. Some cylinder keys don't have shoulders; those keys use the tip as a stop. The *keyway grooves* are millings along the length of a key blade that allow the key to enter a keyway of a corresponding shape.

Tubular Keys

The tubular key has a tubular blade with cuts, or depressions, milled in a circle around the end of the blade (Figure 2.18). The key is used to operate tubular key locks, which are often found on vending machines and coin-operated washing machines.

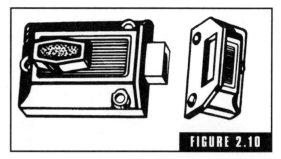

A deadlocking rim lock and strike. *(Courtesy of Ilco Unican Corp.)*

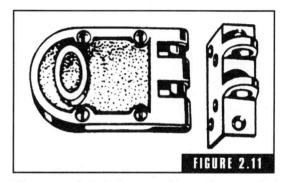

A jimmy-proof rim lock can provide excellent security if its strike is properly installed. *(Courtesy of Ilco Unican Corp.)*

A mortise bit key lock installed on a door. *(Courtesy of Ilco Unican Corp.)*

FIGURE 2.13

Most modern mortise locks are operated with a cylinder key. *(Courtesy of Adams Rite Mfg. Co.)*

Tubular keys are often improperly called Ace keys. The term "Ace key" is a short form of a brand name, but it doesn't apply to all tubular keys. The first tubular key was patented by Chicago Lock Company to operate its Chicago Ace Lock brand tubular key lock. Today many companies manufacture tubular key locks and tubular keys.

Parts of a tubular key include the bow, blade, tumbler cuts, and nib. The *nib* shows which position the key must enter the lock to operate it. The purposes of the bow, blade, and tumbler cuts are similar to the purposes of corresponding parts of a cylinder key.

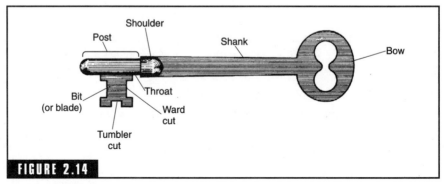

FIGURE 2.14

Parts of a typical bit key. *(Courtesy of Ilco Unican Corp.)*

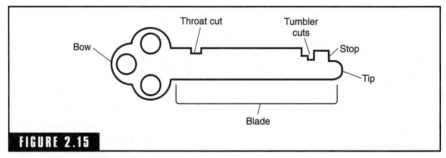

FIGURE 2.15

Parts of a typical flat key.

Angularly Bitted Keys

The angularly bitted key is used with some high-security locks. The key has cuts that angle perpendicularly from the blade.

The key is designed to cause pin tumblers within a cylinder to rotate to specific positions. Medeco Security Locks, Inc. popularized the angularly bitted key (Figure 2.19). Chapter 8 provides more information about Medeco locks.

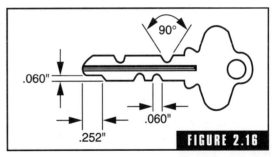

A corrugated key for a Schlage Wafer Lock. *(Courtesy of Schlage Lock Company)*

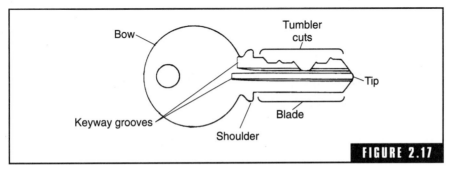

Parts of a typical cylinder key.

Dimple Keys

The dimple key is used to operate some high-security pin tumbler locks. It has cuts that are drilled or milled into its blade surface; the cuts normally don't change the blade silhouette (Figure 2.20). Lori Corporation's Kaba locks are popular locks operated with dimple keys.

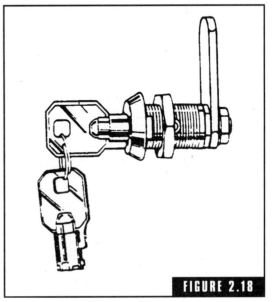

A tubular key lock and tubular keys are used for coin-operated machines.

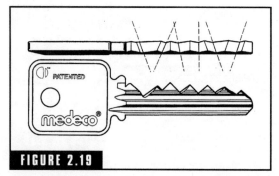

FIGURE 2.19

An angularly bitted key is often used to operate high-security locks. *(Courtesy of Medeco Security Locks, Inc.)*

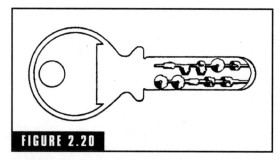

FIGURE 2.20

A dimple key has drilled or milled cuts on its blade.
(Courtesy of Lori Corporation)

Key Blanks and Key Blank Directories

A *key blank* (or blank, for short) is basically an uncut or "uncombi-nated" key. It looks similar to a key, but doesn't have the bitting, or cuts, or other coding that allow it to operate a lock (Figure 3.1).

A key is made by modifying a proper blank, usually by making cuts of different depths across one or both edges of the blade. An *original key blank*, or genuine key blank, is supplied by a lock manufacturer to duplicate keys for that company's locks. Several companies make after-market blanks that can be used in place of original key blanks.

Choosing the Right Blank

Before duplicating a key, you have to choose the right blank. This is easy to do if you know which factors to consider. First decide which basic type of blank you need. It must be the same type as the key you're duplicating. Then select a blank that matches the key in the important areas for the particular key type.

Bit Keys and Barrel Keys

When choosing a blank to duplicate a bit key or a barrel key, consider the thickness of the bit and diameter of the post and shank. The key and blank should closely match in those areas (Figures 3.2 and 3.3). Because there is usually a lot of tolerance in locks that use these types of keys, the blank might not have to match the key perfectly.

FIGURE 3.1

Blanks look like keys without cuts. *(Courtesy of ESP Corporation)*

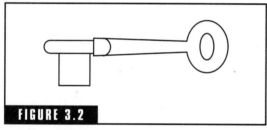

FIGURE 3.2

A bit key blank. *(Courtesy of Ilco Unican Corp.)*

Flat Keys and Corrugated Keys

Thickness, length, width, and shape of the blade are the primary factors to consider when choosing a blank to duplicate a flat or corrugated key. The key and blank should closely match in these areas. Figure 3.4 shows some flat key blanks. A blank for a corrugated key should have the same corrugated configuration as the key (Figure 3.5).

Cylinder Keys

Choosing a blank to duplicate a cylinder key can be a little tricky. There are more varieties of cylinder keys than of other keys, and the differences among cylinder keys are often slight. However, finding the right blank for a cylinder key can be simple if you approach the task methodically. First examine the bow for clues.

THE BOW

When you know the manufacturer of the lock a key operates, your choices of a blank are greatly reduced. Sometimes the key bow provides that information.

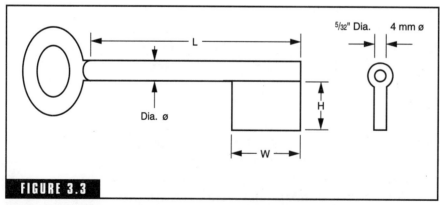

FIGURE 3.3

Before duplicating a barrel key, you need to find the right blank. *(Courtesy of Ilco Unican Corp.)*

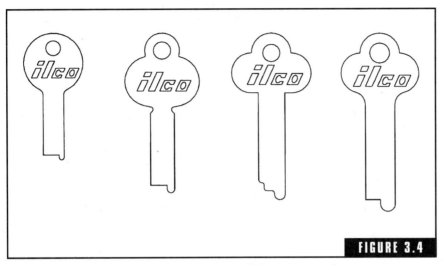

Flat key blanks come in various sizes. *(Courtesy of Ilco Unican Corp.)*

Most major lock man-
ufacturers use distinctive
bow shapes for their fac-
tory original keys and
blanks. Many after-mar-
ket key blank manufac-
turers use similar bows
when making corre-
sponding key blanks.
With a little practice,
you'll be able to quickly
identify distinctive bows
(Figure 3.6).

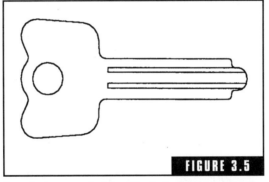

A typical corrugated key blank for warded padlocks. *(Courtesy of Ilco Unican Corp.)*

A company name is on the front of most key bows. The name on factory original keys is that of the manufacturer of the lock the key operates. The name on after-market keys is usually that of the manufacturer
of the key blank that was used to make the key. (Occasionally it's the
name of the locksmith shop that duplicated the key.)

Most bows also have letters and numbers on them. Usually those
letters and numbers are coded in a way that makes it easy for you to
identify the manufacturer of the lock the key operates. For example,
SC1, SC2, SC3, etc., are used to indicate that the key or blank is for a
lock manufactured by Schlage Lock Company. MA3 and MA7 indicate

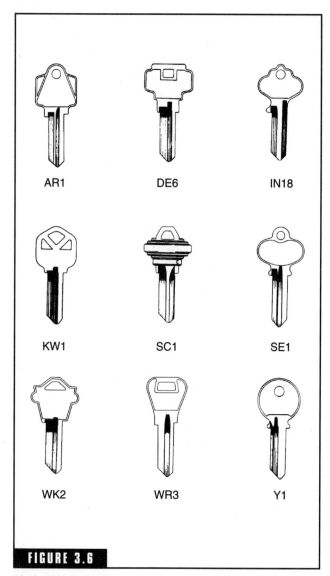

AR1

DE6

IN18

KW1

SC1

SE1

WK2

WR3

Y1

FIGURE 3.6

Distinctive bows of the following lock manufacturers (from top left to bottom right): Arrow, Dexter, Ilco, Kwikset, Schlage, Segal, Weslock, Weiser, and Yale. *(Courtesy of ESP Corporation)*

that the blank or key is for a lock manufactured by Master Lock Company. Different key blank manufacturers use different codes.

It isn't necessary for you to remember all of the codes. However, you will be able to duplicate keys more quickly if you remember the codes most frequently found on keys. After determining the manufacturer of the key you're duplicating, you might still have to choose among several blanks designed for that manufacturer's products, but you've greatly narrowed down your choices.

COMPARE KEYWAY GROOVES

At this point you need to compare the keyway grooves of the key with those of a blank. Pick any blank you think might be the right one. Hold the key and blank in each hand by their bows. Make sure both tips point in the same direction, and the key and blank are on the same side.

See if the blank has the same number of keyway grooves on each side as the key has on each side. If not, find a blank that does. Look at the points where the keyway grooves of the key touch, or nearly touch, the bow. Use those points to compare each keyway groove of the blank to its corresponding groove of the key. Check whether each keyway groove has the same shape as its corresponding groove. Make that comparison on both sides of the key and blank. The five standard shapes are left angle, right angle, square, V, and round. All of these shapes are illustrated in Figure 3.7.

If any of the blank's keyway grooves don't match the shape of its corresponding groove, you don't have the proper blank. After finding a blank with keyway grooves that match those of the key, compare the widths of the grooves with the widths of their corresponding grooves on the key. Then compare the thickness, width, and length of the blank's blade with those of the key. Those dimensions are measured by placing the blank and key together and aligning them at the shoulders. If both blades match in all those respects, you have the right blank.

If the blank matches the key in every respect except blade thickness, width, or length, it can sometimes still be used to duplicate the key. A blank that is longer than the key can be cut down to the length of the key. A blank that is thinner than the key may have a loose fit in the keyway, but it can still be used.

The process of finding a blank to duplicate a cylinder key might seem long and tedious. With a little practice, however, you'll be able to complete the process within a few seconds. You will notice that you're using certain blanks much more frequently than you're using others. In a short period of time, you'll remember what the keyway grooves of those commonly used blanks look like. Then when you see a key with grooves that match one of those blanks, you'll automatically know which blank you need.

> **QUICK»TIP**
>
> If you don't have blanks with which to practice, compare the cylinder keys with each other to study how their keyway grooves differ. Focus on where the grooves meet the bows.

Tubular Keys

Choosing a blank to duplicate a tubular key is very simple, because there are few significant differences among tubular keys. Figure 3.8 shows some tubular keys. The important areas of such keys are the size of the nib and the inside and outside

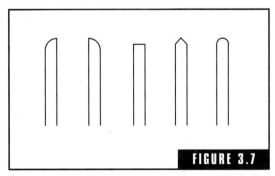

FIGURE 3.7

Five common keyway groove shapes (from left to right): left angle, right angle, square, V, and round.

diameters of the shank. Find a blank that matches a tubular key in those respects and you can duplicate the key.

Key Blank Directories

Several key blank manufacturers publish directories that have drawings of blanks, silhouettes of keyway grooves, and side-by-side listings of the key coding systems of various key blank manufacturers. Although such directories are inexpensive (and sometimes free), they're invaluable to locksmiths who regularly duplicate keys. Figure 3.9 shows a page from a key blank directory. Why would a key blank manufacturer provide information about blanks made by other companies? To let locksmiths know which of that company's blanks can be used in place of blanks made by other manufacturers. The information in a key blank directory can be helpful in other ways.

Using the Directories

Key blank directories are commonly used in two ways. You can compare the numbers and letters on a key with those in the directory to determine which of several blanks to use to duplicate a key. Those key

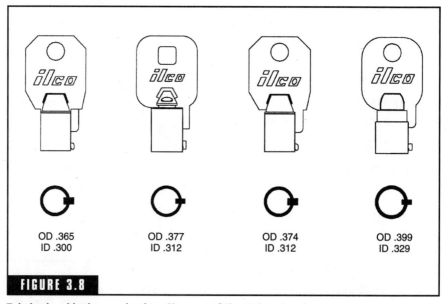

OD .365
ID .300

OD .377
ID .312

OD .374
ID .312

OD .399
ID .329

FIGURE 3.8

Tubular key blanks vary in size. *(Courtesy of Ilco Unican Corp.)*

codes are listed in the directory near drawings of key blanks and in cross-reference charts (Table 3.1).

For example, if you're duplicating a key that has "110" on its bow, you can learn several facts from the directory entries, such as those in Figure 3.9 and Table 3.1. According to the directory, 110 is a number from Illinois's key coding system and Star's blank number IS1 can be

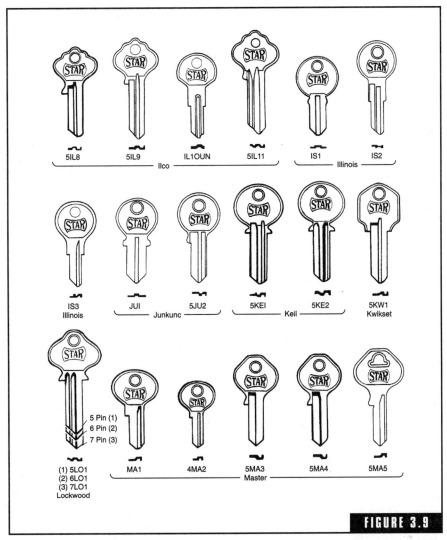

FIGURE 3.9

Some key blank directories show drawings of blanks. *(Courtesy of Star Lock and Key Mfg. Co., Inc.)*

TABLE 3.1 Brass Cylinder Key Blank Comparative List

Hazelton	STAR		
4637	5H01	4936	HBR10J
4647	5WK1	4937	OBR10K
4650	5KW1	4938	HBR12A
4652	5SN1	4939	OBR12B
4655	5AR2	9000	5HD1
4838	HYA4	9015	OFD2
4840	HYA5	9016	HFD7
4844	HPL2	9020	OFD2
4846	OPL2	9025	OFD2
4854	HPL1	9025RH	OFD2
4856	OPL1	9026	HFD7
4858	HPL3	9026-2	HFD7
4864	OPL4	9040	HFD2
4867	OPL5	9041	OFD2
4870/72	HPL68, HPL73	9043	OFD2
		9044	YJ3
4900	HBR11	9046	SYJ1
4902	OBR11	9047	OBR1DB
Hollymade		9058	HFD2
(See Challenger)		9059	OFD2
Huber	STAR	9070	HFD1
700	5HU1	9071	OFD1
Hurd	STAR	9072	HFD1
4932	HBR7	9073	OFD1
4933	OBR7	9074	HFD1
4934	HBR9E	9082	HFD3
4935	OBR9H	9083	OFD3

TABLE 3.1 Brass Cylinder Key Blank Comparative List (*Continued*)

9084	HFD3	9422	HFD9
9086	HFD3	9423	HFD4
9087	OFD5	9424	OFD9
9090	HFD6	9427	HFD9
9091	HFD6	9428	OFD9
9098	HFD4	9431	HFD9
9099	OFD3	9432	OFD9
9124	HFD6	9433	HFD4
9125	OFD6	9434	OFD4
9128	OFD10	9518	HFD5
9129	HFD10	9520	HFD5
9133B	YJ4	9521	OFD5
9147	YJ1	9522	HFD4
9148	YJ4	9523	OFD4
9174	HPL6	9524	HFD4
9175	OPL4	9525	OFD4
9299	HPL6	9526	HFD8
9300	OPL68	9530	HBR2
		9531	OBR2
Hurd	**STAR**	9532	HPL3
9301	HPL68	9533	OPL1
9305	OPL68	9534	OBR1
9337	HFD9	9535	HBR1
9338	OFD9	9537	OPL4
9340	HBR5	9539	OPL5
9341	OBR5	9542	HFD4
9356	HFD9	9543	OFD4
9357	OFD9	9544	HFD4
9421	OFD4	9545	OFD4

TABLE 3.1 Brass Cylinder Key Blank Comparative List (*Continued*)

Hurd	STAR		
9546	HFD4	MZ11	MZ3
9547	OFD4	MZ12	5DA2
9549	OFD4	DA20	5DA1
9556	YJ1	TR26	TO2
9557	YJ4	FT37	FT3
9571	HPL6	FT38	FT2
9572	OPL4	F44	5FT1
9576	HBR3	HO44	HN4
9577	OBR3	P54F	5DO4

Illinois	STAR	Ilco	STAR
110	IS1	RE61F	5RP2
260	IS3	T61C	TO1
360	IS2	T61F	LU1
		RE61N	RP1

Ilco	STAR		
DC1	LDC1	62DP	UN2
MG1	UN4	62DT	DA4
YS1	CP2	62DU	DA3
AA2	HN1	62FS	UN3
FC2	CP1	62VW	VW1
WS2	5DA2	VW67	VW2
YS2	CP3	70S	SM1
MZ4	MZ4	HD70, HD71	HN2-3
MZ5	MZ5	VW71	VW3
PA6	AD1	VW71A	VW5
VO6	6VL1	73VB	VW4
MZ9	MZ1	HD74	HN5
MZ10	MZ2	VR91	5VR1
		VR91AR	5VR3
		VR91B	5VR4
		100AM	CG3

TABLE 3.1 Brass Cylinder Key Blank Comparative List (*Continued*)

995M, 996M	5YA11	1001E	7CO2
997D, 997E	5YA6	1001EA	6CO2
997X	4YA6	1001EB	5CO2
J997M	6YA9	1001EG	6CO1
0997E	6YA6	1001EH	5CO11
998	6YA3	1001EL	7CO1
998GA	6YA12	1001EN	5CO1
998GST	6YA8	1001GH	5CO13
L998GST	7YA8	A1001ABM	6CO12
998R	6YA7	A1001C1/	6CO16
999	5YA1, 5YA1M	C2/D1/D2	
999A	6YA1	A1001EH	6CO11
999B	4YA1	L1001ABM	7CO12
999N	5YA1E	L1001C1/	7CO16
999R	5YA13	C2/D1/D2	
C999	5YA2	L1001EH	7CO11
1000	5CO3	R1001EF	5CO9
1000F	6CO6	R1001EG	6CO5
1000G	5CO6	R1001EL	7CO5
		R1001EN	5CO5
Ilco	**STAR**	1003M, L1003M	5AU1
1000T	LCO15	R1003M	5B01
1000V	LCO7	1004	5LO1
S1000V	CO7	1004A	6LO1
X1000F	6CO10	1004AL	7LO1
X1000FR	6CO14	1004KA	6IL2
X1000KC	5CO8	1004KL	7IL2
X1000KR	5RU3	1004M	5IL6
1001	5CO4	1004N	5IL11
1001ABM	5CO12	1007	5SA4

TABLE 3.1 Brass Cylinder Key Blank Comparative List (*Continued*)

Ilco	STAR
1007K	5SA8
01007K	5SA9
01007KC	5SA10
1007KMA	6SA3
1007KMB	5SA3
1007RMA	6SA6
1007RMB, N1007RMB	5SA6
L1007KMA	7SA3
1009	5SA2
1010	5SA5
1010N	5SA7
L1010N, A1010N	6SA7
01010	5SA1
1011	5RU1
1011D1	5RU7
1011D41	5RU8
1011GH	5CO13
1011M	5RU4
1011P	5RU2
1011PB to PY	5RU5
1011PZ	5RU5
A1011D1	6RU7
A1011D41	6RU8
A1011M/P/S/T	6RU9
A1011P	6RU2

Ilco	STAR
A1011PB to PY	6RU5
A1011PZ	6RU5
L1011D1	7RU7
L1011D41	7RU8
L1011P	7RU2
L1011PZ	7RU5
N1011M/P/S/T	5RU9
1012	5RU6
1014	5EA2
1014A	6EA2
1014D, 1014DX	4EA4
1014F	5EA1

Ilco	STAR
1014J	EA3
1014JS	EA5
1014K	4EA1
L1014A	7EA2
01014S	EA6
X1014F	5EA1
1015	5CH3
1015C	5CH1
1015M	5CH2
A1015M	6CH2
A1015MR	6CH4
L1015M	7CH2
L1015MR	7CH4
1016	5PE2
1016N	5PE1

TABLE 3.1 Brass Cylinder Key Blank Comparative List (*Continued*)

1017	5NW3	1041GR	CG2
1017B	5NW1	1041H	IS1
1017BA	6NW1	1041T	5CG7
01017ML	6NW2	1041Y	5CG4
01017MX	7NW1	1043B	IS2
1019	5RE1	1043D	IS3
1019A	6RE1	1046	5JU2
1019D	5RE2	1047CR, 1047M	5YA2
A1019M	6AR3	1054	5IL3
1020	5HU1	1054F	5IL1
1021BA	5NW3	1054FN, X1054FN	5IL9
1022	5SE1, 5SE1M	1054K	5IL2
1022AB	6SE1	1054KD	5DE1
01022	5SE2	1054MT	5IL11
01022AB	6SE2	1054TW	5IL2
01022AR	6SE4	1054UN	IL10UN
R1022AB	6SE5	1054WB	5WR2
1023	5CL1	A1054F	5DO1
1025	AR1	A1054KD	6DE1
1033N	5UN1	A1054WB	6WR2
1034	5PO1	D1054K	5DE3
1034H	5PO2	D1054KA	6DE3
1041C	JU1	L1054B	IL5
		L1054K	5DO3
Ilco	**STAR**	S1054F	5DO2
1041E	5CG5	X1054F	5IL7
1041G	CG1	X1054JA	5IL8
1041GA	CG6	X1054K	5IL4

TABLE 3.1 Brass Cylinder Key Blank Comparative List (*Continued*)

X1054WA	5WR1	E/C/S1096LN	5EL3
1064, N1069G	4RO2	L1096CN	6EL4
R1064D	5RO4	1098DB	OBR1DB
1069	RO1	1098M	OBR1
1069FL	RO3	1098NR	OBR3
		D1098X	DE2
Ilco	**STAR**	H1098A	HBR5
		H1098A/B	HBR6
1069G	RO5	H1098A/C	HBR5M
1069H, 1069N	RO6	H1098C	HBR7
1069LA	5AU2	H1098LA	HBR2
1071	5WI1	H1098M	HBR1
1073H, 1073K	5FR1	H1098NR	HBR3
1079	5KE2	L1098C/A	HBR8
1079B	5KE1	L1098LA	OBR4
1092	MA1	01098B	OBR5
1092B	4MA2	01098B/A	OBR6
1092D	5MA7		
1092DS	4MA7		
1092H	5MA6		
1092J	6MA8		
1092N	5MA5		
1092NR	5MA3, 5MA4		
1092V	5MA3		
1092VM	5MA4		
1096	5EL2		
1096L	5EL1		
E/C/S1096CN	5EL4		

Courtesy of Star Lock and Key Mfg. Co., Inc.

used to duplicate the key. You can then learn which other manufacturer's blanks are compatible with Star's IS1. That's done by looking at each Star cross-reference chart to find IS1, then seeing what number is beside it.

Keep in mind that the publisher of a directory usually shows drawings of its blanks in its directory. Likewise, all of the listed key code systems in a key blank directory are compared to the system of the publisher.

You can also use a directory to compare a key to the drawings and silhouettes. Many times that comparison makes it unnecessary to handle a lot of blanks. By laying a key on top of the drawing of a blank, aligning both at the shoulders, you can usually determine whether that blank's blade is the right size. By standing the key up on its tip directly above the drawing's corresponding keyway groove silhouette (with the key facing the same direction as the drawing), you can determine whether that blank's keyway groove matches those of the key. Appendix D shows a comprehensive cross-reference key blank chart. Table 3.2 is a quick reference chart that can save you time when searching for many types of key blanks.

Cutting Keys by Hand

Today locksmiths rarely need to cut keys by hand. You can use sophisticated machines to cut virtually any key. Nevertheless, every locksmith should be able to duplicate keys by hand. This skill can be useful in emergency situations when a proper key machine isn't available. Developing the skill can also prepare a locksmith for more technical skills, such as key impressioning.

To duplicate a key by hand you will need a vise, small files (triangle, pippin, and warding), and key blanks. The vise holds the blank in place while you carefully file the proper cuts into the blank. Proper cuts are those with the same angles, depths, and positions, or spacing, as those on the key.

Cutting Procedures

When cutting a bit key by hand, it's a good idea first to make a template from

> **QUICK»TIP** For practice, compare your keys with the keyway groove silhouettes and bow shapes in Figure 3.9. It's likely that at least one of your keys will match.

TABLE 3.2 Common Keyways for Select Locks

	Cole	Ilco	Taylor	Star
Bicycle locks	AM1	1041C	41C	JU1
	CL1	1023	123	5CL1
	M10	1092N	92N	5MA5
	VR6	L67A	—	—
	Y52	997X	7X	4YA6
	—	1136S	—	—
	—	1902	—	—
Boat locks	B1	1098GX	—	HBR3
	NA12	1069LB	174BA	5AU2
Cabinets/desks	AP5	100AM	F41M	CG3
	L1	1054MT	54MT	5IL11
	NA12	1069LB	174BA	5AU2
	RO9	1069N	174J	RO6
	SL1	1120D	120D	SL1
	Y11	H1054L	—	—
	Y12	H1122F	H7F	—
	Y103	K1122B	L54K	—
Campers	BN1	K1122D	L54P	BN1
	IN8	L1954B	L54B	IL5
	IN10	II41H	111TS	—
	IN28	—	—	—
Copiers	RO6	1069-54	174H	—
Club, The	DA22	X6	X6	DA4
(Steering	JA73	X7	X7	DA3
wheel lock)	—	1573A	—	CB1

TABLE 3.2 Common Keyways for Select Locks (*Continued*)

	Cole	Ilco	Taylor	Star
(Steering	—	1573B	—	CB2
wheel lock)	—	1573C	—	CB3
	—	1573D	—	CB4
	—	1573E	—	CB5
	—	1573F	—	CB6
	—	1581G	—	—
	—	1581H	—	—
File cabinets	CB14	1041Y	41Y	5CG4
	CO105	1003D	22R$	—
	CO106	1003M	22R14	5AU1
	SC6	1307A	307A	SH2
Freezers	CG16	1054UN	41RB	IL10UN
	RO1	1069	62	RO1
	RO6	1069-54	174H	—
	Y12	H1122F	H7F	—
	Y103	K1122B	L54K	—
Garage door openers	CG1	1041G	41G	CG1
Garage doors	L1	1054MT	54MT	5IL11
	Y1	BKZ1	—	—
	Y1C	—	—	—
	T4	1141GE	111GE	5TA4
Gas caps	B1	1098GX	—	HBR3
Mail boxes	BO1	R1003M	22B	5BO1
	CO105	1003D	22R4	—

TABLE 3.2 Common Keyways for Select Locks (*Continued*)

	Cole	Ilco	Taylor	Star
Mail boxes	Y14	H1122AR	HRO7NX	—
	NA12	1069LB	174BA	5AU2
Mopeds	M12	1092DS	92F	4MA7
Screen doors	PZ1	—	—	—
Sprinkler boxes	B1	1098GX	—	HBR3
Suitcases	M1	1092	92	MA1
Tool boxes	B1	1098GX	—	HBR3
	CO26	1000V	20V	LC07
	Y11	H1054L	—	—
	Y12	H1122F	H7F	—

the key, then use that template to guide you while you cut the blank. To make a template, tightly wrap a piece of soft metal around the blade of the key to create a pattern of the key's cuts. File the piece of metal to make it match the cuts of the bit. Remove the template, and wrap it around the blade of a bit key blank. Clamp the blank and template into a vise and carefully file down the blank to match the pattern (Figure 3.10).

To duplicate a flat or corrugated key by hand, both the key and the blank need to be clamped into a vise. While holding both in the same direction, align the key and blank at the shoulders (key cuts on top of blade) and clamp them together in the vise. Using the key as a guide, carefully copy the cuts onto the blank with a warded file.

Duplicate a cylinder key by hand by clamping the key and blank together (aligned at the shoulders) in a vise. Use a pippin file or a triangle file to carefully copy the cuts.

Smoking a Key

Some locksmiths find it easier to duplicate a flat, corrugated, or cylinder key by smoking the key before cutting the blank. The soot on a smoked key helps you know when the blank has been filed down enough. When the file wipes the soot off the key, you know you've filed deep enough at that cut.

To smoke a key, use a pair of pliers to hold it over a candle flame, cuts facing down. Move the key over the flame until soot has built up in all of the cuts.

After cutting a smoked key, be sure to clean the soot off because it can damage a lock.

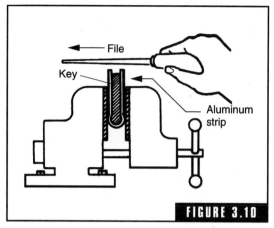

FIGURE 3.10

A strip of thin metal can be used to make a pattern of a bit key.

Warded, Lever Tumbler, Disc Tumbler, and Side Bar Wafer Locks

The locks covered in this chapter—warded, lever tumbler, disc tumbler, and side bar wafer—are all named by their internal construction.

Warded Locks

The Romans are credited with inventing the warded lock. It is the oldest and least secure type of lock commonly in use today. "Warded" refers to a type of internal construction designed to block unauthorized keys from entering or operating a lock. Warded locks come in various shapes and sizes, and are mostly in the form of padlocks and building door locks. From the outside, some warded locks look like more secure locks. You can quickly identify a warded lock by its keyhole or wide keyway (Figure 4.1).

The warded lock relies primarily on wards for its security. Other types of locks also use wards, but not as the primary means of security. *Wards* are fixed obstructions within a lock case; they are designed to prevent unauthorized keys from entering or rotating in the keyway. In theory, only a key with notches corresponding with the sizes and positions of the wards can operate a warded lock. The

FIGURE 4.1

An example of a warded lock. *(Courtesy of Ilco Unican Corp.)*

wards prevent the rotation of other keys into position to open the lock (Figure 4.2).

Warded locks aren't used for high-security applications because the typical warded lock provides fewer than 50 keying possibilities. That means a person with 50 different keys for such locks can open virtually all of them.

Changing ward sizes and configurations provides few keying possibilities because the number of ward changes that can be made depend on the size of the lock. A warded keying system could never be large enough to match modern high-security locks.

A more significant problem with warded locks is that a properly notched key isn't needed to operate them. Wards can be easily bypassed by using a very thin key, known as a skeleton key.

Warded Padlocks

Warded padlocks are the least expensive type of padlock available. They are also the least secure (Figure 4.3). The locks are usually operated with corrugated keys, though some of the more expensive models use flat keys. A group of five skeleton keys sold by locksmithing supply houses can be used to open most warded padlocks. A properly bent paperclip works nearly as well.

Parts

All of the parts of a warded padlock are housed in the lock's case. The case of most warded padlocks consists of several steel plates, or laminations. The parts of a typical warded padlock include a shackle,

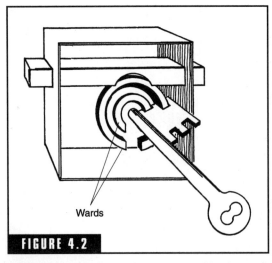

Wards

FIGURE 4.2

A bit key must have cuts that correspond to the wards of a lock.

pins, a shackle spring, a stop plate, a retainer spring, a shackle retainer, several dummy plates, one or more ward plates, and a keyway.

When in the locked position, the shackle spring presses the shackle retainer against the shackle, which holds the shackle in the locked position. The key that bypasses the wards in the lock can be turned to push the shackle retainer against the spring to release the shackle from the lock.

FIGURE 4.3

A warded padlock offers little security.

As the name implies, a *ward plate* is a plate that is used as a ward. The plate has a cutout in the center shaped to allow only certain keys to enter.

A *dummy plate* is used to build the size of a lock case. Such a plate has a large hole in the center. The *stop plate* is directly beneath the shackle and farthest from the keyway. That plate holds one side of the shackle in the lock case at all times. The *pins* are used to hold all of the various plates together.

Because the locks are so inexpensive, locksmiths don't generally repair warded padlocks. If you'd like to disassemble one, just file down the pins. You can then remove the plates and see all of the parts. However, don't expect to find replacement parts at a locksmith supply house.

Warded Bit Key Locks

The oldest type of warded lock is the warded bit key lock. It usually has a metal case and a large keyhole that accepts a bit key. Such locks come in two styles: mortise and rim.

The *mortise bit key lock* is designed to be mortised, or recessed, into a door. The *rim bit key lock* is designed to be surface mounted on a door. Figure 4.4 shows an outside view of a rim bit key lock.

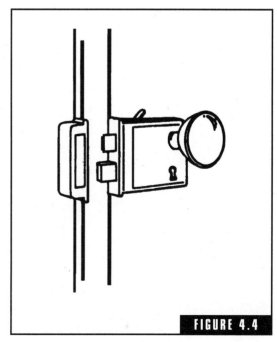

FIGURE 4.4

A rim bit key lock is installed on the surface of a door.

Parts

The construction of most warded bit key locks is very simple. The type and number of parts in those locks depend primarily on the functions of the locks. Those designed for the same function usually have few construction variations among them.

Basic parts found in warded bit key locks include a latch bolt, a hub spindle, a latch bolt spring, an inside latch lock, an inside latch lock spring, a deadbolt, and a lever tumbler. All of these parts are housed in a lock case (Figure 4.5). The front of the lock case is the *cover plate*.

Fixed obstructions on the lock case are positioned to prevent the free motion of the deadbolt when it is in the fully locked or fully unlocked position. When a key designed to bypass the wards is inserted into the keyhole and turned, the key raises the deadbolt over

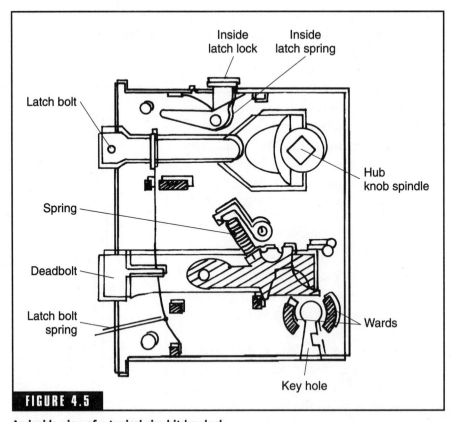

FIGURE 4.5

An inside view of a typical rim bit key lock.

the obstructions and slides it to the locked or unlocked position.

When the deadbolt is in the unlocked position, the latch bolt keeps the door closed. Turning the door knob causes the hub spindle to pull the latch bolt back into the lock case and allows the door to be opened. When the door knob is released, the latch bolt spring pushes the latch bolt back out of the lock case.

The inside latch lock deadlatches the latch bolt. When the inside latch lock is pushed down, it prevents the latch bolt being pulled back by the hub spindle from outside the door.

> **TRADE SECRET**
>
> Disassembling and reassembling locks are great ways to learn. Before removing parts from a bit key lock the first time, carefully remove the cover (probably held in place by one screw), and make a sketch of the parts in the case. The sketch will be helpful when you're reassembling the lock. Also, as you remove parts from the lock, keep them together in the order that you removed them.

The *tumbler spring* applies pressure to keep the deadbolt in the proper position while it's being moved with a key. Some locks use additional springs, but all serve the purpose of applying pressure to parts. Both flat springs and coil springs are commonly used in warded bit key locks.

Servicing

Most problems with warded bit key locks are caused by foreign material—usually dirt or paint—in the lock and/or a weak or broken spring. Often you can service the lock simply by cleaning the lock case and parts, then using a little graphite to lubricate the parts. Don't use oil because it can cause dust to collect on the parts. Servicing the lock occasionally involves replacing a spring.

Lever Tumbler Locks

The lever tumbler lock is so named because it relies primarily on levers within the lock for its security. It is frequently found on luggage, mail boxes, and school lockers.

Most lever tumbler locks sold in the United States, Mexico, and England use flat keys. Many sold in other countries are operated with bit or barrel keys. The type of key used, however, doesn't affect the basic operation of a lever tumbler lock.

Generally speaking, the basic lever tumbler lock offers slightly more security than the warded lock. Some specially designed lever

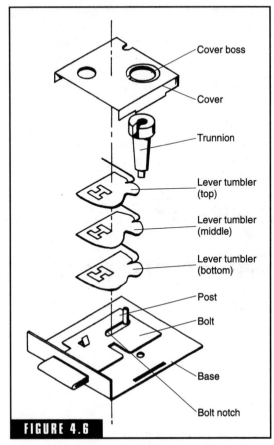

FIGURE 4.6

Cover boss

Cover

Trunnion

Lever tumbler (top)

Lever tumbler (middle)

Lever tumbler (bottom)

Post

Bolt

Base

Bolt notch

An exploded view of a typical lever tumbler lock.

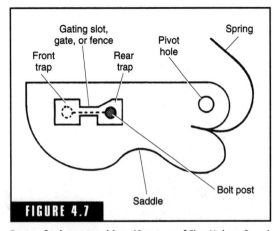

Gating slot, gate, or fence

Front trap

Rear trap

Pivot hole

Spring

Bolt post

Saddle

FIGURE 4.7

Parts of a lever tumbler. *(Courtesy of Ilco Unican Corp.)*

tumbler locks offer a high degree of security. An example is the type found on safe deposit boxes. Unlike a typical lever tumbler lock, the high-security version often has six or more tumblers, is made of high-quality materials, and has little tolerance between its parts.

Parts

The parts of a basic lever tumbler lock are housed in a case consisting of a base, or back cover, and a cover. The parts within the case include the trunnion, or key plug; lever tumblers (usually three or more); and bolt. A post, or bolt post, is fixed on the bolt (Figure 4.6).

The cover boss is a raised opening on the cover; it sits on the trunnion and exposes the keyway. A properly cut key has tumbler cuts that correspond in height and width to the lever tumblers. The key also has a throat cut, which allows it to ride over the raised ridge of the cover boss. The cover boss of a lever tumbler lock acts like a ward in a warded lock.

To understand how lever tumbler locks operate, you have to know the parts of a lever tumbler. They include the front trap; gate, or fence; rear trap; pivot hole; spring; and saddle (Figure 4.7). The lever tumblers sit on the bolt and are held in place by spring tension. The *traps* and *gate* are open areas on the tumbler that restrict the movement of the bolt post.

Operation

When the bolt post moves from one trap to another, the lock bolt extends or retracts. When a properly cut key is inserted, it slides over the saddles of the tumblers and lifts each to the height necessary to allow the bolt post to move from one trap to another.

For increased security, modern lever tumbler locks use tumblers with staggered saddle heights or staggered trap heights. Such tumblers make it difficult to pick the locks.

Servicing

Some lever tumbler lock cases are riveted or spot welded. These locks usually don't cost enough to justify servicing them. To service them you must drill out the rivets or chisel through the case, then spend time putting the case back together.

Other lever tumbler locks can easily be disassembled by removing a screw holding the cover or prying up the metal tabs holding the cover. After removing the cover, look for a broken spring. If you find one, replace it.

Disc Tumbler Locks

The disc tumbler lock is used on automobiles, desks, cabinets, and vending machines. As the name implies, this lock relies primarily on disc tumblers for its security. Sometimes disc tumbler locks are called "wafer tumbler locks."

As a general rule, this lock provides better security and offers more keying possibilities than either the warded or basic lever lock offers. A typical disc tumbler lock allows over 3000 possible key changes.

Parts

Basic parts of a disc tumbler lock include the lock housing, or shell; bolt, or cam; retainer; plug; springs; and disc tumblers, or wafer tumblers (Figures 4.8 and 4.9).

A *disc tumbler* is a flat piece of metal with a rectangular hole in its center. It also has a leg on one side for a spring to sit on. All disc tumblers within a lock are the same height and width, but their center holes vary in height. To operate a disc tumbler lock, a key must have cuts that correspond to the rectangular cutouts on the tumblers. The cutouts are the same size but are positioned at varying places along the tumblers. The position of a tumbler's cutout determines the depth of key cut needed to move the tumbler into alignment along the shear line.

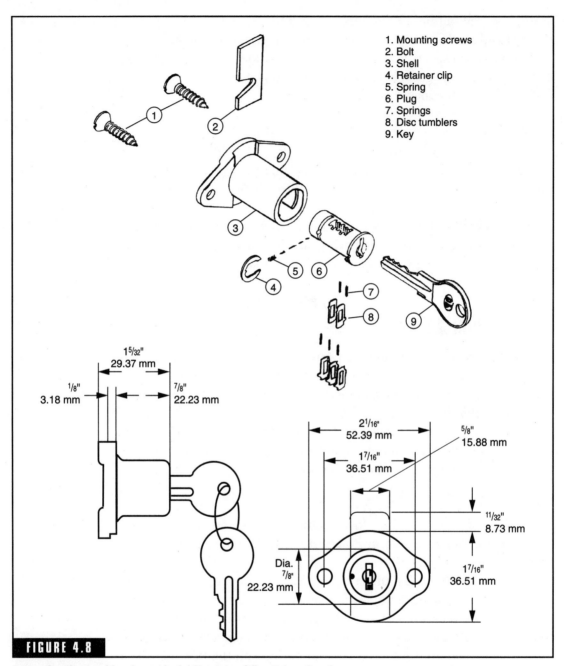

1. Mounting screws
2. Bolt
3. Shell
4. Retainer clip
5. Spring
6. Plug
7. Springs
8. Disc tumblers
9. Key

FIGURE 4.8

Parts of a disc tumbler drawer lock. *(Courtesy of Ilco Unican Corp.)*

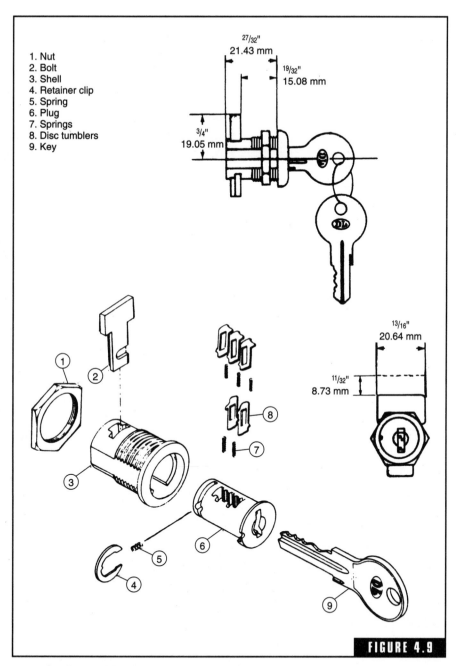

1. Nut
2. Bolt
3. Shell
4. Retainer clip
5. Spring
6. Plug
7. Springs
8. Disc tumblers
9. Key

FIGURE 4.9

Parts of a disc tumbler desk lock. *(Courtesy of Ilco Unican Corp.)*

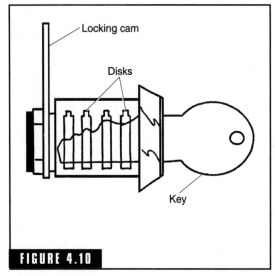

Locking cam

Disks

Key

FIGURE 4.10

A proper key pulls all the disc tumblers of a lock into the plug. Cuts in the key blade align the individual slots in the disk, allowing the cylinder to turn.

The *plug* is the cylindrical part of the lock that contains the keyway. To move the bolt to the locked or unlocked position, the plug must be rotated. Whenever the proper key is not in the keyway, the disc tumblers prevent the rotation of the plug.

The plug has rectangular slots that each hold a spring and a disc tumbler. The springs maintain constant pressure on the tumblers, forcing them to protrude out of the plug and partially enter the shell. In that position, the tumblers connect the plug and shell together. A properly cut key pulls all the tumblers fully into the plug, which allows the plug to rotate (Figure 4.10).

Side Bar Wafer Locks

Many automobiles manufactured by General Motors Corporation use a type of disc tumbler lock called a side bar wafer lock. It has a V-notch on one side of each disc, a V-shaped side bar, and a special slot within the lock housing for a portion of the side bar to protrude into when in the locked position.

The side bar must be fully retracted from the slot in the housing before the plug can be rotated. Before the side bar can fully retract from the housing, all of the V notches of the disc tumblers must be aligned to allow the V-shaped portion of the side bar to fit into those notches.

Spring pressure forces the side bar to constantly press against the discs. When the proper key is inserted into the lock, all of the disc tumblers are properly aligned and the side bar pushes into the V notches and clears the slot in the lock housing.

Pin Tumbler Locks

A pin tumbler is any lock that relies on the pin tumbler cylinder as its primary means of security. The pin tumbler cylinder is the most popular type of cylinder in use today. It's used in many key-in-knob locks, deadbolt locks, rim locks, padlocks, and automobile locks. You can easily identify a pin tumbler lock by looking into its keyway; you'll see the first bottom pin.

Basic parts of a pin tumbler cylinder include: the cylinder case, or "housing" or "shell"; plug, or "core"; keyway; lower pin chambers; upper pin chambers; springs; top pins, or "drivers"; and bottom pins (Figures 5.1 and 5.2). Some pin tumbler cylinders have more parts, but all models basically work the same way.

The cylinder case houses the other basic parts. The plug is the part with the keyway, and that rotates when you're turning the key. When the cylinder is disassembled, you'll see drilled holes, usually five or six, along the length of the plug. Those are lower pin chambers, and each holds a tapered bottom pin. Inside the cylinder case, in alignment with the lower pin chambers, are holes that correspond in size and position, called *upper pin chambers*. The upper pin chambers each house a spring that presses against one or more top pins. Each set of top and bottom pins within corresponding pin chambers is called a *stack*. Usually each stack has only two pins (a top and a bottom), but masterkeyed cylinders may have three or more pins in a stack.

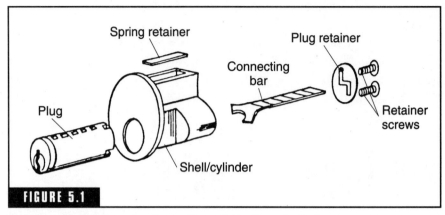

FIGURE 5.1

Partially exploded view of a pin tumbler cylinder for a rim lock.

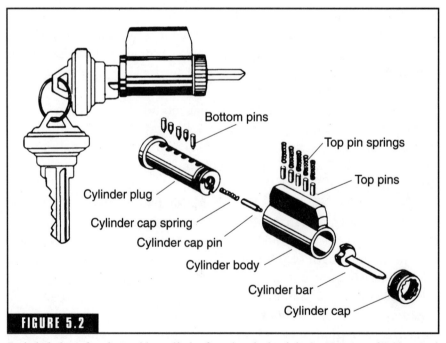

FIGURE 5.2

Exploded view of a pin tumbler cylinder for a key-in-knob lock. *(Courtesy of Schlage Lock Company)*

Operation

The position of each pin determines whether or not the cylinder can be rotated. Pin positions are determined by gravity, pressure from the springs, and pressure from the key (or lockpick; for information on lockpicking, see Chapter 10). When no key is in the keyway, gravity and the downward pressure of the springs drive the top pins into the plug, until they rest on their corresponding bottom pins. Because the bottom pin lengths vary from one lower pin chamber to another, some top pins will drop different depths into the lower pin chambers. When a pin is in its upper pin chamber and in a lower pin chamber at the same time, the pin obstructs the plug from turning. If you tried to rotate the plug forcibly at that time, you would most likely bend the pin causing a serious lockout.

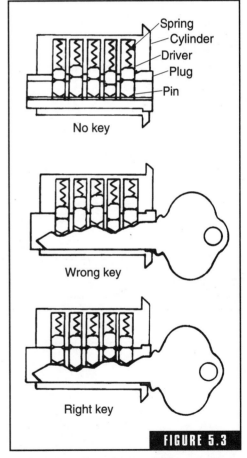

When a cylinder is made, there is always space between the case and its plug. Otherwise the plug would be jammed in so tight that it could never be turned, regardless of the pin positions or which key is used. That space between the case and plug is called a *shear line*. When inserted into the keyway, the proper key slides under all the bottom pins and lifts each to the shear line. The proper key will fit the keyway and have properly spaced cuts of the right depths to match each bottom pin length. When all the top and bottom pins meet at the shear line, none of them are obstructing the plug from being rotated. Figure 5.3 shows how the right key aligns the pins to the shear line. When the plug is rotated, the top pins separate from their respective bottom pins. See Figure 5.4.

FIGURE 5.3

The right key aligns the top and bottom pins to the shear line so the plug is free to rotate.

Repairs

Removing a Broken Key

You might need to remove a piece of broken key from the plug of a pin tumbler lock. First

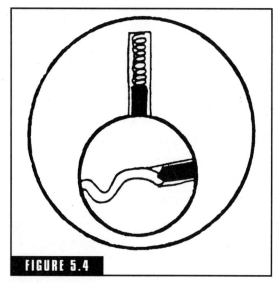

FIGURE 5.4

When the plug is rotated, the top pins rest on its surface.

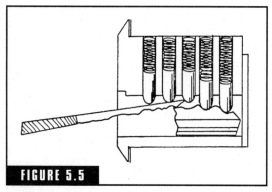

FIGURE 5.5

A thin hooked tool can be used to remove a piece of broken key from a cylinder.

make sure the broken key is in the position that a key is normally inserted to operate the lock (usually either the 12 o'clock or 6 o'clock position). That position ensures that the pins are properly aligned for key removal. You may need to use pliers to turn the key into position. You may then also be able to use the pliers to pull the broken key out of the cylinder, depending on how much of the broken key is protruding from the keyway. Another option is to insert a thin, hooked piece of wire into the keyway, hook pointing towards the key's cuts, and hook into the key to pull it out (Figure 5.5). Sometimes it's easier to use a thin saw blade to poke the broken key and manipulate it out of the plug (Figure 5.6).

Locksmith supply houses sell a wide variety of broken-key extractor tools.

Rekeying

To rekey a pin tumbler cylinder, first remove the device retaining the plug, which will be a retainer clip, cam, or cylinder cap. The device varies among different pin tumbler cylinders.

Remove a retainer clip by carefully prying it off with a small screwdriver (avoid bending or breaking it). Remove a cam by unscrewing the two small screws holding it in place.

To remove a cylinder cap (found on key-in-knob locks), depress the cap pin with an awl or the edge of a small screwdriver, then rotate the cap counterclockwise until it comes off (Figure 5.7). Remove both the cap pin and the small spring beneath it from the plug. (You may find it helpful to place the cylinder in a vise with the tailpiece and cap up. That will allow you to use both hands to remove the cap.)

Rotate the plug about 15 degrees clockwise or counterclockwise. The easiest way is to use a key. If no key is available, you'll need to pick or shim the lock. Do not pull the plug forward while rotating it.

Now hold a plug follower or following bar firmly against the back of the plug (Figure 5.8). Push the tool through the cylinder body. Make sure the plug follower is in constant contact with the back of the plug; if the plug and plug follower separate too soon, the top pins and springs will fall out of the upper pin chambers.

After the plug is pushed out of the cylinder body, set the cylinder body aside and set the plug into a plug holder, or holding fixture (Figure 5.9). It isn't essential to use a plug holder, but using one makes rekeying cylinders easier.

Remove the pins from the plug. Insert a new key. Then add appropriately sized pins into the plug. Use bottom pins that reach the shear line of the plug with the new key in place. Figure 5.10 shows how the pins should be aligned.

There are three ways to find the correct pins. Compare the key bitting numbers written on the bows of some factory original keys to the cross-reference charts listed on most key pinning kits. If the key doesn't have such a number, you can use a key gauge or a caliper to measure the depths of the cuts of the key, then compare your readings with the information listed on your key pinning kit. Appendix E is a chart of the depths and spaces used by many lock manufacturers.

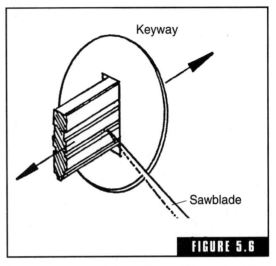

FIGURE 5.6

Sometimes a saw blade can be used to manipulate a piece of broken key out of a cylinder.

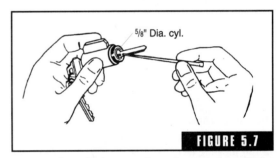

FIGURE 5.7

Depress the cylinder cap pin and rotate the cylinder cap counterclockwise to remove the cap. *(Courtesy of Schlage Lock Company)*

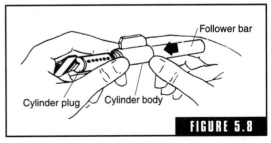

FIGURE 5.8

Use a plug follower to hold the springs and top pins in place while removing the plug. *(Courtesy of Schlage Lock Company)*

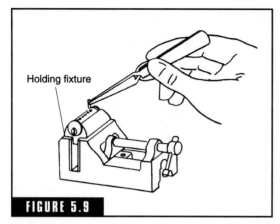

FIGURE 5.9

A plug holder can be used to hold the plug you're working on. *(Courtesy of Schlage Lock Company)*

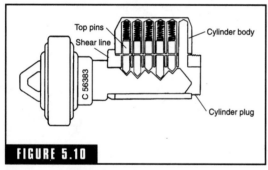

FIGURE 5.10

When a properly cut key is inserted into a cylinder, all the pins are raised to the shear line. *(Courtesy of Schlage Lock Company)*

Another way to find the right pins is trial and error. Look at the key and compare the depths of the cuts to one another. The deeper the cut in the key, the longer the pin for that cut must be. After finding the right pin for the first cut, use the size of that pin as a reference point for locating the other sizes you need.

Ideally, you should find pins that fit perfectly in the plug. In an emergency, you might want to use bottom pins that are too long, then file them down with a fine mill file. Use the key to rotate the plug while filing so you don't flatten the top of the plug (Figure 5.11). Most locksmiths consider it unprofessional to file down pins.

After fitting the pins to the plug, insert the plug into the face of the cylinder body. Push the back of the plug against the plug follower until the tool comes out of the cylinder (Figure 5.12). Do not allow the plug and the plug follower to separate from each other.

Hold the plug and the cylinder body so the plug doesn't slip out of the body, and

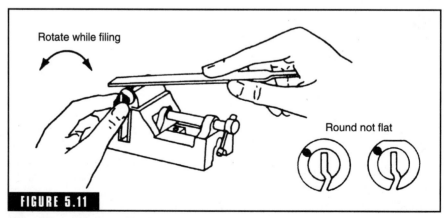

FIGURE 5.11

When filing pins, don't file the plug. *(Courtesy of Schlage Lock Company)*

test the new key. Make sure the plug rotates easily and the key smoothly slides in and out of the plug (Figure 5.13). If there is a problem at this point, use the plug follower to remove the plug, then check the heights of the pins. Put the plug back into the housing and test the key again.

After the key is working properly with the plug in the cylinder body, slowly remove the key. Don't pull hard enough for the plug to slip out of the cylinder body. Reassemble the cylinder by reversing the procedure you used to disassemble it (Figure 5.14).

Replacing Top Pins

Many locksmiths purposely remove the springs and top pins every time they rekey locks. This allows the locksmith to clean the upper pin chambers and replace any worn or broken top pins.

To reload the upper pin chambers, use a pair of tweezers or similar device to hold pins. With this device and a plug follower, you can easily replace the springs and top pins (Figure 5.15). However, it takes a little practice. The first time you try loading upper pin chambers, you'll probably frequently drop pins and springs.

Tubular Key Locks

The tubular key lock is basically a pin tumbler lock that has its tumblers arranged in a circle. Like any other pin tumbler lock, it has springs, top pins, and bottom pins. The tubular key has notches of varying sizes to correspond with the lengths of the pins.

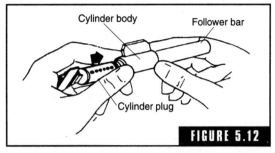

FIGURE 5.12

Push the plug against the plug follower. *(Courtesy of Schlage Lock Company)*

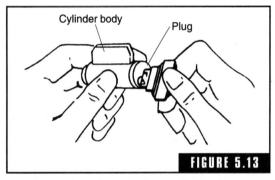

FIGURE 5.13

Test the new key after rekeying a cylinder. *(Courtesy of Schlage Lock Company)*

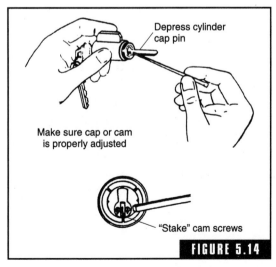

FIGURE 5.14

Put the retaining device back in place after rekeying the cylinder. *(Courtesy of Schlage Lock Company)*

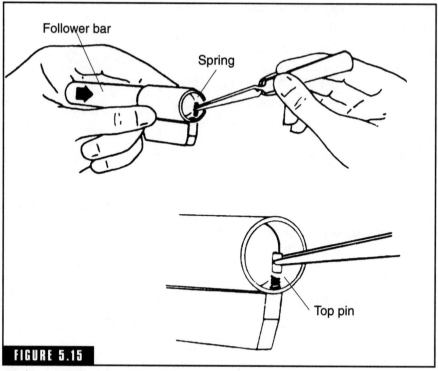

Follower bar

Spring

Top pin

It takes a little practice to feel comfortable replacing springs and top pins. *(Courtesy of Schlage Lock Company)*

QUICK›››TIP It's helpful to practice disassembling pin tumbler cylinders. (Of course, the first time, either buy a cylinder or use an old one that you don't need for anything else.) To handle the pins more easily, you can use tweezers sold in drug stores. If you don't have a plug follower, you can use a wooden dowel, copper piping, a pen, or most any cylindrical object that will fit your cylinder.

When the key is inserted into the keyway, it pushes the pins to the shear line so the plug can rotate.

Locksmithing Tools

In addition to the hand and power tools commonly found in hardware stores, locksmiths work with a variety of special tools. Some of the special tools are used only for locksmithing tasks. This chapter reviews many of those tools and explains how to buy and make some of them. This chapter also includes a list of all of the tools needed to start a locksmithing business.

Any of the locksmithing tools you can't make yourself or find locally can be purchased from locksmith supply houses. Appendix G has a list of such suppliers. You can obtain catalogs from them by sending them a locksmith business card or letterhead, a locksmith license, a copy of your locksmith bond card, or similar evidence that you're a locksmith. Some suppliers only sell to locksmiths, but many also sell to other security professionals.

When buying tools, always get the best quality you can afford. Tools that break or don't work properly will cause you many headaches. Be sure to get a wide variety of basic hand tools—like chisels, screwdrivers, and striking and prying tools (Figure 6.1). Although you can often complete a job using a hand tool that's the wrong size, you'll work faster and do a more professional job with tools that are the right size and weight (Figure 6.2).

1) Common nail hammer
2) Rip hammer
3) Finishing hammer
4) Ball peen hammer
5) Hand drilling hammer
6) Soft-face hammer
7) Magnetic tack hammer
8) Brick hammer
9) Drywall (wallboard) hammer
10) Prybar

FIGURE 6.1

Every locksmith needs a variety of striking and prying tools. *(Courtesy of Vaughan & Bushnell Manufacturing Company)*

Electric Drill

An electric, or "ac powered," drill is a locksmith's most often-used power tool (Figure 6.3). It is used for installing locks, drilling into locks and safes, installing various exit devices, etc. A high-quality drill can cost several times more than a low-quality drill, but it is usually worth the extra money. It will provide many years of heavy-duty service, and save you time and sweat.

There are three basic drill sizes: ¼-inch, ⅜-inch, and ½-inch. A drill's size is based on the largest diameter drill bit shank the drill's chuck can accept without using an adapter. For example, a drill whose chuck can

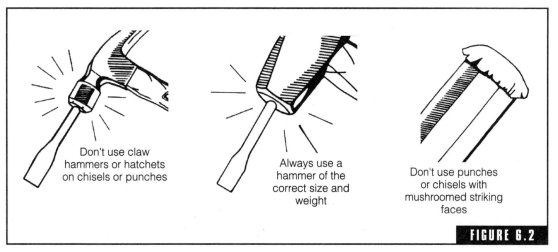

Don't use claw hammers or hatchets on chisels or punches

Always use a hammer of the correct size and weight

Don't use punches or chisels with mushroomed striking faces

FIGURE 6.2

To work efficiently and without hurting yourself, you need to use the right tools. *(Courtesy of Vaughan & Bushnell Manufacturing Company)*

hold a drill bit shank up to ½ inch in diameter is a ½-inch drill.

A drill's power is a combination of chuck speed and torque. Chuck speed is measured in *RPM*, or revolutions per minute when spinning freely in the air. *Torque* refers to the twisting force at the chuck when the drill is being used to drill a hole. RPM alone isn't a good measure of a drill's power, because a drill slows down when doing work. More important than free-spinning speed is the speed of a drill's chuck while it is drilling a hole.

Chuck speed and torque are largely determined by the type of reduction gears on a drill. Reduction gears work somewhat like car gears. One gear, for example, allows a car to move quickly on flat roads; another gives the

Chuck

Removable handle

Chuck jaws

FIGURE 6.3

An electric drill is an important tool for locksmiths. *(Courtesy of Skil Corporation)*

car more power to climb steep hills. The analogy isn't perfect, however, because a drill (unlike a car) comes with a fixed set of reduction gears. You can't shift the gears of a drill.

A drill with a single-stage reduction gear set has a chuck that spins very fast in the air (high RPM) but slows down considerably when drilling a hole. A drill with a three-stage reduction gear set has fewer

RPM but more torque. Generally speaking, the higher the reduction gear set, the slower and more powerful the drill.

Most ¼-inch drills have single-stage reduction gear sets, which can allow a chuck to spin at 2500 RPM or more. Such drills are lightweight and are used primarily for drilling plastic, thin softwood, and sheet metal. Using a drill that has a single-stage reduction gear set to drill hardwood or steel would be time-consuming and could damage the drill.

A ⅜-inch drill is generally faster than the ½-inch drill and provides more torque than the ¼-inch drill. The chuck of a ⅜-inch drill usually spins at about 1000 RPM. The drill can be useful for drilling metals up to ⅜ inch thick and wood up to ¾ inch thick.

A ½-inch drill usually has either a two-stage or a three-stage reduction gear set, and its chuck spins at about 600 RPM. The ½-inch drill is the most popular among locksmiths, because it's most useful for installing locks and door hardware, and for drilling open safes. The wide jaws of a ½-inch drill allows it to hold auger bits, boring bits, and a wide variety of shanks (Figure 6.3a).

Although today's locksmith offers a wide variety of services, lock installation is still a major part of locksmithing.

Not all ½-inch drills are alike, however; they often differ greatly in quality and price. Some manufacturers label their drills as "heavy-duty," "professional," or "commercial." Such labels have no standard meaning. When looking for a high-quality drill, it's best to ignore such labels and look for specific features. Important features to look for include two- or three-stage reduction gear sets, at least 600 RPM, variable speed reversible control switch, double insulation, all anti-friction (needle or ball) bearings, and at least 5 amps of power.

Drills come with one or two fixed speeds or variable speeds. Variable speed drills are the most flexible; they have a switch that allows you to use any speed from 0 RPM up to the drill's highest speed. This enables you to drill different materials at different speeds.

Many drills also have a switch that reverses the direction of the chuck. This is useful for backing out screws or a stuck drill bit. Drills that have both variable speed control and a reversible drive switch are called *variable speed reversible*, or VSR.

Some drills feature double insulation. The drill is housed in non-conductive material such as plastic, and nonconductive material is also used to isolate the motor from other metal parts of the drill. Double insulation is a safety feature that protects the user against being shocked. Most high-quality drills are double insulated, so don't mistake plastic or rubberlike housing as a sign of low quality.

Anti-friction bearings help a drill run smoothly and help it last longer. Low-quality drills use all plain sleeve bearings. A few high-quality drills use a well-planned mixture of both types of bearings.

The amperage (measured in amps) that a drill uses is a good indicator of its power. Usually the more amps a drill uses, the more powerful it is. Look for a drill that uses at least 5 amps.

Cordless Drill

A cordless drill operates with battery power and is usually lighter and more convenient than ac-powered electric drills (Figure 6.4). It can be very useful when no electrical outlets are available, but a cordless drill isn't as powerful as a comparably sized ac-powered model.

Broken-Key Extractor

A *broken-key extractor* is used to remove broken pieces of a key from a lock (Figure 6.5). You can make the tool with a 4-inch piece of a hacksaw blade. Starting at either end of the blade, grind off a 1-inch length of the nontoothed side of the blade until that 1-inch length is about ¼ inch thick. Wrap electrical tape around the other 3 inches of the blade. The taped 3-inch part is used as the handle, and the narrow 1-inch section is used for entering a keyway.

Plug Follower

A *plug follower* is used to hold top springs and pins in the cylinder when the plug is removed. It must be about the same size as the plug. Locksmithing supply houses sell plug followers in various

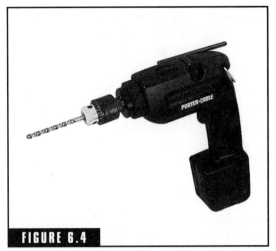

A cordless drill can be useful to a locksmith when no electrical outlet is available. *(Courtesy of Porter Cable Corp.)*

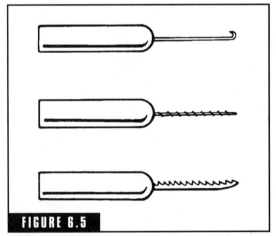

Broken key extractors make it easy to remove broken pieces of keys from locks. *(Courtesy of A-1 Security Manufacturing Corp.)*

sizes; most of them are made of bar stock (Figure 6.6).

You can make your own plug followers out of wooden dowels or copper tubing. They should each be about 4 inches long and about ½ inch in diameter; you might need smaller diameters for some locks.

Plug Holder

A *plug holder* holds a plug while you're servicing or rekeying it (Figure 6.7). You can make one by using a hacksaw to cut off the bottom quarter of an old cylinder that's the same size as the plug you're working on.

Tool Lists

List 1. Common hand and power tools all locksmiths should have.

- Allen wrench set

- Bench grinder with wire wheel

- Bolt cutters, 16-inch

- C-clamps

- Center punch set

- Code books, general set

- Combination square

- Coping saw and blades

- Dent puller

- Disc grinder (Figure 6.8)

- Drill bits, auger assortment

- Drill bits, expansion assortment

- Drill bits, masonry assortment (Figure 6.9)

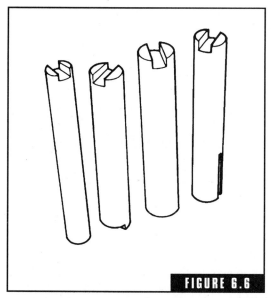

FIGURE 6.6

Plug followers are used for rekeying locks. *(Courtesy of Ilco Unican Corp.)*

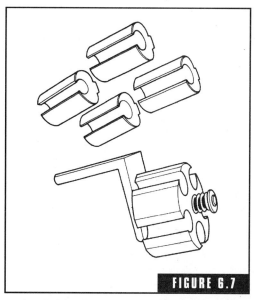

FIGURE 6.7

A plug holder holds plugs while they're being worked on. *(Courtesy of Ilco Unican Corp.)*

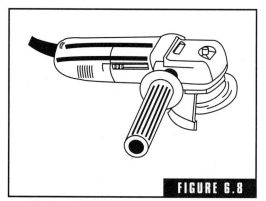

FIGURE 6.8

A disc grinder can be useful for removing high-security screws. *(Courtesy of Skil Corporation)*

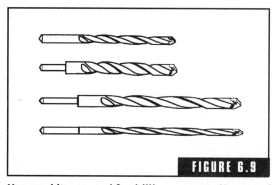

FIGURE 6.9

Masonry bits are used for drilling concrete. *(Courtesy of Keedex Mfg.)*

- Drill bits, spade assortment
- Drill bits, straight assortment
- Drill, cordless
- Drill, electric with ½-inch chuck
- Extension cord, 50-foot
- Files, assorted types and sizes (Figure 6.10)
- Flashlight
- Hacksaw and blades
- Hammers; claw, ball-peen, and soft-face (back in Figure 6.1)
- Hand cleaner
- Hollow mill rivet set
- Lever, carpenter's (from 18 to 96 inches long with three vials)
- Lever, torpedo (up to 9 inches long)
- Lubricant (such as WD-40)
- Mallet, rubber
- Masking tape
- Nails and screws, assorted
- One-way screw removal tool
- Paint scraper
- Pencils
- Pliers, adjustable
- Pliers, cutting
- Pliers, locking
- Pliers, long nose (7-inch)
- Pliers, slip-joint
- Retractable tape measure, 25-foot
- Rivet assortment
- Safety glasses

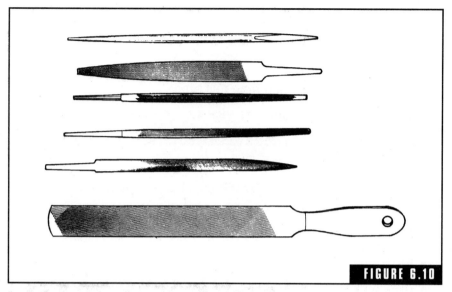

Locksmiths use files to impression keys and to duplicate keys by hand. *(Courtesy of Ilco Unican Corp.)*

- Sandpaper and emery cloth
- Scissors for paper
- Scratch awl
- Screwdriver bits, assorted Phillips and slotted
- Screwdrivers, assorted Phillips and slotted
- Snap ring pliers, assorted sizes
- Socket sets, ½-inch and ¼-inch
- Storage trays
- Tap set
- Tool boxes
- Wrenches, adjustable and pipe

List 2. Tools for shop/bench work. (Needed in addition to all of the tools in List 1.)

- Code books
- Cylinder cap remover

- Dial caliper (Figure 6.11)
- Flat steel spring stock
- Impressioning plate (Figure 6.12)
- Interchangeable core capping machine
- Interchangeable core lock service kit
- Key blanks, assorted
- Key cutting machine, electric (Figure 6.13)
- Key duplicating, or code, machine, electric (Figure 6.14)
- Key marking tools
- Lock parts, assorted (Figure 6.15)
- Lock pick gun
- Lock pick set (Figure 6.16)
- Lock reading tool
- Mortise cylinder removal tools (Figure 6.17)
- Pin kit
- Pin tray (Figure 6.18)
- Pin tumbler tweezers (Figure 6.19)
- Plug followers, assorted sizes
- Plug holders
- Plug spinner (Figure 6.20)
- Retainer ring assortment
- Round spring steel, assorted sizes
- Shim stock (Figure 6.21)
- Spindle assortment
- Spring assortment
- Tension wrenches (Figure 6.22)
- Tubular key decoder (Figure 6.23)
- Tubular key lock picks (Figure 6.24)
- Tubular key lock saw (Figure 6.25)

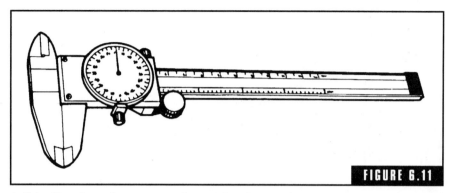

FIGURE 6.11

A dial caliper is used to measure pin tumblers, keys, and blanks. *(Courtesy of Ilco Unican Corp.)*

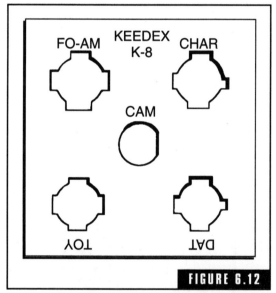

FIGURE 6.12

An impressioning plate is designed to hold locks in place. *(Courtesy of Keedex Mfg.)*

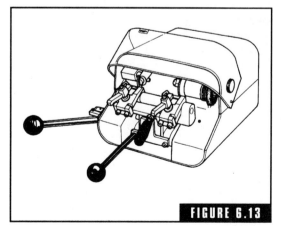

FIGURE 6.13

A key duplicating machine is used to copy keys. *(Courtesy of Ilco Unican Corp.)*

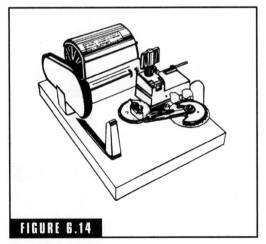

FIGURE 6.14

A key coding machine is used to make a key when the original isn't available. *(Courtesy of Ilco Unican Corp.)*

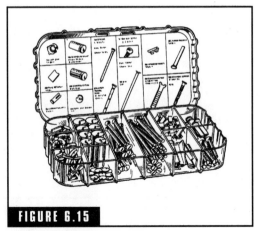

FIGURE 6.15

Lock parts are often needed when repairing locks. *(Courtesy of Ilco Unican Corp.)*

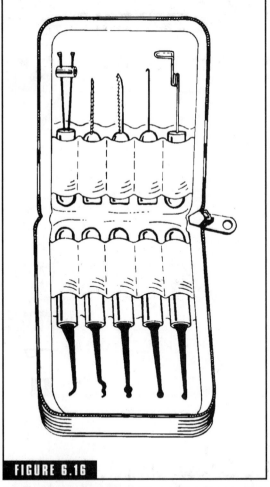

FIGURE 6.16

A lock pick set consists of picks and tension wrenches in a carrying case. *(Courtesy of A-1 Security Manufacturing Corp.)*

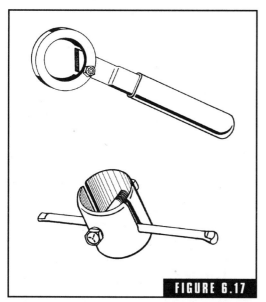

FIGURE 6.17

Cylinder removal tools are used to forcibly remove mortise cylinders. *(Courtesy of A-1 Security Manufacturing Corp.)*

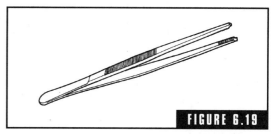

FIGURE 6.19

Pin tumbler tweezers are used for handling pins and small lock parts. *(Courtesy of Ilco Unican Corp.)*

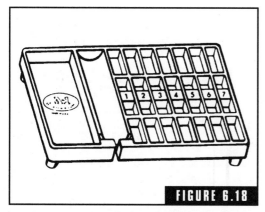

FIGURE 6.18

A pin tray allows a locksmith to keep lock tumblers in order. *(Courtesy of A-1 Security Manufacturing Corp.)*

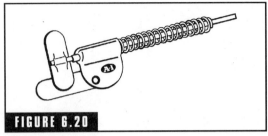

FIGURE 6.20

A plug spinner is used to spin a plug around when a lock has been picked in the wrong direction. *(Courtesy of A-1 Security Manufacturing Corp.)*

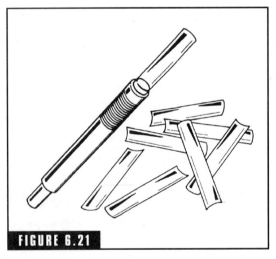

FIGURE 6.21

A shim holder and shims. *(Courtesy of A-1 Security Manufacturing Corp.)*

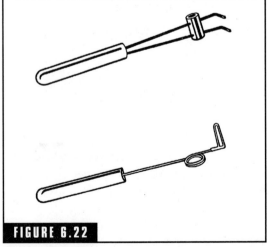

FIGURE 6.22

Tension wrenches, or torque wrenches, are available in assorted shapes and sizes. *(Courtesy of A-1 Security Manufacturing Corp.)*

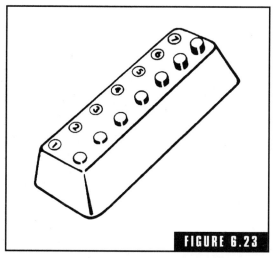

A tubular key decoder helps decode the cuts on tubular keys. *(Courtesy of A-1 Security Manufacturing Corp.)*

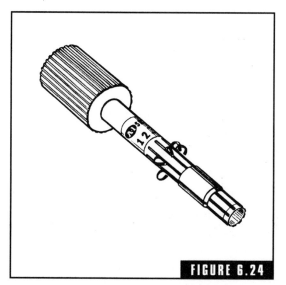

A tubular key lock pick. *(Courtesy of A-1 Security Manufacturing Corp.)*

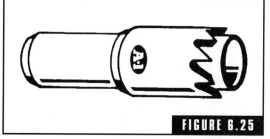

A tubular key lock saw is used to drill the pins in a tubular lock. *(Courtesy of A-1 Security Manufacturing Corp.)*

- Vise

- Whisk broom

- Work bench

List 3. Tools for automotive work. (Needed in addition to all of the tools in Lists 1 and 2.)

- Automobile entry tools and wedges (Figure 6.26)

- Bezel nut wrench (Figure 6.27)

- Broken-key extractors (Figure 6.5)

- Chrysler shaft puller

- Code books, automotive

- Code key-cutting machine, manual (Figure 6.28)

- Door handle clip removal tool (Figure 6.29)

- Door trim pad clip removal tool

- Face cap pliers

- Face caps

- Flexible light

- General Motors lock decoder (Figure 6.30)

- Lock plate compressor

- Steering column lock plate compressor

- Steering wheel pullers

- VATS/PASSKey decoder or key analyzer (Figure 6.31)

- Wedges (Figure 6.32)

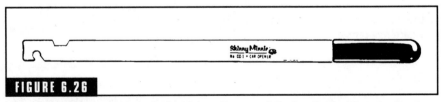

FIGURE 6.26

A versatile tool for opening locked vehicles. *(Courtesy of A-1 Security Manufacturing Corp.)*

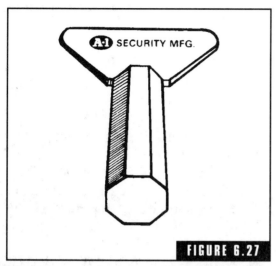

FIGURE 6.27

A bezel nut wrench is necessary for automotive lock servicing. *(Courtesy of A-1 Security Manufacturing Corp.)*

FIGURE 6.28

A manual hand-held code machine can be helpful when a locksmith needs to make keys on the road. *(Courtesy of A-1 Security Manufacturing Co.)*

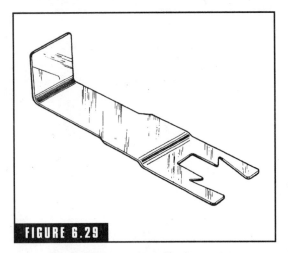

FIGURE 6.29

A door handle clip remover makes it easy to remove a door handle from an automobile. *(Courtesy of A-1 Security Manufacturing Corp.)*

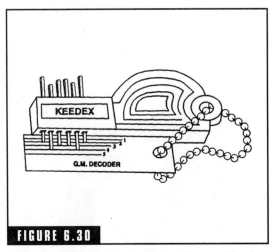

FIGURE 6.30

A GM decoder is used to decode tumbler combinations of GM locks. *(Courtesy of Keedex Mfg.)*

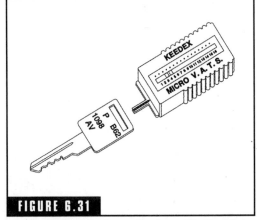

FIGURE 6.31

A VATS/PASSKey Analyzer *(Courtesy of Keedex Mfg.)*

List 4. Tools for servicing safes, vaults, and safe deposit boxes. (Needed in addition to all of the tools in Lists 1 and 2.)

- Borescope
- Carbide drill bits
- Change keys, assorted (Figure 6.33)
- Door puller
- Drill rig (Figure 6.34)
- Hammer drill
- Nose puller
- Safe-moving equipment
- Sledge hammer

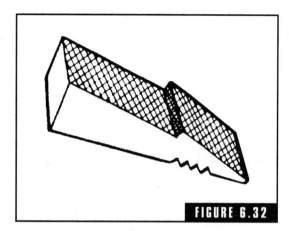

FIGURE 6.32

Wedges are used when opening locked vehicles.
(Courtesy of A-1 Security Manufacturing Corp.)

List 5. Tools/Supplies for installing door locks and other door hardware. (Needed in addition to all of the tools in Lists 1 and 2.)

- Boring jigs
- Broom and dustpan
- Compass, or keyhole, saw
- Door reinforcers, assorted sizes and finishes (Figure 6.35)
- Drop cloth
- Drywall, or wallboard, saw
- Filler plates
- Hole saws, assorted sizes (Figure 6.36)
- Kwikset cylinder removal tool
- Lever
- Nails, assorted types and sizes
- Pry bar
- Reciprocating saw
- Screw-gun

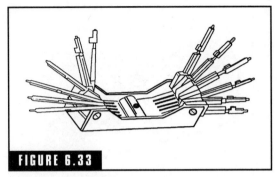

FIGURE 6.33

Change keys are used for changing safe combinations.
(Courtesy of Keedex Mfg.)

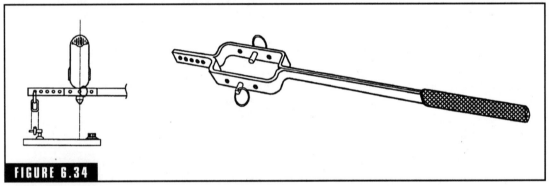

FIGURE 6.34

A drill rig helps hold a drill in position while drilling a safe. *(Courtesy of Keedex Mfg.)*

FIGURE 6.35

Door reinforcers are helpful when installing locks on weak or damaged doors. *(Courtesy of M.A.G. Eng. and Mfg. Co.)*

- Screws, assorted sizes

- Screws, one-way

- Shovel

- Strike plates and strike boxes, assorted types and sizes

- Utility knife and assorted blades

- Vacuum cleaner

- Weiser shim pick

- Wood chisels, assorted sizes

- Wood glue

List 6. Tools for installing alarms and electronic security devices. (Needed in addition to all of the tools in Lists 1 and 2.)

- Electrician's tape

- Fish tape

- Flexible drill bits and extensions

- Multimeter

- Staple guns, or wiring tackers, and staples, assorted sizes for wire and coaxial cable

- Twist connectors

- Under-carpet tape

- Voltage tester

- Wire stripper

- Wire cutters

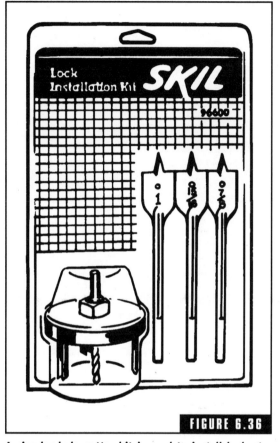

FIGURE 6.36

A circular-hole cutter kit is used to install locksets.
(Courtesy of Skil Corporation)

Key-In-Knob, Deadbolt, and Cylinder Key Mortise Locks

The information in this chapter will help you install and service most standard key-in-knob, deadbolt, and cylinder key mortise locks. Although this chapter provides sound general guidelines and tips that apply to many situations, some of the step-by-step instructions here may not be appropriate for the product with which you're working. Before installing or servicing any lock or door hardware, read and follow the manufacturer's instructions.

Handing of Doors

Door handing, or placement on the right or left hand, is an important consideration for installing most locks. Some locks are nonhanded and can be used with doors of any hand; others are for a specific hand. When a lock is installed on a door of the wrong hand, the lock is upside down. This not only looks unprofessional, but could cause damage to the lock.

The hand of a door is based on the location and direction of swing of the door's hinges from the exterior side of the door. For example, if you're standing outside a door that has hinges on the left side and opens inward, you are looking at a left-hand door. Figure 7.1 shows the four types of door hands.

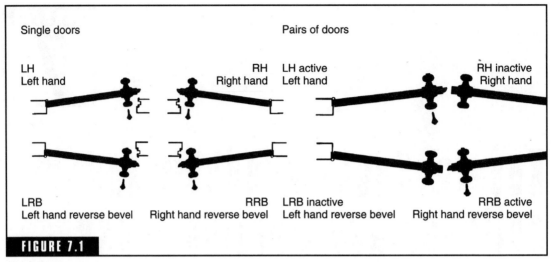

Single doors

Pairs of doors

LH
Left hand

RH
Right hand

LH active
Left hand

RH inactive
Right hand

LRB
Left hand reverse bevel

RRB
Right hand reverse bevel

LRB inactive
Left hand reverse bevel

RRB active
Right hand reverse bevel

FIGURE 7.1

Consider door handing when installing locks. *(Courtesy of Schlage Lock Company)*

Key-In-Knob Locks

A *key-in-knob lock* is operated by inserting a key into its knob (Figure 7.2). The knobs of key-in-knob locks come in a variety of designs. Figure 7.3 illustrates one of these. Schlage Lock Company invented this type of lock in 1925.

Installation

Install key-in-knob locks in the following way.

1. Mark the door using the template packaged with the lock. Mark the height line (the center line of the latchbolt) on the edge of the door. The suggested height from the floor is 38 inches. Mark the center point of the door's thickness. Position the center line of the template on the height line. Hold it in place and mark the center point for a 2⅛-inch hole (Figure 7.4).

2. Bore a 2⅛-inch hole in the door on the face near its lock edge. To avoid splintering the door, drill on both sides of the door (instead of from one side only). Bore a ⅞- or 1-inch hole, depending on the latch housing diameter, straight into the door edge to intersect with the center of the 2⅛-inch hole (Figure 7.5). Then use the latchfront faceplate as a pattern for the cutout. The front should fit flush with the door surface. Install the latch with screws.

For circular latch installation, drill a 1-inch-diameter latchbolt hole. Place a wooden block against the bolt. Apply enough pressure to depress the bolt. Tap the block with a hammer or mallet to drive the latch into the hole. The surface of the latch faceplate should be flush with the edge of the door (Figure 7.6).

3. Mark the vertical line and height line on the jamb exactly opposite the center point of the latch hole. Clean out the hole and install the strike.

   For a T-strike, bore two $\frac{7}{8}$-inch holes, $\frac{11}{16}$ inch deep in the frame on a vertical line $\frac{3}{8}$ inch above and below the height line.

   For a full lip strike, mark screw holes for the strike so that the screws lie on the same vertical center line as the latch screws. Cut out the frame, providing for clearance of the latch bolt and the strike tongue. Install the strike (Figure 7.7).

4. Remove the inside trim by depressing the knob catch, sliding the knob off the spindle, and removing the appropriate rose design (Figure 7.8).

5. Adjust the rose by rotating it $\frac{1}{16}$ inch short of the housing for a 1⅜-inch-thick door. Rotate it out to $\frac{3}{16}$ inch for a 1⅞-inch door (Figure 7.9).

FIGURE 7.2

A cutaway view of an A Series key-in-knob lock.
(Courtesy of Schlage Lock Company)

TRADE SECRET

To avoid damaging the door, and to ensure that the lock works properly, it's critical that you drill straight. If you're not used to boring straight holes, you might want to use a lock installation kit that includes a boring jig and a boring bit. Such kits, sold by locksmithing supply houses, allow anyone to bore lock holes like a professional. A less expensive way to help you drill straight is to tape a small level to your drill.

6. The latch unit must be in place before installing the lock. Be sure the lock housing engages with the latch prongs and that the retractor interlocks with the latch bar (Figure 7.10).

   For proper installation, the deadlocking plunger on the latch bolt must stop against the strike, preventing forcing when the door is closed. Do not attempt to mount the lock unit with the door closed.

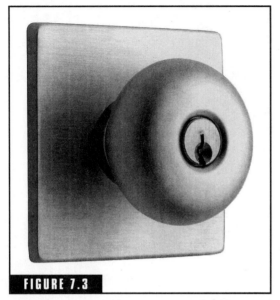

FIGURE 7.3

A popular knob design. *(Courtesy of Schlage Lock Company)*

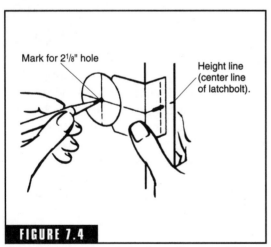

Mark for 2⅛" hole

Height line (center line of latchbolt).

FIGURE 7.4

Use a template to mark the door. *(Courtesy of Schlage Lock Company)*

7. Snap on the rose. Slip the mounting plate over the spindle and fasten it securely with two machine screws. Snap the rose over the spring clip on the mounting plate (Figure 7.11). Depress the knob catch slide all the way onto the spindle so the catch engages into the slot.

For a threaded rose, slip the rose over the spindle and screw it onto the threaded hub. Turn it clockwise and tighten it with a spanner wrench (Figure 7.12).

Servicing

When a key-in-knob lock isn't working properly, you may need to disassemble it to discover the problem. You might find a worn or broken spring, or perhaps the lock needs cleaning and lubricating. The exploded lock views in Figures 7.13 through 7.16 show the parts you'll find in typical key-in-knob locks. Table 7.1 is the list of part names corresponding to the numbered parts in Figures 7.13 through 7.16.

Deadbolt Locks

Figure 7.17 illustrates a typical deadbolt lock. A deadbolt is installed in much the same way as a key-in-knob lock. Figures 7.18 through 7.21 are exploded views of several types of deadbolt locks. Table 7.2 is the list of part names corresponding to the numbered parts in Figures 7.18 through 7.21.

Cylinder Key Mortise Locks

Commercial and industrial buildings are common places where cylinder key mortise locks are used (Figure 7.22).

Table 7.1

Sym.	No.	Description	A10S	A20S	A25D	A30D	A40S	A43D	A44S	A53PD	A55PD	A70PD	A73PD	A79PD	A80PD	A85PD
1	01-018 **	Knob & sleeve, cylinder								•	•	•	•	•	•	•
2	01-001 **	Rose, outside	•	•		•	•	•	•	•	•	•	•	•	•	•
3	01-009 **	Knob/lever, open				•	•	•	•	•	•	•	•			•
4	01-008 **	Knob/lever, closed	•	•	•	•							•		•	
5	01-002 **	Rose, inside	•		•	•	•		•	•	•	•	•			•
6	A201-399 *	Hub & cap, outside				•				•	•	•	•		•	•
7	A201-406 *	Hub & cap, outside	•	•			•	•	•							
8	A508-598	Frame	•	•	•	•	•		•	•	•	•	•	•	•	•
9	A508-399	Plate, outside	•	•	•	•	•	•	•	•	•	•	•	•	•	•
10	A301-387	Spindle & catch, outside	•	•		•	•	•	•	•	•	•	•	•	•	•
11	A301-402	Cam, outside				•		•	•							•
12	A590-158	Slide				•	•		•				•			•
13	A590-159	Slide	•	•	•					•		•		•	•	
14	A508-597	Seat, spring (knob designs)	•	•	•	•	•		•	•	•	•	•	•	•	•
14a	A501-525	Seat (2), spring (lever designs)	•	•	•	•			•	•	•	•	•		•	•
14b	A501-645	Separator, spring (lever designs)	•	•	•	•			•	•	•	•	•		•	•
15	A501-311	Spring (2), slide (knob designs)	•	•	•	•	•	•	•	•	•	•	•	•	•	•
15a	A508-605	Spring (2), slide (lever designs)	•	•	•	•	•		•	•	•	•	•		•	•
16	A501-305	Plate, inside	•	•	•	•	•	•	•	•	•	•	•		•	•
17	01-055 ***	Plunger & button, inside				•										
18	01-056 ***	Plunger & button, inside					•		•							
19	01-057 ***	Plunger & button, outside					•									
20	01-058 ***	Plunger & button, outside						•								
21	01-059 ***	Plunger & button, outside							•							
22	01-060 ***	Plunger & button, inside								•						
23	01-061 ***	Plunger & button, inside									•					
24	01-062 ***	Plunger & button, inside											•			
25	01-063 ***	Plunger & button, inside														•
26	A301-403 *	Housing & cap, 1 ⅜"–1 ⅞" drs.	•		•	•	•			•	•	•	•		•	•
	A301-404 *	Housing & cap, 2"–2 ¼" drs.	•		•	•	•			•	•	•	•		•	•

Table 7.1 *(Continued)*

Sym.	No.	Description	A10S	A20S	A25D	A30D	A40S	A43D	A44S	A53PD	A55PD	A70PD	A73PD	A79PD	A80PD	A85PD
	A301-405 *	Housing & cap, 2 ½" drs.	●		●	●	●		●	●	●	●			●	●
	A301-406 *	Hsg. threaded 1 ⅜"–1 ⅞" drs.	●		●	●	●		●	●	●	●	●		●	●
27	A508-600	Housing		●				●						●		
28	C503-008	Cotter pin (2)	●	●	●	●	●	●	●	●	●	●	●	●	●	●
29	A301-386	Spindle & catch, I/S, 1⅜"–1⅞" drs.	●		●	●	●		●	●	●	●	●		●	●
	A301-409	Spindle & catch, I/S, 2"–2¼" drs.	●		●	●	●		●	●	●	●			●	●
	A301-410	Spingle & catch, I/S, 2½" drs.	●		●	●	●		●	●	●				●	●
30	A501-633	Spindle, I/S, 1⅜"–1⅞" drs.		●				●								
	A500-001	Spindle, I/S, 2"–2¼" drs.		●				●								
	A500-002	Spindle, I/S, 2½" drs.		●				●								
31	A501-498	Hub, 1⅜"–1½" drs.			●											
	A501-499	Hub, 1⅞"–2½" drs.			●											
32	A301-391	Cam					●									
33	A201-421	Slide							●							
34	A501-721	Plug, cam										●	●	●		
35	A501-776	Spiral cam										●	●	●		
36	A501-791	Spacer, cam										●		●		
37	A501-768	Plate, inside												●		
38	A201-370	Cam													●	
39	A501-901	Plate, outside													●	●
40	A501-615	Wedge													●	●
41	A201-782	Sleeve, cam											●			
42	A201-558	Rose, outside*			●											
43	A201-688	Turn & plate, inside*		●				●								
44	A501-766	Rose, inside**												●		
45	A501-767	Plate, mounting												●		
46	A501-710	Sleeve, swivel														●
47	G570-232	Plug, spindle, lever designs only	●	●												
48	A201-377	Mounting plate, inside	●		●	●	●		●	●	●	●	●		●	●
49	A501-874	Plate, outside			●											

Table 7.1 *(Continued)*

Sym.	No.	Description	A10S	A20S	A25D	A30D	A40S	A43D	A44S	A53PD	A55PD	A70PD	A73PD	A79PD	A80PD	A85PD
50	A201-774	Keyway											●			
51	01-019	Cylinder knob (less sleeve)**								●	●	●	●	●	●	●
52	01-020	Sleeve, knob, cylinder**									●	●	●		●	●
53	A501-161	Screw (2), mtg., 1⅜"–1⅞" drs.	●		●	●	●		●	●	●	●	●		●	●
	A501-818	Screw (2), mtg., 2"–2½" drs.	●		●	●	●		●		●	●	●		●	●
54	A501-634	Screw (2), mtg., 1⅜"–1⅞" drs.		●				●								
	A501-635	Screw (2), mtg., 2"–2½" drs.		●				●								
55	A501-769	Screw (2), mtg., 1⅜"–2" drs.												●		
	A501-770	Screw (2), mtg., 2"–2¾" drs.												●		
56	21-002	Cylinder unit, 6 pin*								●	●	●	●	●	●	
	21-002-122	Cylinder unit, 6 pin, orb design*								●	●	●		●	●	
57	21-002-149	Cylinder unit, 6 pin, orb design*											●			
58	21-003	Indicator cylinder unit*														●
	21-003-168	Indicator cylinder unit, orb design*														●

*Specify finish.
**Specify design and finish.
***Specify design, finish, and door thickness.

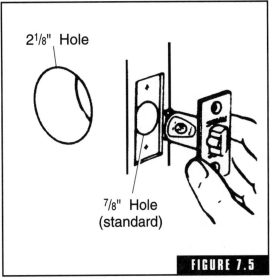

Drill two holes in the door. *(Courtesy of Schlage Lock Company)*

2⅛" Hole

⅞" Hole
(standard)

FIGURE 7.5

Table 7.2 Schlage Parts Index

Sym.	No.	Description	160 260 460	261 461	162 262 462	263 463	264 464	180 280 480	560	562	250	251	252	270
A	22-017	5-pin cylinder unit, outside	•	•	•	•					•	•	•	
	22-019	6-pin cylinder unit, outside	•	•	•	•					•	•	•	
B	22-018	5-pin cylinder unit, inside			•		•						•	
	22-020	6-pin cylinder unit, inside			•		•							
C	36-067	⁷⁄₁₆" trim ring	•	•	•	•	•				•	•	•	
D	36-066	⅛" trim ring	•	•	•	•	•				•	•	•	
E	36-069	⁷⁄₁₆" security insert, std. B400 series	•	•	•	•	•							
F	36-068	⅛" security insert, std. B400 series	•	•	•	•	•							
G	B202-323	Cyl. bar, 5- or 6-pin, 1⅜" or 1¾" dr., std.	•				•		•		•			
H	B202-453	Cyl. bar, 5-pin, 1⅜" or 1¾" dr., (2 req.), std.			•								•	
	B202-269	Cyl. bar, 6-pin, 1⅜" dr. (2 req.)			•									
	B202-369	Cyl. bar, 6-pin, 1¾" dr. (2 req.)			•								•	
I	B202-267	Cyl. bar, 5- or 6-pin, 1⅜" or 1¾" dr., std.		•								•		
J	E205-204	Cyl. bar, 5-pin, 1⅜" or 1¾" dr., std.					•							
	B202-269	Cyl. bar, 6-pin, 1⅜" dr.					•							
	E205-204	Cyl. bar, 6-pin, 1¾" dr.					•							
K	12-181	Deadbolt, ⅝" throw, 2⅜" bs., B100 std.	•		•			•						
	12-073	Deadbolt, 1" throw, 2⅜" bs., B400/B500 std.	•	•	•	•	•	•	•	•				
	12-193	Deadbolt, ⅝" throw, 2⅜" bs., B200 std.	•	•	•	•	•	•						
L	12-100	Deadlatch, ⁹⁄₁₆" throw, 2⅜" bs., std.									•	•	•	•
M	B202-321	Rose & turn, no holdback	•					•						
N	B502-815	Blank rose		•								•		
O	B202-322	Rose & turn, one way				•								
P	B202-320	Rose & turn, with holdback									•			•
Q	B520-086	Mtg. screw, #10-32 × 2¼", 1⅜"–1¾" dr., 5- or 6-pin (2 req.)	•	•	•	•					•	•		
R	B520-092	Mtg. screw, #10-32 × 2½", 1⅜" or 1¾" dr., 5-pin (2 req.)			•								•	
	B520-094	Mtg. screw, #10-32 × 3", 1⅜" or 1¾" dr., 6-pin (2 req.)			•								•	

Table 7.2 *(Continued)*

Sym.	No.	Description	160 260 460	261 461	162 262 462	263 463	264 464	180 280 480	560	562	250	251	252	270
													Functions	
S	B502-894	Drive screw, (2 req.)			●		●						●	
T	B502-472	Wrench			●		●						●	
U	B520-112	Bar turn, 1⅜" or 1¾" dr.						●						●
V	B502-409	Backplate						●						
X	F506-359	Screw, backplate, (2 req.)						●						
Y	B502-711	Support												●
Z ⌐	B502-821	Mtg. screw, wood drs.						●						●
└	B502-823	Mtg. screw, metal drs.						●						●
AA	B520-090	Mtg. screw, #10-32 × 1¾", 5- & 6-pin					●							
AB	B502-497	Anchor					●							
BB	B202-317	Cylinder housing & trim, outside							●	●				
BC	B520-098	Mounting plate							●	●				
BD	B520-097	Cylinder housing, inside								●				
BE	B202-319	Rose & turn							●					
BF	B520-101	Trim, housing, inside								●				
BG	B520-103	Cylinder guard							●	●				
BH	B520-104	Cyl. guard retainer clip							●	●				
BI	22-002	Cylinder, 6-pin, (no cylinder bar)							●					
BK	B202-269	Cyl. bar, 1⅜" to 2⅛" dr., std. (2 req.)								●				
BL	B520-102	Cyl. retainer, outside							●	●				
BM	B520-108	Screw, cylinder retainer, (2 req.)							●	●				
BN	B520-107	Screw, mtg. plate (4 req.)							●	●				
BO	B520-110	Screw, rose & turn (2 req.)							●					
BP	A501-634	Screw, cyl. hsg., inside (2 req.)								●				
BQ	B520-105	Plug, cyl. hsg. screw (2 req.)								●				
BR	B520-111	Screw, hsg. trim, inside (1 req.)								●				
BS	22-043	Cylinder, 6-pin (no cylinder bar)								●				

Courtesy: Schlage Lock Company

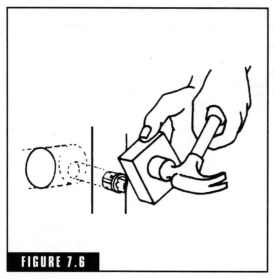

Drive the latch into the hole. *(Courtesy of Schlage Lock Company)*

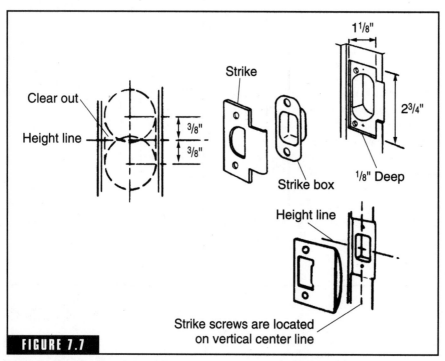

Mark the lines to install the strike. *(Courtesy of Schlage Lock Company)*

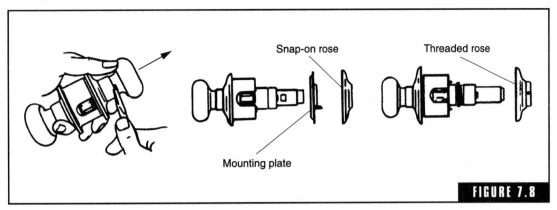

Snap-on rose

Threaded rose

Mounting plate

FIGURE 7.8

Remove the rose. *(Courtesy of Schlage Lock Company)*

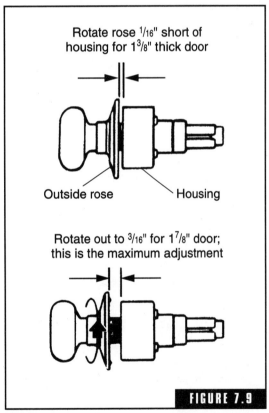

Rotate rose $1/16''$ short of housing for $1^3/8''$ thick door

Outside rose

Housing

Rotate out to $3/16''$ for $1^7/8''$ door; this is the maximum adjustment

FIGURE 7.9

Adjust the rose. *(Courtesy of Schlage Lock Company)*

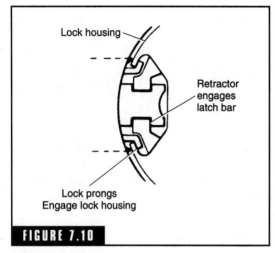

FIGURE 7.10

Lock housing

Retractor engages latch bar

Lock prongs Engage lock housing

Interlock the units. *(Courtesy of Schlage Lock Company)*

FIGURE 7.12

Use a spanner wrench on a threaded rose. *(Courtesy of Schlage Lock Company)*

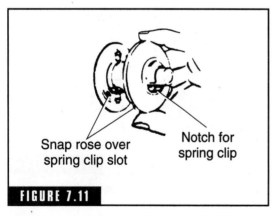

Snap rose over spring clip slot

Notch for spring clip

FIGURE 7.11

Attach the trim and rose. *(Courtesy of Schlage Lock Company)*

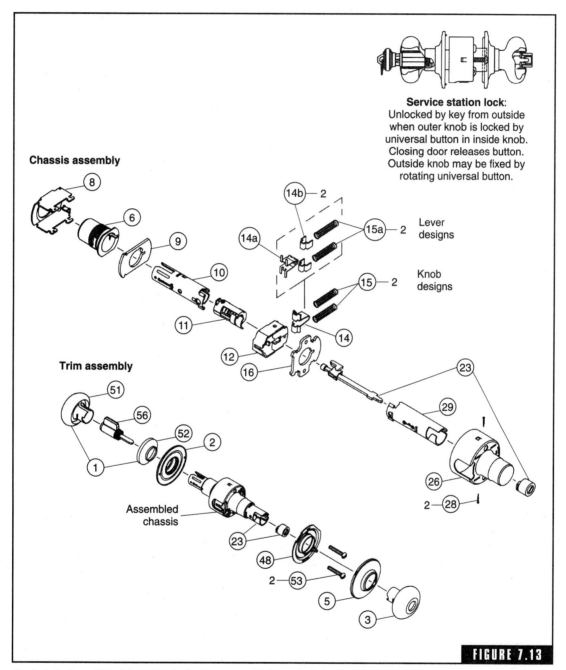

Service station lock:
Unlocked by key from outside when outer knob is locked by universal button in inside knob. Closing door releases button. Outside knob may be fixed by rotating universal button.

Chassis assembly

14b — 2
14a
15a — 2 Lever designs

15 — 2 Knob designs

14

Trim assembly

23
29
26
2 — 28

Assembled chassis

23
48
2 — 53
5
3

FIGURE 7.13

Exploded view of Model A55PD lock. *(Courtesy of Schlage Lock Company)*

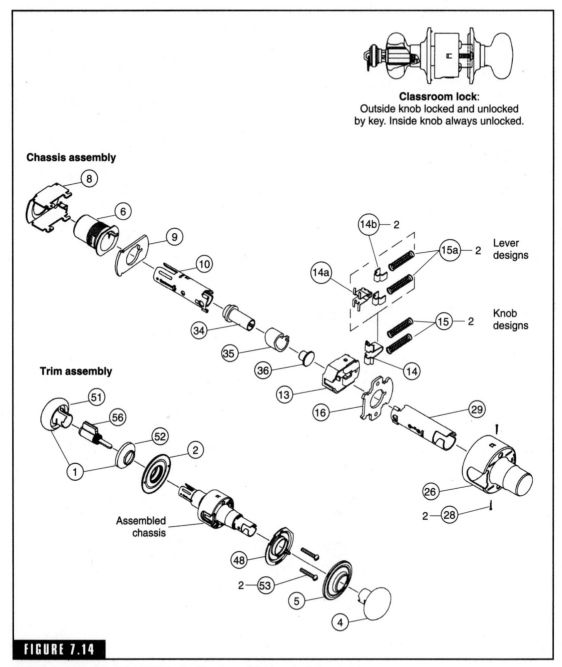

Classroom lock:
Outside knob locked and unlocked
by key. Inside knob always unlocked.

Chassis assembly

Lever designs

Knob designs

Trim assembly

Assembled chassis

FIGURE 7.14

Exploded view of Model A70PD lock. *(Courtesy of Schlage Lock Company)*

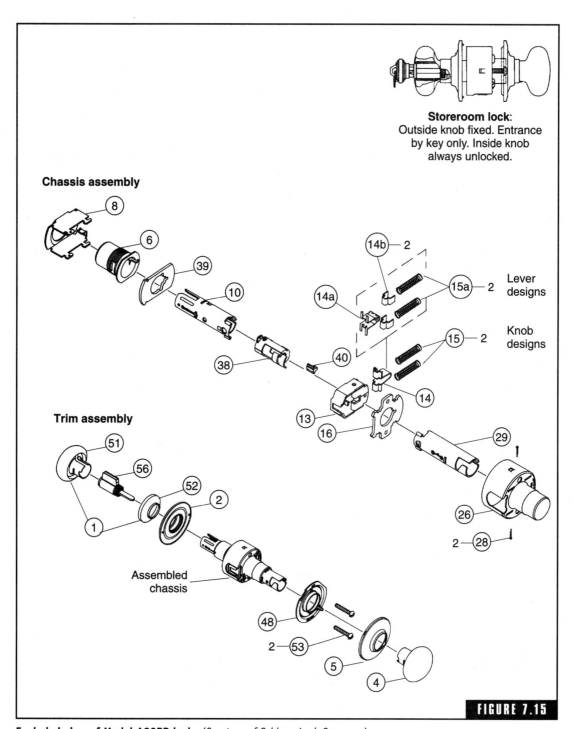

Storeroom lock:
Outside knob fixed. Entrance
by key only. Inside knob
always unlocked.

Chassis assembly

Trim assembly

Lever
designs

Knob
designs

Assembled
chassis

FIGURE 7.15

Exploded view of Model A80PD lock. *(Courtesy of Schlage Lock Company)*

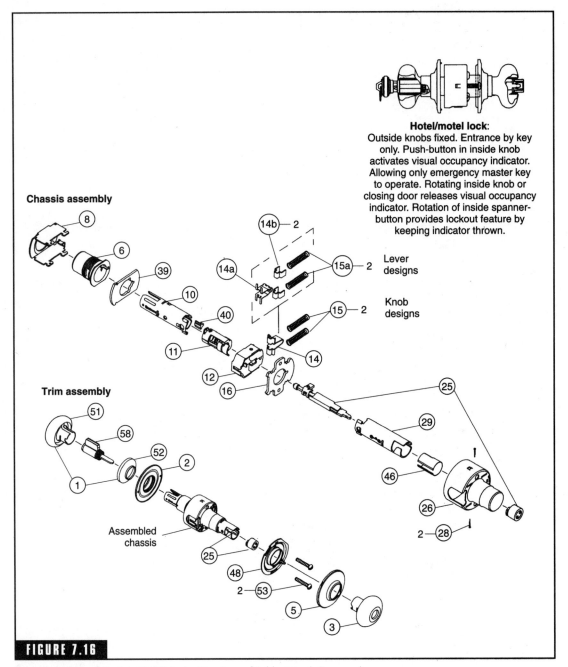

Hotel/motel lock:
Outside knobs fixed. Entrance by key only. Push-button in inside knob activates visual occupancy indicator. Allowing only emergency master key to operate. Rotating inside knob or closing door releases visual occupancy indicator. Rotation of inside spanner-button provides lockout feature by keeping indicator thrown.

Chassis assembly

Lever designs

Knob designs

Trim assembly

Assembled chassis

FIGURE 7.16

Exploded view of Model A85PD lock. *(Courtesy of Schlage Lock Company)*

Schlage deadbolt. *(Courtesy of Schlage Lock Company)*

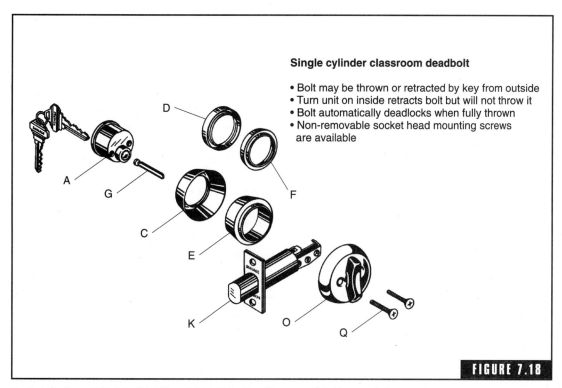

Single cylinder classroom deadbolt

- Bolt may be thrown or retracted by key from outside
- Turn unit on inside retracts bolt but will not throw it
- Bolt automatically deadlocks when fully thrown
- Non-removable socket head mounting screws are available

Exploded view of Models B263P and B463P locks. *(Courtesy of Schlage Lock Company)*

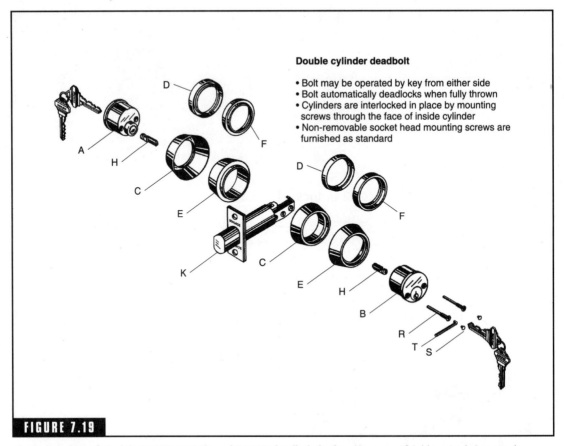

Double cylinder deadbolt

- Bolt may be operated by key from either side
- Bolt automatically deadlocks when fully thrown
- Cylinders are interlocked in place by mounting screws through the face of inside cylinder
- Non-removable socket head mounting screws are furnished as standard

FIGURE 7.19

Exploded view of Models B162P, B262P, and B462P deadbolt locks. *(Courtesy of Schlage Lock Company)*

Installation

Cylinder key mortise locks manufactured by Schlage Lock Company (L Series) are installed in the following way.

1. Measure the desired height from the finished floor, both sides, and the edge of the door. Mark horizontal lines on the door and the door edge (Figure 7.23).

2. Align the template on the edge of the door with the applicable horizontal at the height line. Mark the drill points (Figure 7.24).

    Caution: The outside and inside of the door might require different preparation. Read the instructions thoroughly and use the proper template for the outside (exterior or corridor side) and inside of the door.

3. Mortise the door edge 1 inch. Drill 4½ inches deep by 6¾ inches high (Figure 7.25).

4. Drill the proper holes for the trim and lock function (Figure 7.26).

   Note: For through holes, drill halfway from each side of the door to prevent splintering or otherwise damaging doors.

5. Recess to the dimensions of the lock face (Figure 7.27).

6. Align the strike template on the jamb. Be sure to match the center line on both the strike and the lock trim templates (Figure 7.28). Bore 1-inch-diameter holes into the door

> **TRADE SECRET**
>
> **Many mistakes made while drilling deadbolt or key-in-knob lock holes can be covered by using low-cost scar plates.**

> **TRADE SECRET**
>
> **If a key turns hard in a lock, first check to see if the bolt easily and fully extends and retracts while the door is open. If it does, then the problem is likely a misalignment between the bolt and door strike. If the bolt doesn't work properly with the door open, the bolt probably needs to be lubricated.**

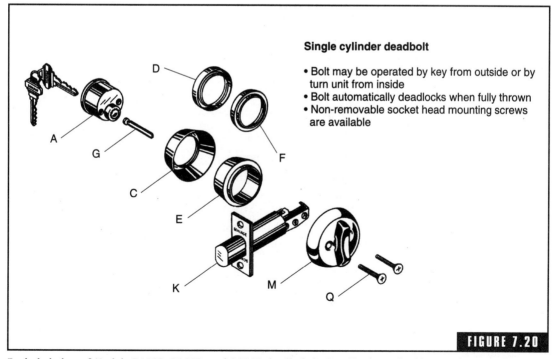

Single cylinder deadbolt

- Bolt may be operated by key from outside or by turn unit from inside
- Bolt automatically deadlocks when fully thrown
- Non-removable socket head mounting screws are available

FIGURE 7.20

Exploded view of Models B160P, B260P, and B460P deadbolt locks. *(Courtesy of Schlage Lock Company)*

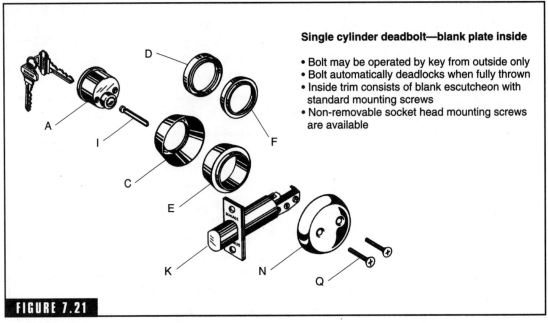

Single cylinder deadbolt—blank plate inside

• Bolt may be operated by key from outside only
• Bolt automatically deadlocks when fully thrown
• Inside trim consists of blank escutcheon with standard mounting screws
• Non-removable socket head mounting screws are available

FIGURE 7.21

Exploded view of Models B261P and B461P deadbolt locks. *(Courtesy of Schlage Lock Company)*

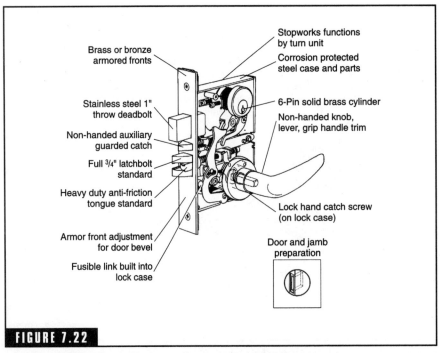

Stopworks functions by turn unit

Corrosion protected steel case and parts

Brass or bronze armored fronts

Stainless steel 1" throw deadbolt

6-Pin solid brass cylinder

Non-handed auxiliary guarded catch

Non-handed knob, lever, grip handle trim

Full 3/4" latchbolt standard

Heavy duty anti-friction tongue standard

Lock hand catch screw (on lock case)

Armor front adjustment for door bevel

Door and jamb preparation

Fusible link built into lock case

FIGURE 7.22

L Series cylinder key mortise lock. *(Courtesy of Schlage Lock Company)*

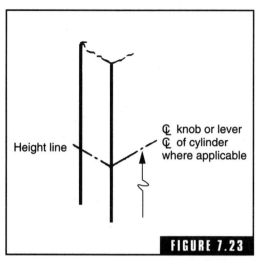

Mark the horizontal lines. (*Courtesy of Schlage Lock Company*)

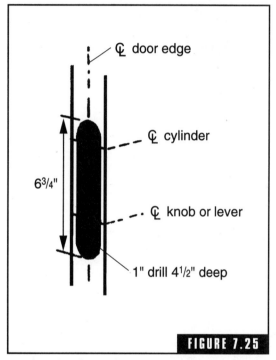

Mortise the door edge. (*Courtesy of Schlage Lock Company*)

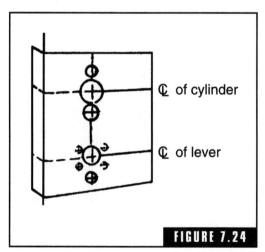

Mark the drill points. (*Courtesy of Schlage Lock Company*)

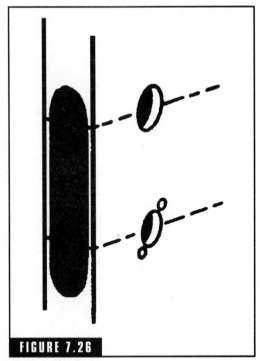

FIGURE 7.26

Drill holes for the trim and lock function.
(Courtesy of Schlage Lock Company)

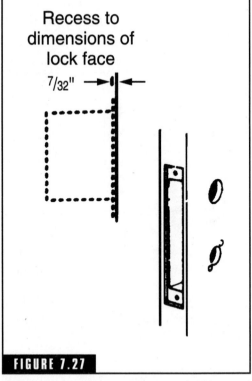

Recess to
dimensions of
lock face

7/32"

FIGURE 7.27

Recess for the lock face. *(Courtesy of Schlage Lock Company)*

edge, 1⅛ inches deep. Recess ⁵⁄₃₂ inch for flush fit of the strike and box. (Additional recess is required when using a strike reinforcement.)

Caution: Be certain that the auxiliary latch does not enter the strike opening.

7. Adjust for the door bevel by loosening the two screws on the top and bottom of the lock case. Position the faceplate tabs at the correct angle and tighten the screws (Figure 7.29).

   Insert the lock case into the mortise cutout (armor front removed) and fasten it to the door (Figure 7.30). The catch screw must always be on the inside of the lock chassis.

8. Insert and install the inside and outside spindle and springs so that the pin stop is in contact with the hub of the lock case (Figure 7.31).

9. Trim the installation (rose trim) levers. Thread the screw posts onto the outside rose. Place the spring cage onto the screw posts with the arrows pointing in the direction of the lever rotation. Install the outside trim onto the spindle with the screw posts through the holes in the lock case (Figure 7.32).

10. Install the inside lever trim. Join the spring cage and mounting plate. Slide the mounting plate over the screw posts. Insert and tighten the mounting screws. Place the inside rose over the mounting plate. Slide the lever into position and tighten the bushing with a spanner wrench (Figure 7.33).

11. Thread the posts onto the outside rose mounting plate (Figure 7.34).

12. Install the inside knob trim. Slide the mounting plate onto the spindle. Insert and tighten the mounting screws. Place the inside rose over the mounting plate. Slide the knob into position and tighten the bushing with a spanner wrench (Figure 7.35).

13. Install the cylinders (exposed type). Exposed cylinders are installed after the escutcheon trim (Figure 7.36). Tighten the set screws against the cylinders. Install the armored front.

14. Install the cylinders (concealed type). The cylinder plug must project approximately ⁷⁄₁₆ inch from the face of the door. Tighten the set screws against the cylinders. Install the armored front.

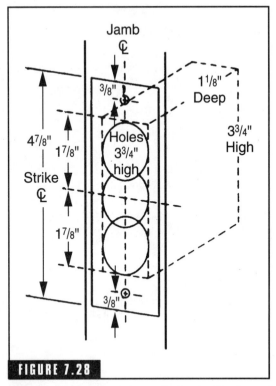

FIGURE 7.28

Align the strike template on the jamb. *(Courtesy of Schlage Lock Company)*

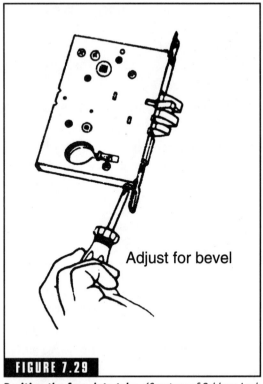

FIGURE 7.29

Position the faceplate tabs. *(Courtesy of Schlage Lock Company)*

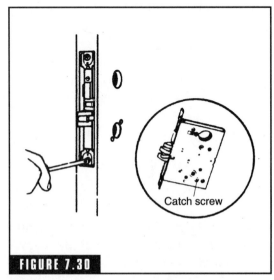

FIGURE 7.30

Install the lock case. *(Courtesy of Schlage Lock Company)*

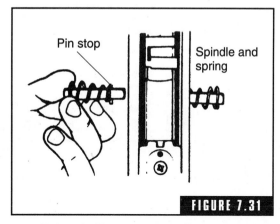

Install the spindle. *(Courtesy of Schlage Lock Company)*

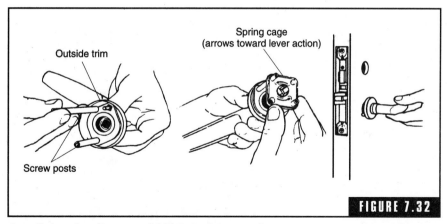

Install the trim. *(Courtesy of Schlage Lock Company)*

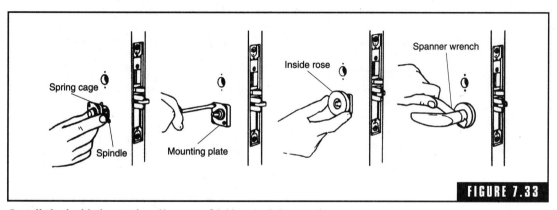

Install the inside lever trim. *(Courtesy of Schlage Lock Company)*

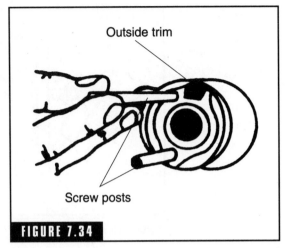

Thread the screw posts. *(Courtesy of Schlage Lock Company)*

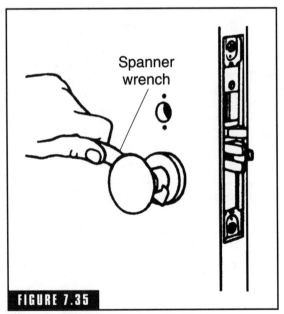

Tighten the bushing with a spanner wrench. *(Courtesy of Schlage Lock Company)*

15. Install the escutcheon trim (lever trim only). Position the spring cages on the spindles with the arrows pointing in the direction of the lever rotation. Slide the outside trim unit onto the spindle and the mounting posts through the door. Hold the unit in place.

Place the inside trim unit onto the spindle. Insert and tighten the mounting screws (inside of door only). The turn piece must be vertical when the bolt is retracted (Figure 7.37).

16. Install the turn piece and project the deadbolt. Align the screw holes on the vertical and fasten them with screws (Figure 7.38).

17. Install the emergency button by snapping it into place (refer to the template).

18. Install the "Do Not Disturb" indicator plate (hotel function) and cylinder collar. Fasten it with the screw provided. Refer to the template (⁹⁄₁₆-inch-diameter hole).

Changing Lock Handing

To change latch handing, first remove the armor front. Pull the anti-friction tongue and latch bolt away from the chassis and rotate the complete unit, adjusting for door handing. Reinstall the armor front (Figure 7.39).

To change chassis handing, remove the catch screw from one side of the chassis and install it on the opposite side. The catch screw must always be on the inside of the latch chassis for proper functioning of the lock (Figure 7.40).

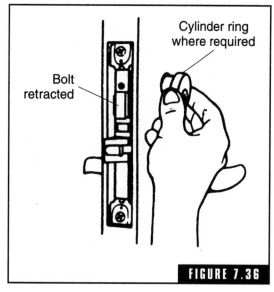

Install the cylinder. *(Courtesy of Schlage Lock Company)*

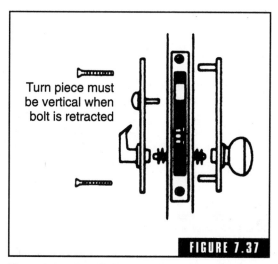

Figure 7.37 Install the escutcheon trim. *(Courtesy of Schlage Lock Company)*

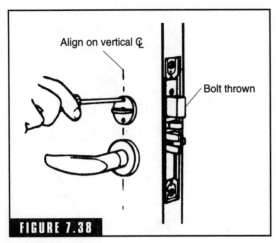

FIGURE 7.38

Install the turn piece. *(Courtesy of Schlage Lock Company)*

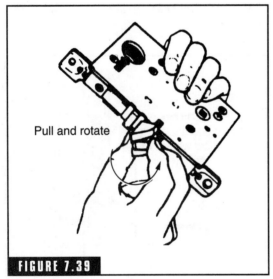

FIGURE 7.39

Changing latch handing. *(Courtesy of Schlage Lock Company)*

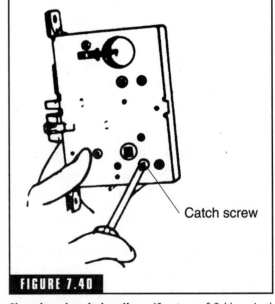

FIGURE 7.40

Changing chassis handing. *(Courtesy of Schlage Lock Company)*

Grip Handle Installation

1. Insert the outside spindle and inside spindle and spring. The inside spindle pin stop should be in contact with the hub of the lock case (Figure 7.41).

2. Thread the mounting posts and screws onto the inside of the grip handle. Lift the thumbpiece while grasping the handle and place it on the outside door (Figure 7.42). Install a wood screw at the bottom of the grip handle after completing assembly of the inside trim. For a metal door, tap a ⁷⁄₆₄-inch-diameter pilot hole.

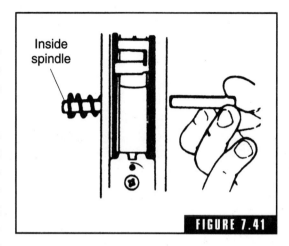

Insert the spindles and springs. *(Courtesy of Schlage Lock Company)*

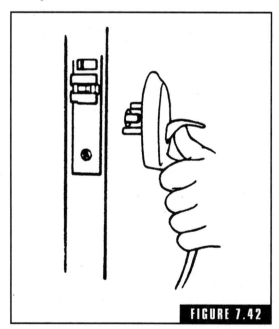

Attach the grip handle to the door. *(Courtesy of Schlage Lock Company)*

High-Security Cylinders

A *lock cylinder* is a complete operating unit that usually consists of a shell, tumblers, springs, a plug, a cam/tailpiece or other actuating device, and other necessary operating parts. It contains a keyway and is installed into locks to allow them to be operated with keys. Most high-security cylinders are designed to be used in locks made by many different manufacturers.

A high-security cylinder has special features to thwart attempts to operate it without a proper key. Most high-security cylinders have built-in safeguards against picking, impressioning, and drilling. Such cylinders are usually operated by special keys and provide various levels of key control.

The cylinders covered here reveal the many differences among high-security cylinders. This chapter also discusses how the cylinders are constructed, rekeyed, serviced, and installed.

The CorKey System

CorKey Control Systems, Inc. has patented kits that are used as replacement doorknobs and cylinders on most major brands of dead-bolt, key-in-knob, and rim locks. The kits turn standard mechanical locks into card-operated access control systems, usually without modifying the locks.

The card-operated replacement kits, or Cor-Kits, have been used at the U.S. Mint building in San Francisco, at the Honolulu International Airport, and at numerous hotels and universities throughout the world. Figure 8.1 shows a Cor-Kit used with a deadbolt.

With a Cor-Kit, locks can be opened by sliding a key into a slot at the top of the knob or cylinder.

This slot then becomes the lock's new keyway. Figure 8.2 shows a Cor-Kit replacement knob and key. The key, called a CorKey, can be coded to operate one or several locks within a system.

The CorKey is flat and looks like a military dog tag. It is a magnetically coded card, usually encased in a steel housing. Plastic housings are available for light-duty applications.

The keys and locks within a CorKey system can be decoded and recoded as often as the user chooses to do so. Coding of the locks and keys is controlled by the user of a Cor-Kit system. The manufacturer provides encoding equipment with the original setup.

Installing Cor-Kits on Deadbolt Locks

Models in the Cor-Kit 400 Series are used to operate deadbolt locks and panic locks. The following instructions are for installing model 400R on rim cylinder lock hardware, such as deadbolts and panic locks.

If you are installing a new deadbolt lock, follow the lock manufacturer's instructions to locate and drill the hole through the door for the cylinder. Do not mount the lock or strike. Go on to Step 1 below.

If you are replacing the cylinder on a lock, remove the lock from the door. Then follow these simple instructions to mount the Cor-Kit on the outside of the door.

1. Place the two mounting screws through the two outside holes in the round steel plate that has three holes in it (Figure 8.3).

2. Feed the screws through the hole in the door from the inside.

3. Hold the Cor-Kit on the outside of the hole, feeding the tailpiece through the center hole of the round steel plate.

4. Position the Cor-Kit in the hole and press to locate the point to drill a ¼-inch hole for the pin, which secures the lock on the door against wrenching. Drill the hole for the pin ½ inch into the door.

5. Screw the two screws into the threaded holes of the Cor-Kit until it is snug on the door, but not too tight.

6. Place the hardware in position on the inside of the door, engaging the Cor-Kit tailpiece. You will need the steel plate or washer that originally secured the cylinder.

7. If the hardware was previously installed, make sure you can replace it in the same position as before. Otherwise, it might be necessary to turn the Cor-Kit housing or to file the inside of the hole in the door to accommodate the two new screws.

8. Tighten the Cor-Kit to the door.

9. Secure so there is no binding of the Cor-Kit tailpiece.

10. If you are mounting the deadbolt lock for the first time, secure it to the inside of the door, keeping alignment with the tailpiece of the Cor-Kit so it will not bind. Then mount the strike to match the bolt location as the lock manufacturer directs.

FIGURE 8.1

A Cor-Kit can be used with a deadbolt lock. *(Courtesy of CorKey Control Systems, Inc.)*

Operating the Cor-Kit

Follow these steps to operate a Cor-Kit.

1. Insert the CorKey, arrow side out, into the slot.

2. When it meets resistance, start to turn the complete front cylinder while applying added pressure on the CorKey.

3. CorKey will go farther into the slot, engaging the tailpiece mechanism. Continue to turn to actuate the bolt.

FIGURE 8.2

A Cor-Kit, with key, installed on a key-in-knob lock. *(Courtesy of CorKey Control Systems, Inc.)*

4. The CorKey may be inserted or removed from any point around the housing. The Cor-Kit free spins whenever the CorKey is released or removed.

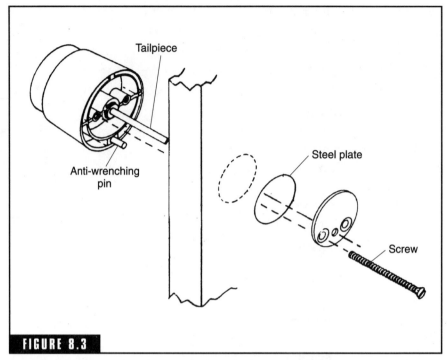

Tailpiece

Anti-wrenching pin

Steel plate

Screw

FIGURE 8.3

An exploded view of a Cor-Kit for a rim lock. *(Courtesy of CorKey Control Systems, Inc.)*

Installing Cor-Kits on Kwikset Tubular Deadbolts

The Cor-Kit Model 400K is used to operate Kwikset 800 Series tubular deadbolts. Model 485K is used for the Kwikset 885 Series. If you are installing a new deadbolt, follow the manufacturer's instructions to locate and drill the holes through the door for the cylinder, bolt, and strike. The following installation instructions apply to both series.

1. Remove the inside thumbturn by removing the two screws in the rose, or if 885 Series (double cylinder unit), remove the inside cylinder.

2. Back out the two mounting screws until the front cylinder and ring can be removed.

3. File or drill a notch in the bottom of the hole in the outside of the door to accommodate the anti-wrench projection on the 400K housing for a single cylinder and on both the outside and inside for a double cylinder. If you are putting the Cor-Kit on the outside of the lock with the thumbturn on the inside, continue to Step 4. If

you have Model 485, skip to Step 8. (*Note:* For the double cylinder, you must use the new type of bolt shown in Figure 8.4.)

4. Determine if your Kwikset is a new or old type by inspecting the tailpiece hole in the bolt. If you have the new type, insert two spacer bars to prevent the turning of the tailpiece in the large hole (Figure 8.5).

5. Install the Cor-Kit in the outside hole in the door, feeding the tailpiece through the hole in the bolt and into the thumbturn hole. If it is too long, cut it off. Remove the thumbturn.

6. Secure the Cor-Kit with mounting the screws and plate, just as the original cylinder was secured.

7. Replace the thumbturn and the rose on the inside and secure with two screws.

   Note: If you are installing a Kwikset deadbolt, follow the manufacturer's instructions up to "Install Exterior Mechanism." Also follow these additional steps:

8. Identify the inside and outside Cor-Kits. The outside unit has a snap ring on the center coupling; the inside unit has a hole in the housing bottom for the set screw (Figure 8.6).

9. To disassemble for coding or installation, remove the snap ring on the outside unit. Pull out the Cor-Kit cylinder and push out the cylinder from inside unit. Make sure the key works the Cor-Kits.

10. Reassemble the outside unit and install the snap ring.

11. Use Kwikset's instructions to install the bolt.

12. Place the Cor-Kit in the outside hole so the tailpiece goes through the bolt drive hole. Mark the tailpiece ¼ inch from the bolt body. Cut off the excess.

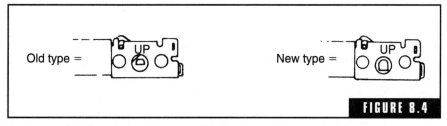

Two types of Kwikset bolts. (*Courtesy of CorKey Control Systems, Inc.*)

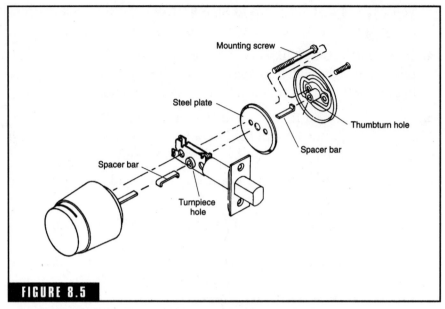

A Model 400K Cor-Kit. *(Courtesy of CorKey Control Systems, Inc.)*

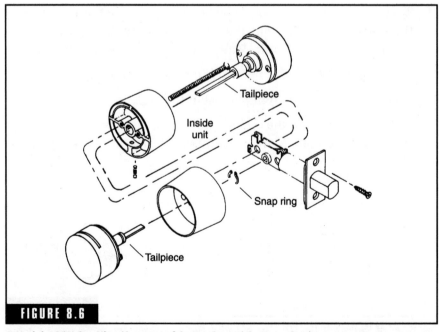

A Model 485K Cor-Kit. *(Courtesy of CorKey Control Systems, Inc.)*

13. Temporarily assemble the inside Cor-Kit. Hold it in the inside door hole with the tailpiece through the bolt drive hole. Mark it ¼ inch from the bolt body. Cut off excess.

14. Replace the outside Cor-Kit in the hole with the tailpiece in the bolt.

15. Remove the inside cylinder from its housing.

16. Place eight 32-x-⁵⁄₁₆-inch Nylok Allen screws on a ⁵⁄₁₆-inch Allen wrench. Feed carefully into the hole in the bottom of the housing, into the second hole in the bottom of the housing, and into the second hole in the hub. This starts the Allen screws.

17. Place the housing in the inside hole and secure it to the outside housing, through the bolt with the two screws provided.

18. Insert the inside Cor-Kit, feeding the tailpiece through the bolt hole. Push the Cor-Kit firmly all the way into the housing.

19. Use the Allen wrench to tighten the screw.

20. Use Kwikset's instructions to install the door strike.

DOM IX KG System Cylinder

The cylinders in the DOM IX KG system (Figure 8.7) have a horizontal keyway and two rows of teardrop-shaped and mushroom pin tumblers that are virtually impossible to pick. The tumblers are arranged in an offset position to one another. The heads of these pins are in the form of cutaway, beveled half-discs, which are stabilized in their lateral position by the elliptically shaped cross-sectional design of the pin tumblers.

Special dimple keys are used to operate the cylinders (Figure 8.8). The keys are designed to make unauthorized duplication very difficult. Key control is through DOM's registration certificate program; duplicate keys can be obtained from the factory with proper identification.

The keys include a patented floating ball that is integrated with the key. No locking is possible without that ball. Only after a deflection pin inside the keyway has been overridden by the floating ball is it possible for the ball to actuate the tenth blocking pin. The ball is just mobile enough in its ball cage to enable it to override the deflection pin.

When the key is completely inserted, the floating ball is pressed down by the lifting pin and operates the blocking pin. Only when all

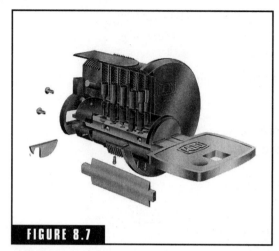

FIGURE 8.7

A DOM IX KG cylinder is extremely burglar resistant.
(Courtesy of DOM Security Locks)

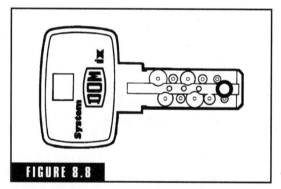

FIGURE 8.8

A DOM IX KG key can be duplicated only by the factory. *(Courtesy of DOM Security Locks)*

pin tumblers and profile control pins are in the right position and the blocking pin has been operated correctly is it possible to operate the cylinder.

The profile pins, which are not controlled by springs and which operate laterally and vertically, are guided into position. When the key is inserted, the pins each fall into their own respective borings, either from above or from the side. When all pin tumblers are in position and all profile control pins are resting correctly in their key borings, the cylinder can be operated.

A rigid instrument, such as a lock pick, cannot operate the blocking mechanism of this lock because the deflection pin protruding into the keyway prevents the insertion of such an instrument. In addition to this safety measure, each row of tumblers is equipped with two tapered core pins, which jam whenever an opening attempt is made with a picking instrument, thus rendering it virtually impossible to turn the core of the cylinder.

Construction Keys

The construction key for the DOM IX KG cylinder (Figure 8.9) allows temporary operation during the construction period. These cylinders are fitted with an insert that prevents the use of the permanent keys during the construction period. Only the construction key can be used during that phase. When the building is finished and handed over to the owner, the temporary inserts are removed so that only the original keys operate the cylinder. All construction keys become inoperative at this time.

Split Keys

Any DOM IX KG cylinder can be equipped with a split key (Figure 8.10). The split key is in two separate parts, meaning that two people are required to operate the cylinder together. The "two-party compulsory locking" guarantees that the cylinder cannot be opened or closed by one person alone. This is especially useful to protect places like drug cabinets, banks, computer rooms, and evidence rooms.

Kaba Gemini

Lori Corporation's Kaba Gemini cylinder is operated by dimple keys that have cuts drilled at precise angles. Figure 8.11 shows several types of such cylinders. They are Underwriters Laboratories-listed (UL-listed) and extremely difficult to pick or impression.

The cylinder can be used in deadbolt locks, key-in-knob locks, and padlocks. It fits the DIN standard profile cylinders (Hahn or Euro types), as well as American key-in-knob cylinder configurations. The American style cylinder is manufactured at the Lori plant in Connecticut.

Excerpt: *Kaba High-Security Manual*

Note: Lori Corporation and Anthony "A. J." Hoffman have given permission for the section of the Kaba High Security Manual (copyright ©1987) that pertains to Kaba Gemini cylinders to be reprinted here. A. J. Hoffman, CML, is the author of the manual. Slight modifications have been made to allow the information to fit the format of this book. The following information is, in substance, a reprint of section CST-2 of the manual.

The Kaba Gemini Cylinder has two rows of side pins (Figure 8.12). Keys for the cylinder have cuts made at 15-degree angles. Most dimple key machines are not capable of cutting Kaba Gemini keys. (Lori Corporation offers a machine designed to cut Kaba keys.) Many key machines that

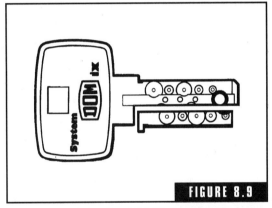

FIGURE 8.9

Construction keys for DOM IX KG cylinders allow temporary operation of cylinders. *(Courtesy of DOM Security Locks)*

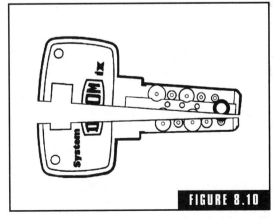

FIGURE 8.10

Any DOM IX KG cylinder can be equipped with a split key. *(Courtesy of DOM Security Locks)*

Kaba Gemini cylinders are available for a variety of lock types. *(Courtesy of Lori Corporation)*

have 15-degree vises can't maintain the accuracy in spacing and depth required for consistent results on Gemini.

The edge has three active cut depths, plus a #4 cut depth used in masterkeying (Figure 8.13). Four depths are used on the sides. Remember, #1 depth is the deepest and #4 the shallowest. The increment is .35 millimeter (.0138 inch) for side and edge cuts.

There are ten edge positions available, but because of their close spacing, no two can be drilled adjacent to one another in the cylinder. The #1 position is not used at this time.

Stock cylinders (Figure 8.14) are all drilled at right-hand or odd positions (3, 5, 7, 9) on the edge.

This means that any stock Gemini cylinder may be rekeyed to any stock Gemini key. For the factory to guarantee that no stock Gemini key

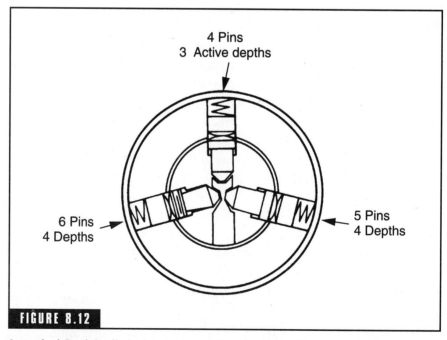

A standard Gemini cylinder has 15 active pins. *(Courtesy of Lori Corporation)*

will ever operate a cylinder in a factory-designed keying system, cylinders furnished for keying systems (Figure 8.15) are normally drilled at left-hand or even positions (2, 4, 6, 8, 10) on the edge. This means that people servicing factory keying systems as well as stock cylinders will need both hands of the cylinders.

Gemini architectural hardware cylinders are UL-listed. They are furnished with hardened steel pins as standard. This provides a high degree of drill resistance to the cylinder. The drill resistance runs the entire length of a Kaba Gemini cylinder, rather than only on the front portion. A minimum of two and a maximum of four mushroom bottom pins are used in each Gemini cylinder to provide resistance to both picking and impressioning. All pins have a hard electrolysis nickel plating to prevent corrosion.

Because the cylinder diameters are small, the drivers are compensated. The longer the bottom, the shorter the top pin (Figure 8.16). For this reason, it isn't practical to service the cylinder with a plug follower.

When combinating a cylinder, remember that the edge bottom pins are different from the side bottom pins. The same top pins, however, are used for both sides and the edges.

Because it isn't practical to use a plug follower, a special holding fixture is used for combinating and sleeving these cylinders. With practice, it should take you about five minutes to combinate a Kaba Gemini cylinder.

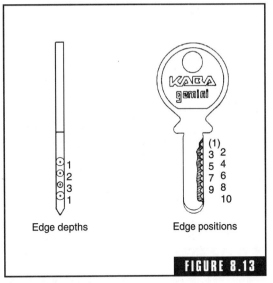

FIGURE 8.13

Kaba Gemini keys have four cut depths and ten edge positions. *(Courtesy of Lori Corporation)*

FIGURE 8.14

Any stock Gemini key can be used to rekey any stock Gemini cylinder. *(Courtesy of Lori Corporation)*

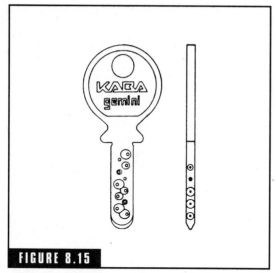

FIGURE 8.15

Gemini key for factory-designed keying system.
(Courtesy of Lori Corporation)

The replacement cylinder product line for American architectural hardware is built around two basic units: the cylinder body and the core. The cylinder body (Figure 8.17) is used for all key-in-knob cylinders. It is recognizable by the three tapped holes in the cylinder shell, which accept "bible" screws, and by the horizontal hole in the rear of the plug. The core (Figure 8.18) is used for all rim and mortise cylinders and some tubular deadlock cylinders. It has a hole in the shell to receive the core retaining screw.

Kaba Gemini Key-in-Knob Cylinders

All Kaba Gemini key-in-knob cylinders are built around one cylinder body.

Bibles, adapters, and tailpieces of various shapes and sizes are attached to the cylinder body (Figure 8.19), enabling it to assume many forms. This chameleon effect greatly reduces the investment required to retrofit a wide variety of locksets with high-security cylinders.

Here's how this "build-a-cylinder" concept works. If most of your retrofit high-security sales are for "brand X" key-in-knob locks, you

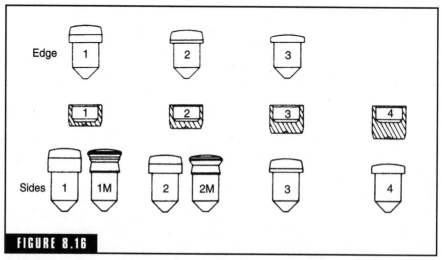

FIGURE 8.16

Gemini pins come in various shapes and sizes. *(Courtesy of Lori Corporation)*

can stock only Kaba cylinders designed for that brand. Then if a customer needs a high-security cylinder for another brand, you can take the necessary parts from the build-a-cylinder kit and attach them to the body of one of your cylinders. There's no need to wait for distributor or factory shipments or to stock dozens of different types of cylinders.

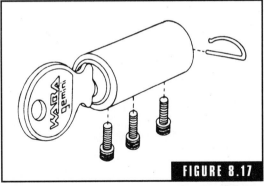

A Gemini key-in-knob cylinder body uses three bible screws. *(Courtesy of Lori Corporation)*

Using Kaba Gemini Cylinders in Padlocks

When padlocks are needed with Gemini cylinders, Master Lock Company's 29 Series can be used. If you use the company's original cylinder retaining plate on the bottom of the padlock, the plate must be altered slightly.

Because the bible attaches to the Gemini cylinder at the bottom of the keyway rather than at the top, the plate must be installed 180 degrees from the position in which it was designed to be installed. There is a chamfer only halfway around the inside edge of the plate. The non-

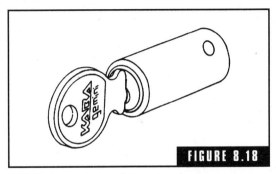

A Gemini core. *(Courtesy of Lori Corporation)*

chamfered portion keeps the plate from being installed in the opposite position. You simply need to finish the chamfer, using a grinder or belt sander, then install the plate in a rotated position for the Kaba Gemini cylinder.

Kaba Gemini Core Cylinders

Although technically not an "interchangeable core," the Kaba Gemini core is identical for all mortise, rim, and tubular deadlock cylinders (Figure 8.20). To use the same core in various types and lengths of cylinders, a cam driver is used. This piece makes up for differences in the types of cams and tailpieces among cylinders.

The core is held into the housing by several screws, including a hardened retaining screw.

This makes the core resistant to slide hammer attacks.

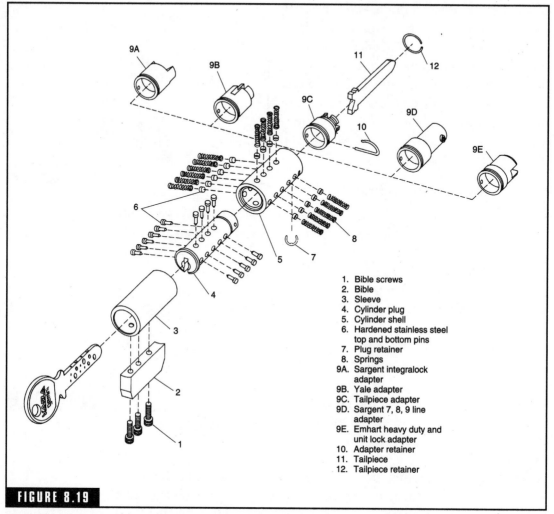

1. Bible screws
2. Bible
3. Sleeve
4. Cylinder plug
5. Cylinder shell
6. Hardened stainless steel
   top and bottom pins
7. Plug retainer
8. Springs
9A. Sargent integralock
    adapter
9B. Yale adapter
9C. Tailpiece adapter
9D. Sargent 7, 8, 9 line
    adapter
9E. Emhart heavy duty and
    unit lock adapter
10. Adapter retainer
11. Tailpiece
12. Tailpiece retainer

FIGURE 8.19

Gemini's "Build-a-Cylinder" is built around one cylinder body. *(Courtesy of Lori Corporation)*

Medeco Cylinders

Since the 1960s, Medeco Security Locks, Inc. has been a leading manufacturer of high-security locks and cylinders. The company's cylinders are UL-listed and designed to resist picking, impressioning, hammering, wrenching, and prying. They are available for a wide assortment of lock types, including mortise, rim, deadbolt, and key-in-knob (Figure 8.21).

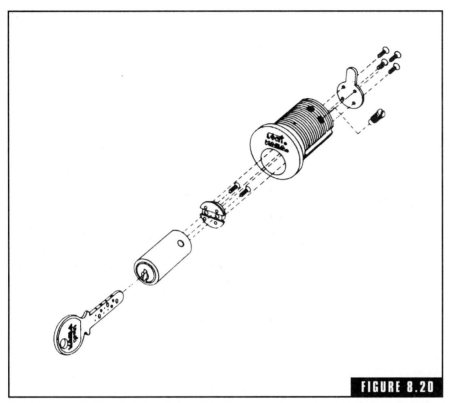

FIGURE 8.20

Gemini's core is identical for all mortise, rim, and tubular deadlocks. *(Courtesy of Lori Corporation)*

Principles of Operation

Figure 8.22 is an exploded view of a typical Medeco cylinder, showing the important elements of Medeco's dual locking system. The first important element is a set of pin tumblers that must be elevated by the cuts of the key. The second element is the sidebar within the cylinder that requires the pin tumblers to be rotated to specific positions by the key. This rotation aligns a slot in each pin tumbler. When the pin tumblers have been properly elevated and rotated, the fin-

FIGURE 8.21

Medeco cylinders are available for a variety of lock types. *(Courtesy of Medeco Security Locks)*

gers, or projections, on the sidebar can enter the pin tumbler slots, which frees the plug to rotate to the locked or unlocked position (Figure 8.23).

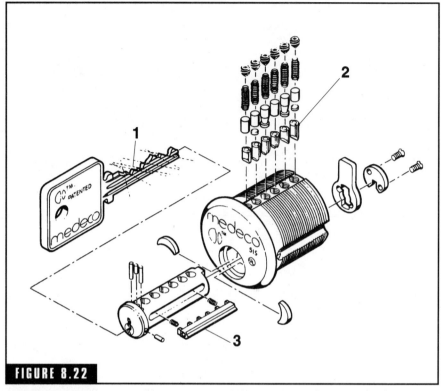

FIGURE 8.22

1. Medeco key. 2. Bottom pins. 3. Side bar with hardened insert. *(Courtesy of Medeco Security Locks)*

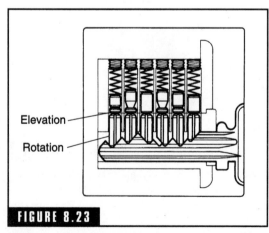

FIGURE 8.23

Pins in a Medeco cylinder must be elevated and rotated by a key. *(Courtesy of Medeco Security Locks)*

For additional security, Medeco cylinders are equipped with hardened steel inserts that protect strategic areas of the cylinder from drilling and surreptitious entry. Anti-drill rods surround the keyway, and hardened inserts protect the shear line and sidebar areas of the cylinder.

A Medeco cylinder requires a key that must be made on a special key machine. This limits the availability of duplicate keys.

Medeco Biaxial Cylinders

The Biaxial cylinder is an improved version of Medeco's original cylinder. The two cylinders look similar and operate on the same principle. The primary differences between them are the angles of the bottom pins and the corresponding angles of the keys used to operate the cylinders.

Like the original Medeco cylinder, the Biaxial is UL-listed, extremely burglar-resistant, and available for a wide variety of locks. The Biaxial offers over 1 billion possible key changes—more than 50 times the changes the original cylinder design offered.

> **TRADE SECRET**
>
> Because Medeco locks are designed at very close tolerances, sometimes the key may 'stick' a little, and be hard to insert, remove, or turn. To solve the problem, and to keep the lock operating smoothly, regularly lubricate the bolt and cylinder.

Schlage Primus Cylinders

Manufactured by Schlage Lock Company, the Schlage Primus Security Cylinder offers a new dimension in security cylinders. It is operated by a unique, "patent protected" key.

These cylinders are used for highly sensitive government installations, public and private institutions, and commercial and residential applications. They are available for Schlage's A, B, C/D, E, H, and L Series locks and allow for simple, cost-effective retrofitting.

Construction

Figures 8.24 and 8.25 show exploded views of Primus cylinders. The Primus is a six-pin cylinder, precision-built to extremely close tolerances. It is machined to accept a side bar and a set of five finger pins.

The side bar and finger pins, in conjunction with Schlage's conventional six-pin keying system, provide two independent locking mechanisms that are operated simultaneously by a specially designed Primus key. Hardened steel pins are incorporated in the cylinder plug and housing to protect it from drilling and other forceful attacks.

Primus Key Control

To meet a wide variety of security needs, Schlage has created four levels of control for Primus keys. Each level requires special registration and an identification card for duplication of the Primus key. Figure 8.26 shows the differences among the levels.

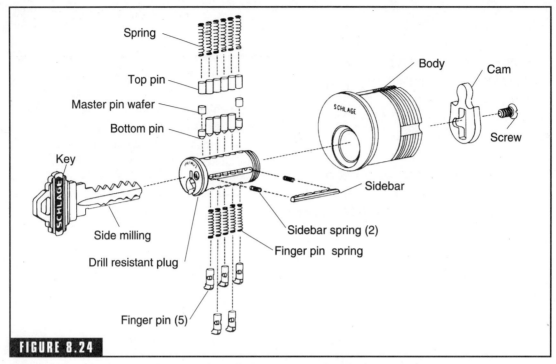

FIGURE 8.24

Exploded view of a Schlage Primus mortise cylinder. *(Courtesy of Schlage Lock Company)*

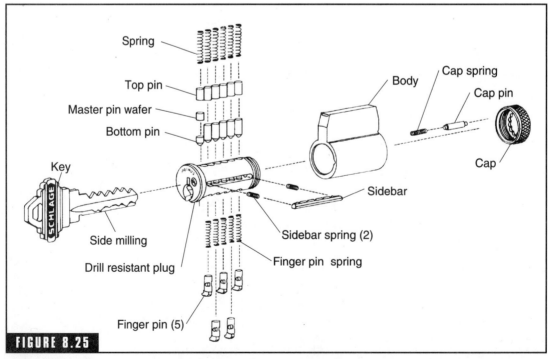

FIGURE 8.25

Exploded view of a Schlage Primus key-in-knob cylinder. *(Courtesy of Schlage Lock Company)*

Assembling Primus Cylinders

To assemble a Schlage Primus cylinder, do the following:

1. Insert two sidebar springs into the cylinder plug. Insert the cylinder plug upside down into a plug holding fixture, with the sidebar engaging the slot in the holding fixture (Figure 8.27).

2. Insert five finger pin springs into the holes at the bottom of the plug (Figure 8.28).

3. Determine the correct finger pins for each position as required by the side milling of the keys (Figure 8.29).

4. Insert the finger pins while advancing the key upside down into the cylinder plug to capture the pins in position (Figure 8.30). Maintain light pressure on the finger pins while inserting the key.

5. With the key fully inserted, rotate the plug slightly to ensure the correct selection of finger pins (Figure 8.31). The plug will not rotate if the wrong finger pin(s) have been installed.

   Note: When masterkeying, use a key with the deepest cuts to complete plug and body assembly. If no one single key allows all bottom and master pins to be at or below the shear line, cut a key to all #9 cuts (deepest depth) for final assembly.

6. Select the bottom and master pins from the key bitting list and load the cylinder plug. Add a small pinch of graphite into the plug holes (Figure 8.32).

7. Use the chart to determine the stack height of the combined bottom and master pins and select the correct top pins (Figure 8.33, top).

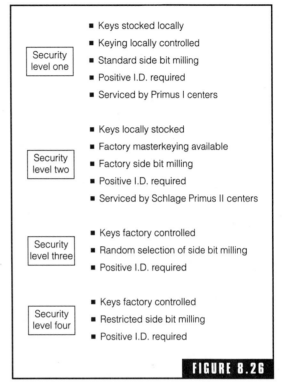

- Security level one
  - Keys stocked locally
  - Keying locally controlled
  - Standard side bit milling
  - Positive I.D. required
  - Serviced by Primus I centers

- Security level two
  - Keys locally stocked
  - Factory masterkeying available
  - Factory side bit milling
  - Positive I.D. required
  - Serviced by Schlage Primus II centers

- Security level three
  - Keys factory controlled
  - Random selection of side bit milling
  - Positive I.D. required

- Security level four
  - Keys factory controlled
  - Restricted side bit milling
  - Positive I.D. required

FIGURE 8.26

Four levels of key control are available for Schlage cylinders. *(Courtesy of Schlage Lock Company)*

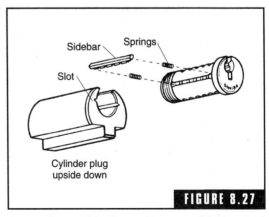

Sidebar   Springs

Slot

Cylinder plug upside down

FIGURE 8.27

Insert plug upside down. *(Courtesy of Schlage Lock Company)*

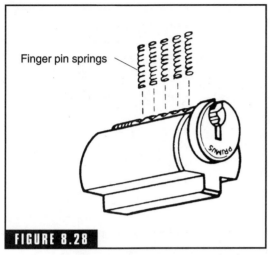

FIGURE 8.28

Finger pins are inserted into the bottom of the plug.
(Courtesy of Schlage Lock Company)

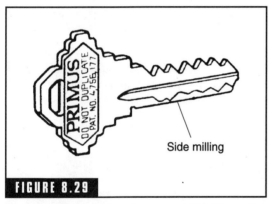

FIGURE 8.29

The side milling of a key shows you which finger pins to use. *(Courtesy of Schlage Lock Company)*

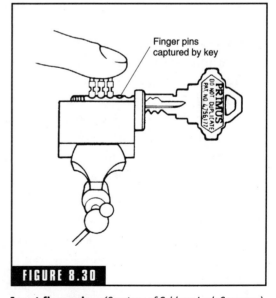

FIGURE 8.30

Insert finger pins. *(Courtesy of Schlage Lock Company)*

Insert the top pins and springs into the appropriate holes in the loading rod (bottom).

8. Slide the sleeve into the loading rod. Depress the springs with a knife tip and advance the sleeve along the rod to the guide groove (Figure 8.34).

9. Slide the cylinder body onto the loading rod. Keep the cylinder body slightly rotated (about 15 degrees) and push the sleeve off until the body is in line with the groove in the loading rod. Remove the sleeve (Figure 8.35).

10. Rotate the cylinder body so that the holes in the loading rod align with the holes in the cylinder body. Use a knife to transfer the pins and springs into the cylinder body. Rotate the cylinder body to capture the pins and springs (Figure 8.36).

11. Remove the cylinder plug from the holder, with the assembly key fully inserted, by maintaining pressure on the sidebar (Figure 8.37). Keep the cylinder body slightly rotated and slide the body onto the cylinder plug. When assembling mortise cylinders, use the opposite end of the loading rod.

12. Rotate the key and plug to align the bottom and top pins. Maintain finger pressure on the cylinder plug face while removing the key (Figure 8.38).

13. Complete cylinder assembly with the cap, pin spring, cap pin, driver bar, and cap or mortise cylinder cam (Figure 8.39).

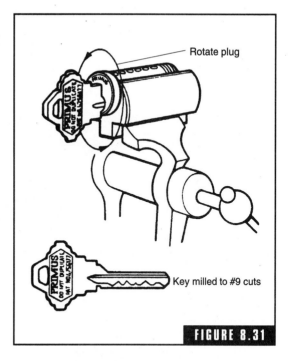

Rotate plug

Key milled to #9 cuts

FIGURE 8.31

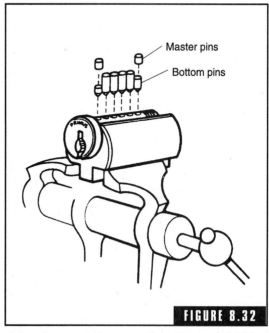

Master pins

Bottom pins

FIGURE 8.32

Select bottom and master pins. *(Courtesy of Schlage Lock Company)*

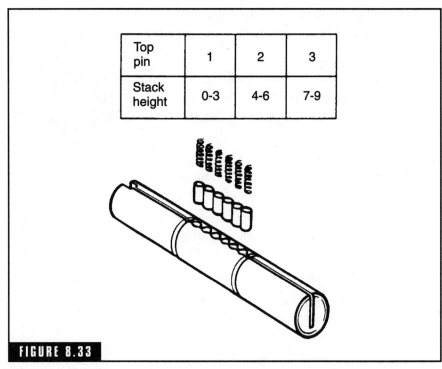

Top pin	1	2	3
Stack height	0-3	4-6	7-9

FIGURE 8.33

Use chart to determine stack height (top) and insert top pins (bottom). *(Courtesy of Schlage Lock Company)*

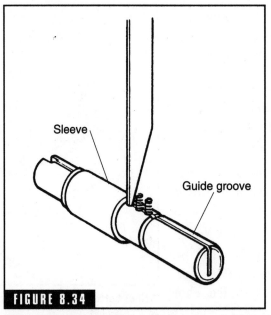

Sleeve

Guide groove

FIGURE 8.34

Slide sleeve onto loading rod. *(Courtesy of Schlage Lock Company)*

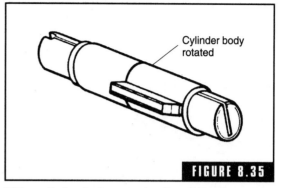

Slide cylinder body onto loading rod. *(Courtesy of Schlage Lock Company)*

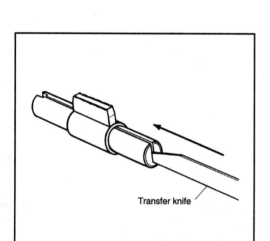

Rotate cylinder body. *(Courtesy of Schlage Lock Company)*

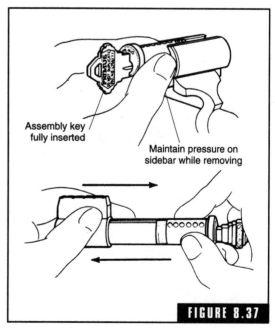

Remove cylinder plug from holder. *(Courtesy of Schlage Lock Company)*

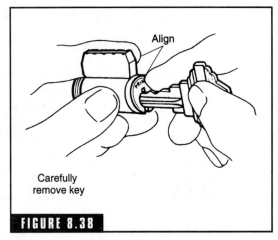

Rotate key and plug. *(Courtesy of Schlage Lock Company)*

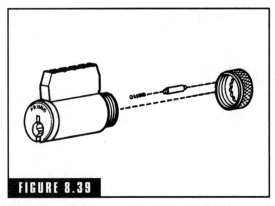

Complete cylinder assembly. *(Courtesy of Schlage Lock Company)*

Pushbutton Combination Locks

A pushbutton combination lock is operated by pushing a series of buttons (usually labeled with letters or numbers) in unison or in sequence. It might also be operated by a key. If a key is used, it is usually an override feature for emergencies only.

These locks are most often designed for commercial applications such as employee entrances, dormitories, and apartment lobbies, but some are available for residential applications.

Modern pushbutton combination locks are ideal for a high-traffic business because they offer thousands (and in some cases, millions) of possible combinations. It can be very hard to guess the combination of a lock with as few as five buttons, if the owner uses only random combinations (as opposed to more guessable choices, such as a name or part of a phone number).

The combinations on pushbutton locks can usually be changed quickly and easily by authorized personnel. These locks can greatly reduce or even eliminate costs of issuing, collecting, and reissuing keys.

Simplex Access Controls Corporation is a major manufacturer of pushbutton combination locks.

This chapter reviews how to install and service some of the company's most popular models.

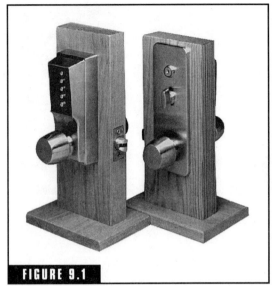

FIGURE 9.1

Simplex 1000 Series pushbutton combination locks are used in high-security areas. *(Courtesy of Simplex Access Controls Corp.)*

1000 Series Locks

Simplex's Unican 1000 Series locks (Figure 9.1) are completely mechanical; they don't require batteries or electrical wiring. The locks offer thousands of possible combinations, and any combination can be changed in seconds by any authorized person.

To install the Models 1000-1 and 1000-2 (those without passage set) on 1⅜- to 1⅞-inch doors, follow these instructions:

1. First carefully check windows, frame, door, etc., to make sure these procedures will not cause damage.

2. Carefully fold the paper template included with your lock (Figure 9.2) as indicated. Tape the template securely to the door so that all indicated folds are properly aligned with the edge of the door. Using an awl or similar marking tool, make the marks for drilling the four holes at precisely the points indicated on the template (Figure 9.3). Remove the template.

    Caution: When a metal frame features an existing strike, locate the strike template so the latch hole center is directly aligned with the center of the strike cutout.

3. Use a hole saw with a center guide drill bit for drilling the 2⅛-inch (54 mm) hole and the two 1-inch (25 mm) holes. Use standard drilling bits for the two ¼-inch (6 mm) holes (Figure 9.4).

    Place the tip of the drill bit against the mark made by the awl. Apply pressure evenly until the circular blade cuts the first side of the door and the tip of the pilot bit emerges through the other side, then stop. Drill through the other side until the 2⅛-inch circular hole is completed. Use the same procedure to drill the 1-inch hole in the door face.

    Using a ¼-inch bit, drill the two holes. Drill the final 1-inch hole through the edge of the door. Carefully drill until the hole saw is

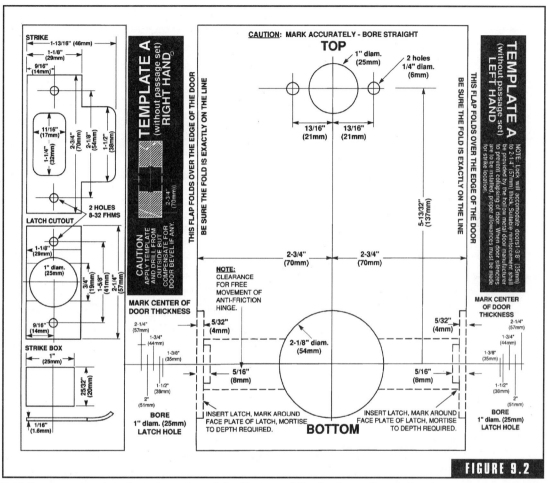

Fold the paper template (not shown to scale). *(Courtesy of Simplex Access Controls Corp.)*

visible through the 2⅛-inch hole, then stop.

Caution: Make a mortise cutout for antifriction hinge of latch.

For metal doors: Cut the opening according to the latch face plate. Mount the top and bottom brackets to accept two latch mounting screws.

For wood doors: Insert the latch into the 1-inch hole until the face plate abuts the door edge. Draw a line around the face plate. Then remove the latch from the door. Using a sharp 1-inch wood chisel, remove approximately ⅛ inch (3 mm) of material, or enough for the face plate to be perfectly flush with the edge of the door (Figure 9.5).

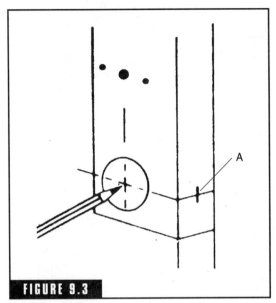

FIGURE 9.3

Mark the door. *(Courtesy of Simplex Access Controls Corp.)*

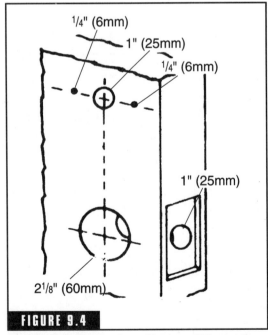

FIGURE 9.4

Drill the holes in the door. *(Courtesy of Simplex Access Controls Corp.)*

FIGURE 9.5

Make latch cutout on wood doors. *(Courtesy of Simplex Access Controls Corp.)*

4. Insert the latch into the 1-inch door edge hole until the latch face plate is flush with the edge of the door. Secure the latch face plate with two Phillips head screws, which are provided (Figure 9.6).

5. Remove the inside knob by depressing the spring-loaded retaining pin that is visible through the poke hole. Pull the handle as the pin is depressed. Release the retaining pin. Continue to pull the handle. The handle has now been separated from the lock body.

6. Properly align the latch unit and the cylindrical drive unit by depressing the latch bolt slightly. Referring to Figure 9.7, make sure that the latch case clips (A) engage the front opening of cylinder drive unit cover (B). Then engage the end of the tailpiece (C) with the shoe retracting hood hooks (D).

7. Test the operation of the lock by depressing the factory-set combination: Press buttons 2 and 4 simultaneously, then press button 3 (Figure 9.8).

Turn the outside knob clockwise to the stop position. As the knob is turned, the latch is retracted until it is flush with the latch face plate. Release the outside knob. The latch will return to the fully extended position. Turn the inside sleeve clockwise or counterclockwise to the stop position. The latch will retract until it is flush with the latch face plate. After the inside sleeve is released, the latch bolt will return to the fully extended position.

8. Position the reinforcing plate onto the sleeve as illustrated in Figure 9.9. Insert the two mounting screws through the reinforcing plate

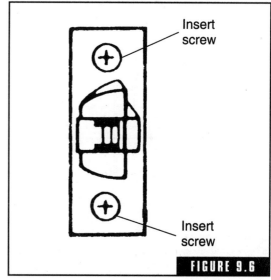

Install the latch. *(Courtesy of Simplex Access Controls Corp.)*

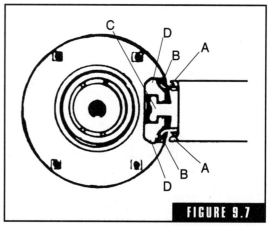

Install the lock. *(Courtesy of Simplex Access Controls Corp.)*

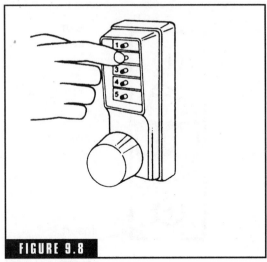

FIGURE 9.8

Test operation of the lock. *(Courtesy of Simplex Access Controls Corp.)*

FIGURE 9.9

Install reinforcement plate. *(Courtesy of Simplex Access Controls Corp.)*

and into the two ¼-inch holes. Tighten the screws to secure the front lock housing to the door.

9. Position the trim plate over the reinforcing plate. Gently screw the threaded ring onto the cylindrical drive unit (Figure 9.10). Tighten the threaded ring using the spanner wrench provided.

   Note: If you have difficulty screwing the ring onto the drive unit, remove the cover and readjust the reinforcing plate: Do not force the ring.

10. Locate the retaining pin through the poke hole in the collar of the knob (Figure 9.11). If the threaded ring in the trim plate covers this poke hole, then loosen the ring and align the hole in the ring with the hole in the collar. Depress the knob retaining pin using the pointed tip of the spanner wrench. Slide the inside knob until the retaining pin snaps back into place.

11. Tighten the threaded ring. Turn the knob clockwise to the stop position. The latch should retract smoothly until it is flush with the face plate. Release the knob and the latch will return to the fully extended position.

12. Insert the correct key into the cylinder of the threaded plug assembly (Figure 9.12). Engage the lock screw through the hole in the trim cover. The mounting stud is located in the 1-inch-diameter cutout. If necessary, shorten the lock screw.

   Turn the key clockwise until the threaded plug assembly abuts the trim plate. The key can only be removed in either the vertical or horizontal position.

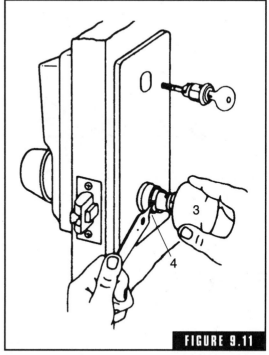

FIGURE 9.11

Install the inside knob. *(Courtesy of Simplex Access Controls Corp.)*

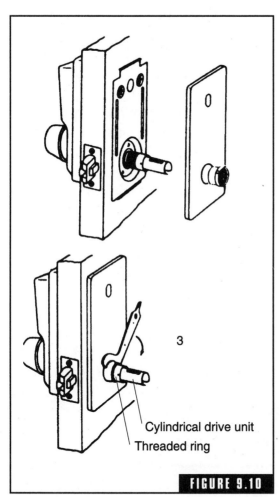

Cylindrical drive unit

Threaded ring

FIGURE 9.10

Install the inside trim plate. *(Courtesy of Simplex Access Controls Corp.)*

FIGURE 9.12

Install threaded plug assembly. *(Courtesy of Simplex Access Controls Corp.)*

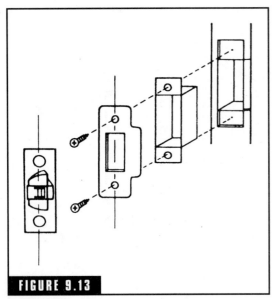

FIGURE 9.13

Install the strike. *(Courtesy of Simplex Access Controls Corp.)*

13. Mark the location of the strike on the door frame. Make sure the line through the screw holes of the strike is well aligned with the line through the screw holes on the face of the latch when the door is closed (Figure 9.13).

14. Mortise the frame for the strike box to a minimum depth of ¾ inch (19 mm). This guarantees that the latch can be fully extended into the door jamb. Place the strike box in the mortised cutout. Secure the strike plate with the screws provided. If necessary, draw a line around the strike. Use this line as a guide to cut out a minimum of ¹⁄₁₆ inch (2 mm) of material, or enough to make the strike plate flush with the door jamb.

Caution: Check the operation of the latch by making sure that the latch deadlocking plunger stops against the strike plate and does not slip into the strike opening when the door is closed. If this situation occurs, then a total lockout can result. This will cancel the warranty of the complete lock mechanism.

If there is a gap between the edge of the door and frame (or in the case of double doors, the edge of door and the edge of door) of more than ¼ inch, the latch will fail to engage the strike jamb. If necessary, adjust the gap using the rubber bumpers included in the lock box.

Installation on 1³⁄₈- to 1¹⁄₂-Inch Doors

The lock has been preset at the factory to accommodate 1⅝- to 1⅞-inch doors. For 1⅜- to 1½-inch doors, adjust the lock as follows (Figure 9.14).

1. Remove the back plate and the cylindrical drive unit from the back plate.

2. Remove and discard the spacer between the back plate and the cylindrical drive unit. Remount the cylindrical drive unit onto the back plate using the shorter screws provided.

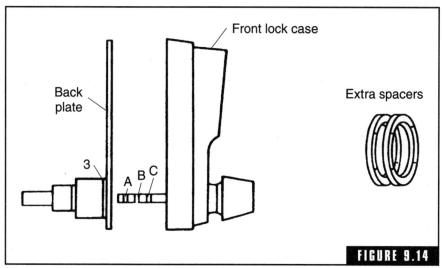

Adjust the lock for varying door thicknesses. *(Courtesy of Simplex Access Controls Corp.)*

3. Remove the cross pin from position B (refer to Figure 9.14). Place the new cross pin in position C. Reinstall the back plate onto the front of the lock case.

Installation on 2- to 2¼-Inch Doors

To adjust the lock to accommodate 2- to 2¼-inch doors, proceed as follows.

1. Remove the back plate and the cylindrical drive unit from the back.

2. Insert the extra spacer provided in the accessory pack between the cylindrical drive unit and the back plate. Be sure that the sharp edges are adjoining.

3. Remount the cylindrical drive unit onto the back plate using the longer screws provided. Add a cross pin in position A (refer to Figure 9.14).

4. Remount the back plate onto the front lock case.

Warning: Damage may result if the knob hits against the wall or wall stop. If such is the case, all warranties are null and void.

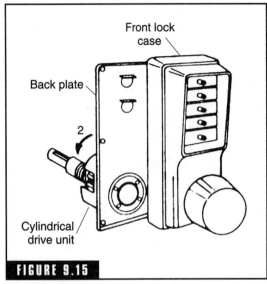

FIGURE 9.15

Changing the hand of the lock. *(Courtesy of Simplex Access Controls Corp.)*

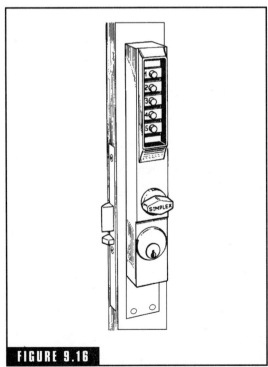

FIGURE 9.16

Simplex 3000 Series locks are fully mechanical. *(Courtesy of Simplex Access Controls Corp.)*

Reversing Lock Location

Unless otherwise stated in the manufacturer's literature included with a lock, all locks are factory-assembled for left-hand operation. To reverse the hand of a lock, proceed as follows (Figure 9.15).

1. Remove the back plate, which contains the cylindrical drive unit, from the lock case. Unscrew the cylindrical drive unit from the back plate.
2. Turn the cylindrical drive unit so that the cutout for the latch faces in the opposite direction.
3. Reattach the cylindrical drive unit to the back plate. Remount the back plate onto the lock case.
4. Tighten all screws securely.
5. Test the lock to make sure it is still working properly.

Series 3000

The Simplex Series 3000 pushbutton combination locks (Figure 9.16) are made for narrow stile doors. The locks are fully mechanical and can be recombined by authorized personnel in less than a minute.

A key can be used to deactivate the pushbutton combination to prevent unauthorized reentry after hours and to reactivate the combination for the next day's shift. Management's key can also activate the latch hold-back feature, which removes all security from the door.

For a complete installation, you need both a lock housing and a drive assembly; they are sold separately. Those narrow stile doors already equipped with Adams

Rite hardware (latches, key cylinders, and egress devices) need only the Simplex Series 3000 lock for a complete installation.

Lock Housing Assembly

You need a large Phillips head screwdriver and small and medium flat blade screwdrivers to install a 3000 Series lock. The installation procedure is as follows.

1. Remove the mounting plate assembly (Figure 9.17) by removing one round-head screw and one flat-head screw.

2. Install the mortise cylinder by turning the cylinder until the cam contacts lock in the plate. Turn the cylinder counterclockwise less

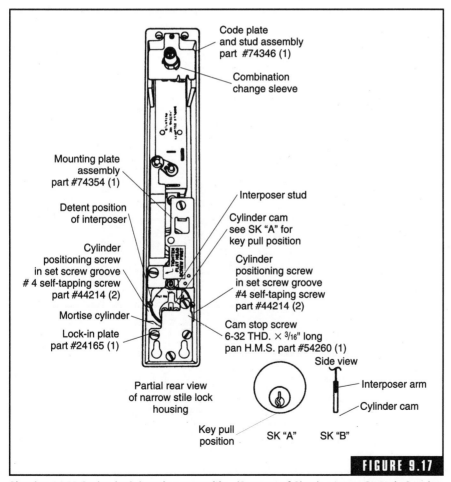

FIGURE 9.17

Simplex 3000 Series lock housing assembly. *(Courtesy of Simplex Access Controls Corp.)*

than one turn until the key is positioned in the pull position, also aligning to the cylinder set screw grooves.

3. Assemble two cylinder-positioning screws. Make sure the heads of these screws are below the underside of the cylinder cam. Reassemble the mounting plate assembly.

4. The interposer arm should be positioned central to the cylinder cam. If it is not, adjust the cylinder depth. Assemble the cam stop screw.

Note: The interposer stud is to be centered as shown in Figure 9.17 before mounting the combination lock housing.

Mounting Lock to Stile

To mount a Series 3000 lock to the stile, proceed as follows.

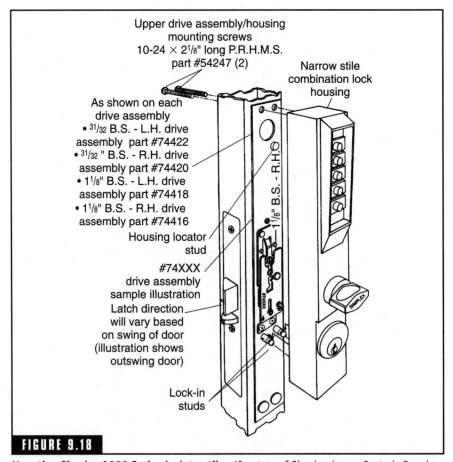

Upper drive assembly/housing
mounting screws
10-24 × 2¹/₈" long P.R.H.M.S.
part #54247 (2)

Narrow stile
combination lock
housing

As shown on each
drive assembly
• ³¹/₃₂ B.S. - L.H. drive
assembly part #74422
• ³¹/₃₂ " B.S. - R.H. drive
assembly part #74420
• 1¹/₈" B.S. - L.H. drive
assembly part #74418
• 1¹/₈" B.S. - R.H. drive
assembly part #74416

Housing locator
stud

#74XXX
drive assembly
sample illustration
Latch direction
will vary based
on swing of door
(illustration shows
outswing door)

Lock-in
studs

FIGURE 9.18

Mounting Simplex 3000 Series lock to stile. *(Courtesy of Simplex Access Controls Corp.)*

1. Place the combination lock over the lock-in studs and slide downward until a stop position is attained—approximately ⅛ inch of movement (Figure 9.18). The top of the lock housing and the top of the drive assembly should be flush when properly positioned.

2. Fix two long round-head machine screws as shown in Figure 9.18.

3. Using the key, thread the control lock assembly into the combination change sleeve (Figure 9.19) until the trim plate is snug against the stile. The key can only be removed in the vertical or horizontal position. Before closing the door, refer to the operating instructions to check the operation of all lock functions.

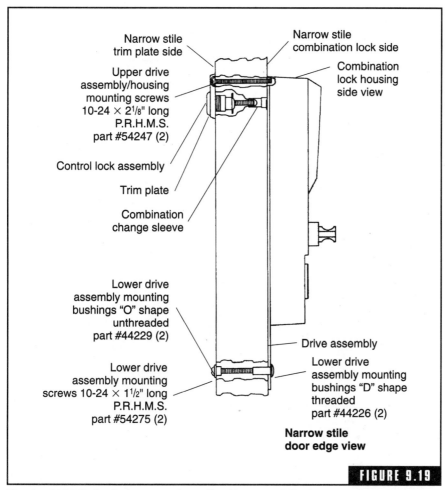

FIGURE 9.19

Simplex 3000 Series lock mounted to stile. *(Courtesy of Simplex Access Controls Corp.)*

Lock Picking, Impressioning, and Forced Entry

Entry techniques used for locksmithing generally differ from those used for burglary. Although locksmiths and burglars share the goal of getting into a locked place quickly, burglars aren't concerned about causing damage, and they generally have little or no specialized knowledge of locking devices. They mainly take advantage of unlocked doors and windows and of entry points with blatant security weaknesses.

A locksmith, on the other hand, relies on a variety of sophisticated skills, and causes as little damage as possible. Few customers would expect their locksmith to gain entry into their locked home by kicking the door in or by breaking a window. In addition to not causing damage, a good locksmith has the expertise to point out a wide variety of security problems that burglars may exploit.

This chapter explains in detail two of the most sophisticated lock-opening techniques: lock picking and key impressioning. Both take patience and practice to master. Also in this chapter are some of the most common forced-entry techniques used by burglars, which take minutes to master. Knowledge of how burglars work is important for helping you better advise and help your customers.

Lock Picking

You may have seen movies and television shows where people pick open locks as fast as they would using a key. Perhaps that's why some people get agitated when a locksmith takes more than a minute to pick open their lock. In real life, it isn't uncommon for an experienced locksmith to spend five minutes picking open a common pin tumbler lock. It can take much longer (from hours to days) to pick a high-security lock.

In theory, any mechanical lock that is operated with a key can be picked. That is, tools can be made to simulate the action of the key. There are many locks with patented cylinders and keys, however, that would be impractical for burglars or locksmiths to try to pick open. To pick open those locks, a person would need intimate knowledge of their internal construction, custom-made tools, and someone to bring him food and water occasionally. Highly pick-resistant locks are almost never picked open because it's faster and easier either to bypass the lock or open it in some other way.

Before you can learn to pick locks professionally, you need to become familiar with the internal construction of the basic types of locks. That information is in Chapters 2, 4, 5, 7, and 8. Knowing how a lock is designed will help you visualize what's going on in the lock while you're picking.

Tools

The only tools needed for picking most types of locks are picks and torque wrenches, also called tension wrenches or turning tools. The pick is used to align the tumblers into a position that frees the plug so it can be turned. The torque wrench is used to place tension on the lock plug to help hold the tumblers in place as the pick places them into position. After the tumblers are in position to free the plug, the torque wrench is then used like a key to turn the plug.

There are a wide variety of types, styles, and sizes of picks and torque wrenches (Figures 10.1 and 10.2). It's good to have a wide variety of picking tools, so you'll be prepared to handle different situations. There are many brands of picking tools. Which brand is best is largely a matter of personal preference.

Picking Pin Tumbler Locks

The ability to pick pin tumbler locks quickly is one of the most important skills a locksmith needs, because the pin tumbler lock is so commonly used. Being able to pick locks quickly can help you get hired as a locksmith, and can help you do various locksmithing tasks better.

There are several ways people go about trying to pick open locks. The "feel" method is the most professional, and will work most consistently. It's also hardest to become proficient at. Learning the basics is simple (just a matter of reading this chapter), but lots of practice is needed to develop the feel. Nevertheless, you'll benefit greatly by becoming proficient at using the feel method before learning other methods.

The Feel Method

Before trying to pick open a pin tumbler lock, make sure that the tumblers aren't sticking. Insert the flat edge of a half diamond pick into the keyway to the last stack of pins (usually about 1-inch into the plug), and try to raise all the pin stacks evenly together in the cylinder. While lifting them, slowly pull the tool toward the front of the cylinder, listening for each stack to drop one at a time. If you can't raise all the pin stacks evenly, or if all of them don't drop, you'll need to fix the problem before picking the lock. Foreign matter in the cylinder may be blocking the tumblers.

Many locksmiths use a diamond or hook pick (see Figure 10.1) when using the feel method to pick a pin tumbler lock. Hold the pick as you would hold a pencil.

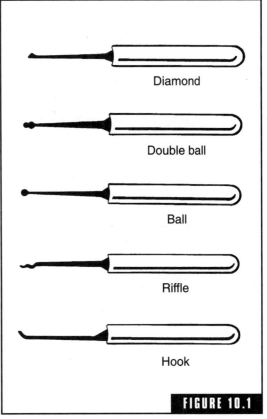

Diamond

Double ball

Ball

Riffle

Hook

FIGURE 10.1

Some common types of lock picks. *(Courtesy of A-1 Security Manufacturing Corp.)*

T)OOLS

You can make lockpicks and torque wrenches by filing or grinding spring steel. Good sources of spring steel are hacksaw blades, piano wire, and the bristles left behind on the streets from street sweepers.

With the pick's tip pointing toward the pins (which is usually upward, unless the lock was installed upside down), insert it into the keyway to the last pin stack (the one furthest from the face of the cylinder).

With your other hand, place the small bent end of your torque wrench (see Figure 10.2) into the top or bottom of the keyway,

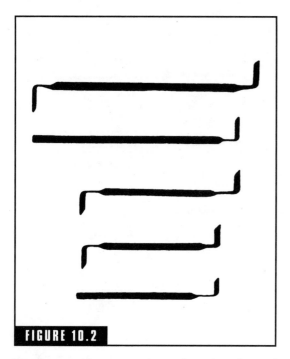

FIGURE 10.2

Torque wrenches come in various lengths and thicknesses.

whichever position gives you the most room to work your pick properly. Make sure the torque wrench doesn't touch any pins. Use the index finger of the hand with which you're holding the torque wrench to apply light pressure on the end of the torque wrench in the direction you want the plug to turn. While maintaining that pressure, slowly lift the last pin to the shear line. Release the torque wrench pressure, letting that pin stack drop back into place. Then move on to the next pin and do the same thing. Repeat that with each pin to figure out which pin stack has the most and least resistance.

Release the pressure on the torque wrench. Then go to the pin stack that has the most resistance, and lift its bottom pin while varying pressure on the torque wrench. When the top and bottom pins for that chamber meet at the sheer line, apply enough pressure on the torque wrench to hold the top pins in place, out of the lower pin chamber. Then gently move on to the next most resistant stack, and lift it into place. Continue lifting each stack into place, from most resistant to least resistant, until the plug is free to be turned.

PRINCIPLES OF THE FEEL METHOD

Understanding the principle behind the feel method is important for learning to perform it.

The method works for two reasons. First, the lower pin chambers of a pin tumbler cylinder are never perfectly aligned with their corresponding upper pin chambers. Second, the sets of upper and lower pin chambers are never perfectly aligned with one another. Instead of forming a straight line, the sets of pin chambers form a slight zigzag pattern across the plug and cylinder case (Figure 10.3).

Sometimes the variation from one set of pin chambers to the next set is less than .0002 inch.

There's always some variation because mass production techniques can't create perfect locks. The higher the quality of the lock, the less

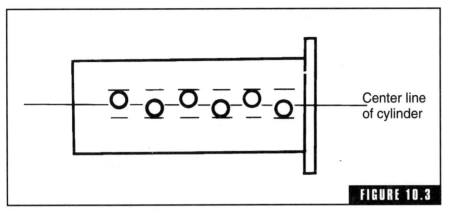

Center line
of cylinder

FIGURE 10.3

Pin chambers within a cylinder are not perfectly aligned with one another.

variation the lock will have among its sets of pin chambers (and between each upper and lower pin chamber).

The slight misalignments within a cylinder allows the cylinder to be picked. When a bottom pin is lifted to the shear line while pressure is applied to the torque wrench, the top pin that's resting on that bottom pin

> **QUICK»»TIP**
> At first, you may want to practice lock picking by holding the cylinder you're working on. But to develop the skills you'll need for real work conditions, you'll need to practice picking stalled locks.

is also being lifted. As the top pin is being lifted, it leans against a wall within its upper pin chamber. When the bottom of that top pin reaches the shear line (which occurs the same time the top of its corresponding bottom pin reaches the shear line), the plug is able to turn slightly. When it turns, a small ledge is created on the plug. This ledge prevents the top pin from falling back into the lower pin chamber.

Even when the pick is moved away from the corresponding bottom pin and the bottom pin falls back into the plug, that top pin will stay on that ledge at the shear line as long as adequate pressure is being applied to the plug.

As each top pin is set on the ledge, the ledge gets bigger because the plug is able to turn more.

When all the top pins are sitting on the ledge, all the bottom pins will be at or below the shear line. The plug is then free to be rotated into position to operate the lock.

How can you tell when a bottom pin has reached the shear line? When a ledge is formed by the plug to prevent the top pin from dropping into the lower pin chamber, a slight ceiling is formed below the upper pin chamber that makes it a little more difficult for the bottom pin to go into the upper pin chamber. If you're lifting the bottom pin slowly enough, you will feel when it bumps against that ceiling; that's when you stop lifting the pin. Lifting each pin exactly to the shear line is only part of the task of picking a pin tumbler cylinder. You also have to apply just the right amount of turning pressure to the plug. The proper amount of pressure varies among the sets of pin chambers within a cylinder. While lifting one bottom pin you might need to use an amount of pressure that differs from the amount you used with another bottom pin.

If too much turning pressure is applied to the plug, the pins will be bound between the upper and lower pin chambers and you won't be able to lift the pins to the shear line. If too little pressure is applied, the ledge on the plug will be too small to prevent the top pins from dropping into the lower pin chambers.

Applying too little turning pressure to the plug is seldom the problem. In most cases, people apply far too much pressure. A very small ledge is needed to hold the top pins in place.

Practicing The Feel Method

Even though you know the principle behind the feel method and the steps required to perform it, you will need to practice a great deal before you can use the method proficiently. It will probably seem very difficult at first—perhaps even impossible! With enough proper practice, you will become an expert at picking locks.

You'll learn this method faster if you first practice picking a lock that has only one set of pin tumblers (one bottom pin and one corresponding top pin and spring). After you feel comfortable picking the lock, add another set of pin tumblers to it. Continue adding sets of pins until you can pick the lock with five sets of pin tumblers in it.

When practicing, don't rush the learning process. It takes a while to develop the feel you need to pick pin tumbler locks. Visualize what's happening in the lock as you're picking it, and take your time. Just as you developed the feel to ride a bike, you can develop the feel to pick locks.

The Rake Method

The most common method used to pick locks is the rake method, or raking. The rake method is based primarily on luck. People who only use the rake method to pick locks have never taken the time to learn the feel method.

To rake a lock, insert a pick (usually a half diamond or a riffle) into a keyway past the last set of pin tumblers, then quickly move the pick in and out of the keyway while varying tension on the torque wrench. The scrubbing action of the pick causes all the pins to jump up to (or above) the shear line, and the varying pressure of the torque wrench helps catch the top pins in place. Raking sometimes works very quickly.

Many times locksmiths use both the rake method and the feel method to pick a lock. You can rake a few times first to bind some top pins into position, and then switch to the feel method to finish the job. With experience, you'll know which method is best to use in a given situation.

Picking Lever Tumbler and Disc Tumbler Locks

Lever tumbler and disc tumbler locks are picked in much the same way as pin tumbler locks. The same types of picks are used for all three lock types. If you're able to pick pin tumbler locks, you'll have no trouble picking lever tumbler or disc tumbler locks.

When picking a lever tumbler lock, you lift lever tumblers instead of pins. When picking disc tumbler locks, you pull the disc tumblers down instead of lifting them up.

When picking double-bitted disc tumbler locks, you might need to use a two-sided pick. If so, use the rake method.

The side bar wafer lock is a type of disc tumbler lock that is difficult to pick using common picking tools. Bringing the tumblers to the shear line isn't hard, but until all of them are aligned at once, the side bar will prevent the lock from being operated.

To pick a side bar wafer lock, apply pressure to the side bar to force it against the tumblers so that each tumbler you put in place with your pick will stay in place until all the tumblers have been properly positioned. One way to do that is to drill a small hole in the face of the cylinder beside the side bar and insert a thin wire into the hole to press the side bar against the tumblers.

Using a Lock-Picking Gun

A lock-picking gun (Figure 10.4) is a tool that is shaped like a gun. It can't automatically open locks, but it can sometimes make the job of picking easier.

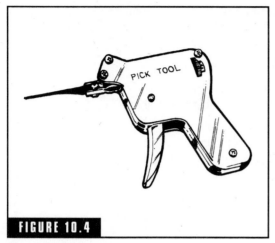

FIGURE 10.4

A lock-picking gun can be a helpful tool. *(Courtesy of Ilco Unican Corp.)*

When using a lock-picking gun, you also need to use a torque wrench. Insert the pick end of the gun into the keyway beneath the last bottom pin. Insert the torque wrench. Squeeze the trigger a few times while varying the pressure on the torque wrench. The pick end of the gun will slap the bottom pins, causing them to jump up. The torque wrench catches the pins in place, much like the rake method of lock picking.

Lock Picking Tips

Locks with worn tumblers are usually easier to pick than new locks. When picking a lock, work on one that's most often used. For homes, that's usually the main entry door; for automobiles, it's usually the driver-side door.

Thinner picks are usually easier to work with than thicker picks.

The more loosely a lock is mounted, the harder it will be to pick. Use shims or a wedge to stiffen a lock's mounting, if necessary.

While you're picking the lock, visualize how the tumblers and other parts of the cylinder are being moved.

Lubricating a lock's keyway can make it easier to pick. If you expect to impression the lock, however, don't lubricate it.

Key Impressioning

The ability to impression keys can help you quickly make a working key without having another working key to copy and without disassembling the lock. Unlike lock picking, key impressioning lets a locksmith quickly gain entry and make a new key at the same time. However, a great deal of practice is required to develop the skill.

Basically, impressioning is a technique in which a blank is methodically marked by the lock and then bitted (or cut) until the blank becomes a working key. For most locks, the only tools needed for impressioning a key are a blank, a file, and a tool for holding the blank (such as locking pliers).

To impression, insert a properly prepared blank into a keyway and move the blank so the tumblers scratch the bitting surface of the blank. When tumblers scratch the blank, they leave small marks.

Those marks indicate where and how deep to cut the blank. In most cases, the process of preparing, inserting, and cutting the blank must be attempted several times before the blank can be made into a key that will operate the lock.

> **QUICK>>>TIP**
>
> Although a lock-picking gun can be a nice accessory for the locksmith who has everything, if you can afford only a few lockpicking tools you'll get more for your money from a standard set of picks and torque wrenches in a carrying case.

The markings are small; sometimes they are barely visible. They won't be positioned in a straight line. Some may be near the center along the blank's bitting edge; others may be off center to the left or right. The type and position of markings you get depend on many factors, including the type of lock you're working on, the condition of the lock, the type of blank you're using, how you move the blank in the lock, how hard you move the blank, and the quality of lighting you're using.

It wouldn't be helpful to try to describe all the types of marks you're likely to see while impressioning, because each situation is unique. The best way to understand impression marks is to become familiar with the internal construction of the lock you're working on, and to practice impressioning a lot. When it comes to developing key impressioning skills, nothing can take the place of practice.

Your choice of a blank is critical for impressioning. The blank not only must match the lock's keyway, but must also be soft enough to get good marks, and hard enough to resist easily breaking while you're trying to get the mark. Aluminum blanks are soft enough to mark easily, but are also brittle. Nickel silver blanks are strong, but are too hard for tumblers to mark. Brass is the most popular blank material among locksmiths for impressioning. It can get good marks, and is fairly strong. The blank must also be long enough to reach all the pin stacks.

Although the principle behind key impressioning is the same for all basic types of locks, the specific steps differ depending on the type of locks.

Impressioning Keys for Warded Locks

To impression a key for a warded padlock, you need a pair of locking pliers, the correct key blank, a lighted candle, and a small warding, or square cut, file. Proceed as follows.

1. Clamp the vise grips to the bow of the proper blank. Using the locking pliers as a handle, hold the blank over the candle flame until the blade is covered with soot on both sides.

2. Insert the blank into the lock and gently twist the blank left to right a few times. Remove the blank from the lock, being careful not to rub the soot off the blade.

There are several marks on the blade; they show where you must make the cuts. The marks should be on both sides and on both cutting edges of the blade.

3. Use a corner of the file to scratch the center of each mark. You need the scratches to show where to make the cuts because much of the soot will come off the blade while you're handling the blank.

4. Use your warding file to make a 90-degree (squared) cut at each scratch you made and on both sides of the blank. Make all of the cuts about ¼ inch deep.

5. You should now have a key that will operate the lock. If it doesn't, you might need to widen the cuts or make them a little deeper. Use the locking pliers and candle to put more soot on the key, then twist it in the lock again. The new marks will tell you where the key needs to be cut again.

Impressioning Keys for Pin Tumbler Locks

The pin tumbler lock is the most difficult type of lock for which to impression a key. The tumbler marks left on a key blank are usually very small and can sometimes be misleading. It takes a lot of practice to learn to notice the marks and to understand what they indicate. The procedure for impressioning a key for a pin tumbler lock is as follows.

1. Find out which cut depths and spaces are used for keys that operate the lock you're impressioning. That information can be obtained from depth and space charts.

2. Select the proper blank and file the length of its bitting edge on both sides at about 45-degree angles to create a

knife edge. It's somewhat like sharpening the blade of a single-edge knife. Use smooth strokes, and file in one direction. Don't decrease the width of the blade—only the thickness of the bitting edge.

3. Clamp pliers to the bow of the blank, and using the pliers as a handle, insert the blank into the lock's keyway. (That will raise all the pins in the lock to their highest level.) Gently twist the blank from left to right a few times, and gently rock it up and down a few times.

4. Remove the blank from the lock and notice the small marks on or near the shallow cuts on your blank. Find the cut that has the heaviest tumbler mark near it; the pins don't always leave marks in the center of proper spaces. Use your file and caliper to make the shallowest cut depth, for the lock you're working on. Don't deepen any other cuts.

5. Use your file to replace the knife edge on the blank. Then insert it back into the lock and gently twist and rock the blank again. Remove the blank and notice the tumbler marks left on the cutting edge of the blade. If the heaviest mark is on the cut you just deepened, deepen the cut to the next depth for that lock. If the heaviest mark is near another cut, deepen that cut to its next depth.

6. Replace the knife edge on the blank and reinsert it into the lock. Look at the marks and find the heaviest one. Cut one depth at the proper spacing nearest the heaviest mark. (See Appendix E for depth and space charts.)

7. Continue replacing the knife edge on the blank, reinserting it into the lock, deepening the heaviest mark, etc., until you have a working key. Remember, never file a cut deeper once it stops getting the heaviest tumbler mark, even if it later gets the heaviest mark.

When filing cuts, you need to make them the same shape and angle as the original key that was made for the lock you're working on. Figure 10.5 shows the three types of cuts most commonly found on keys. If the cut shapes and angles are made improperly, the key you've impressioned will not allow the pin tumblers to seat properly in the cuts; the pins will either seat too high or too low. Many depth and space charts have drawings that show the shapes and angles key cuts should be.

Forced Entry Techniques

Most locksmiths consider it unethical to use forcible entry techniques except in emergencies when professional techniques won't work or when professional techniques would not be cost-effective. It usually isn't sensible to waste time trying to pick a lock open, for example, if someone inside a building needs immediate medical attention. Nor is it in a customer's best interest for a locksmith to impression a key to open an inexpensive lock.

Loiding

Locks with spring-loaded latch bolts, such as most key-in-knob locks and some rim locks, can be opened by using a thin piece of plastic or metal (a credit card or a knife) to press the latch bolt out of a strike and back into the lock. This process is called *loiding*. The card or knife is inserted between the door and jamb at the beveled edge of the latch bolt and is pushed against the latch bolt.

Loiding is harder to do with a spring-loaded latch bolt that has a deadlatching bar attached to it. When the lock is properly installed, the bar is depressed against the strike plate and prevents depression of the bolt. You have to free the deadlatching bar before loiding will work on the lock.

Jimmying

Many deadbolt locks and most spring-loaded locks (including those with deadlatching bars) can be opened by jimmying. To jimmy a lock, simply insert a prying bar between the door and jamb near the lock's bolt. Pry the door far enough away from the jamb to allow the bolt to

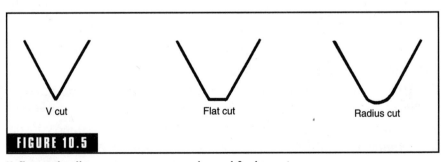

V cut   Flat cut   Radius cut

FIGURE 10.5

V, flat, and radius grooves are commonly used for key cuts.

come out of the strike. The more loosely a door is fitted and the smaller the lock's bolt, the easier it is to jimmy a lock.

Drilling Pin Tumbler Locks

Most pin tumbler locks can be easily drilled open by drilling through the top pins. Position a ⅛-inch or ³⁄₃₂-inch drill bit on the face of the cylinder about ⅛ inch above the shear line, directly in line with the top pins. As you drill through the cylinder, you will feel the drill jerk forward each time you go through a pin. After you've drilled through the last pin, use a key blank or a screwdriver to rotate the plug.

QUICK»»TIP

When you first begin practicing key impression, start with a 4-pin padlock. Those small keys are easier to impression than keys for 5- and 6-pin locks.

QUICK»»TIP

Always wear eye protection when cutting padlocks, because often pieces of the shackle will fly through the air at dangerous speeds.

Some pin tumbler cylinders have hardened pins or plates protecting the pins. They too can be drilled through, but drilling them takes a little longer. A tungsten carbide drill bit can make it easier to drill through hardened pins and plates.

Locksmithing supply houses sell jigs for properly aligning a drill bit to a cylinder. The jigs can be useful but aren't necessary for drilling through a cylinder.

Removing Mortise Cylinders

A mortise cylinder can be forcibly removed by first prying off the cylinder collar, then using a wrench to twist the cylinder out. After wrenching out the cylinder, replace it because its threads will be stripped. Many locksmith supply houses sell mortise cylinder removal tools; these work in much the same way as wrenches.

Opening Padlocks

The most common way of opening an inexpensive padlock is to cut the shackle with bolt cutters. The process is quick and allows a locksmith to earn extra money selling new padlocks. When cutting a shackle, make sure people aren't standing too close. Sometimes the lock will fly off its hasp. To open a high-quality padlock, it might be in the customer's best interest for you to drill out the cylinder plug or pick the lock.

TRADE SECRET   The longer the bolt cutter handles, the thicker the bolt shackle it will easily cut through. It's best to have bolt cutters at least two feet long. If necessary, you can attach piping to the handles for extra leverage.

Another way to enter a padlocked area is to use a bolt cutter to cut the hasp loop, or staple, that the padlock's shackle is in. Sometimes you can simply unscrew the hasp and remove both it and the padlock intact.

Masterkeying

Contrary to a popular myth, there is no master key that can open every lock (or even most locks). The closest thing to such a mythological key is a skeleton key. As explained in Chapter 4, a skeleton key can be used to operate a large number of warded locks. A *master key* in locksmithing terminology is simply a key that has been cut to operate two or more locks that have different key combinations. It can only operate locks that have been modified to allow it to operate them.

To *masterkey* means to modify a group of locks in such a way that each can be operated by a uniquely bitted key that can't operate the others, and all can be operated by a master key. A key that operates only one lock, or two or more locks keyed alike, within a master system is called a *change key*.

Some people confuse masterkeying with locks that are keyed alike. The latter all have the same keying combination and are operated by the same key. In a house, for example, the front and back door might be keyed alike so that a single key can be used to operate both locks. Two masterkeyed locks, however, are combinated differently from each other; neither's change key can operate the other lock.

Masterkeying is frequently done on locks in hotels and apartment complexes. In an apartment complex, for example, a master key system can allow each tenant to have a change key to operate only the lock for his or her apartment, and the apartment manager can have a master key that operates all the locks in the complex.

Some master key systems consist of more than one level. In a multi-level system, different locks are modified to be operated by different master keys and all of the locks can be operated by the top-level master key. For example, a hotel might have a system that allows each guest to have a change key, each maid to have a master key to open one group of rooms, and the manager to have a top-level master key that can open all the doors in the hotel. Figure 11.1 shows how a multi-level master key system works.

Often some locks within a masterkeyed system are *maison keyed.* That is, they are modified to be operated by two or more change keys. The front door of an apartment building, for example, may be maison keyed so that each tenant's change key unlocks that door.

Both maison keying and masterkeying systems are used primarily for convenience. Without them, an apartment or hotel would need to have and control the use of many more keys. However, both types of keying systems reduce security. Whenever a lock is modified to be operated by more than one key, the lock becomes less secure. Likewise, a lock that can be operated by two levels of master keys is less secure than one that can be operated by only one master key.

How a group of locks are masterkeyed depends on the type and model of the locks. Some general masterkeying principles apply to each type of lock, but certain models with each type require special treatment. This is especially true for many high-security pin tumbler locks that have unique features.

Warded Locks

Groups of warded locks are masterkeyed by the manufacturer. Masterkeying is accomplished by placing wards of various sizes and shapes within each lock. A change key is cut in such a way that it will bypass the wards of one of the locks, so it can operate that lock but none of the others. A master key is cut to bypass the wards in all the locks, so it can operate all of them.

As explained in Chapter 4, warded locks offer little security. They are seldom used in situations that require masterkeying and therefore are seldom masterkeyed.

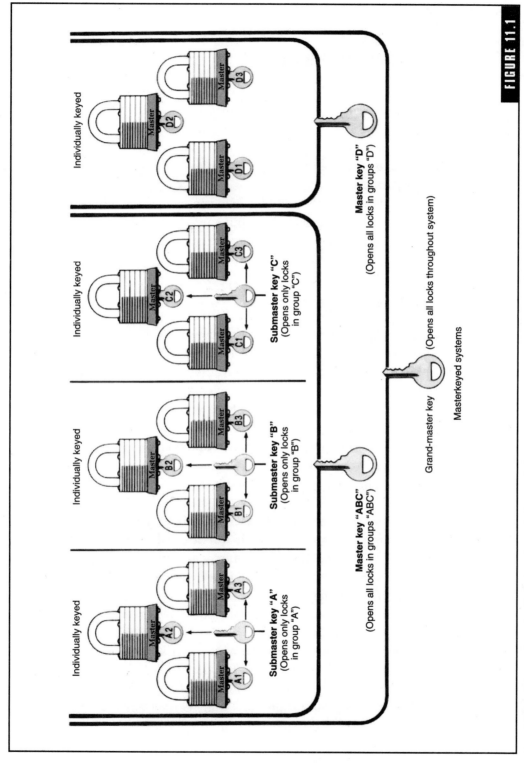

A multi-level masterkeyed system has several change keys and master keys. *(Courtesy of Master Lock Company)*

FIGURE 11.1

Lever Tumbler Locks

Lever tumbler locks are also usually masterkeyed by the manufacturer. Masterkeying such locks is time-consuming and seldom a practical job for a locksmith.

A lever tumbler lock can be masterkeyed by using double-gated levers. One set of gates is operated by the change key; the other set by the master key.

Another way a lever tumbler lock can be masterkeyed is by using a control lever tumbler that has a pin running through it connecting the tumbler to all of the other tumblers in the lock. The master key is cut to operate the lock by lifting the control tumbler.

Disc Tumbler Locks

A disc tumbler lock that isn't part of a masterkeyed system usually has a rectangular cutout in each tumbler. The lock is masterkeyed by using tumblers with cutouts shaped to allow more than one key combination to operate it. One side of the tumbler is operated by the change key, the other side by the master key. In addition to having different cuts, the keys have different (reversed) keyway grooves. The keyway of a masterkeyed disc tumbler lock is designed to accept two different keyway groove patterns.

Pin Tumbler Locks

Although most other types of locks are usually masterkeyed by lock manufacturers, locksmiths are frequently called upon to masterkey pin tumbler locks. Such locks offer many more keying possibilities than do other types and can be masterkeyed in several different ways.

Some pin tumbler locks have keyways that are specially designed for masterkeying. Such keyways are called *sectionals.* They allow certain keys within a masterkeyed system to fit into them and prevent the fitting of certain keys within the system. With sectional keyways (Figure 11.2) a person can combinate two or more locks the same and issue a distinct change key for each lock. Even though the change keys have the same spacing depths and cuts, they cannot enter the other's lock. Another specially designed key can enter both locks. Sectional keyways are especially useful for a large master key system because they provide many master key levels.

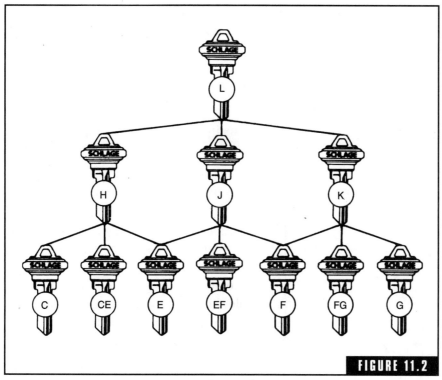

Sectional keys come in groups and are used for masterkeying. *(Courtesy of Schlage Lock Company)*

Pin tumbler locks can also be masterkeyed by creating more than one shear line within each cylinder. This is accomplished by placing master pins between the top and bottom pins. A masterkeyed pin tumbler lock has one shear line for a change key and others for master keys (Figure 11.3). In a well-designed system, none of the change keys will bring the pins of any lock to the shear line used by a master key; likewise, none of the master keys will bring the pins of any lock to the shear line used by other master keys.

Key interchange is when a key in a masterkeyed system causes the pins of a lock to reach a shear line that the key wasn't meant to use. That condition is undesirable and is easy to avoid by properly planning the masterkeying system.

You can easily masterkey two pin tumbler locks without planning a system. Assuming each lock is already operated by a distinctly bitted key of the same length and keyway grooves, proceed as follows:

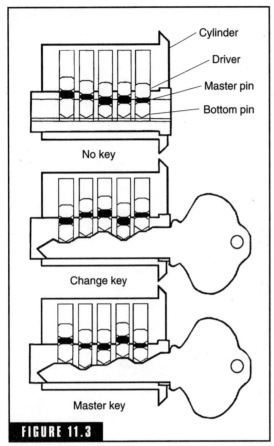

Cylinder

Driver

Master pin

Bottom pin

No key

Change key

Master key

FIGURE 11.3

Pin tumbler locks can be masterkeyed by using master pins to create more than one shear line in each lock.

1. Select a cylinder key of the same length and keyway grooves of the other two (the key can be taken from another lock). Make sure the key bitting differs from the bitting of the other two keys.

2. Using a plug follower to keep the top pins in place, remove the plug from the cylinder.

3. Using variously sized bottom and master pins (the master pins should set on top of the bottom pins), rekey the lock so that the original key causes the pins to create one shear line and the master key causes them to form a second shear line. Reassemble the cylinder and make sure both keys operate it. Set the original key for that lock aside.

4. Repeat Steps 2 and 3 with the other lock, using that lock's original key and the master key. You then have a simple masterkeyed system.

Locksmith supply houses sell charts for designing more complicated master key systems.

Some of the charts are available on computer discs. To use them you need to know how many pins are in the locks you're using, how many change keys you want, how many levels of master keys you want, and how many master keys you want for each level.

Nonlocking Door Hardware

Locks represent a small part of the hardware commonly used on or with doors.

Other hardware includes hinges, strikes, and door reinforcers. A locksmith who is familiar with the wide range of door hardware can profit greatly by selling and installing them.

Butts and Hinges

A door that binds or sags can be an eyesore and can hinder the performance of locks and door closers. Often these problems can be resolved by simply replacing the door's butts or hinges.

Many people use the terms "butt" and "hinge" synonymously. However, there is a distinction between the two. All butts are hinges, but all hinges are not butts. Hinges designed for applications in which their leaves normally abut each other—such as on the edge of a door and door jamb—are called *butt hinges,* or butts (Figure 12.1). Usually one or both leaves of a butt are swaged, or bent slightly at the knuckles. That brings the leaves into closer contour with the barrel and allows for a tighter fit.

Butts and hinges come in a variety of shapes, styles, and types to be used for many different functions and applications. A butt or hinge usually consists of three basic parts: two metal leaves or plates, each

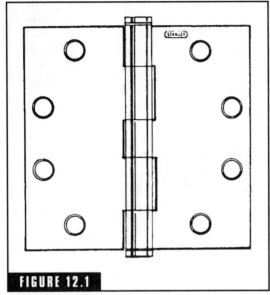

FIGURE 12.1

A butt hinge. *(Courtesy of Stanley Hardware)*

with knuckles on one edge; and one pin that fits through the knuckles of both leaves. When the knuckles of both leaves are joined, they form the barrel of the butt or hinge.

The pin may be removable or nonremovable. A *removable pin* can be pulled out of the barrel. A *nonremovable pin* is typically retained by a small retaining pin or a set screw. Ordinarily, the retaining pin or set screw is concealed when the door is closed.

Nonremovable pins are especially useful for exterior doors where the barrel of the butt or hinge is exposed to the outside. Without such pins, a person could enter a door simply by pulling the pins out of the door's hinges.

Fast, or rivet, pins have both ends machined on and are factory sealed. This type of nonremovable pins is often used in prisons and psychiatric hospitals.

Classification

Butts and hinges are classified in three ways: by screw hole pattern, by type of installation, and by function. Those that have standard screw hole sizes and patterns are called *template hinges.* They're used mostly on metal doors and pressed metal frames.

Nontemplate hinges are those with staggered screw hole patterns; such hinges are used on wooden doors and wood frames. *Blank face,* or plain, hinges have no predrilled screw holes. These are used when it's necessary to field-drill screw holes or weld hinges into place.

In addition to screw hole pattern, butts are classified by type of installation.

Full-mortise butts are installed by mortising both leaves (Figure 12.2). *Full-surface butts* are installed by surface-mounting both leaves. Butts that have one leaf mounted to the door frame and the other mortised into the edge of the door are *half- mortise butts. Half-surface butts* are installed in the reverse manner (Figure 12.3).

Sometimes butts and hinges are identified by how they function. For example, a *clear swing hinge* allows a door to swing clear of the passageway (usually a 180-degree swing), permitting full use of the door opening.

Regardless of the door type, weight, or size, a butt can usually be used on it. Butts come in four standard sizes, based on barrel length: 3-inch, 3½-inch, 4-inch, and 5-inch. These are made in a variety of finishes to match other door hardware. The following list describes the many different kinds of butts and hinges.

- Simple butts are nonhanded; they can be used on both left-hand and right-hand doors. These butts have nonremovable pins.

- Loose-pin butts also have nonremovable pins. Their pins are fixed into one leaf. Loose-pin butts are designed to allow the door to be removed without disturbing the pin or unscrewing the leaves. The door is removed by lifting it up so the leaves attached to the pins will clear the fixed pins. Loose-pin butts are handed.

- Rising butts are also handed. They have knurled knuckles and are designed to lift a door up as it swings open. They can be used to allow a door to clear a heavy carpet.

- Ball-bearing butts turn on two or more lubricated ball bearings instead of on pins. The lubricant and ball bearings are housed in "ball bearing

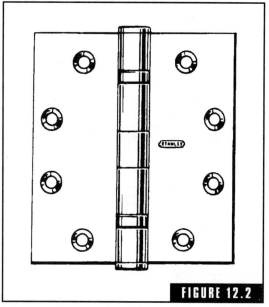

FIGURE 12.2

A full-mortise template hinge. *(Courtesy of Stanley hardware)*

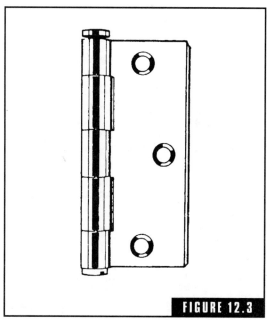

FIGURE 12.3

A half-surface hinge is installed by mortising the jamb leaf. *(Courtesy of Stanley hardware)*

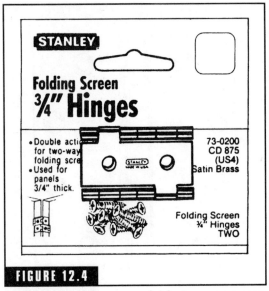

FIGURE 12.4

Double-acting hinges are useful for two-way screens.
(Courtesy of Stanley Hardware)

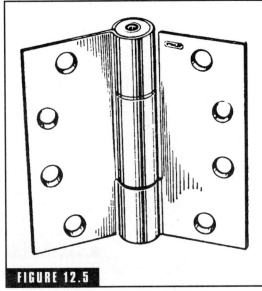

FIGURE 12.5

A spring hinge. *(Courtesy of Stanley Hardware)*

raceways" that look like small knuckles resting between the knuckles of the barrel. Ball-bearing butts are used on heavy doors.

- Concealed hinges are used on folding doors and look very different from most other types of hinges. They're installed by drilling two properly sized parallel holes, one in each meeting edge of the door. One cylindrical end of the concealed hinge is inserted into one hole, and the other end is inserted into the other hole. Then both ends are screwed into place, resulting in a completely concealed hinge.

- Gravity-pivot hinges allow a door to swing either way. Some have a hold-open feature.

- Double-acting hinges, as the name implies, permit folding doors to swing either way (Figure 12.4).

- Spring-loaded hinges can be used as door closers on fire doors and large screen doors. Some models have adjustable spring tension (Figure 12.5).

- Pivot reinforced hinges don't require a door frame. Such hinges are used for recessed, flush, or overlay doors.

J-U-5 Replacement Hinges

Manufactured by Brookfield Industries, Inc., J-U-5 hinges are designed for replacement and new installation on store fronts, public buildings, apartment buildings, and other places where the doors are used frequently.

J-U-5 hinges come as part of a kit. The kit includes two hinges, 12 aluminum expanders, 12 steel fasteners, four security strips, one expanding tool, and one instruction sheet. The kit makes installing J-U-5 hinges easy. To install a J-U-5 hinge, proceed as follows.

1. Strip the door and jamb of old, worn hinges, broken pivots, or slip-ins. Chuck the door up, leaving equal clearance on the top and bottom and side to side. To allow for vertical door adjustment, set hinge barrel gap between ⅛ and ³⁄₁₆ inch.

2. Using the hinge as a template, set the barrel of the hinge in the center line of the clearance between the door and jamb approximately 6 inches from both top and bottom (Figure 12.6). On doors where butts or slippings were removed, cover the old cutout with the new hinge.

3. Scribe the center hole of the leaf with a pencil, and drill a ¼-inch hole (Figure 12.7).

4. Insert a blind-threaded fastener through both hinge and frame, expanding the fastener with the tool provided (Figure 12.8). Make sure the hinge is straight.

5. Drill the center hole and insert the fastener on the opposite leaf. Then drill the remaining four holes and expand the fasteners (Figure 12.9). Repeat this procedure on the lower hinge.

6. Install 12 steel screws (supplied with the kit) and tighten (Figure 12.10).

7. Clean the hinges. Apply self-adhering cover strips, remove chucks, and test the door for a free swing. Balance up and down with the vertical adjustments

FIGURE 12.6

Use the hinge as a template. *(Courtesy of Brookfield Industries, Inc.)*

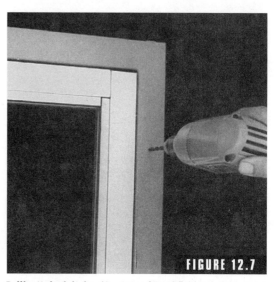

FIGURE 12.7

Drill a ¼-inch hole. *(Courtesy of Brookfield Industries, Inc.)*

Expand the fasteners. *(Courtesy of Brookfield Industries, Inc.)*

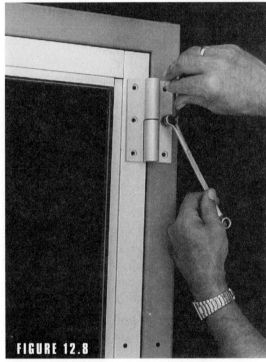

Insert a blind threaded fastener. *(Courtesy of Brookfield Industries, Inc.)*

Install steel screws. *(Courtesy of Brookfield Industries, Inc.)*

screw, if necessary. The installation is now complete (Figure 12.11).

High-Security Strike Plates

When customers go to a locksmithing shop to buy a good lock, they are often shocked to hear the price of a lock that's highly resistant to picking, impressioning, and drilling. A less expensive lock combined with a high-security strike box can be sold to such customers as an alternative. Although such strike boxes are relatively inexpensive, they provide strong resistance to the most common form of forcible entry: kick-ins (Figure 12.12).

Burglary statistics show that picking, drilling, and impressioning are rarely used for gaining entry into residences. Most standard strike plates are held to a frame by two small wood screws and can easily be popped out of the frame by a well-placed kick.

FIGURE 12.11

A completed J-U-5 hinge kit installation. *(Courtesy of Brookfield Industries, Inc.)*

Strike 3

Manufactured by M.A.G. Eng. & Mfg., Inc., the Strike 3 is a popular high-security strike box. It's made of heavy-gauge steel (one-piece construction) and fits all standard door frames. Four hardened screws anchor it to the stud. When properly installed, the Strike 3 makes the frame as strong as the deadbolt (Figure 12.13). To install a Strike 3, proceed as follows.

1. Mark the center of the bolt on the frame.

2. Locate the center mark on the template with the center mark on the frame (Figure 12.14 shows a sample that's for illustrative purposes only, and not for installation use. It isn't reproduced to scale). Tape the template in place.

3. Draw around the outside of the template. Using an awl, mark four holes per template. Drill the holes.

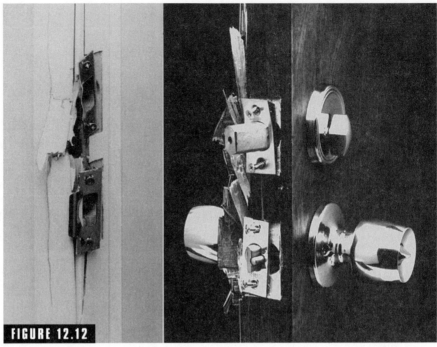

FIGURE 12.12

Kicking in a door is the leading method of forced entry. *(Courtesy of M.A.G. Eng. & Mfg., Inc.)*

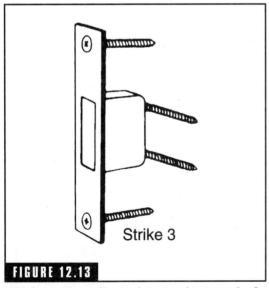

Strike 3

FIGURE 12.13

A high-security strike can increase the strength of a door frame. *(Courtesy of M.A.G. Eng. & Mfg., Inc.)*

4. Chisel out between 1-inch holes and fit the strike box. (Figure 12.15).

5. Cut ⅛ inch deep for the strike.

6. Install the strike and faceplate with the top and bottom screws. Be sure the two holes in the strike box are toward the center of the frame (Figure 12.16).

7. Drill two ⅛-inch pilot holes at the bottom of the strike box toward the center of the frame and install the screws. Angle the screws as shown in Figure 12.16.

Install-A-Lock Door Reinforcers

Manufactured by M.A.G. Eng. & Mfg., Inc., the Install-A-Lock door reinforcer makes a door as strong as the door's lock. In addition to guarding against kick-in attacks, the door reinforcer is excellent for lock conversions and improperly drilled holes (Figure 12.17).

Original Series

The original standard series Install-A-Lock is used with recessed latches. The 2000 series is used with both recessed and drive-in latches. Both types are available in several popular finishes and in sizes to fit all doors.

To install an indented unit Install-A-Lock, proceed as follows.

1. First, make sure the unit you're using matches the backset, door thickness, and hole size for your installation. Drill holes in the door using the instructions furnished with the lockset purchased, or remove the old lockset from the door.

2. Cut out the door edge (Figure 12.18). For double units, the "A" dimension, or centers between the lock holes (Figure 12.19), is 3⅝ or 4 inches.

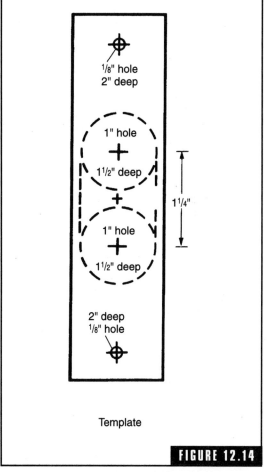

Template

FIGURE 12.14

Locate the center mark on the high-security strike's template. *(Courtesy of M.A.G. Eng. & Mfg., Inc.)*

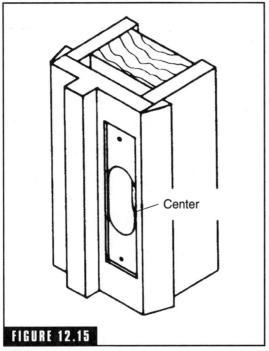

FIGURE 12.15

Chisel out between 1-inch holes. *(Courtesy of M.A.G. Eng. & Mfg., Inc.)*

FIGURE 12.17

An Install-A-Lock reinforces the strength of a door. *(Courtesy of M.A.G. Eng. & Mfg., Inc.)*

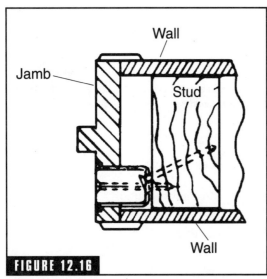

FIGURE 12.16

Drill holes and angle screws. *(Courtesy of M.A.G. Eng. & Mfg., Inc.)*

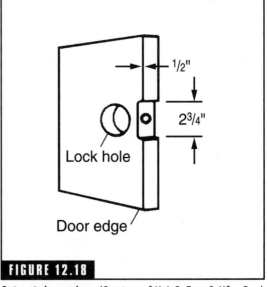

FIGURE 12.18

Cut out door edge. *(Courtesy of M.A.G. Eng. & Mfg., Inc.)*

3. Slide the unit over the door.

4. Install the latch with the ⅜-inch machine screws provided. Then install the lockset. Tighten the lockset to hold the Install-A-Lock in position. Push the unit flush against the edge of the door, then tighten the lockset. Install the four mounting screws.

Note for tight-fitting doors: If the Install-A-Lock hits the jamb when closing, remove it and cut out ¹⁄₃₂ inch on the door edge so the unit fits flush with the door edge.

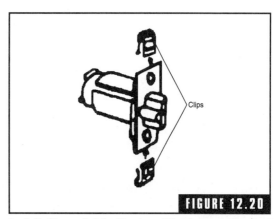

The "A" dimension is 3⅝ inches or 4 inches. *(Courtesy of M.A.G. Eng. & Mfg., Inc.)*

2000 Series

To install a 2000 Series (flat edge unit) Install-A-Lock, proceed as follows.

1. Drill holes in the door using the instructions furnished with the lockset purchased, or remove the old lockset from the door. Remove the latch screws, but don't remove the latch. If the door is damaged, install the clips on the latch as shown in Figure 12.20. Place the latch in the Install-A-Lock, and insert the 1½-inch screws.

Install clips on latch. *(Courtesy of M.A.G. Eng. & Mfg., Inc.)*

2. Slide the unit over the door (Figure 12.21).

3. Replace the latch screws with the 1½-inch furnished screws (Figure 12.22).

4. Install the four mounting screws, and the installation is complete (Figure 12.23).

Uni-Force Door Reinforcer

The Uni-Force is another type of door reinforcer manufactured by M.A.G. Eng. & Mfg. Like the company's Install-A-Lock, the Uni-Force

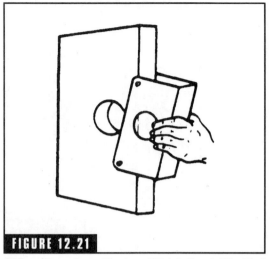

FIGURE 12.21

Slide unit on door. *(Courtesy of M.A.G. Eng. & Mfg., Inc.)*

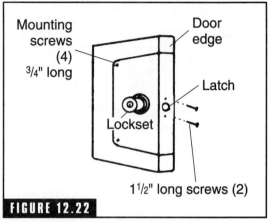

FIGURE 12.22

Install mounting screws. *(Courtesy of M.A.G. Eng. & Mfg., Inc.)*

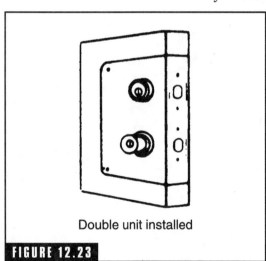

Double unit installed

FIGURE 12.23

An installed unit. *(Courtesy of M.A.G. Eng. & Mfg., Inc.)*

greatly increases a door's strength. The Uni-Force is for doors with deadbolt and key-in-knob locks. It is installed on the edge of a door, but not underneath the door's lock (Figure 12.24).

To install the Uni-Force, proceed as follows.

1. Remove the two latch screws, but not the latch (Figure 12.25).

2. Place the unit over the door.

3. Replace the latch screws with the two 1½-inch-long screws provided.

4. Drill ⅛-inch pilot holes 2 inches deep for the screws. Install the 2-inch screws.

5. Install the four ¾-inch-long screws.

Miscellaneous Products

In addition to the products previously mentioned in this chapter, locksmiths can profit from selling all types of door hardware. Hasps,

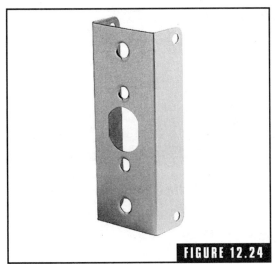

FIGURE 12.24

The Uni-Force is a door reinforcer for deadbolt and key-in-knob locks. *(Courtesy of M.A.G. Eng. & Mfg., Inc.)*

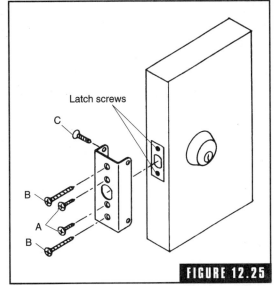

Latch screws

C

B

A

B

FIGURE 12.25

Uni-Force installation. *(Courtesy of M.A.G. Eng. & Mfg., Inc.)*

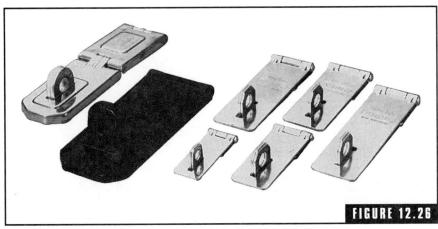

FIGURE 12.26

Hasps are good products for locksmiths to lock. *(Courtesy of Abus Lock Co.)*

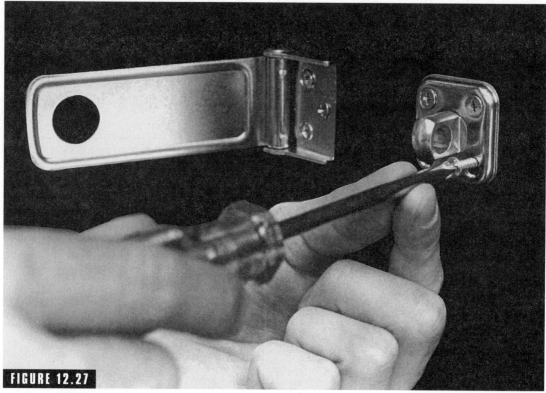

FIGURE 12.27

Hasps are easy to install. *(Courtesy of Stanley Hardware)*

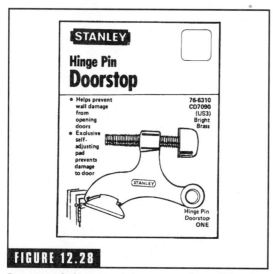

FIGURE 12.28

Doorstops help prevent damage to the wall by door knobs. *(Courtesy of Stanley Hardware)*

for example, are used by many people in conjunction with padlocks (Figure 12.26). Because hasps are very easy to install, you probably won't make much money installing them (Figure 12.27).

Likewise, door stops (Figure 12.28), door holders (Figure 12.29), and door viewers (Figure 12.30) are also easy to install. Smart locksmiths will stock all of these items in their store-front shops because people often go to a locksmith shop when they need such products.

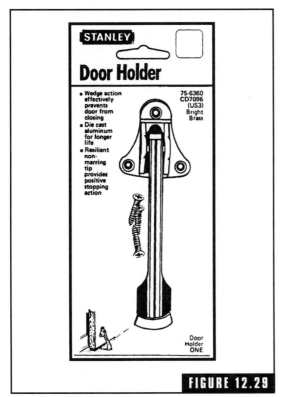

FIGURE 12.29

A door holder props a door open. *(Courtesy of Stanley Hardware)*

FIGURE 12.30

A door viewer lets you see who's knocking on a door. *(Courtesy of Stanley Hardware)*

Emergency Exit Door Devices

To comply with building and fire codes, businesses and institutions often have to keep certain doors as emergency exits that can be easily opened by anyone at any time. (That's to help prevent not having enough quick ways out during a fire or other emergency.) In some cases, however, those doors that must remain easy to exit also need to be secured from unauthorized use (such as when the door may allow shoplifters to slip out unnoticed).

Most institutions and commercial establishments use emergency exit door devices as a cost-effective way to handle both matters (Figure 13.1). Such devices are easy to install and offer excellent money-making opportunities for locksmiths.

Typically such devices are installed horizontally about 3 feet from the floor, and have a bolt that extends into the door frame to keep the door closed. They also usually incorporate either a push-bar or clapper arm that retracts the bolt when pushed.

Some models provide outside key and pull access when an outside cylinder and door pull is installed. In these models, entry remains unrestricted from both sides of the door until the deadbolt is relocked by key from inside or outside the door.

Many emergency exit door devices feature an alarm that sounds when a door is opened without a key. The better alarms are dual piezo (double sound).

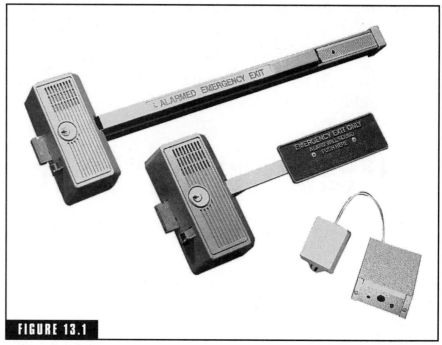

FIGURE 13.1

Emergency exit door devices are used to keep doors locked from the outside while allowing easy egress from the inside. *(Courtesy of Alarm Lock Systems, Inc.)*

Other useful features to consider on an emergency exit door device include for which hand it is installed (nonhanded models are the most versatile); the length of the deadbolt (a 1-inch throw is the minimum desirable length); and special security features (such as a hardened insert in the deadbolt).

This chapter explains how to install, operate, and service some of the models manufactured by Alarm Lock Systems, Inc. Much of the information also applies to most other popular models.

This chapter also tells how exit devices are tested and rated.

Distinctive Exit Devices Also Provide Safety

By Ashley Rolfe

Exit devices now come in such a wide range of styles (such as pushbar and crossbar) and finishes (such as aluminum, stainless, brass, and bronze) that they complement doors in a variety of applications and can enhance the design integrity of a building, whether it is traditional or modern. More important, however, is an exit device's safety function.

You may use the same exit devices day after day without realizing that some are panic devices and others are fire-rated devices. The four common types of both panic and fire-rated devices are mortise, rim, surface vertical rod, and concealed vertical rod. They have the same designs and finishes, and for the most part, function similarly. You can get both panic and fire-rated devices for light-, medium-, or heavy-duty traffic installations.

QUICK»TIP As you walk around businesses and institutions notice, the brands and models of emergency exit devices they have. Then get installation and technical information on the most popular ones. You can usually get such information from the manufacturer or trade associations (if you have access to the Internet, do an online search for the information).

Even though you may not be able to tell a panic device from a fire-rated device at a quick glance, there are big differences in application, material, and product testing.

Which Exit Device to Choose

Panic devices, which provide no guaranteed protection against fire, are for life safety; they allow a person to get out through the door quickly. Conversely, fire-rated exit devices are designed to keep fire from getting in through the door. A fire-rated device is designed to stay latched so the door doesn't open during a fire.

There is a quick way to tell the difference between panic and fire-rated exit devices. Panic (life safety) devices usually have dogging. In a school, for instance, a custodian can use a dogging key to lock the latchbolt in. Since the latchbolt cannot project when it's dogged, it basically becomes a push-pull door, allowing people easy entrance and exit. Fire-rated exit devices are not allowed to have dogging. Every time the door shuts, it latches, creating a secure fire wall. Such exit devices have a label somewhere in view that says they are fire rated.

The type of door device installed depends on specifications set by local building codes, the Fire Marshall, or whoever has jurisdiction. Most often, internal exit devices are fire-rated and external doors have panic devices. Panic devices on external doors allow quick exit, while internal doors have fire-rated exit devices to create a safe barrier against any fire outside the door.

The most essential difference between fire-rated and panic devices is the material used to make the latchbolts. Latchbolts in fire-rated hardware are generally made of stainless steel because of the material's ability to withstand fire. On the other hand, panic devices are made with forged brass, which can't stand up to fire as well as stainless steel, but is more economical and meets the requirements of panic devices. You can use the same trim on both fire and panic exit devices.

Many manufacturers perform in-house testing of panic devices and use Underwriters Laboratories (UL) to test fire-rated devices. The American National Standards Institute (ANSI) and Builders Hardware Manufacturers Association (BHMA) set the standards and UL enforces them. UL doesn't rate quality, but simply ensures that manufacturers meet industry guidelines.

Currently, ANSI and BHMA don't set stringent guidelines for manufacturers to follow when setting up their panic device testing facilities, so each apparatus is a little different than others.

Since most manufacturers have their own testing apparatus for panic devices, a UL field representative comes to the factory to supervise the testing of each type of product. A randomly selected exit device is attached to a door that is specially mounted to I-beams or similar rigging for testing. UL then puts the device through a series of tests:

EXIT TESTS (GRADES 1 & 2)

With the door latched, a maximum of 15 lbf (pounds of force) is applied against the bar and the door swings open. The device also must work when the force is applied anywhere along the bar in the direction of the swing. The door also must swing open when a maximum 250 lbf is applied against the door and a maximum of 50 lbf is applied against the bar.

SECURITY TEST (GRADE 1)

A pull of 400 lbf is applied to the door. The door shouldn't open and the device should function properly after the test.

INSIDE PULL TEST (GRADE 1)

A 400 lbf is applied at the center of the locked bar in the opposite direction of the swing.

After the force is removed and the bar released, the device should still function and no damage should be apparent.

PUSH TEST (GRADE 1)

With the touchbar free and the door securely fastened to prevent it from swinging open, a 400 lbf is applied at the center of the bar in the direction of the swing. The device should work when the test is finished and there should be no apparent damage.

TORQUE TO RETRACT LATCHBOLT TEST

A torque load is applied to the knob, lever, or turn to retract the latchbolt of an unlocked device. The torque is applied slowly until the latchbolt clears the strike. Where applicable, the test is repeated in the opposite direction. For thumbpieces, the load is applied at a point $\frac{1}{4}$ inch from the end of the thumbpiece until the latchbolt clears the strike. Values can't exceed 15 lbf/inch for levers, 15 lbf/inch for thumbpieces, and 22.5 lbf/inch for turns.

FORCE TO LATCH DOOR TEST

Force is applied to the face of the door 1 inch from the lock edge of the door and on the centerline of the latchbolt when the door is just clear of the latch contacting the lip of the strike.

The door is closed slowly by pushing the force gauge against the door until the latchbolt fully engages the strike. The maximum measured force to fully latch the door cannot exceed 4.5 lbf.

TRIM DURABILITY TEST

Outside Grade 1 trim is tested for at least 250,000 cycles and outside Grade 2 trim for at least 100,000 cycles. The Torque to Retract Latchbolt Test is then repeated. The opening values should not exceed by more than 20 percent those in the earlier test.

CYLINDER TEST

The cylinder used in the exit device must meet ANSI/BHMA requirements for Auxiliary Locks and Associated Products. The cylinder is to have been tested in other locks and have met the applicable requirements. Additionally, the torque necessary to retract the latchbolt(s) by key or to lock and unlock the trim by key must be measured.

UNLOCKED OUTSIDE KNOB OR LEVER TORQUE TEST

With the device in the latched position, 250 lbf/inch torque to Grade 1 knobs or turns, 150 lbf/inch torque to Grade 2 knobs or turns,

450 lbf/inch torque to Grade 1 levers, and 225 lbf/inch torque to Grade 2 levers is applied. At the end of the test, the maximum torque to retract the latchbolt cannot exceed 18 lbf/inch for knobs, 27 lbf/inch for turns, or 50 lbf/inch for levers.

Devices should operate in all respects.

Locked Outside Knob Torque Test

A torque is applied to a locked knob or thumbturn of 300 lbf/inch for Grade 1 and 150 lbf/inch for Grade 2. After the load is released, the torque to retract the latch cannot exceed an 18 lbf/inch torque for knobs or 27 lbf/inch for turns.

Locked Outside Thumbpiece Test

A load of 150 lbf for Grade 1 and 150 lbf for Grade 2 is applied at a point ¼ inch from the end of the thumbpiece until the latchbolt clears the strike. After the load is released, the force to retract the latch cannot exceed a 50-lbf/inch torque.

Axial Load Test

A load dynamometer force of 400 lbf for Grade 1 and 300 lbf for Grade 2 is applied to the outside knob, lever, turn, or thumbpiece grip along the axis of the trim perpendicular to the face of the door to load the latchbolt against the strike. After the load is released, the force to retract the latch can't exceed 18 lbf/inch for knobs, 27 lbf/inch for turns, or 50 lbf/inch for levers. The load is applied at the highest points of knobs and for levers 1 inch from the face of the door or escutcheon if present.

Vertical Load Test

A load dynamometer force of 360 lbf for Grade 1 and 250 lbf for Grade 2 is applied vertically downward to the outside knob, lever, or turn, perpendicular to the trim axis. After the load is released, the force to retract the latch can't exceed 18 lbf/inch for knobs, 27 lbf/inch for turns, or 50 lbf/inch for levers. The load is applied at the highest point of knobs and for levers 1 inch from the face of the door or escutcheon if present.

Outside Knob or Lever Crush Test

A knob or lever is positioned in a tensile loading device and compressed with 1000 lbf.

Deformation cannot exceed 10 percent for Grade 1 or 25 percent for Grade 2.

OUTSIDE ROSE AND ESCUTCHEON DENT TEST

An 8-ounce projectile is dropped from a height of 12 inches in a tube between the edges of the rose or escutcheon. The depth of the dent cannot exceed 0.075 inch for Grade 1 or 0.100 inch for Grade 2.

OUTSIDE ROSE AND ESCUTCHEON DEFORMATION TEST

Outside trim is mounted to simulate its installation on a door. A compression of 650 lbf for Grade 1 or 560 lbf for Grade 2 is applied on the horizontal centerline of the rose or escutcheon assembly. The side bars to apply the compression load must be 6 inches long. When testing escutcheons, the vertical centerline of the 6-inch-long bars must be opposite the centerline of the escutcheon. Deformation shall not exceed 10 percent. Finish tests ensure consistent trim quality. Trim parts must meet minimum values given.

SALT SPRAY TEST

Clear-coated materials are exposed for 96 hours, lock fronts and strikes for 24 hours, uncoated base materials for 200 hours, and painted and powder-coated materials for 96 hours.

HUMIDITY TEST

Clear-coated materials are exposed for 240 hours, lock fronts and strikes for 48 hours, and painted and powder-coated materials for 240 hours.

PENCIL HARDNESS TEST

Materials with organic coatings are tested in lieu of the Tabor Abrasion Test at the manufacturer's option.

ULTRAVIOLET LIGHT AND CONDENSATION TEST

Exterior grade finishes are tested eight hours UV at 60°C and four hours humidity at 50°C for 144 hours.

TABOR ABRASION TEST

This test is conducted in lieu of the Pencil Hardness Test at the manufacturer's option for 500 cycles.

After all of these tests and others, the UL representative takes apart the exit device and checks for wear points. The most obvious spots for wear are the strike and latchbolt. Manufacturers commonly go through the same procedure on both metal and wooden doors.

UL will also check the follow-up service books on each product to ensure the descriptions and drawings in the book match the tested device.

The examiner then checks to ensure that the device the manufacturer is having tested is the same product they are selling. That often means a trip to the factory warehouse to check inventory against the test product. The inspector won't necessarily run a randomly selected product through a cycle test, but may conduct a parts inspection, again to ensure the parts match the drawing. UL will also occasionally take a panic device off the shelf to test it.

Most likely, if the testing does not meet ANSI standards, the manufacturer makes a change that UL finds acceptable. No American manufacturer of exit devices will sell their products without a UL label.

How a Fire Rating is Determined

To have their hardware fire-rated, manufacturers go to the UL fire division in Chicago, where the device is attached to a door. The door is hung on a brick fire wall so that the opposite side of the exit device faces a powerful furnace. The hardware is subjected to the intense fire from the furnace for a period of time, depending on the rating the manufacturer seeks. There isn't much left of the door when the test is finished, and the exit device isn't in very good shape either. However, the latchbolt should still maintain engagement with the strike.

If the door doesn't stay locked throughout the test, the device fails. In that case, the manufacturer's engineers either go back to the drawing board or make relatively minor adjustments and retest the device. The manufacturer's cost for each fire test runs tens of thousands of dollars.

Fire-rated doors have several different grades and tests. A-label devices are fire-rated for three hours, which means they withstood three hours of a fire while staying locked. B-label devices have a 1½-hour fire rating, and C-label doors have a 45-minute rating. Some buildings may only need C- and B-label devices, while others exclusively require A-label hardware.

Most manufacturers would test double egress doors as standard, therefore complying with the test requirement of burning the active and inactive door to the fire. Those that choose not to do so would be subject to two tests—one with the device to the fire, the other with the device away from the fire.

Although panic devices must pass a 250,000-cycle test minimum, fire-rated devices, which often are subjected to less routine wear and tear than panic hardware, must only pass a 100,000-cycle test. Many manufacturers often try to do two, three, even four times the minimum when doing their own testing.

Every manufacturer is on a testing schedule. For instance, a manufacturer may have five different series of exit devices and each must be tested every two years. No matter how long a product has been on the market, it must be retested to ensure it still meets ANSI standards.

No industry standard exists for the apparatus used in testing panic devices. Each manufacturer does it their own way. There is, however, a consensus to reach the same conclusions.

The external appearance of exit devices hasn't changed much in several years and may not for years to come. So the average person probably will never notice the difference between panic and fire-rated exit devices. But the differences are real and essential. And engineers continually look for ways to improve quality and endurance.

ANSI and BHMA also continue to look for ways to strengthen industry standards. Even though the industry is essentially self-governing, the stringency and frequency of testing ensures the performance and safety of exit devices made in America.

Pilfergard Model PG-10

One of the most popular emergency exit door devices is the Pilfergard PG-10 (Figure 13.2). It has a dual piezo alarm, can be armed and disarmed from inside or outside a door, and is easy to install on single or double doors.

The device is surface-mounted approximately 4 to 6 feet from the floor on the interior of the door with a magnetic actuator on the frame (or vice versa). It is armed or disarmed with any standard mortise cylinder, which is not supplied. Opening the door, removal of the cover, or any

FIGURE 13.2

The Pilfergard PG-10 is a popular emergency exit door device among locksmiths. *(Courtesy of Alarm Lock Systems, Inc.)*

attempt to defeat the device with a second magnet, when armed, activates the alarm.

Installation

To install the PG-10 Pilfergard,

1. Remove the cover by depressing the test button and lift the cover out of the slot.

2. Mark and drill holes per the template directions and drill sizes (5 for alarm unit, 2 for magnetic actuator).

3. For nonoutside cylinder installation, proceed to the next step. For outside cylinder installation, drill a 1¼-inch hole as shown on the template. Install a rim type cylinder through the door and allow flat tail piece to extend 1 inch inside door. Position cylinder so that keyway is vertical (horizontal if PG-10 is installed horizontally). Hold PG-10 in position over mounting holes and note that outside cylinder tailpiece is centered in clearance hole in base of PG-10 (rotate cylinder 180 degrees if not). Tighten outside cylinder mounting screws.

4. Install the PG-10 and magnetic actuator with seven screws.

5. Install the threaded 1¼-inch mortise cylinder in the PG-10 cover using the hardware supplied (Figure 13.3). The keyway must be horizontal so that the tailpiece extends toward the center of the unit when the key is turned.

6. Move the slide switch to Off (Figure 13.4). Connect the battery. Hook the cover on the end slot and secure with the two cover screws. *Note:* One of these screws acts as the tamper alarm trigger, so be sure the screws are fully seated.

   Caution: When installing the PG-10 on a steel frame, it might be necessary to install a nonmagnetic shim between the magnetic actuator and the frame. This prevents the steel frame from absorbing the magnet's magnetic field, which could cause a constant alarm condition or occasional false alarms. The shim should be ½ × 2½ × ⅛ inch thick and may be constructed from plastic, Bakelite, or aluminum.

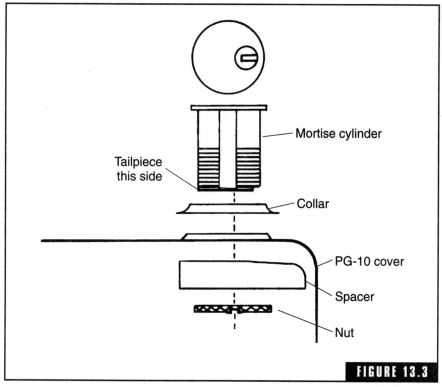

Install mortise cylinder. *(Courtesy of Alarm Lock Systems, Inc.)*

Testing and Operating

To test and operate the PG-10, first depress the test button with the slide switch in the off position. Horns should sound.

To test using the magnetic actuator, proceed as follows.

1. Close the door.

2. Arm the PG-10 by turning the key clockwise 170 degrees.

3. Open the door; the alarm should sound.

4. Close the door; the alarm should remain sounding.

5. Silence the alarm by turning the key counterclockwise until it stops.

6. Close the door and rearm the PG-10 by turning the key clockwise until it stops.

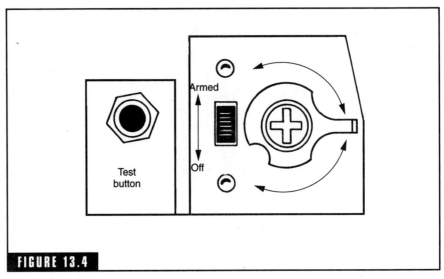

FIGURE 13.4

Move slide switch to Off. *(Courtesy of Alarm Lock Systems, Inc.)*

The unit should be tested weekly using the test button to ensure that the battery is working. The test button only operates when the PG-10 is turned off.

Pilfergard Model PG-20

The Pilfergard PG-20 (Figure 13.5) is a sleek, modern version of the PG-10. The PG-20 is designed to fit all doors, including narrow stile doors. It has a flashing LED on its alarm and is as easy to install as the PG-10.

Installation

To install the PG-20, remove the cover from the mounting plate. Install the mortise cylinder (which is not supplied), keeping the key slot pointing down in the six o'clock position. Screw the lock ring on the cylinder.

Select the proper template for the specific type of door. Mark and drill %₄-inch-diameter holes per the template directions on the door and jamb. This requires four holes for the mounting plate and two holes for the magnetic actuator. *Note:* Certain narrow stile doors require only two holes for the mounting plate.

For the outside key control only: Drill a 1¼-inch-diameter hole as shown on the template.

Install a rim-type cylinder (not supplied) through the door and allow the flat tailpiece to extend 5/16 inch beyond the door. Position the cylinder, keeping the key slot pointing down, in the six o'clock position. Tighten the cylinder screws.

Knock out the necessary holes from the mounting plate and install the plate on the door with the No. 8 sheet metal screws (supplied). Make sure that the rim cylinder tailpiece fits in the cross slot of the ferrule if the outside cylinder is used.

Install the magnetic actuator on the door jamb with the two No. 8 sheet metal screws supplied.

Note: It is sometimes necessary on steel frames to install a nonmagnetic shim between the magnetic actuator and the frame. This prevents the absorption by the steel frame of the magnet's magnetic field, which could cause a constant or occasional false alarm. The shim should be 1/2-×-2 1/2-×-1/8-inch-thick nonmagnetic material such as plastic, Bakelite, or rubber.

Make sure the battery is connected. Cut the white jumper only on the side of the unit on which the magnet will not be installed. The unit will not function otherwise. Select the options desired as follows.

- Cut the yellow jumper for a 15-second entry delay. (The alarm will sound 15 seconds after any entry through the door if the unit is armed.) To avoid the alarm upon entry, reset the unit within 15 seconds. This feature is used for authorized entrance.

- Cut the red jumper for 15-second exit delay. (The unit will be activated after 15 seconds each time the unit is turned on with a key.) This feature allows authorized nonalarmed exit.

- Place the shunt jumper plug in position C or 2. If the jumper is in position C, the alarm will sound continuously until the battery is discharged. If the jumper is in position 2, the alarm will

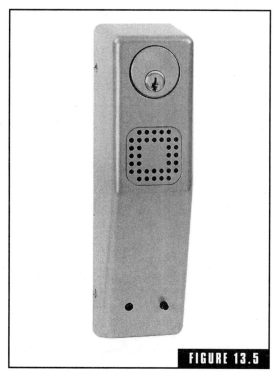

The Model PG-20 emergency exit door device can be used on narrow stile doors. *(Courtesy of Alarm Lock Systems, Inc.)*

be silenced after two minutes and the unit will rearm. However, the LED will continue to flash, indicating an alarm has occurred.

Install cover on the mounting plate, making sure that the slide switch on PC board fits into the cam hole. Secure the cover with the four screws supplied.

Testing

To field test the PG-20, proceed as follows.

1. With the door closed, turn the key counterclockwise until it stops (less than one-quarter turn). Unit is now armed instantaneously or delayed.

2. Push the test button and the alarm should sound, verifying that the unit is armed.

3. Open the door, then close it. Alarm should sound instantaneously or delayed.

4. Note the pulsating sounder and flashing LED, indicating an alarm.

5. To reset the unit, turn the key clockwise until it stops (less than one-quarter turn). Unit is now disarmed. This can be done at any time.

Exitgard Models 35 and 70

To install Exitgard Models 35 or 70 panic locks, proceed as follows.

1. With the door closed, tape the template to the inside face of the door with the center line approximately 38 inches above the floor. Mark all hole locations with a punch or awl. Note that the keeper is surface installed on the jamb for single doors, on the other leaf for pairs of doors.

2. If an outside cylinder is being used, mark the cylinder hole center. If an alarm lock pull #707 is furnished, mark the four holes on the template for the pull, in addition to the cylinder hole.

3. Drill the holes as indicated for the lock and keeper. Drill the holes for the outside pull, if used.

4. Loosen the hex head bolt holding the cross bar to the lock and pull the bar off the clapper arm.

5. Remove the lock cover screws. Depress the latch bolt. Lift up and remove the lock cover.

6. (Disregard this step if the cylinder or thumb turn is already installed.) Remove the screws holding the cylinder housing (Figure 13.6) to the bolt cover. Install the rim cylinder with the keyway horizontal facing the front of the lock, opposite the slot in the rear of the cylinder support.

7. Reinstall the support while guiding the tailpiece into the slot cam.

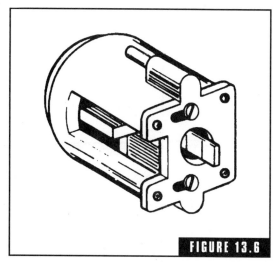

FIGURE 13.6

Remove screws holding cylinder. *(Courtesy of Alarm Lock Systems, Inc.)*

8. Use the key to try proper operation. The key should withdraw in either the fully locked or fully unlocked position of the deadbolt. If not, the cylinder and cam are mistimed. The cylinder housing must be removed, the cam turned a quarter turn to the right, and the cylinder housing reinstalled.

9. Attach the lock to the door. For single doors, remove the keeper cover and roller, install the keeper, replace the roller and cover. Double door keeper #732 is installed on the surface of the inactive leaf, as furnished.

10. Remove the hinge pivot cover. Reinstall the push bar section on the lock clapper as far forward as it will go. Tighten the hex head bolt under the lock clapper. Attach the hinge side pivot assembly, using a level or tape to assure the cross bar is level. If the cross bar is too long, loosen the hex head bolt on the underside of the clapper and remove the pivot assembly. Cut the bar to the proper length, deburr the edges, and reinstall the pivot assembly on the cross bar. Only after the pivot base has been installed should the dogging screw (Figure 13.7) be loosened and the pivot block removed and discarded.

11. The dogging screw should face the floor. If not, remove it and reinstall it from below. Replace the pivot cover with the hole for the dogging screw facing the floor.

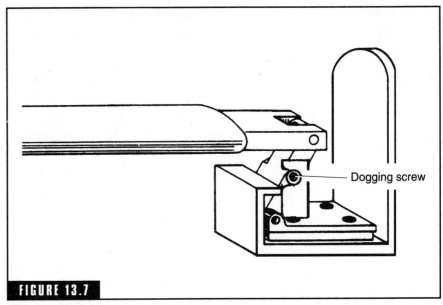

Loosen dogging screw. *(Courtesy of Alarm Lock Systems, Inc.)*

12. Test lock operation by projecting the deadbolt by key into the keeper. Depress the crossbar fully to retract the deadbolt, then release the latchbolt and open the door.

13. On single doors, close the door and adjust the keeper so the door is tightly latched. After final adjustments, install the holding screw in the keeper to maintain the position permanently. On pairs of doors, adjust the plastic slide on the keeper so the door is tightly latched.

14. (If installing Model 35, disregard this step.) Connect the power plug. Repeat Step 12. Horns should sound until the deadbolt is projected by key. Attach the self-adhesive sign to the bar and door.

15. Replace the lock cover.

Alarm Lock Models 250, 250L, 260, and 260L

Models 250, 250L, 260, and 260L by Alarm Lock Systems, Inc. are used to provide maximum security on emergency exit doors. Each of the models features sleek architectural design and finishes, a dual piezo sounder, a low-battery alert, a simple modular construction, selectable 2-minute alarm or constant alarm, and a hardened insert in the deadbolt.

Installation

Install these models in the following way.

1. With the door closed, select the proper template. Tape it to the inside face of the door with the center line about 38 inches above the floor, according to template directions.

2. Mark and drill the holes.

3. Remove the lock cover and four screws holding the cylinder housing to the bolt cover. Install the rim cylinder (CER) with the keyway horizontal, facing the front of the lock in the nine o'clock position. Cut the cylinder tailpiece ⅜ inch beyond the base of the cylinder. Reinstall the cylinder housing, guiding the tailpiece into the crosshole of the cam with the four screws.

4. Use the key to test for proper operation of the deadbolt. You should be able to withdraw the key from the lock in either the fully locked or fully unlocked position of the deadbolt. If not, the cylinder and the cam are misaligned and the cylinder housing must be removed. Turn the cam one-quarter turn to the right, and reinstall the cylinder housing. *Note:* The deadbolt can be projected into the keeper by turning the key counterclockwise. Likewise, it can be withdrawn from the keeper by turning the key clockwise one full turn.

5. For outside cylinder only (CER-OKC): Install the rim cylinder with the keyway horizontal facing the front of the door in the three o'clock position. Use the screws supplied. Cut the tailpiece ⅜ inch beyond the inside face of the door.

6. For outside cylinder only: Guide the tailpiece of the outside cylinder into the crosshole of the cam.

7. Install the lock to the door with the four screws supplied.

8. For single doors only: Remove the keeper cover, roller, and pin. Install the keeper base on the door with the two screws supplied. Reinstall the pin, roller, and cover with two screws.

9. For double doors only: Install the rub plate for a 1¾-inch-wide door from inside the door.

10. Install the keeper with two screws. Do not tighten the screws fully because the keeper will require adjustment.

11. For single doors only: Close the door, project the deadbolt, and adjust the keeper so that the door latches tightly. Retract the deadbolt, hold the keeper, release the latch, and open the door. Open the keeper cover and tighten the screws. Drill a .157-inch-diameter hole, as shown on the template, for the holding screw. Fasten the keeper with a screw. Reinstall the pin, roller, and cover with two screws.

For double doors only: Close the door, project the bolt, and adjust the plastic slide on the keeper so the door is tightly latched. Tighten the screws.

Electronic Exit Lock Model 265

The Alarm Lock Systems, Inc. Model 265 emergency exit door device has the following features: a nonhanded unit; a deadbolt with a hardened-steel insert that can be operated with an outside key; 15-second delay before the door can be opened after the clapper arm plate has been pushed; a lock that only requires 5 to 10 pounds of force to operate; a dual piezo horn; and a disarming beep when the bolt is retracted with a key (Figure 13.8).

Installation

To install the Model 265's lock and keeper, proceed as follows.

1. With the door closed, select the proper template. Tape it to the inside face of the door with the center line approximately 38 inches above the floor, according to template directions.

2. Mark and drill the following holes (see template for details):

   ~ For single and double doors mark six .157-inch-diameter holes, four for the lock mounting plate and two for the keeper.

   ~ Mark a ¼-inch-diameter hole for the rub plate on double doors that are 1¾ inches thick.

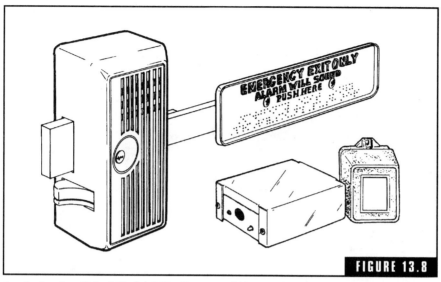

An electronic exit lock Model 265. *(Courtesy of Alarm Lock Systems, Inc.)*

~ If an outside cylinder (CER-OKC) is used, mark the center of the 1½-inch-diameter hole.

3. If mounting the lock on a hollow metal door and wires are run through the door, align the lock with the holes drilled in Step 2A above. Mark and drill a ⅜-inch hole in the door to align with the hole in the baseplate near the terminal strip (Figure 13.9).

4. Remove the lock cover and four screws holding the cylinder housing to the bolt cover. Install rim cylinder (CER) with the keyway horizontal, facing the front of the lock in the nine o'clock position. Cut the cylinder tailpiece ⅜ inch beyond the base of the cylinder. Reinstall the cylinder housing, guiding the tailpiece into the cross-hole of the cam with four screws.

5. Use the key to test for proper operation of the deadbolt. You should be able to withdraw the key from the lock in either the fully locked or fully unlocked position of the deadbolt. If not, the cylinder and the cam are misaligned and the cylinder housing must be removed. Turn the cam one-quarter turn to the right, and reinstall the cylinder housing. *Note:* The deadbolt can be projected into the keeper by turning the key counterclockwise one full turn.

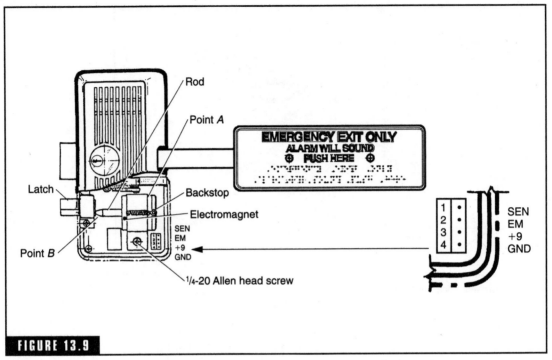

FIGURE 13.9

Connect one end of the 4-conductor cable to the control box. *(Courtesy of Alarm Lock Systems, Inc.)*

6. For outside cylinder only (CER-OKC): Install the rim cylinder with the keyway horizontal facing the front of the door in the three o'clock position. Use the screws supplied. Cut the tailpiece ⅜ inch beyond the inside face of the door.

7. For outside cylinder only: Guide the tailpiece of the outside cylinder into the crosshole of the outside cam.

8. Install the lock to the door with the four No. 10 screws that are supplied.

9. For single doors only: Remove the keeper cover, roller, and pin. Install the keeper base on the door with the two screws that are supplied. Reinstall the pin, roller, and cover with two screws.

10. Do not tighten the screws fully, because the keeper will require adjustment.

11. For single doors only: Close the door, project the deadbolt, and adjust the keeper so that the door is tightly latched. Retract the deadbolt, hold the keeper, release the latch, and open the door.

12. Open the keeper cover and tighten the screws. Drill a .157-inch-diameter hole, as shown on the template, for the holding screw, and fasten the keeper with a No. 10 screw. Reinstall the pin, roller, and cover with two screws.

13. For double doors only: Close the door, project the bolt, and adjust the plastic slide on the 732 keeper so the door is tightly latched. Tighten the screws.

14. A fine adjustment in the latch and electromagnet mechanism might be necessary. With the door pulled fully closed, check to see that the backstop is in complete contact with the electromagnet.

15 There will be a small gap, approximately $\frac{1}{32}$ inch or less, between the rod and latch. If not, loosen the Allen head screw and slide the electromagnet to the right or left until adjusted.

16. Retighten the Allen head screw.

Installing the Control Box

Install the control box for Model 265 as follows.

1. Remove the control box cover.

2. Select a location for the control box on the hinge side of the door and mount it to the wall, using the three No. 10 × $\frac{3}{4}$-inch self-tapping screws.

Wiring

Model 265 is wired in the following way.

1. A four-conductor No. 22-AWG cable is needed to connect the control box to the lock. There are two ways of bringing electric current from the hinge side of the door frame to the door: Use the Armored Door Loop Model 271 and disconnect one of the 271 end boxes. Insert the loose end of the armored cable into the ½-inch hole on the control box and secure it with the retaining clip. Or, use a continuous conductor hinge with flying leads.

2. Connect one end of the four-conductor cable to the control box terminal strip P2 and the other end of the cable to the lock terminal strip P3. The terminal strips are marked as follows.
   (1) SEN -sence (2) EM electromagnet (3) +9VDC (4) -ground.
   Note: Do not cross wires.

3. Connect one end of an approved twin lead cable to the terminal strip at P1-1 and P1-2 (see Figure 13.9), and connect the other end of the cable to the transformer provided. Do not plug in the transformer at this time.

4. Connect one end of another approved twin lead cable to the terminal strip at P1-3 and P1-4 (see Figure 13.9). Connect the other end to the normally closed alarm relay contacts of either an approved supervised automatic fire detection system or an approved supervised automatic sprinkler system.

5. Install the control box cover.

Operating

Before installing the lock cover, do the following.

1. For a continuous alarm, leave the black jumper plug on the terminal strip installed. For 2-minute alarm shutdown, remove the black jumper plug from the terminal strip.

2. Connect the 9-volt battery to its connector. A short beep will sound, ensuring that the 265 is powered and ready.

3. Plug the transformer into a continuous 115 ac volt source. Note the red pilot lamp on the control box is lit.

4. Open the door and install the lock cover with the four screws that are supplied.

Testing

To test the 265, lock and unlock the door using the cylinder key. Note that a small beep sounds when the bolt is retracted, indicating a disarmed condition. The door can be opened by pushing the clapper plate, after a 15-second wait, without causing an alarm.

Lock the door again and push the clapper plate. Immediately the alarm will pulse loudly and the 265 latch will impede the opening of the door for approximately 15 seconds, then remain unimpeded until it is manually reset with the key. If continuous alarm was selected above, the piezo sounder will remain on for two minutes then reset.

In the event of a power failure, the impeding latch will be disabled, but the 9-volt battery will provide standby power for the alarm circuit. This can be tested by disconnecting the transformer from the 115-volt source and pushing the clapper plate. The door should now open immediately and the alarm should sound.

In the event of a fire panel alarm, the impeding latch will also be disabled. This can be tested by disconnecting the wire going to the control box at P1-3 and pushing the clapper plate. The door should open immediately and the alarm should sound.

Test the unit's battery by pushing and holding the test button on the control box and pushing the clapper plate to alarm the unit. If the piezo sounder is weak or doesn't operate at all, replace the 9-volt battery.

Alarm Lock Models 700, 700L, 710, and 710L

Standard features for each emergency exit door device in Alarm Lock Systems, Inc. 700 and 710 Series include a nonhanded unit; a deadbolt with a hardened steel insert that can be operated by outside key and can be used for single or double doors; a deadlatch for easy access from inside without alarm; a loud dual piezo horn; a selectable continuous or two-minute alarm shutdown; a disarming beep when the bolt is retracted with key; a low-battery beep when the battery needs to be replaced; and a retriggerable alarm after two-minute shutdown (for Model 710 only). Figure 13.10 shows a Model 700.

Installation

The 700 and 710 series models are installed as follows.

1. With the door closed, select the proper template. Tape it to the inside face of the door with the center line approximately 38 inches above the floor, according to template directions.

2. Mark and drill the following holes (see template for details):

   ~ For single and double doors mark six .157-inch-diameter holes, four for the lock mounting plate and two for the keeper.

   ~ Mark a $\frac{1}{4}$-inch-diameter hole for the rub plate on double doors $1\frac{3}{4}$ inches thick.

   ~ If outside cylinder (CER-OKC) is used, mark the center of the $1\frac{1}{4}$-inch-diameter holes.

   ~ If outside pull Model 707 is used, mark the center of the four $\frac{1}{4}$-inch-diameter holes.

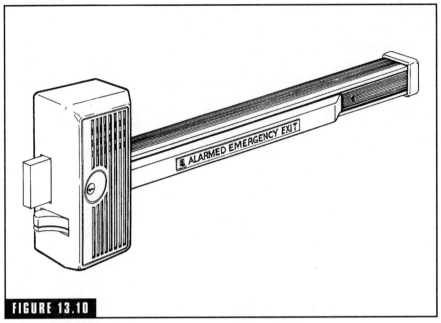

A panic exit alarm Model 700. *(Courtesy of Alarm Lock Systems, Inc.)*

~ If mounting the lock on a hollow metal door and wires are to be run through the door, drill hole x (see template). *Note:* If outside pull is used, drill four ¼-inch-diameter holes through the door from the inside. Then drill ¾-inch-diameter holes 1¼ inches deep from the outside of the door.

3. Remove the lock cover and four screws holding the cylinder housing to the bolt cover.

4. Install rim cylinder (CER) with the keyway horizontal, facing the front of the lock in the nine o'clock position. Cut the cylinder tailpiece ⅜ inch beyond the base of the cylinder. Reinstall the cylinder housing, guiding the tailpiece into the crosshole of the cam with four screws.

5. Use the key to test for proper operation of the deadbolt. You should be able to withdraw the key from the lock in either the fully locked or fully unlocked position of the deadbolt. If not, the cylinder and the cam are misaligned and the cylinder housing must be removed. Give the cam one-quarter turn to the right, and reinstall the cylinder housing. *Note:* The deadbolt can be

projected into the keeper by turning the key counterclockwise and can be withdrawn from the keeper by turning the key clockwise one full turn.

6. For outside cylinder only (CER-OKC): Install the rim cylinder with the keyway horizontal facing the front of the door in the three o'clock position, using the screws supplied. Cut the tailpiece ⅜ inch beyond the inside face of the door.

7. For outside cylinder only: Guide the tailpiece of the outside cylinder into the crosshole of the outside cam.

8. Install the lock loosely to the door with four No. 10 screws as supplied. Do not tighten them at this time.

9. Insert the bar and channel assembly under the channel retainer bracket, which is mounted to the lock baseplate. Hold the bar and channel assembly horizontally against the door using a level.

10. Slide the end cap bracket into the end of the channel and, using the bracket as a template, mark and drill the two .157-inch-diameter mounting holes on the door. If the channel is too long, cut the channel and channel insert to the proper length and deburr the edges.

11. Attach the pushbar to the lock at the clapper arm hinge bracket, using the ½-inch screw and No. 10 internal tooth lockwasher provided.

12. Mount the end cap bracket to the door with the two No. 10 screws provided, and tighten the lock securely to the door.

13. Attach the end cap to the end cap bracket using the ½-inch oval head screw provided.

14. For single doors only: Remove the keeper cover, roller, and pin. Install the keeper base on the door with the two screws supplied. Reinstall the pin, roller, and cover with two screws.

15. For double doors only: Install the rub plate for a 1¾-inch-wide door from inside the door. Also install the 732 keeper with the two No. 10 screws supplied. Do not tighten the screws fully because the keeper will require adjustment.

16. For single doors only: Close the door, project the deadbolt, and adjust the keeper so that the door is tightly latched. Retract the deadbolt, hold the keeper, release the latch, and open the door.

17. Open the keeper cover and tighten the screws. Drill a .157-inch-diameter hole, as shown on template, for holding screw. Fasten the keeper with a No. 10 screw. Reinstall the pin, roller, and cover with two screws.

18. For double doors only: Close the door, project the bolt, and adjust the plastic slide on the 732 keeper so the door is tightly latched and tighten the screws.

Operating 700 and 710 Series Models

Before installing the lock cover, do the following.

1. For continuous alarm, leave the black jumper plug on the terminal strip, as installed.

2. For two-minute auto-alarm shutdown, remove the black jumper plug from the terminal strip.

3. Connect the battery connector to the 9-volt battery, observing the proper polarity. A short beep will sound, ensuring that the lock is powered and ready.

4. Install the lock cover with the four screws supplied.

5. Close the door.

Testing

To test a 700 or 710 Series model, do the following.

1. Lock and unlock the door using the cylinder key. Note that a small beep sounds when the deadbolt is retracted, indicating a disarmed condition. The door can now be opened without an alarm, by pushing the push bar.

2. Lock the door again and push the push bar to open it. Immediately the alarm will pulse loudly and, if continuous alarm was previously selected, the alarm will sound until the lock is manually reset by locking the deadbolt with the key. If auto-alarm shutdown was selected, the alarm will sound for two minutes then reset.

When the battery becomes weak, the sounder will emit a short beep approximately once a minute, indicating the battery needs replacing.

Special Operations

If the unit has a retriggerable alarm (Model 260), after the initial two-minute alarm and auto shutdown, the alarm will retrigger if the door is opened again. This function will remain retriggerable until the door is relocked with the key. Whenever an alarm is caused by opening the door, and the door is left open, the two-minute alarm shutdown will be inhibited.

To use the unit's dogging operation, insert the $\frac{3}{16}$-inch Allen wrench into the dogging latch through the hole in the channel insert. Turn the dogging latch counterclockwise a half turn, push in the pushbar, and turn the dogging latch clockwise a quarter turn until it stops. Release the pushbar and notice that it stays depressed and the door is unlatched.

Alarm Lock Model 715

Standard features of the Model 715 include: the unit is nonhanded; a deadbolt with a hardened steel insert that can be operated by an outside key; a 15-second delay before door can be opened after pushbar has been pushed; a lock that only requires 5 to 10 pounds of force to operate and can be used for single or double doors; loud dual piezo horn; selectable, continuous, or two-minute alarm shutdown; and a disarming beep when bolt is retracted with key.

Installation

The Model 715 electronic exit lock is installed in the following way.

1. With the door closed, select the proper template and tape it to the inside face of the door with the center line approximately 38 inches above the floor.

2. Mark and drill the following holes (see template for details):

   ~ For single and double doors: Mark six .157-inch-diameter holes, four for the lock mounting plate and two for the keeper.

   ~ Mark a $\frac{1}{4}$-inch-diameter hole for the rub plate on double doors $1\frac{3}{4}$ inches thick.

   ~ If outside cylinder (CER-OKC) is used, mark the center of the $1\frac{1}{4}$-inch-diameter hole.

~ If mounting the lock on a hollow metal door and wires are to run through the door, align the lock with the holes drilled in Step 2A. Mark and drill a $\frac{3}{8}$-inch hole in the door to align with the hole in the baseplate near the terminal strip P3 (Figure 13.11).

3. Remove the lock cover and four screws holding the cylinder housing to the bolt cover.

4. Install rim cylinder (CER) with the keyway horizontal, facing the front of the lock in a nine o'clock position. Cut the cylinder tailpiece $\frac{3}{8}$ inch beyond the base of the cylinder. Reinstall the cylinder housing, guiding the tailpiece into the crosshole of the cam with four screws.

5. Use the key to test for proper operation of the deadbolt. You should be able to withdraw the key from the lock in either the fully locked or fully unlocked position of the deadbolt. If not, the cylinder and the cam are misaligned and the cylinder housing must be removed. Turn the cam a quarter turn to the right, and reinstall the cylinder

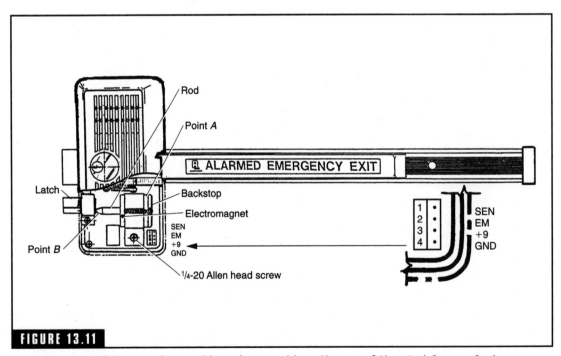

FIGURE 13.11

Connect one end of the 4-conductor cable to the control box. *(Courtesy of Alarm Lock Systems, Inc.)*

housing. *Note:* The deadbolt can be projected into the keeper by turning the key counterclockwise and can be withdrawn from the keeper by turning the key clockwise one full turn.

6. For outside cylinder only (CER-OKC): Install the rim cylinder with the keyway horizontal facing the front of the door in the three o'clock position. Use the screws supplied. Cut the tailpiece ⅜ inch beyond the inside face of the door.

7. For outside cylinder only: Guide the tailpiece of the outside cylinder into the crosshole of the outside cam.

8. Install the lock loosely to the door with the four No. 10 screws supplied. Do not tighten them at this time.

9. Insert the bar and channel assembly under the channel retainer bracket, which is mounted to the lock baseplate. Using a level, hold the bar and channel assembly horizontally against the door.

10. Slide the end cap bracket into the end of the channel and, using the bracket as a template, mark and drill the two .157-inch-diameter mounting holes on the door. If the channel is too long, cut the channel and channel insert to the proper length and deburr the edges.

11. Attach the pushbar to the lock at the clapper arm hinge bracket using the ½-inch screw and No. 10 internal tooth lockwasher provided.

12. Mount the end cap bracket to the door with the two No. 10 screws provided, and tighten the lock securely to the door.

13. Attach the end cap to the end cap bracket using the ½-inch oval head screw provided.

14. For single doors only: Remove the keeper cover, roller, and pin. Install the keeper base on the door with two screws supplied. Reinstall the pin, roller, and cover with two screws.

15. For double doors only: Install the rub plate for a 1¾-inch-wide door, from inside the door. Also install the 732 keeper with the two No. 10 screws. Do not tighten the screws fully because the keeper will require adjustment as mentioned in the next step.

16. For single doors only: Close the door, project the deadbolt, and adjust the keeper so that the door is tightly latched. Retract the deadbolt, hold the keeper, release the latch, and open the door.

17. Open the keeper cover and tighten the screws. Drill a .157-inch-diameter hole, as shown on the template, for the holding screw, and fasten the keeper with a No. 10 screw. Reinstall the pin, roller, and cover with two screws.

18. For double doors only: Close the door, project the bolt, and adjust the plastic slide on the 732 keeper so the door is tightly latched. Tighten the screws.

Installing the Control Box

To install the control box for Model 715, remove the control box cover. Select a location for the control box on the hinge side of the door and mount it to the wall using the three ¾-inch self-tapping screws.

Wiring

Model 715 is wired in the following way.

1. A four-conductor No. 22-AWG cable is needed to connect the control box to the lock. There are two ways of bringing electric current from the hinge side of the door frame to the door. Use the Armored Door Loop Model 271 by disconnecting one of the 271 end boxes and inserting the loose end of the armored cable into the ½-inch hole on the control box. Secure it with the retaining clip. Or, use a continuous conductor hinge with flying leads.

2. Connect one end of the 4-conductor cable to the control box terminal strip P2 (see Figure 13.11) and the other end of the cable to the lock terminal strip P3. The terminal strips are marked as follows: (1) SEN -sence (2) EM -electromagnet (3) +9 VDC (4) -ground. *Note:* Do not cross wires.

3. Connect one end of an approved twin lead 18-2 cable to the terminal strip at P1-1 and P1-2 (see Figure 13.11), and connect the other end of the cable to the 12 Vac 20 VA transformer provided. Do not plug in the transformer at this time.

4. Connect one end of another approved twin lead 22-2 cable to the terminal strip at P1-3 and P1-4, connect the other end to the normally closed alarm relay contacts of either an approved supervised automatic fire detection system or an approved supervised automatic sprinkler system.

5. Install the control box cover.

Operating

Before installing the lock cover, do the following.

1. For continuous alarm, leave the black jumper plug on the terminal strip, as installed.

2. For two-minute auto-alarm shutdown, remove the black jumper plug from the terminal strip.

3. Connect the 9-volt battery to its connector. A short beep will sound, ensuring that the 715 is powered and ready.

4. Plug the transformer into a continuous 115 ac volt source. Note the red pilot lamp on the control box is lit. Open the door and install the lock cover with the four screws that are supplied.

Testing

To test a Model 715, do the following.

1. Lock and unlock the door using the cylinder key. Notice the small beep when the deadbolt is retracted, indicating a disarmed condition. The door can be opened by pushing the push bar, after a 15-second wait, without causing an alarm.

2. Lock the door again and push the push bar. Immediately the alarm will pulse loudly and the 715 latch will impede the opening of the door for approximately 15 seconds, then remain unimpeded until it is manually reset with the key. Or, if continuous alarm was selected above, the piezo sounder will remain on for two minutes, then reset.

3. In the event of a power failure, the impeding latch will be disabled, but the 9-volt battery will provide standby power for the alarm circuit. Test this by disconnecting the transformer from the 115-volt source and pushing the pushbar. The door should now open immediately and the alarm should sound.

4. In the event of a fire panel alarm, the impeding latch will also be disabled. Test this by disconnecting the wire going to the control box P1-3 and pushing the pushbar. The door should open immediately and the alarm should sound.

Test the battery by pushing and holding the test button on the control box and pushing the pushbar to alarm the unit. If the piezo sounder sounds weak or doesn't operate at all, replace the 9-volt battery.

Electricity for Locksmiths

lectric strikes, electronic exit devices, and electromagnetic locks are just a few of the many electrical items locksmiths regularly install and service. More items are constantly being added to that list. Today it's difficult for a locksmith to stay competitive without working with electricity.

Not long ago, few locksmiths bothered to learn about electricity. Most just worked with mechanical locking devices and left the installation and servicing of electrically controlled devices to electricians and alarm installers. This situation has changed within the last few years for two reasons. First, hardware and department stores were fiercely competing with locksmiths.

Frequently such stores were so large they could afford to cut keys and sell and install locks at much lower prices than could locksmiths. Locksmiths had to offer new services to compete with those stores. Second, many locksmiths sell and install electrically controlled security devices because manufacturers now make such devices easy to install.

An extensive understanding of electricity isn't needed for installing most electric security devices.

Usually the major difference between installing a mechanical locking device and an electric one is that the latter requires running wires. The instruction manual that comes with the device explains how to mount the various parts of the device and how to hook up the wires to those parts. The wires are color-coded, which makes it easy to make proper connections.

Running the wires can be the most difficult part of installing an electrically controlled device. You should keep in mind, however, that this is usually more a matter of aesthetics than function. Even if the wires were just laying in a heap in the middle of a room, the electrically controlled device would operate if the wires were connected properly. However, most people prefer the wires to be less noticeable. Some wires must also be hidden to prevent people from tampering with them.

To install electrically controlled security devices, you need to know three things: the basic principles of electricity, how to run wires properly, and how to work safely with electricity.

Basic Principles

For an electrically controlled device to operate, electric current must flow in a complete, or continuous, circuit. In a complete circuit, a power source such as a battery must contain the amount of voltage needed to force a sufficient amount of current to flow through a wire, called a conductor, to an electrically controlled device, called a load, and then to flow through another conductor to return to the power source. That cycle continues until the power source runs down or the current flow is interrupted (Figure 14.1).

In addition to wires, terminals, screws, and strips of various types of metals are also used as conductors. Usually a combination of several types of conductors are used with an electrically controlled device. Regardless of which conductors are used, they must be connected to one another in such a way that current flows in an unbroken path.

When you turn an electrically controlled device off, you are simply disrupting the current flow.

For example, when you push a button or flip a switch to turn a light off, the button or switch moves a conductor, usually a small piece of wire or metal, away from a connecting conductor to prevent the flowing of current (Figure 14.2).

Types of Current

The two types of current are ac (alternating current) and dc (direct current).

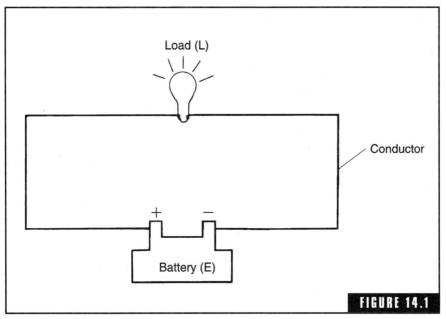

Electricity flows through a complete circuit.

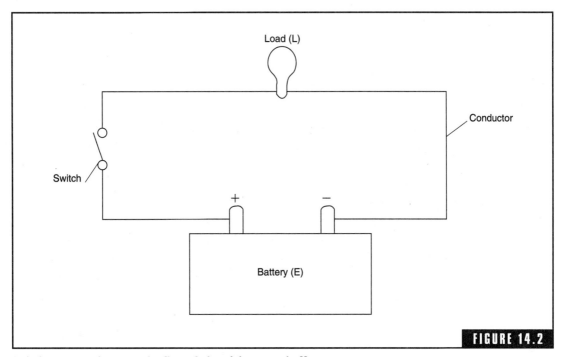

Switches are used to turn the flow of electricity on and off.

Alternating current flows through wires within the walls of your house; direct current flows from batteries. There are two practical differences between the two: ac can be more dangerous to work with, and polarity doesn't have to be observed when using an ac power source.

Polarity refers to negative and positive terminals of a power source. When using a battery, it's important to consider which terminal (negative or positive) to which each conductor must be connected. When using ac power from a wall socket, either conductor can be connected to either terminal. For example, if you insert an ac-powered device into a wall socket with the plug upside down, the device will still operate. However, if you insert batteries upside down in a dc-powered device, the device will not operate.

Resistance

Any opposition to electrical current flow is called *resistance*. There is some resistance in every circuit because every load and every conductor contains resistance.

Different types of material provide varying amounts of resistance. Rubber offers resistance to current flow, while copper conducts current very well. This is why rubber is often used to insulate electrical devices and why copper is often used to make conductors.

Controlling Electricity

Electricity is controlled in two ways: by limiting its force and by directing its flow. The force must be controlled because too much can damage electrically controlled devices and too little won't power the device. Force is controlled by using a power source that has the proper amount of voltage; by using the proper type, length, and thickness of conductors; and by using various circuit components.

Circuit Components

The various components within an electrically controlled device are the circuit components. Each serves a specific function within the device. Examples of such components include resistors, capacitors, and transformers. Each component and various types of each component are identified by a letter or a schematic symbol. This makes it easier to illustrate on a schematic diagram the components of a device and the relationships of those components.

Resistors

Resistors are circuit components designed to reduce the amount of current flowing to other components within a circuit. Because different components in a circuit require different amounts of current, resistors are used in virtually every electrically controlled device. They are available in both fixed and variable types. *Fixed resistors* provide a certain level of resistance. *Variable resistors*, sometimes called potentiometers or rheostats, can provide more than one level of resistance.

Capacitors

A *capacitor* stores electricity. It is made of two plates that are separated by insulation, such as air or glass. The insulation prevents a direct electrical connection of the plates, which would cause the current to flow rather than be stored. Some current does flow through a capacitor, but some is also stored. Both fixed and variable capacitors are available.

Transformers

Most of the electronic devices locksmiths install use transformers.

Transformers allow you to use an ac power source from one circuit, such as is found in your wall socket, to power a device on another circuit. Depending on the type of transformer used (step-up or step-down), it will increase or decrease the current flow to make the level of current flow suitable for the device. Most of the transformers used by locksmiths are step-down transformers. Because they decrease the level of current flow, such transformers make it safe to install electrically controlled devices.

Ohm's Law

Voltage, the force that powers current, is measured in volts. Current is measured in amperes (also called amps). Resistance is measured in ohms.

The relationship between the basic elements of an electric circuit is expressed by Ohm's Law. The law states that a resistance of 1 ohm passes a current of 1 ampere in response to an applied potential of 1 volt. Mathematically, Ohm's Law is expressed as: $E = I \times R$, where E is voltage, I is current, and R is resistance.

Ohm's Law expresses a basic principle of electricity that is very important to understand. When installing an electrically operated device, Ohm's Law makes it possible to figure out how much voltage, current, and resistance is needed to properly power the device.

Running Wires

Where wires can be run depends on the locations of the various parts of the locking system and the physical characteristics of the facility in which the system is installed.

When deciding where to run wires, consider where they would be most unobtrusive and tamper resistant. This usually requires running the wires over a drop ceiling, under carpet near a wall, or along or behind baseboards.

When running a wire from one room to another, you might need to drill a small hole through a wall, preferably above a drop ceiling or at another place where it can't be seen. To run a wire from one floor to a floor on another level, you might be able to use an exiting hole such as one used for an air vent or water pipe.

Wire can be protected by running it through a conduit. Electrical metallic tubing (EMT) is commonly used for that purpose. Many local building codes require the use of EMT.

Safety

Working with electricity can be very dangerous, unless you strictly adhere to certain safety factors. Before doing any electrical work, shut off the current coming into the building or automobile. In a building, the current can be shut off at the service entrance panel by turning off the main circuit breaker or by pulling the main fuse. In an automobile, remove the battery cables from the battery. Be sure to wrap electrical tape around the ends of the cables.

All of the tools you use should be properly insulated. Wear rubber-soled shoes and stand on a rubber mat to resist electrical shock. Because water is a very good conductor of electricity, make sure your hands are dry before working with electricity.

Finally, always use properly insulated wires. Never use wires that are encased in frayed or torn insulation.

Electromagnetic Locks

The electromagnetic lock was introduced in the United States in 1970 and has gained considerable popularity. Today it's a popular part of access control systems throughout the world.

Electromagnetic locks are often used to secure emergency exit doors. When connected to a fire alarm system, the lock's power source is automatically disconnected when the fire alarm is activated. That allows the door to open freely so people can exit quickly.

Although the principle of operation of an electromagnetic lock is very different from that of a conventional mechanical lock, the former has proven to be a cost-effective, high-security locking device. Unlike a mechanical lock, an electromagnetic lock doesn't rely on the release of a bolt or a latch for security, but instead relies on electricity and magnetism.

A standard electromagnetic lock consists of two components: a rectangular electromagnet and a rectangular, ferrous metal strike plate. The electromagnet is installed on a door's header; the strike plate is installed on the door in a position that allows it to meet the electromagnet when the door closes (Figure 15.1). When the door is closed and the electromagnet is adequately powered (usually by 12 to 24 dc volts at 3 to 8 watts), the door is secured. Typically, the locks have 300 to 3,000 pounds of holding power.

FIGURE 15.1

The strike plate of an electromagnetic lock is usually mounted on the top of a door in alignment with the electromagnet. *(Courtesy of Securitron)*

One of the biggest fears people have about electromagnetic locks is power failure. What happens if the power goes out or if a burglar cuts the wire connecting the power source to the lock? Standby batteries are often installed with the lock to provide continued power in such cases. Also, the lock can't be tampered with from outside the door because it is installed entirely inside the door. No part of the lock or power supply wires is exposed from outside the door.

Another important security feature of electromagnetic locks is that they are fail-safe. That is, when no power is going to the electromagnet, the door will not be locked. That is why the lock meets the safety requirements of many North American building codes.

There are two major disadvantages to electromagnetic locks. The locks often cost from four to ten times more than typical high-security mechanical locks. Also, many people think electromagnetic locks are much less attractive than mechanical locks.

The electromagnetic lock reviewed in this chapter is the Model 62 Magnalock, manufactured by Securitron. This lock can secure any door with a force of 1200 pounds. It is UL-listed and contains no moving parts. The electromagnet is housed in a compact stainless steel case and operates on 3 watts of dc power. Internal electronics awarded two patents ensure compatibility with all standard card-reader access control systems (Figure 15.2).

Installing a Model 62 Magnalock

The Model 62 Magnalock has several features to make installation easy. The lock includes blind nuts to allow the installer to mount it to the frame without having to tap the mounting holes. The mounting holes are recessed into the lock and covered by tamper-resistant finish caps. The wire can be hidden in the frame of the door or run through conduit fitting from the lock.

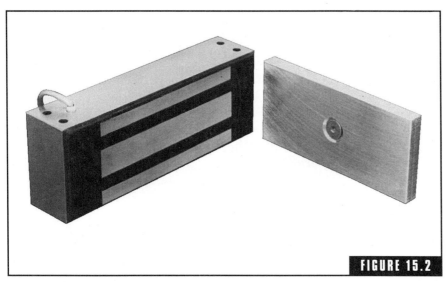

FIGURE 15.2

The Model 62 Magnalock. *(Courtesy of Securitron)*

To further help the installer, Securitron offers an installation kit that includes various tools and templates that make it easy for anyone to install a Model 62 Magnalock. Figure 15.3 shows an installation kit.

First, survey the physical area in which the unit is to be placed, and determine the best method of mounting it. In this initial planning, two considerations come into play. The mounting method must be strong enough that the full holding power of the Magnalock can be effective, and the Magnalock and wiring must be protected from damage by intruders or vandals. Often an accessory bracket is necessary, either furnished by Securitron or made by the installer.

When installing the lock on an outswinging door, mount the lock under the door frame header in the corner farthest from the hinges (Figure 15.4). It is most commonly positioned horizontally, but vertical positioning should also be considered. In some cases the horizontal header on an aluminum frame glass door is not as

FIGURE 15.3

The Magnalock installation kit makes it easy to install Magnalocks. *(Courtesy of Securitron)*

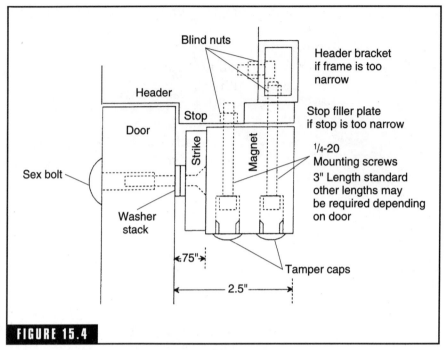

FIGURE 15.4

Typical mounting on out-swinging door. *(Courtesy of Securitron)*

strong as the vertical extrusion; vertical mounting might be preferred in such an instance.

This type of installation places the Magnalock so the door swings away from it. This configuration is necessary for all facility doors; otherwise, the Magnalock would be on the outside of the building. For interior doors, the Magnalock should still be mounted in the same manner, unless security planning anticipates a physical assault on the Magnalock from that side of the door.

Mounting the Strike

Mount the strike before the magnet on the upper corner of the door. Position the top of the strike about $\frac{1}{10}$ inch below the point where the door meets the door stop to permit free closing even if the door shifts. Left/right positioning of the strike is dictated by the desired position of the magnet. The strike must be centered on the magnetic poles (three bars) and the magnet may be moved an inch or so in from the frame, so that the magnet mounting holes will not have to be drilled awkwardly in the corner.

After you choose the strike position, drill three holes in the door, following the template.

Install the roll pins (metal for standard, plastic for Senstat) in the strike, using a hammer. If metal roll pins have been supplied, be careful not to strike them too hard with the hammer because it is possible to dent the strike surface of the pins by overdriving. This can degrade the strike flatness and therefore the holding force.

The strike is secured by the centrally located strike mounting screw. Place a washer stack consisting of two flexible washers between the strike and the door with the strike mounting screw passing through the two washers to provide flexibility. Do not place the washers around the roll pins. The roll pins should float in their holes and not bind. Their only purpose is to prevent the rotation of the strike.

Securing the strike to the door is crucial because it is the only point of attack for an intruder from the outside. Accordingly, Securitron provides a 1¼-inch-diameter sex bolt, machined from case-hardened tool steel, to terminate the strike mounting screw. Commercial sex bolts made of brass or aluminum can be defeated with a chisel and should not be used.

Secure the strike to the door using the supplied sex bolt. It is sometimes difficult to align the strike mounting screw with the sex bolt. The following technique is recommended. Start the sex bolt in its ½-inch hole, but thread the strike mounting screw into it before hammering the sex bolt down flush. When the strike mounting screw is started, hammer the sex bolt down, then screw the strike mounting screw in the rest of the way. This makes alignment much easier.

When the strike is mounted, make sure it flexes freely around the washer stack. This flexing allows the Magnalock to pull the strike into perfect alignment for maximum holding force, regardless of inaccuracies of alignment between the strike and the Magnalock that can occur during initial installation or during subsequent warping of the door or settling of the frame. The most common error made during installation of a Magnalock is mounting the strike in a rigid position.

Mounting the Magnet

The magnet mounts in the door frame header with four socket cap machine screws for metal frames or wood screws for wood frames. In mounting the Magnalock, you must adhere to the following conditions.

- The frame header must present a flat surface for the magnet to mount to.

- The frame area selected must be structurally strong enough to yield a properly secure installation.

- The magnet face must be parallel to the strike plate.

- The magnetic poles (three metal bars on the Magnalock) must be centered on the strike.

- The magnet must make solid contact with the strike but still allow the door to close properly.

- The direction of the door opening must pull the strike directly away from the magnet rather than sliding it away. Electromagnets hold only weakly in the shear direction of pull.

Taking these points in order, the first is satisfied if the frame presents a flat surface wide enough for the magnet. If not, the use of stop filler plates and header brackets, available from Securitron, can usually solve the problem. A 2¼-inch space is required from the door to the rear of the magnet for proper mounting.

The issue of the frame strength must be considered in selecting vertical or horizontal mounting.

On aluminum headers the horizontal extrusion is often weak and can be snapped off, so vertical mounting is preferred. It is also possible to reinforce the header by adding a steel plate. Avoid mounting the magnet to a wobbly or weak support, or the intrinsic security of the lock will be diminished.

Once a flat surface has been prepared for the magnet, the magnet must be positioned so that its face is parallel to the strike plate and door. The magnetic poles must be centered on the strike plate, and the door must close properly with the magnet making firm contact to the strike plate.

When the magnet has been experimentally positioned so that these criteria have been met, it is ready for mounting.

Drill four holes for the mounting screws and a ½-inch-diameter wire hole for electrical hookup.

For proper strength, the mounting machine screws must be secured by nuts. To facilitate this, special blind finishing nuts with star washers are supplied with each Magnalock.

To use the nuts, drill a ⅜-inch (9.5 mm) hole according to the template for each finishing nut.

Press the nut up into the hole and lightly seat with a hammer tap so its knurl engages. Run the mounting screws through the magnet and into the finishing nuts. Place the star washers between the magnet case and the blind nuts to provide friction, allowing the nuts to self-collapse. If you use the blind nut collapsing tool furnished in the installation kit, you do not need the star washers.

Use the gold flat washers on the magnet mounting screw heads; they prevent the narrow screw heads from digging into the resin body of the magnet.

If the mounting screws don't line up with the blind nuts installed in the header, it is possible to enlarge certain of the mounting holes in the magnet to achieve alignment. Note that all Magnalock versions have a cable exiting on one end of the magnet. Never enlarge the two mounting holes on the end where the cable exits. Wiring runs through the resin in that part of the magnet, and drilling out the mounting holes on that end can easily destroy the product and void the warranty.

You may enlarge either or both of the mounting holes on the opposite side of the magnet from cable exit, although you shouldn't go beyond $\frac{9}{32}$ inch. If the holes still don't line up, you can mount only three of the four screws and still achieve a strong installation. Installers doing multiple jobs should obtain Securitron's installation tool kit, which includes a drill guide that yields excellent mounting hole alignment.

As you tighten the screws, you will feel an initial resistance which is the nuts collapsing, then a second, stronger resistance as the screws seat. Do not overtorque. The collapsed nuts coupled with machine screws provide extremely strong mounting. The purpose of the star washers is to dig into the case of the magnet and into the base of the nuts. This helps the nuts collapse and prevents them from spinning. The nuts will work on metal frames of any thickness, including concrete-filled headers. Once the nuts have collapsed, the star washers can be removed for a slightly neater installation.

In-swinging Door Mounting

In cases where the Magnalock must be mounted on the in-swinging side of the door to protect it from physical assault, mount the Magnalock body flush on the wall above the door frame. Affix a Z-bracket to the door, which positions the strike plate in front of the Magnalock. Use Securitron's F Series Magnalocks because they have mounting holes through the face of the magnet and wire exit to the rear (Figure 15.5).

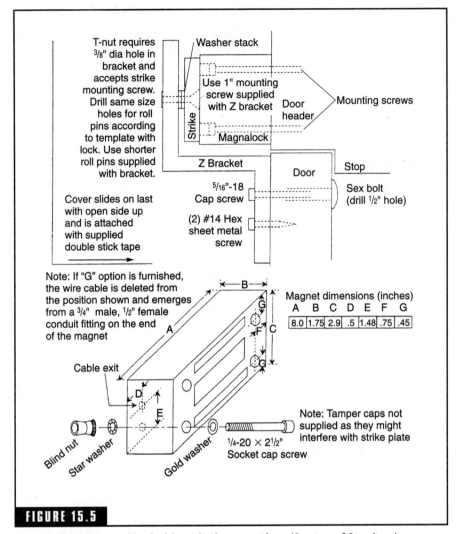

Magnet dimensions and typical in-swinging mounting. *(Courtesy of Securitron)*

Finishing nuts are supplied because often the lower two screws are mounted in the metal door frame header. The top two screws might require appropriate anchors when used in drywall, for instance. Securitron offers a Z-bracket to allow mounting on a wide range of commercial door/frame configurations.

Aluminum Frame Glass Door Mounting

The aluminum frame glass door is probably the most common door type used with the Magnalock. Certain mounting problems can arise depending on the exact configuration of the door and frame. Often the header is not wide enough to support the depth of the magnet.

This can mean that none of the mounting screws can be run into the header or that only two of the four will fit. Another aspect of the mounting screw problem is that two of the mounting screws might line up with the end of the header extrusion. Also, the wires might exit beyond the end of the header so that they will be exposed and vulnerable to tampering.

Most of these problems are solved by using Securitron's universal header bracket (part UHB-62). This extends the depth of the header either 1 or 1½ inches, depending on which way it is oriented. This usually allows mounting of all four screws, and because the bracket is a hollow extrusion, the wire is run inside the bracket and therefore is hidden.

Even if you use the bracket, it is possible that one set of mounting screws may line up with the end of the header. Note that some adjustment of the magnet mounting position is possible. Instead of the two rubber washers supplied with the strike, one or three may be used. If the door is secured only by the Magnalock (there is no mechanical deadbolt), the door's closed position may be altered to allow use of all four mounting screws. Finally, note that an installation of this type of door is acceptable if only two mounting screws are used.

Because the screws run into steel nuts, the fastening technique is very strong. In fact, when the design decision was made to employ four mounting screws, one reason was to allow at least a pair to be used in the event of alignment problems with the header. It is best to use all four screws, but on this type of door, which is inherently not high security because the glass can be shattered for forced entry, firmly mounting two screws is acceptable.

Another problem that can arise with aluminum frame glass doors is that, in certain cases, the height of the aluminum rail at the top of the door is not sufficient to mount the strike and sex bolt.

If the sex bolt is installed in the lowest area of the top rail, the top edge of the strike will protrude above the rail. To solve this problem, Securitron offers the offset strike. The holes in the strike plate are offset ¼ inch from the center of the strike; this allows successful mounting on a narrow top rail. Approximately 10 percent of the holding force is lost because of the skewed position of the strike mounting screw. However, this is not significant on aluminum frame glass doors because they are not high-security barriers. The offset strike can be supplied with the lock or ordered separately.

Solid Glass Door Mounting

The Magnalock is useful for securing 100 percent glass doors that have no aluminum rail. The magnet is suspended in normal fashion from the header. The difficulty in the installation is mounting the strike plate on the glass because glass cannot be drilled. This is accomplished by using Securitron's Model GDB (glass door bracket) and Model AKG (adhesive kit for glass). The bracket is affixed to the glass surface by a special adhesive, and the strike screws into the bracket conventionally. The adhesive provides a bond stronger than the holding force of the Magnalock and is permanent (Figure 15.6).

Some doors that appear to be glass are laminated with plastic. The Magnalock with glass door bracket might fail if used on such a door.

In some cases the header of a glass door is vertical glass. The magnet can be mounted on such a header by using a 3-×-3-inch aluminum angle bracket, available from Securitron. The bracket is glued to the vertical glass header with Securitron's adhesive kit for glass, and the magnet is screwed to the bracket.

Double Door Mounting

It is very common to use Magnalocks on double doors. Several mounting possibilities exist. In some cases one of the door leaves is pinned so only one leaf is used. It is secured by a single Magnalock in standard fashion. If both leaves are to be active, two Magnalocks can be used. For the most attractive installation, the leaves should be abutted, but if obstructions exist in the header that interfere with mounting, the magnets can be separated.

Another possibility is to use Securitron's split strike. In this method, a single Magnalock is mounted in the center of the header, and a half-size strike is mounted on each leaf. This reduces the holding force to under 600 pounds for each leaf and lowers the door security to a "traffic control" level. It must be strictly understood that a strong kick will open this door, whereas if two complete Magnalocks are used, the lock strength typically exceeds that of the door. The split strike is available either as part of a complete Magnalock or supplied separately as a replacement for the standard strike. (*Note:* Certain electronic considerations also apply when Magnalocks are used on double doors.)

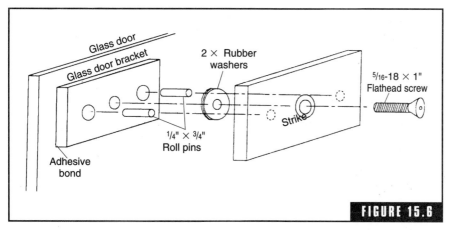

Strike installation on a 100 percent glass door. *(Courtesy of Securitron)*

Wood Frame Mounting

With a wooden frame, you can use long wood screws to mount the Magnalock.

If, however, the frame is not solid enough to secure the Magnalock adequately, you can use a wood frame bracket available from Securitron (part WF-62). The Magnalock mounts to the bracket with machine screws, and the bracket permits the wood screws to penetrate more deeply into the header (Figure 15.7).

Steel Header Filled with Concrete Mounting

The blind nuts function normally despite the presence of concrete, but a problem can occur in pulling the hookup wires. To help, Securitron offers the concrete header bracket (part CHB-62), which permits a range of techniques (see Figure 15.7). The center of the bracket forms a splice chamber, which makes it less difficult to pull the wires back into the header.

Alternately, you can pull the wires through the edge of the bracket by drilling a hole, if it's impractical to drill the concrete.

Another technique for concrete headers is the use of Securitron's G version Magnalock. It incorporates a ½-inch female and ¾-inch male universal threaded conduit fitting. The conduit fitting is placed on the end of the magnet body, and the problem of pulling wires into concrete is bypassed because the wires can be run in pipe in a surface-mounted configuration. The mounting holes on G-locks are counterbored from

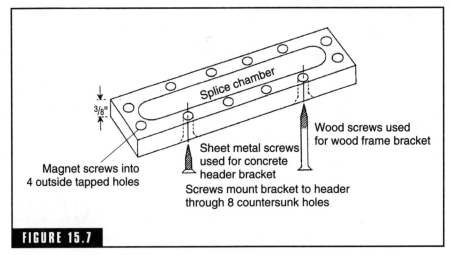

Splice chamber

3/8"

Wood screws used
for wood frame bracket

Sheet metal screws
used for concrete
header bracket

Magnet screws into
4 outside tapped holes

Screws mount bracket to header
through 8 countersunk holes

FIGURE 15.7

Wood frame and concrete header bracket. *(Courtesy of Securitron)*

both sides to make the lock nonhanded. To collapse the blind nuts (which otherwise would fall into the counterbore), flat washers are supplied to close the magnet surface. Discard the flat washers after the nuts have been collapsed.

Exterior Gate Mounting

A popular application for the Magnalock is to secure motorized or manual exterior gates. The Magnalock provides several benefits in this application. Gates tend not to be precisely fitted, so electric bolts suffer from alignment failures. The Magnalock is designed to be self-aligning and tolerates considerable inconsistency in the gate-closed position regarding upward/downward alignment, side alignment, and twisting. The Magnalock is also fully sealed and waterproof, so it is generally unaffected by tough environments.

Because of the wide variety of gates in existence, each installation has to be considered special. You must usually make up bracketry on site. The concept is to mount the magnet on a fixed post and the strike plate to the swinging or sliding member of the gate. Both components should be positioned so that the strike plate slaps against the magnet face on closure.

Usually, the GF version of the Magnalock is preferred for gate installation. "G" refers to a conduit fitting mounted on the magnet end, and "F" refers to mounting holes through the face (see Figure 15.5). The magnet typically screws onto a back plate fashioned on site, and the back plate is welded onto the fixed post.

A back plate or Securitron's Z-bracket should also be provided for the strike plate. The strike plate cannot be welded directly to the gate because it will not be able to flex and self-align. It must be screwed onto a surface with the washer stack used to provide flexibility. If Securitron's Z-bracket is used, it typically bolts to the gate rather than being welded because it is aluminum.

In the case of very tall and large gates, a levering problem can exist. An intruder might be able to flex the gate enough to take up the slack in the strike mounting screw, then lever off the strike plate. If the installer or user determines that this might happen, a single Magnalock will not provide adequate security. Two must be used, typically at the top and bottom of the gate.

Figure 15.8 shows preferred special techniques for Magnalock mounting on three types of gates.

The first drawing shows a single swinging gate. The general technique follows the principles discussed above, but use of Securitron's Z-bracket, which creates a neat installation, is also shown. Note that in some cases the post that mounts the magnet is hollow. It is possible to use the F version (without conduit fitting) and pull the wires through the post, which might yield a neater and more secure installation.

The second drawing in Figure 15.8 shows a double swinging gate, which presents a unique problem.

The Magnalock is mounted in the same general way as on a single swinging gate, but because both arms move, an intruder pushing on the gate exerts a shearing force on the Magnalock.

Electromagnets are not at all strong in this type of attack. Therefore, as the drawing shows, Securitron's Z-bracket should be used with an interference piece. This blocks the shearing effect, while the strength of the magnet blocks one arm moving when the other is stationary. For this technique to work, the motorized operator must be coordinated. One arm must move first to clear the interference piece before the other arm starts moving. Gate operators can normally accomplish this.

The final drawing on Figure 15.8 shows a special mounting technique for sliding gates. Use the GF-type magnet and two 3-inch angle brackets (available from Securitron) for a neat installation.

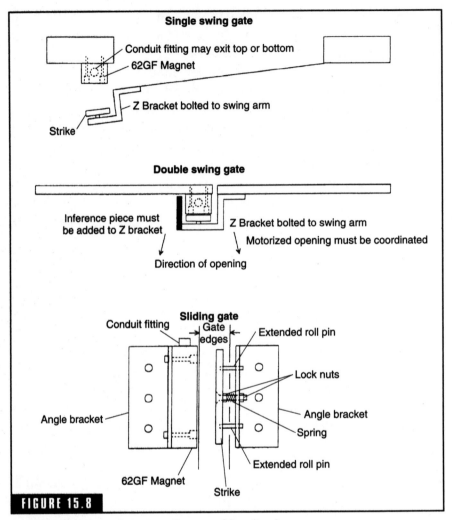

FIGURE 15.8

Mounting techniques for gates. *(Courtesy of Securitron)*

A special strike-mounting technique that improves the reliability of the installation is shown in the drawing. The problem is that if the strike is mounted normally to the angle bracket and the gate is a powerful one that slams shut, the magnet might be impacted to the point where its mounting screws loosen or the bracket bends.

The strike mounting technique shown creates a shock absorber effect through the use of lock nuts at the rear of the strike and the rear of the bracket, together with a spring. Drill a through-hole in the angle bracket mounting the strike, and use extra-long roll pins. When the gate closes, the strike moves in against the spring and creates a shock-absorbing action.

Tamper-Proofing the Magnalock

In situations where vandalism is more probable, the Magnalock should be protected from tampering. The magnet is inherently tamper-proof because it is totally sealed.

However, the magnet mounting screws are vulnerable because the magnet can be dismounted if the screws are loosened. The Allen holes on the screws can be filled with a potting compound such as silicon.

Alternately, the entire hole in the magnet where the screw heads fit can be filled. Butyrate caps are supplied to close the mounting holes. These provide tamper proofing because they can't be removed by hand, but they can be pried off with a tool. The strike plate mounting screw is covered by the strike when the magnet is energized. If tampering is anticipated when the door is open, the screw socket head may be filled.

For added safety, Securitron carries special tamper-proof screws for both magnet and strike mounting. These screws are identical Allen head types, but a special key is needed to install and remove the screws. It is highly unlikely that a vandal would have access to this type of key.

Securitron supplies the tamper-proof screw sets with keys both in the form of a manual Allen wrench and in a bit key for use with a drill.

General Electrical Characteristics

The Magnalock constitutes an electric load that draws 3 watts of power. Because of its patented internal circuitry, the Magnalock does not show the normal characteristics of an electromagnetic or other inductive load. Magnalock resistance also cannot be read with an ohmmeter because of the internal circuitry. Inductive kickback is suppressed, so arcing across control switch contacts need not be a concern.

This suppression also protects nearby access control or other computer equipment from possible interference and, for the same purpose, microwave radiation is also suppressed internally.

The circuitry performs the additional functions of canceling residual magnetism ("stickiness" on release) and accelerating field collapse so that the Magnalock releases instantly when power is removed from it.

Standard Lock

For operation, dc voltage (24 or 12 volts, depending on the model selected), must be provided to the lock. The red wire receives +12 volts or +24 volts, and the black wire receives 0 volts (negative). The lock will not function if it is connected with reverse polarity. The voltage source may be regulated, filtered, or pulsating dc (using transformer plus bridge rectifier).

Half-wave pulsating dc generated by a transformer and single diode will not properly operate the Magnalock. An exact voltage level is not necessary. Less than standard voltage will proportionately reduce the holding force but will cause no harm. Over-voltage up to 30 percent is acceptable.

The current draw is 125 mA (milliamperes) for 24-volt versions or 250 mA for 12-volt. It is good practice to use power supplies with one-third extra capacity beyond the current requirements of the load. This greatly reduces the possibility of heat-induced power supply failure and allows for future expansion. Power supply cost is a small fraction of the job cost and should not be skimped on.

Switches can be wired as necessary between the Magnalock and power source. Internal circuitry eliminates inductive kickback, so neither electromechanical switches nor solid state devices will be damaged by arcing when the Magnalock is shut off.

Securitron recommends switching the Magnalock on the dc side of its power supply. If switched on the ac side, the power supply capacitor (in the case of a filtered supply) will discharge through the magnet, slowing its release.

Wire Gauge Sizing

If the power supply is distant from the lock, voltage will be lost, or dropped, in the connecting wires, and the Magnalock will not receive full voltage. The 24-volt Magnalock version is a much better choice for long wire runs because it gives four times the resistance of the 12-volt version. Note that the correct calculation of wire sizing is very important because the installer is responsible for ensuring that adequate voltage is supplied to any load. In multiple device installations, the calculation can become quite complex.

The general practice of wire sizing in a dc circuit is to avoid causing voltage drops in connecting wires, which reduces the voltage available to operate the device. Because Magnalocks are low-power devices, they can be operated long distances from their power source. For any job that includes long wire runs, the installer must be able to calculate the correct gauge of wire to avoid excessive voltage drops.

To calculate the correct gauge, add the resistance of the Magnalock to the resistance in the power wires, then divide the wire resistance by the total resistance. This yields the fraction of voltage drop in the wires. For example, a single 24-volt Magnalock has a resistance of 192 ohms. If the wires completing the circuit between the Magnalock and its power source have a resistance of 10 ohms, the total resistance is 202 ohms. Dividing 10 ohms (the wire resistance) by 202 (the total resistance) yields roughly $\frac{1}{20}$ or 5 percent. If the input voltage is 24 volts, 5 percent of this voltage will be dropped in the wires (1.2 volts), leaving 22.8 volts to operate the Magnalock. This will cause a small reduction in holding force but is generally acceptable.

To calculate the wire resistance, you need to know the distance from the power supply to the Magnalock and the gauge (thickness) of the wire. Magnalock resistances are 192 ohms for the 24-volt (dc) version and 48 ohms for the 12-volt version.

Suppose a single 24-volt Magnalock is 1200 feet from its power supply, and you're using 20-gauge wire. The total length of the power wires is 2400 feet. Remember that you combine the wire lengths from the power supply to the lock and back to the power supply to get the total circuit wire length. The wire resistance then becomes 2.4×10.1 ohms, which is 24.2 ohms.

Adding this to the Magnalock resistance of 192 ohms yields a total resistance of 216.2 ohms. 24.2 divided by 216.2 yields an 11 percent drop in the wires, which Securitron would consider excessive.

This problem can be dealt with in two ways. Either use 16-gauge wire, which reduces the drop to a more acceptable 5-percent range, or provide extra voltage at the power supply. For instance, Securitron 24-volt power supplies are adjustable from 24 to 28 volts. You can therefore easily set the power supply to output 11 percent over-voltage, which will then deliver 24 volts at the lock.

As mentioned, the Magnalock will accept up to 30 percent over-voltage without ill effects.

Note that the 12-volt dc Magnalock has one-fourth the resistance of the 24-volt version (48 ohms versus 192 ohms). This means that wire voltage drops are four times more significant in a 12-volt system than in a 24-volt system. In any job that has wire runs long enough to be of concern, always use 24 volts.

Note also that it is common to mount two Magnalocks on a double door and operate them as one lock (only two power wires). In this case, the resistance of the pair of locks is half the resistance of a single lock (96 ohms for 24 volts, 24 ohms for 12 volts).

If a common power wire is used in a loop structure, for instance, the many locks powered by the single loop will have an increasingly low combined resistance, so the loop wire resistance will become more significant to the point that the locks don't receive enough voltage.

To find the combined resistance of multiple locks powered by a common wire, divide the resistance of one lock by the number of locks. For example, eight 24-volt Magnalocks have a combined resistance of 192 divided by 8, which is only 24 ohms. Another method is to calculate the current in amps and divide that into the circuit voltage. Because each 24-volt Magnalock draws ⅛ of an amp, eight would draw 1 amp. Dividing this into the same 24-volt input voltage yields a 24-ohm combined resistance.

In general, you have to be cautious about using common wires for loads in long-distance situations, unless you're very confident of your ability to calculate the correct configuration. Bear in mind, however, that whenever you are uncertain about the voltage drop in wiring, you can meter the voltage at the lock while it's connected, and you will be able to see if it's receiving adequate voltage. If the lock is not connected when you make this measurement, the result will be false because the circuit will not see any lock resistance to compare with wire resistance. You will read the full input voltage. Also, you cannot measure Magnalock resistance with an ohmmeter. It has semiconductors inside that render ohmmeter readings meaningless.

Senstat Magnalocks S and C

Securitron's optional patented Senstat electronics package provides lock status sensing. In many electrically controlled door security systems, status sensing is provided by a magnetic switch on the door. This indicates the door is closed, but not necessarily secured.

Securitron's Senstat monitors the lock rather than the door and therefore provides a higher level of security.

S Senstat Magnalock

S versions provide a voltage signal on a third wire equal to the input voltage that is on when the door is secure. This is accomplished by conducting the input voltage through the strike, which ensures a flush fit of the strike to the magnetic core. Input power is also monitored so that if the lock is not powered, it will not report secure, even if the strike and magnet are flush.

The output signal is typically used to drive a load such as a relay coil, light, or buzzer, which indicates lock status. The load must not draw more than 1 amp of current. Securitron monitoring control panels are designed to work with S Senstat Magnalocks. When using an S Magnalock on a metal door, it's important to insulate the strike from the door to prevent low-voltage leakage into the door frame. The strike is furnished with insulating hardware (Figure 15.9).

C Senstat Magnalock

C versions provide an isolated contact closure on a third and fourth wire that is closed when the lock is secure. The contact closure is between the strike and magnet face, so a flush fit is required for the lock to report secure. Although the C version does not directly monitor input power to the lock, it will generally not report secure if the strike merely lays on the magnet without power. If the C version is used on a metal door, the strike should be insulated from the door by using the insulating hardware supplied with it. The C version is normally used because of its direct compatibility with popular access control and alarm monitoring circuits.

Double Door Procedure for Status Reporting

Often two Magnalocks are mounted on a double door and are turned on and off together, having no separate control. It is possible to receive a separate Senstat status signal from each door, or you can combine the outputs so that if both locks are secure, the double door is secure, and if either lock is not secure, the double door is not secure.

If the desired status output from the double door is of the dry contact type (C Senstat), the connection connects the C outputs in series. Connect one of the C status wires (white or green) from each lock together and take your output from the two wires (one from each lock).

When both locks are secure, both Senstat circuits will be closed and the double door will report secure as if it was a single lock.

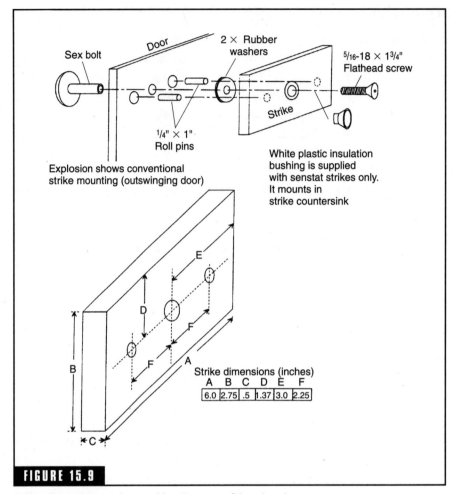

FIGURE 15.9

Strike dimensions and assembly. *(Courtesy of Securitron)*

If the desired status output from the double door is of the voltage type (S Senstat), use an S Magnalock together with a C Magnalock. The voltage output of the S Magnalock is passed through the C contacts and both locks must be secure for a single voltage output to be present from the pair (Figure 15.10).

Magnalock L Version with Indicator Light

Magnalocks equipped with indicator lights have an LED mounting socket permanently installed in the magnet body. The indicator can be replaced easily in the event of vandalism or failure, because both the LED lamp and lens screw into the permanently mounted socket. On

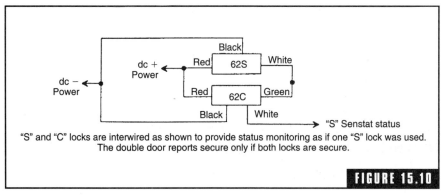

Double door wiring with S and C lock. *(Courtesy of Securitron)*

standard or C Senstat Magnalocks, the amber-colored light indicates the magnet is powered. On S Senstat Magnalocks, the light is driven by the Senstat voltage output, and a green color indicates the door is secure. A vandal who removes the light and attempts to tamper with the socket will not be able to harm the function of the Magnalock because the socket is short-circuit protected.

If a light is desired on an F-type Magnalock, it must be mounted on the end of the lock because the rear of the lock is the mounting surface. This position interferes with Securitron's Z-bracket cover, so Securitron does not recommend ordering lights with F Magnalocks, although lights can be supplied on a special-order basis.

Emergency Release

Magnalocks are often wired into a system such that they can be simultaneously released in an emergency, either manually from one switch or automatically, often from the fire alarm system. It is the user's responsibility to accomplish this hookup correctly according to these instructions and good electrical practices. In general, Securitron recommends that a switch or relay be used to perform a series break of all dc power, which is the simple and sure way to make sure the doors release. Securitron power supplies have terminals for interconnection of such emergency release switches.

Troubleshooting a Magnalock

This section contains a list of problems that can occur with the Magnalock and instructions for fixing them.

No Magnetic Attraction Between Magnet and Strike Plate

Make sure the lock is being correctly powered with dc voltage. This includes connecting the power wires with the correct polarity. Positive must go to red and negative to black. If the Magnalock is wired in reverse polarity, it will not be damaged, but it will not operate. If the unit continues to appear dead, it must be electrically checked with an ammeter. It must be powered with the correct input voltage and checked to see if it draws the specified current (125 mA at 24 dc volts or 250 mA at 12 dc volts).

The Magnalock cannot be checked with an ohmmeter because it has semiconductors that render an ohmmeter reading meaningless. If the unit draws the correct current, it is putting out the correct magnetic field, and the problem must be in the mounting of the strike.

Reduced Holding Force

If reduced holding force is the problem, usually the door can be kicked in without much effort. Check the strike and magnet face to see if some small obstruction is interfering with a flat fit. Even a small air gap can greatly reduce the holding force. If the strike and magnet are flat and clean, the cause is nearly always improper mounting of the strike: It is mounted too stiffly. The strike must be allowed to float around the rubber washer stack, which must be on the strike center mounting screw. The magnet then pulls it into flat alignment.

To correct the problem, try loosening the strike mounting screw to see if the lock then holds properly. It is also possible that the input voltage is too low. Be sure that you are not operating a 24-volt lock on 12 volts. If you are using 12 volts and suspect that you have a 24-volt lock, the only way to check it is to use an ammeter. If it is a 24-volt lock, it will draw 60 mA (milliamperes) at 12 volts instead of the correct 250 mA.

Lock Buzzes or Hums and Does Not Hold

The lock will buzz if it's operated on ac or half-wave rectified dc power (transformer plus single diode). Make sure you are using full-wave rectified dc (transformer plus bridge), or filtered or regulated dc power.

It is also possible that the strike and magnet are not flat together, owing to some obstruction or dent that must be corrected. This can cause a fluttering noise.

The Senstat Output Does Not Report Secure

Because of the simplicity of Securitron's patented Senstat design, this is almost always a case of the lock status sensor doing its job. It is not reporting secure because a small obstruction or a stiffly mounted strike is causing the Magnalock to hold at reduced force.

Correct the problem by cleaning the surfaces of the magnet and strike or establishing proper play in the strike mounting. If this doesn't work, verify function of the Senstat feature as follows.

Note that there are two thin, vertical lines on the magnet face that can be said to separate the core into three sections, from left to right. The Senstat output is created by the strike establishing electrical contact between the leftmost and rightmost core segments. With the lock powered, use a pair of scissors and press the points respectively into the leftmost and rightmost core segments.

The Senstat output should then report secure. This shows that the problem lies in the strike not making flat contact with the magnet face. If the scissors technique doesn't cause the lock to report secure, check to see if there is a broken Senstat wire. If this is not the case, the lock must be returned to the factory for replacement.

Lock Does Not Release

When the power is removed from it, the Magnalock must release. If internal circuitry, which eliminates residual magnetism, were to fail completely, the lock would only exhibit "stickiness" at a rough level of 5 pounds. Therefore, if the lock will not release, the problem is either mechanical bonding via vandalism, meaning glue has been applied between the strike, or a failure to completely release power.

Failure to completely release power is generally a wiring integrity problem. An upstream switch removes power from the wires going to the Magnalock, but through an installation error, the wires have their insulation abraded between the switch and lock. Partial or full power can leak in from another Magnalock or other dc device with similarly abraded wiring. This is most likely to occur at the point where the wire cable leaves the lock case and enters the door frame. Another potential problem area is an improper splice on wiring in conduit.

Either a metal door frame or the metal conduit is capable of leaking power between multiple devices with abraded wires, thereby bypassing switches. A good way to check this electrically (as opposed to visually removing and inspecting the wires) is to use a meter. Check for leakage between the power supply positive or negative and the door frame and conduit. Magnalocks should be powered by isolated dc voltage without any earth ground reference to positive or negative.

Rusted Lock

Both the Magnalock core and strike plate are cadmium plated and sealed following a military specification. Cadmium provides the highest degree of rust-proofing possible on ferrous metal. Because of this plating and the sealed nature of the magnet, the Magnalock is weatherproof and may be used outdoors. If rusting appears, the most common cause is improper cleaning. If steel wool is used, for instance, it can strip off the relatively soft cadmium. Once the plating has been removed, it cannot be restored in the field, so the lock will have to be periodically cleaned and coated with oil or other rust inhibitor. A rusty Magnalock will still function, but at reduced holding force. If the product is installed in a heavily corrosive atmosphere, such as near the ocean, it will eventually rust, even if nonabrasive cleaners are used. The only solution in this case is periodic removal of the rust.

Electronic Noise Interference with Access Control System

Electric locks, being inductive devices, return voltage spikes on their power wires and emit microwave radiation when switched. This can interfere with access control electronics, causing malfunctions, particularly with those units employing high-speed dynamic RAM. Access control contractors often employ installation techniques designed to isolate the access control electronics from the electric lock. These include separate circuits for the lock, shielded wiring, and other techniques. The Magnalock, however, is heavily used in access control installations and includes internal electronics that suppress both inductive kickback and radiation.

The Magnalock has been extensively tested and accepted by numerous access control manufacturers and has been used in thousands of installations without incident. An apparent noise problem is therefore usually not caused by the Magnalock. The access control equipment might be faulty or installed improperly. Check with the manufacturer for proper installation procedures.

A problem can arise with the Magnalock: if you are using the Senstat version, you must isolate the strike plate (which passes current) from a metal door and frame. Securitron supplies insulating hardware to accomplish this, but the hardware might not have been used or the strike might be scraping against the header. When the door is secure, use an ohmmeter to check for full isolation between the strike and the door frame. The presence of lock voltage potential in the door frame can interfere with the ground reference of access control system data communication and cause a problem.

Other Magnalocks

In addition to the Model 62 discussed in this chapter, Securitron manufactures two other Magnalock models (Figure 15.11). Model 92 is the company's strongest model; it secures a door with a holding force of 3000 pounds. It is for extremely high-security applications. Model 32 Magnalock provides for 600 pounds of holding force (Figure 15.12). It is especially useful for internal traffic control doors and sliding doors, where high security is not a requirement.

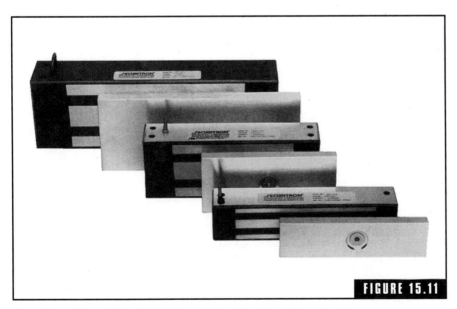

FIGURE 15.11

Securitron offers a "family" of Magnalocks. *(Courtesy of Securitron)*

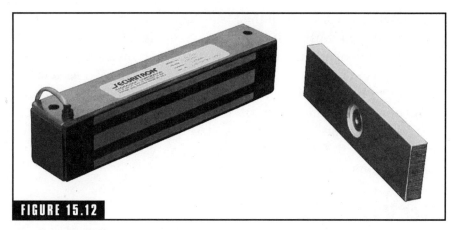

FIGURE 15.12

The Mini-Mag Model 32 Magnalock has 600 pounds of holding force. *(Courtesy of Securitron)*

Model 32 comes in a convenient size ($8 \times 1\frac{1}{2} \times 1\frac{3}{4}$ inches) and is the smallest of the three models. Called the "Mini-Mag," Model 32 has many of the same features as Model 62, including vandal- and weather-resistant stainless steel casing, mil-spec cadmium plating for rust resistance, and low power consumption (300 mA at 12 dc volts or 150 mA at 24 ac volts).

Pairs of Model 32s can be mounted at the top and bottom of a door to yield a total holding force of 1200 pounds.

Electric Strikes

An electric strike is architectural hardware designed to make frequently used doors more secure and convenient (Figure 16.1). These strikes are usually mounted in the frame of a door and use electricity to either hold or release a latch. A switch, which can be located close to or far away from the strike, can activate and deactivate a strike.

There are several popular manufacturers of electric strikes. This chapter reviews some of the models made by Adams Rite Manufacturing Company.

Strike Selection

Most Adams Rite electric strikes have flat faces. Two exceptions are the 7801 and the 7831 models, which have radius faces to match the nose shape of paired narrow stile glass doors.

The basic Adams Rite size conforms to American National Standards Institute (ANSI) strike preparation, 1¼ × 4⅞ inches. However, two other sizes are offered to fill or cover existing jambs or opposing stiles from previous installations of M.S. deadlock strike (7830 and 7831) or discontinued Series 002 electric strikes (7810).

Strikes are available with round corners for installation in narrow stile aluminum, where preparation is usually done by router, and with square corners for punched hollow metal ANSI preparation or wood mortise.

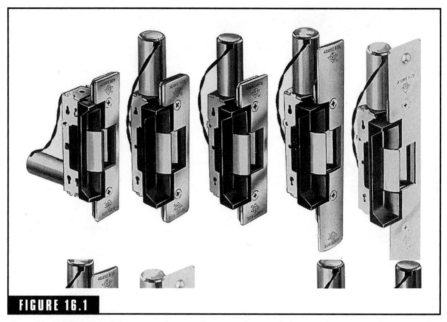

FIGURE 16.1

Electric strikes provide control over frequently used doors. *(Courtesy of Adams Rite Manufacturing Co.)*

Strikes with vertically mounted solenoids are designed to slip into hollow metal stile sections as shallow as 1.6 inches. Horizontal solenoids for wood jambs require an easily bored 3⅝- to 4½-inch-deep mortise, depending on the model.

If the jamb was previously fitted with an 002 electric strike, the new 7810 unit will fit with minor alterations. If a hollow jamb was originally prepared to receive the bolt from an Adams Rite M.S. deadlock and you plan to substitute a 4710 latch, the 7830 (flat jamb) or 7831 (radius inactive door) will cover the old strike cutout.

The standard lip on all basic Adams Rite electric strikes accommodates 1¾-inch-thick doors that close flush with the jamb. If the door/jamb relationship is different, a long clip can be added if it is so specified.

Adams Rite electric strikes 7800 through 7831 mate with all Adams Rite Series 4500 and 4700 latches. The 7840, 7840 ANSI, and 7870 are designed for mortise latches of the makes shown.

All standard operation strikes are unhanded and can be installed for either right- or left-hand doors.

Electrical Considerations

The first electrical factor to determine is whether the operation is to be intermittent or continuous. If the door is normally locked and released only momentarily from time to time, it is *intermittent*. If it is rare that the strike is activated (unlocked) for long periods, the duty is *continuous*. A seldom-used requirement is *continuous/reverse action*, also called fail safe, in which the strike is locked only when its current is switched on.

For a normal intermittent application, specify an electric strike using 24 ac volts. This gives enough power for almost any entrance, even one with a wind-load situation. Yet this low-voltage range is below that requiring UL or Building Code supervision. Reliable transformers are available in this voltage.

The buzzing sound inherent in ac-activated strikes is usually not considered offensive in intermittent use. In fact it acts as the "go" signal to a person waiting to enter. However, if silence is desired, specify a strike using 24 dc volts. This dc current operates the strike silently. A buzzer or pilot light can be wired in if a signal is required.

Continuous duty is required when the strike will be energized for more than 60 seconds at a time.

Most continuous-duty applications can be supplied through the same 115/24-volt ac transformer used for intermittent jobs. The factory will automatically add those components necessary to achieve continuous performance at the voltage specified.

For long periods of unlocking, a Fail-Safe Reverse Action strike can be obtained. This might be required to provide the same service as a continuous-duty strike, but will preserve current because it is on dc power. It could also be used to provide a fail-safe unlocked door in case of power failure.

If a visual or other signal is required to tell the operator what the electric strike is doing, a monitoring strike is needed. This feature is specified by adding the proper dash number to the strike's catalog number. Two sensor/switches are added. One is activated by the latchbolt's penetration of the strike and the other by the solenoid plunger that blocks the strike's release.

Low voltage for electric strike operation is obtained by using a transformer, which steps down the normal 115-volt ac power to 12, 16,

24 or other lower voltage. For this operation, three items must be specified: input voltage (usually 115 volts); output voltage (12, 16, or 24 volts); and capacity of the transformer, measured in volt-amps.

Skimping on the capacity of the transformer to save a few dollars will not provide adequate power for the door release. Adams Rite electric strikes for intermittent duty models draw less than 1 amp (regardless of duty) and use a 4602 current limiter, which stores electrical energy for high-use periods.

The wire must carry the electrical power from the transformer through the actuating switch (or switches) to the door release. It must be large enough to minimize frictional line losses and deliver most of the output from the transformer to the door release. For example, a small-diameter garden hose won't provide a full flow of water from the nozzle, particularly if it's a long run. Neither will an undersized wire carry the full current.

When you suspect insufficient electrical power in a weak door release, simply measure the voltage at the door release while the unit is activated. If the voltage is below that specified on the hardware schedule, the problem is in the circuit—probably an under-capacity transformer if the current length is short. A long run might indicate both a transformer and wire problem.

Questions and Answers

How Do You Define Intermittent or Continuous Duty?

When there are only short periods of time during which the switch will be closed and the coil energized, the duty is classified as continuous.

What is the Electrical Voltage Source?

For the majority of electric strikes, 115-ac volt, 60-cycle alternating current is the power source. Unless there are specific customer demands to do otherwise, it is recommended that the 115-volt, 60-cycle source be stepped down to a 24-volt, 60-cycle source using the Adams Rite 4605 transformer. Why 24 volts? There are two reasons. First, at 24 volts there are few safety problems. Second, popular low-voltage replacement transformers are readily available at any electrical supply house. (*Caution:* Make sure any replacement transformer has minimum rating of 20 volts.)

SHOULD THE STRIKE BE AUDIBLE OR SILENT?

First, understand what causes the strike to be audible or silent. Alternating current changes direction 60 times per second. The noise you hear in the audible unit is that very brief period of time during which the solenoid plunger is released from the pole piece as the current builds back up to a peak. This is why a continuous-duty, alternating current system is not recommended. The solenoid simply beats itself to death. By contrast, dc current flows in one direction, and when the coil is energized the plunger remains seated until the circuit is broken. Silent operation can be achieved in an ac circuit by specifying an Adams Rite 4603 rectifier be installed between the transformer secondary and the solenoid coil, which then sees only dc current.

WHAT ABOUT CURRENT DRAW?

The Adams Rite Electric Strike combines standard components that provide the maximum mechanical force necessary to do the job. To the overwhelming majority of intermittent-duty applications, the current draw for this heavy-duty performance poses no problem. However, there are applications where, because of sensitive components somewhere else in the electrical system, a low maximum amount of current flow can be tolerated. In this case, specific hardware is used.

You can use specially wound coils to compromise the mechanical force range through which the strike gives peak performance. This means substituting a solenoid that meets the current draw requirements but doesn't have the strong plunger "pull" of the high-current solenoid. In most instances, customer's requirements have been satisfactorily met with standard available parts without the added expense of specially wound coils.

WHAT IS SURGE CURRENT?

Surge current is the momentary high draw necessary to start the plunger moving from its rest position. Considerably less current is required to hold the plunger, the same way it requires more energy to start a freight train moving than it does to keep it moving.

WHAT IS A CURRENT LIMITER?

A *current limiter* is simply a combination of known electrical components wired in such a way as to provide the extra surge of current without damaging effects on other equipment in the circuit. One such combination uses capacitors to store electrical energy in exactly the same way an air reservoir stores pneumatic energy, diodes, resistors of correct value, and switches.

This combination stores electrical energy and, upon demand (closing a switch), provides the solenoid coil extra momentary charge. It does so outside the circuit so that the circuit sees only the current required to hold the coil in position.

Troubleshooting

Accurate checking of an electrical circuit requires the proper tool. Purchase a good 200,000-volt-per-ohm volt-ohm-milliammeter (VOM). Simpson Model 261, one of several on the market, costs about $130. Read the instructions and make some practice runs on simple low-voltage circuits.

Checking Voltage

1. Zero the pointer.

2. Turn off the power to the circuit being measured.

3. Set the function switch to the correct voltage to be measured (+dc or ac).

4. Plug the black test lead into the common (−) jack. Plug the red test lead into the (+) jack.

5. Set the range selector to the proper voltage scale. *Caution:* It is important that the selector be positioned to the nearest scale above the voltage to be measured.

6. Connect the black test lead to the negative side of the circuit and the red lead to the positive side. This is applicable to dc circuit only. Turn power on to circuit to be tested. If the pointer on the VOM moves to the left, the polarity is wrong. Turn the switch function to −dc and turn power back on. Pointer should now swing to the right for proper reading on the dc scale.

7. Turn off the circuit before disconnecting the VOM.

Note: For an ac circuit, connections are the same, except you don't have to worry about polarity.

Checking DC Current

1. Zero the pointer.

2. Turn off the power to the circuit being measured.

3. Connect the black test lead to the −10-amp jack and the red test lead to the +10-amp jack.

4. Set the range selector to 10 amps.

5. Open the circuit to be measured by, for example, disconnecting the wire that goes to one side of the solenoid. Connect the meter in series. Hook the black lead to one of the disconnected wires and the red lead to the other wire.

6. Turn the power on to the circuit and observe the meter. If the pointer moves to the left, reverse the leads in the −10-amp and +10-amp jacks.

7. Turn power back on to the circuit and read amperage on dc scale.

8. Turn the power off before disconnecting the VOM.

Checking Line Drop

Measure line drop by comparing voltage readings at the source (the transformer's secondary or output side) with the reading at the strike connection.

Locating Shorts

The VOM is the most reliable instrument for detecting a short. This is accomplished by setting up the VOM to measure resistance.

1. Set the range switch at position Rx1.

2. Set the function switch at + dc.

3. Connect the black test lead to the common negative jack and the red test lead to the positive jack.

4. Zero the pointer by shorting test leads together.

5. Connect the other ends of the test lead across the resistance to be measured. For a solenoid, connect one end of test lead to one coil terminal and the other to the other terminal.

6. Watch the meter. If there is no movement of the pointer, the resistance being measured is open. If the pointer moves to the peg on the right-hand side of the scale, the resistance being measured is shorted closed. If you get a reading in between these two extremes, there is probably no problem with the solenoid.

Strike Will Not Activate After Installation

1. Check fuse or circuit breaker supplying system.

2. Check that all wiring connections are securely made. When wire nuts are used, be sure that both wires are twisted together.

3. Check the solenoid coil rated voltage (as shown on coil label) to make sure it corresponds to the output side of the transformer within plus or minus 10 percent.

4. Using the VOM, check the voltage at the secondary (output) side of the transformer.

5. Using the VOM, check the voltage at the solenoid to make sure there are no broken wires, bad rectifiers, or bad connections.

6. Check the coil for a short.

Strike Will Not Activate After Use

1. Check the fuse or circuit breaker supplying system.

2. Make sure you have a transformer. One shot of 115 ac volts will ruin the coil.

3. Make sure the rated voltage of the transformer and the rated voltage of the coil correspond with plus or minus 10 percent.

4. Check the coil for a short.

Overheating

If transformer overheats, proceed as follows.

1. Make sure the rated voltage of the transformer and the rated voltage of the coil correspond within plus or minus 10 percent.

2. Make sure the volt-amp rating is adequate. We recommend a minimum of 40 to 20 volts.

If rectifier overheats, proceed as follows.

1. The rectifier might be wired wrong, which means the overheating is a temporary situation because it burns out.

2. There might also be too many solenoids supplied by a single rectifier, and more current is being pulled through than the diodes can
handle.

If solenoid overheats, proceed as follows.

1. First, define overheating. The coils used by Adams Rite have a
temperature rise rating of 65°C (149°F) above ambient. However,
all 7800 Series continuous-duty units should run 200°F or less in a
72°F environment.

2. The vast majority of these intermittent-duty units never see the
kind of use that brings the coil to maximum rating. If a coil gets
extremely hot on very short pulses at two- or three-second intervals, either the wrong coil or the wrong transformer output is being
used. The same is basically true for continuous-duty coils. If the
coil temperature exceeds the ratings, it has to be because the coil
voltage or the transformer are improperly coordinated.

3. Set the meter up as if testing for a short and obtain the exact resistance.

Figures 16.2 through 16.13 on the following pages are installation
instructions for several models of Adams Rite electric strikes.

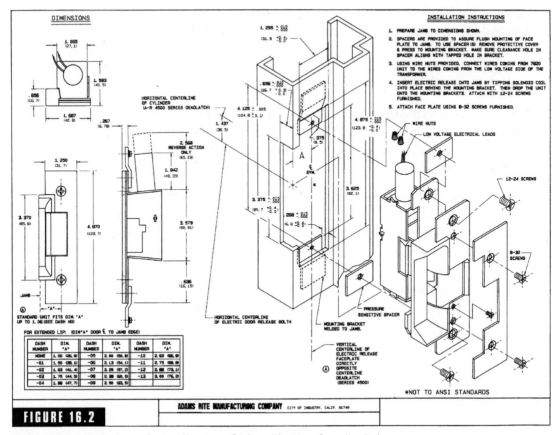

ADAMS RITE MANUFACTURING COMPANY CITY OF INDUSTRY, CALIF. 91749

FIGURE 16.2

Model 7800 electric door release. *(Courtesy of Adams Rite Manufacturing Co.)*

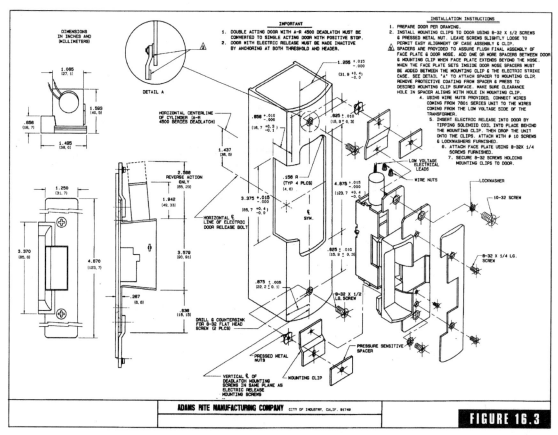

Model 7801 electric door release. *(Courtesy of Adams Rite Manufacturing Co.)*

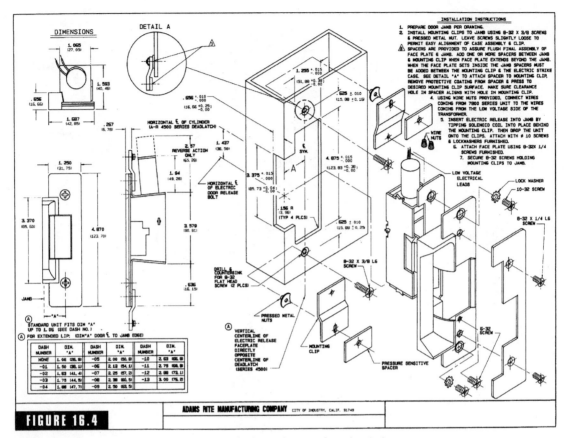

FIGURE 16.4

Model 7810 electric door release. *(Courtesy of Adams Rite Manufacturing Co.)*

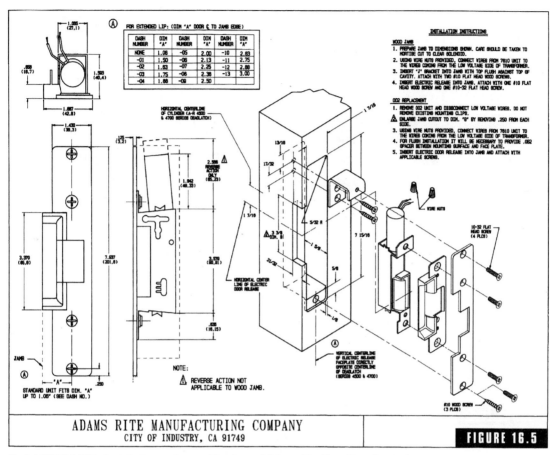

ADAMS RITE MANUFACTURING COMPANY
CITY OF INDUSTRY, CA 91749

FIGURE 16.5

Model 7820 ANSI electric door release. *(Courtesy of Adams Rite Manufacturing Co.)*

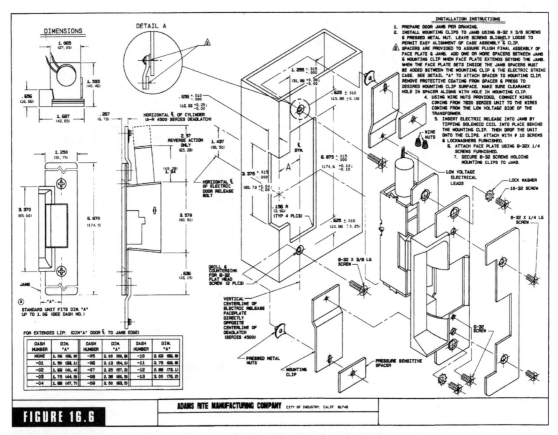

Model 7830 electric door release. *(Courtesy of Adams Rite Manufacturing Co.)*

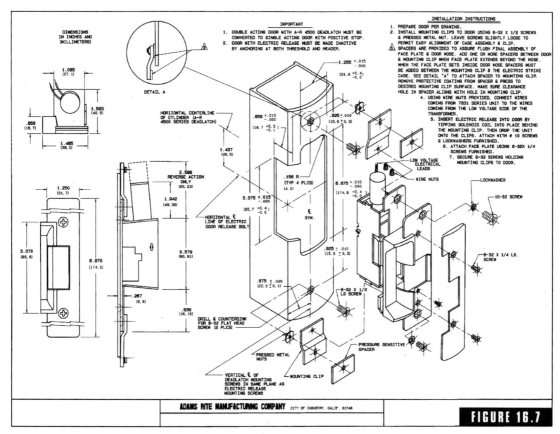

Model 7831 electric door release. *(Courtesy of Adams Rite Manufacturing Co.)*

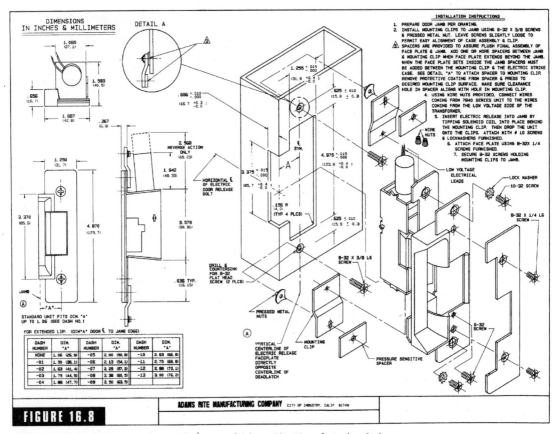

FIGURE 16.8

Model 7840 electric door release. *(Courtesy of Adams Rite Manufacturing Co.)*

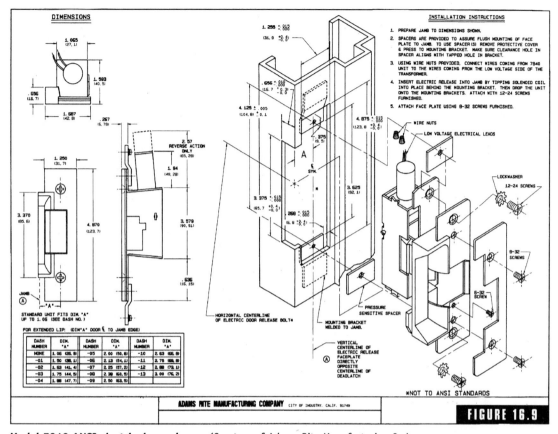

Model 7840 ANSI electric door release. *(Courtesy of Adams Rite Manufacturing Co.)*

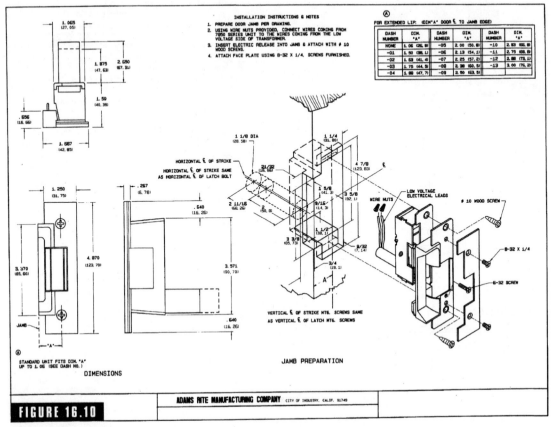

INSTALLATION INSTRUCTIONS & NOTES
1. PREPARE DOOR JAMB PER DRAWING.
2. USING WIRE NUTS PROVIDED, CONNECT WIRES COMING FROM 7850 SERIES UNIT TO THE WIRES COMING FROM THE LOW VOLTAGE SIDE OF TRANSFORMER.
3. INSERT ELECTRIC RELEASE INTO JAMB & ATTACH WITH # 10 WOOD SCREWS.
4. ATTACH FACE PLATE USING 8-32 X 1/4, SCREWS FURNISHED.

Ⓐ FOR EXTENDED LIP: (DIM "A" DOOR ₵ TO JAMB EDGE)

DASH NUMBER	DIM. "A"	DASH NUMBER	DIM. "A"	DASH NUMBER	DIM. "A"
NONE	1.06 (26.9)	-05	2.00 (50.8)	-10	2.63 (66.8)
-01	1.50 (38.1)	-06	2.13 (54.1)	-11	2.75 (69.9)
-02	1.63 (41.4)	-07	2.25 (57.2)	-12	2.88 (73.1)
-03	1.75 (44.5)	-08	2.38 (60.5)	-13	3.00 (76.2)
-04	1.88 (47.7)	-09	2.50 (63.5)		

JAMB PREPARATION

DIMENSIONS

FIGURE 16.10

ADAMS RITE MANUFACTURING COMPANY CITY OF INDUSTRY, CALIF. 91749

Model 7850 electric door release. *(Courtesy of Adams Rite Manufacturing Co.)*

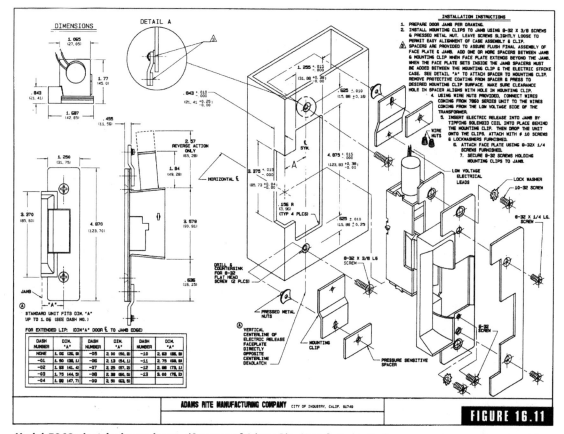

ADAMS RITE MANUFACTURING COMPANY CITY OF INDUSTRY, CALIF. 91749

FIGURE 16.11

Model 7860 electric door release. (*Courtesy of Adams Rite Manufacturing Co.*)

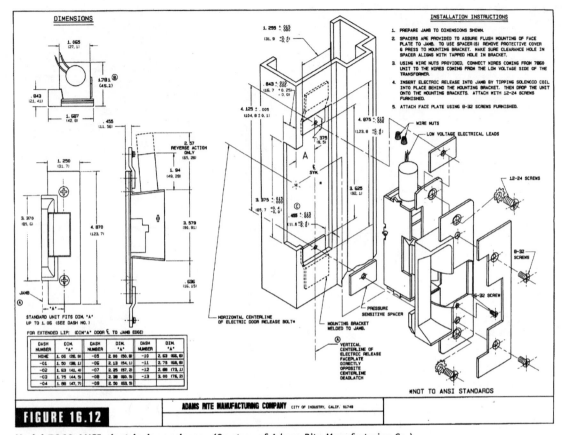

FIGURE 16.12

Model 7860 ANSI electric door release. *(Courtesy of Adams Rite Manufacturing Co.)*

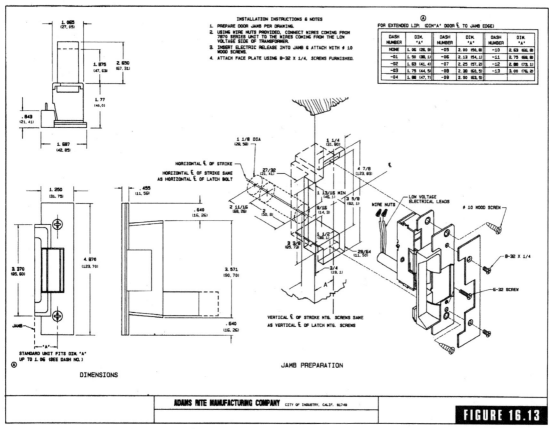

Model 7870 electric door release. *(Courtesy of Adams Rite Manufacturing Co.)*

Key Duplicating Machines

A key duplicating, or key cutting, machine makes keys by simultaneously tracing the pattern of a key and cutting that pattern onto a key blank. The machine includes three basic parts: a pair of small vises; a stylus, or "key guide"; and a cutter wheel. One vise securely holds the key in place; the other holds the blank. The stylus moves along the cuts of the key to guide the cutter in making corresponding cuts into the blank.

Some machines can duplicate only one type of key; others are designed to duplicate a wide variety of keys. This chapter explains how to operate and service several popular key duplicating machines.

Half-Time Key Machine

Manufactured by Precision Products, Inc., the Half-Time key machine is designed to cut two flat keys at a time (Figure 17.1). L-shaped vise handles allow fast seating of all flat keys. The rotating stylus changes to four guide widths: .055, .062, .072, and .088 inch.

Operate the machine as follows.

1. Place the key to be duplicated into the right side vise, securely against the key stop.

QUICK »TIP **If you can afford only one key duplicating machine, make sure it cuts standard cylinder keys. Machines that cut only flat, tubular, or high-security keys generally aren't good choices for a first machine.**

2. Select the proper key blank for duplication. Secure a pair of these keys into the left side vise, against the key stop.

Note: The Half-Time is designed so that the vise jaws need be lightly tightened. Do not overtighten. To release keys, only a quarter turn of the handle is required.

Caution: If the vise spring-loaded handle is forced, the internal stud may be stripped. To place the handle in a convenient position, lift up and rotate it around the post to a comfortable position and let it rest.

3. Turn on the Half-Time.

4. Push the carriage forward to lift the key to the tip of the tracing stylus. Move the carriage left or right to locate the stylus into the first bitting to be duplicated.

5. Push the carriage forward until the stylus collar stops against the stylus block.

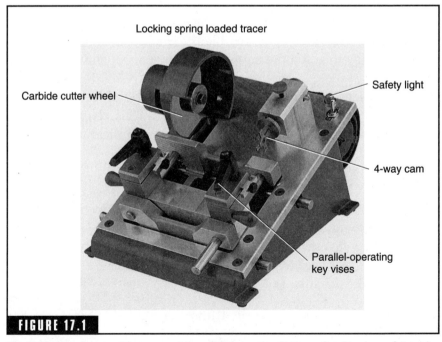

Locking spring loaded tracer

Carbide cutter wheel

Safety light

4-way cam

Parallel-operating key vises

FIGURE 17.1

The Half-Time key machine can cut two flat keys simultaneously. *(Courtesy of Precision Products, Inc.)*

The cutter on the Half-Time is not a side-milling slotter. All carriage movements must be straight in and out when the stylus is engaged with the key. Any lateral movement will cause damage to the solid carbide cutter.

6. Lower the carriage until the stylus is clear of the key. Move the carriage left or right to locate the stylus into the next bitting to be duplicated. Push the carriage forward until the collar stops against the stylus block.

7. Repeat Step 6 until all bits of the key have been duplicated onto the pair of blanks.

8. Allow the carriage to rest at the bottom of its stroke.

9. Inspect the pair of new keys. If there is any material left in a bitting, locate that bit under the cutter and gently push forward until the collar stops against the block. If there is no excess material, the pair of new keys are completed.

10. Turn off the machine.

11. Remove the pair of keys.

12. Remove any burring on the side of the bottom key with a small file or deburring brush. The top key will not have any burring on it.

13. Repeat Steps 6 through 12 to duplicate as many new keys as needed.

To make adjustments in the depths of the bits, the stop collar has been indexed with increments of .001 inch. To make an adjustment in the depth of cuts, loosen the two set screws on the stylus collar. Rotate the collar clockwise to make the cuts shallower. Rotate the collar counterclockwise to deepen the cuts. To measure the amount of adjustment, rotate and count the increments on the collar against the index centered on the stylus block.

To check for proper cutter height against the stylus, secure the same type key blank in each vise.

> **TRADE SECRET**
>
> To use a file to deburr a key, hold the key by the bow with the cuts on top of the blade leaning slightly away from you with the key's tip pointing downward at about a 90-degree angle. Using long strokes, gently file across the sides and tops of the cuts, moving from bow to tip. Then twist your wrist so that the key cuts are on top of the blade and the unfiled side of the cuts are leaning slightly toward you. Gently file the cuts from that side also. Remember that you're only removing burrs and slightly rounding the tops of the cuts. (Slightly rounded tips allow the key to slide in and out of the lock easier than do sharp points.) Don't file into the bottom of any cut.

Slide the carriage forward until the stylus engages the key blank and is stopped against the block.

Rotate the cutter slowly by hand. It should make light contact with the blank under it. If the cutter will not rotate, the stylus is too deep. If it turns freely, it is too shallow. Make corrections by rotating the stop collar on the stylus, then retighten the set screws.

Maintenance

- Keep the Half-Time free of excess dirt, dust, and chip debris.

- Occasionally lubricate bearing surfaces with a very light amount of oil, then wipe off with a clean dry cloth. The motor is a sealed bearing type and requires no lubrication.

- Inspect all screws and keep them snug.

Borkey 986

Distributed by DiMark International, the Borkey model 986 is a semi-automatic key machine designed to cut cylinder keys (Figure 17.2). Operate the machine in the following way.

1. Place the machine on a strong, stable workstand or bench. Bolting isn't necessary. Check the current on your power supply, which

- If the new keys don't operate the lock, check the depths of the cuts. Make corrections by adjusting the stop collar. **TROUBLE-SHOOTING**

- If the carriage movements feel binding or sluggish, check the hardened rods for cleanliness. Also, if the Half-Time has been bolted down to the work surface, release the pressure from each securing screw until the binding has been released. The securing screws must have balanced pressure.

- If the vise jaws do not slide up and down smoothly, check under the top jaw against the beating post for cleanliness. Apply a very light coat of oil, then wipe off with a clean dry cloth.

- When the cutter blade becomes dull, remove it with two open-end wrenches and have it sharpened. When it is replaced, make adjustments to zero the stylus to the cutter. *Note:* The blade securing nut is reverse threaded.

must be two-phase ac, and compare with that shown on the machine. Unplug the machine before undertaking any repairs, removing housing, or moving the machine. The hand lever (Figure 17.3) for moving the slide car-

riage is on top of the machine body. Loosen the screw and the hand lever can be turned to any working position.

2. Firmly fasten the key in left-hand vise, with shoulder about 2 mm from the vise side (Figure 17.4). Use the alignment gauge lever to line up accurately. Place the key blank in the same manner into the right-hand vise. Tighten down. Disengage the alignment gauge levers.

   Note: When cutting very small keys, place the delivered pins behind the key and the blank. To prevent the key and blank from slipping during the duplicating process, insert small pins into the keyway grooves or place the bolts, mounted on left side of vises, below the bows.

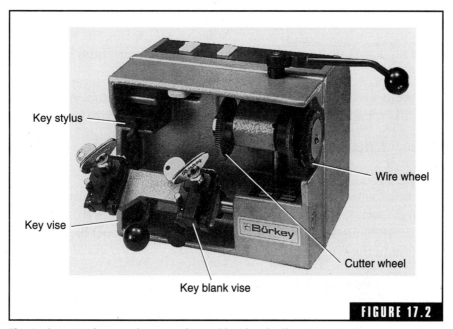

FIGURE 17.2

The Borkey 986 is a semi-automatic machine for duplicating cylinder and cross keys.
(Courtesy of DiMark International)

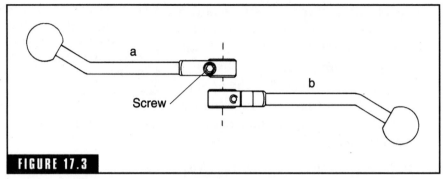

FIGURE 17.3

Loosen the screw to turn the hand lever. *(Courtesy of DiMark International)*

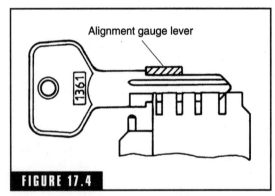

FIGURE 17.4

Engage the feeler on side of key near shoulder. *(Courtesy of DiMark International)*

3. Turn the machine on. You should see a red light. Hold the carriage knob with your left hand. Loosen the security device on the right side below the slide carriage by pulling out the bolt. Gently engage the feeler on side of key near shoulder. Start cutting from left to right using the lever on right side of the machine.

Note: Special springs ensure correct pressure against the cutter, obviating need to press by hand.

4. Return the lever and slide carriage into start position, remove the cut key, and pass it on a wire brush to remove swarf.

Adjustments

CUTTING KEYS WITHOUT SHOULDERS

By using the flat bars (without cutout sections) that are delivered with the accessories, shoulderless keys can be aligned at the tip of the key (Figure 17.5). Depending on the length of the key, the flat bars are to be inserted in the left or right slots of the vises.

CUTTING CROSS KEYS (100 MM)

Depending on the length of cross key shoulder, insert the flat bars with cutout section (Figure 17.6) on top into the exterior or interior left slot of the vises. The edges of the cutout section are used as stops (Figure 17.7), and depending on the position of the key shoulder, they are lifted or pressed down or up. After fastening the key and blank in the vises, the flat bars are pushed back.

It's important that both key and blank are always fastened in the vises with the same rip. Cross keys with ring or shoulder are to be aligned at the left outside of the vises (Figure 17.8). The upper part of the vise must be protected against moving by placing the flat bars into the right slot of the vises.

CHECKING THE CUTTING DEPTH

Place check-up keys into the vises and tighten down. Bring slide carriage forward to feeler and cutter. Feeler (#2 in Figure 17.9) and cutter must now equally touch the edges of the check-up keys.

READJUSTING CUTTING DEPTH

Loosen nut (#8 in Figure 17.9) and threaded pin (#3 in Figure 17.9) of the feeler. Adjust cutting depth by turning the adjustment screw (#1 in Figure 17.9) to the right to withdraw the feeler or to the left to advance the feeler. Tighten threaded pin and nut again.

CHECKING LATERAL DISTANCE

Place check-up keys into the vises. Push them against the left side of the vises and tighten down.

ALIGNMENT GAUGE LEVERS

Both gauge levers must now touch the shoulders of the check-up keys equally. To readjust, loosen screws (#6 of Figure 17.10) of one of the

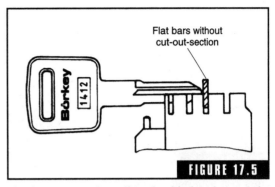

FIGURE 17.5

Flat bars are used to align shoulderless keys at the shoulder. *(Courtesy of DiMark International)*

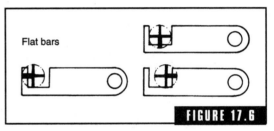

FIGURE 17.6

Insert the flat bars with cutout section. *(Courtesy of DiMark International)*

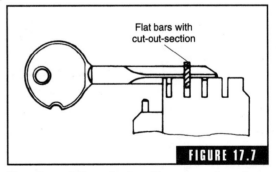

FIGURE 17.7

The edges of the cutout section are used as stops. *(Courtesy of DiMark International)*

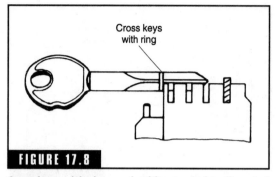

FIGURE 17.8

Cross keys with ring or shoulder are to be aligned at the shoulder. *(Courtesy of DiMark International)*

gauge levers. Push gauge lever against shoulder of check-up key and tighten down screw (#6 of Figure 17.10) again.

DISTANCE FEELER AND CUTTER

Bring slide carriage forward to feeler and cutter. Feeler and cutter must equally touch the cut of the check-up keys. To readjust, loosen screw (#7 of Figure 17.10) of feeler base. Move feeler base until feeler and cutter equally touch the cut of the check-up keys. Tighten screw (#7 of Fig. 17-10) again.

To change the cutter, switch off the machine. Unscrew the cutter nut, turning to the right. Retain the spindle by using the 6 millimeter bar.

Borkey 954 Rexa 3/CD

Distributed by DiMark International, the Borkey 954 Rexa 3/CD (Figure 17.11) precisely duplicates a variety of key types.

The carriage is released by lowering slightly and pulling out on the trigger release below the vises and carriage. After cutting the key, it is not necessary to pull out the release to lock the carriage back down. It will automatically lock down.

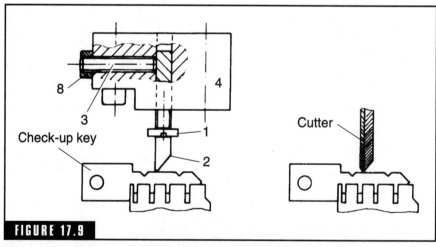

FIGURE 17.9

Place check-up keys into the vises. *(Courtesy of DiMark International)*

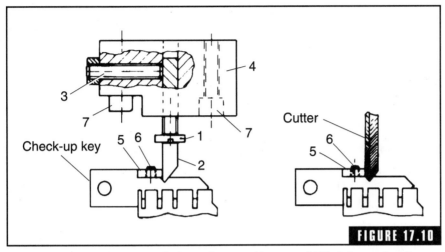

FIGURE 17.10

Bring slide carriage forward to feeler and cutter. *(Courtesy of DiMark International)*

When releasing the carriage, hold it firmly or the spring tension will cause the carriage to fly forward, which will damage the vises, feeler, and cutter. Always return the top shoulder alignment gauge to the rear before bringing the carriage assembly into the cutting position. If the cutter hits the alignment gauge lever, it might knock out a cutter tooth.

Cutting a Key

1. Select either the front or rear sets of vises. This depends on whether keys can be gripped flat on the bottom of the vises or can ride on their milling along the top of the front set of vises, or whether the keys should be gripped on a center milling. In the latter case, use the rear jaws.

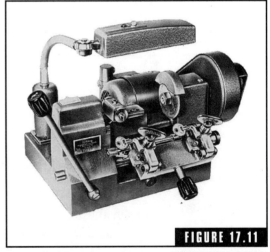

FIGURE 17.11

The Borkey 954 Rexa 3/CD is simple to use and duplicates keys accurately. *(Courtesy of DiMark International)*

2. Place the key in the left vise and the blank in the right vise. The key may be gauged by the top shoulder using the alignment gauge, by the bottom shoulder using the lower side of the vise, or by the tip using the slots in the vise and the flat tip gauges provided.

For double-sided keys, the milling or ridges of the key may rest on the top of the vise, but not at the bottom of the vise. The Rexa vises grip keys that have a bare minimum to grasp.

3. Pull down the carriage slightly, holding the carriage firmly as the trigger release is pulled out. Turn on the machine and, using the lever handle to move the carriage, begin cutting from the bow of the key to the tip. Do not cut over the tip. Reverse back to the bow.

4. Pull the carriage down to lock it in place, and turn the machine off. The entire process of cutting a key takes only a few seconds.

Changing the Cutter

1. Remove the cutter guard. Using the wrench provided, turn the cutter nut toward you in the direction of the arrow on the cutter. Stabilize the cutter axle by inserting the round rod provided into the hole which is drilled in the cutter axle to the left of the belt guard.

2. Remove the cutter nut and the cutter. When placing the new cutter on the machine, remember to note the direction indicated on the side of the cutter. The cutter will be ruined if placed on the shaft in the wrong direction.

Maintenance

The Rexa should be maintained regularly to guarantee the long life for which it was designed. Maintenance includes cleaning the filings from the machine with a soft brush and oiling certain areas with a 20–30 W motor oil, not with a cleaner like LPS or WD-40. Oil the following areas regularly.

- On the top of the cutter shaft at the V grooves, next to the belt guard and the cutter.

- Along the main carriage axle shaft at all exposed points, moving the lever to the right and left to bathe the shaft in oil. (Then lightly wipe with a cloth to remove excess oil.) At the oil cup at the left side of the machine, near the main axle shaft.

- On the alignment gauge axle where it rides in the casting.

- Under the wing nuts where the pressure washers are located, and along the threaded posts on which the wing nuts tighten. (This keeps the vises gripping well.)

Framon DBM-1 Flat Key Machine

Manufactured by Framon Mfg. Co., Inc., the DBM-1 key machine (Figure 17.12) is designed to duplicate flat keys. Use the machine as follows.

1. Set all keys from the tip for spacing.

2. Insert the key in the right-hand vise, with the tip of the blank protruding slightly beyond the left side of the vise (Figure 17.13). This position allows cutting of tip guide on blank, if blank tip can be cut without cutting vise.

3. Push the guide shaft rearward and lock into this position by tightening the locking knob (Figure 17.14). This relieves the spring pressure so tip setting is easier. Lift the yoke and set the tip of the key against the right side of the guide. While holding this position, insert the blank and set the tip of the blank against the right side of the cutter (Figure 17.15). This procedure assures proper spacing.

4. Release the guide by loosening the locking knob, and key is ready to be cut.

5. Set the cut in the key against the guide and lift the yoke into the cutter to make the cut (Figure 17.16). Lower the yoke and repeat for the next cut. Follow this procedure until all cuts (including throat cut) are made and the key is complete. All cuts should be made with a straight in motion. This will ensure clean square cuts.

You will notice that there is no side play in the guide assembly, so all cuts on

FIGURE 17.12

The DBM-1 is designed to accurately duplicate flat keys. *(Courtesy of Framon Manufacturing Co., Inc.)*

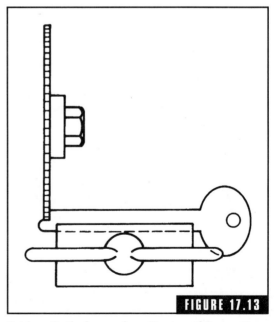

FIGURE 17.13

Set keys to tip for spacing. *(Courtesy of Framon Manufacturing Co., Inc.)*

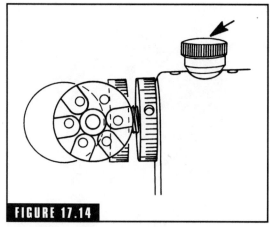

FIGURE 17.14

Push guide shaft rearward. *(Courtesy of Framon Manufacturing Co., Inc.)*

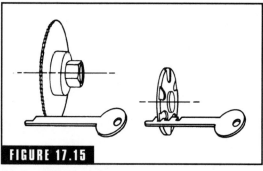

FIGURE 17.15

Set tip of blank against right side of cutter. *(Courtesy of Framon Manufacturing Co., Inc.)*

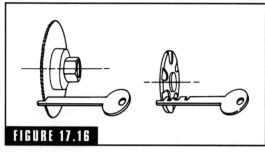

FIGURE 17.16

Set cut in pattern key against guide. *(Courtesy of Framon Manufacturing Co., Inc.)*

the duplicate key will be the same width as the key.

Adjustments

SPACING

With tip setting for spacing, there is no problem with improper spacing.

CHECK DEPTH SETTINGS

Use two blanks that are the same and draw the blank against the cutter guide. If depth adjustments are needed, simply loosen the set screw on the depth ring and adjust the ring until the cutter barely touches the blank. To make cuts deeper, rotate the depth ring counterclockwise. To make cuts shallower, rotate the ring clockwise. Tighten the set screw after adjustment is made, but do not overtighten.

Another way to check depth is to make one cut on the duplicate key and check the depth cut on both the key and the duplicate key. For example, if the cut on the duplicate key is .003 inch deeper than the cut on the key, loosen the set screw on the depth ring, rotate the ring .003 inch clockwise, and tighten the set screw. *Note:* Calibrations on the depth ring are in increments of .001 inch.

CHECK CUTTER GUIDE SETTING

The guide must be set to the same width of the cutter used. The DBM-1 is supplied with one .045-inch-width cutter. This is the best width for general work. Cutter widths of .035, .055, .066, and .088 inch are available if needed. A cutter width of .100 (LeFebure) can be obtained by using an .045- and an .055-inch at the same time. All of these cutters are solid carbide.

To set the guide, simply loosen the cap screw. Rotate the guide to the cutter width and tighten the cap screw. The screw-in guide shaft will align the guide. No adjustment is required when changing guide settings.

Maintenance

The yoke rod, guide shaft, and vise studs should be lubricated sparingly using very fine oil. Do not use motor oil. Wipe off all excess oil. To lubricate the guide shaft, unscrew the locking knob and put one or two drops of oil in the opening, then replace the knob.

On all other parts, cleanliness is the best maintenance.

Ilco Unican Model .023 Key Machine

Manufactured by Ilco Unican Corporation, the model .023 key machine (Figure 17.17) is designed to duplicate a variety of cylinder keys.

Setup

1. Place the machine on a level, sturdy surface before cutting keys. Unlatch the cover and lift to a completely open position. Remove the hook from the eye on the left side of the carriage (Figure 17.18).

2. Insert the appropriate plug into an available power supply. The machine operates on 110 volts (220-volt optional) or 12 dc volts, with no other attachments or converter required. The machine is equipped with cords for both ac or dc application and will work equally well from either power source. It automatically converts from one to the other without touching any switches. If both plugs are installed in separate receptacles at the same time, the power pack will draw current from the strongest source only and will not cause damage to the machine.

   The motor is protected against overload by a circuit breaker type starting switch. To reset this switch, simply depress the start button after a delay of a few seconds.

Transportation

1. Disengage the electrical cord from the power source and wrap the cord on the metal angles provided in the cover.

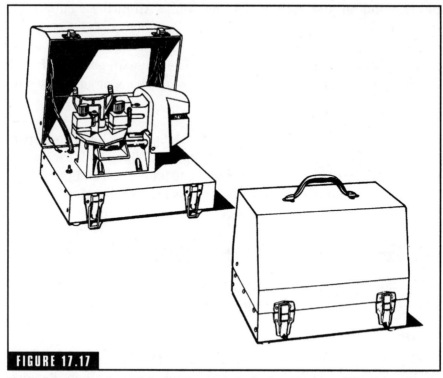

FIGURE 17.17

The Model .023 is a manual dual-voltage key duplicator. *(Courtesy of Ilco Unican Corp.)*

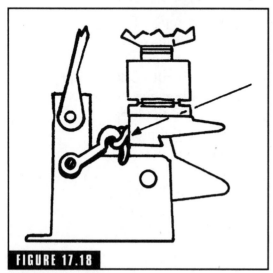

FIGURE 17.18

Remove the hook from the eye. *(Courtesy of Ilco Unican Corp.)*

2. Slide the carriage to the extreme left position and engage the hook and eye.

Note: For transportation, the hook and eye must be secure to prevent possible damage to the machine.

3. Close the cover and engage both latches.

General Instructions

- Do not make adjustments on this machine. It has been adjusted and thoroughly tested at the factory.

- Never work on this or any machine without disconnecting the power cord.

- Do not attempt to cut keys until you have read the operating instructions and are sure that you understand the mechanism and its operation.

- Wear eye protection when operating the machine.

- Keep the carriage spindle clean of chips and lightly lubricated with a thin film of 3-in-1 or light machine oil. Keep the cutter shaft bearings well lubricated using the oil cup.

- Do not use pliers to tighten the wing nuts. They are designed to give adequate pressure when tightened by hand.

- Take proper care of the cylinder key duplicating cutter. Cutters can be dulled or broken by improper handling. They are shipped in perfect condition and will last a long time if handled with reasonable care. Accurate duplication requires proper seating of key and blanks in four-way jaws. Keep jaws and machine free from chips. Brush off regularly. The accumulation of dirt and chips shortens the life of the machine and reduces its accuracy.

- Periodically remove the top jaws of each vise to check the springs and to clean the jaw thoroughly. After doing so, apply a few drops of light machine oil or a touch of grease on the four vertical surfaces that guide the top jaw.

- When duplicating a key, avoid an irregular jerk in the movement of the carriage. Practice a smooth, steady motion, using both hands on the carriage and holding it behind the key clamps.

- Apply the same degree of pressure each time you duplicate a key. Excessive pressure may cause over-cutting; too light pressure will result in under-cutting. Practice on a few keys to learn to apply a uniform pressure to the carriage.

- The motor speed varies with the force of the cutter. This is normal for any battery-operated motor. Too much pressure on the cutter will cause the motor to draw excessive current and trip the circuit breaker.

- After removing key from clamp, remove any burrs that remain on the edge of the cut surface by drawing lightly through the deburring brush.

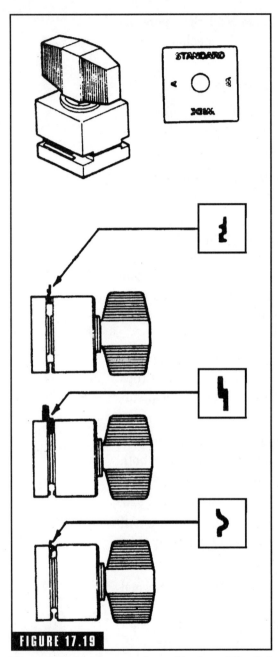

FIGURE 17.19

The machine has four-way jaws. *(Courtesy of Ilco Unican Corp.)*

Selecting Jaw Position

The .023 is equipped with four-way jaws that do not require adapters (Figure 17.19). The jaw positions are labeled Standard, Wide, A, and W.

- Standard width is used on most commercial keys and house keys. Examples include keys made by Dominion, Schlage, and Weiser.

- Wide width is used on wide blade large keys, and for some European locks that are cut on both sides where the center milling of the key can rest on the top of the jaw. Examples include keys made by Ford and Chicago.

- The A-width jaw is for duplicating Schlage "A" double-sided keys, some foreign automobile keys, and other keys that require a firm grip.

- The W-width jaw is for duplicating Schlage "W" double-sided keys. The center of the key is held on ridge in jaw.

With experience, you'll find many other uses for the various jaw positions.

Changing Jaw Positions

1. Turn the wing nut at least seven complete turns counterclockwise (Figure 17.20).

2. Place your fingers in the recessed holes provided, then lift upward and rotate until the desired position is reached. Be sure to raise the lower jaw enough to clear its seat.

Duplicating Regular Cylinder Keys

1. Select the proper key blank.

2. Make sure the machine's jaws are in the required position.

3. Place the blank in the right-hand jaw (Figure 17.21). Using the wing nut, lightly clamp the blank in place. Swing the shoulder guide over the rest on the blank. With the wing nut loose enough, slide the blank using your thumb. Push on the head of the blank until the shoulder abuts the guide. Use your index finger to press down the tip of the blank, making sure the blank is seated in the jaw. Tighten the wing nut securely. Swing the shoulder back out of the way.

4. Insert the key in the left jaw in the same manner.

Duplicating Irregular Keys

The majority of the keys presented for duplication are easily cut. The four-way jaws simplify the job of holding irregularly shaped keys such as Ford, Schlage double-sided, etc. (Figure 17.22). The following instructions will help you with the duplication of most irregular cylinder keys.

Duplicating Ford double-sided, Best, Falcon, and other keys without shoulders:

1. Rotate the jaws to Standard or Wide, as required by the size of the key.

2. Place the key blank in the right-hand jaw. The blank should be located in the jaw so the tip of the blank is parallel with the back portion of the jaw.

3. Move the carriage to the extreme left until the tip of the key abuts the key gauge. Maintaining this position, place the key in the left

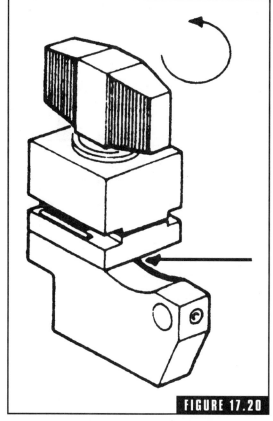

FIGURE 17.20

Turn wing nut counterclockwise. *(Courtesy of Ilco Unican Corp.)*

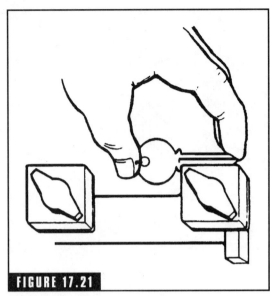

FIGURE 17.21

Place the key blank in the right-hand jaw. *(Courtesy of Ilco Unican Corp.)*

vise and slide the key until it abuts the opposite end of the key gauge.

4. Tighten keys securely and return the key gauge to the upright position.

5. Turn the machine on and proceed as outlined in duplication of regular keys.

6. If the key is cut on two sides, turn it over and duplicate the reverse side. For Ford keys and most foreign double-sided keys, only the blank needs to be turned over because the cuts are the same on both sides.

Note: The aforementioned procedures can also be used in duplicating broken keys that do not have a shoulder to gauge from.

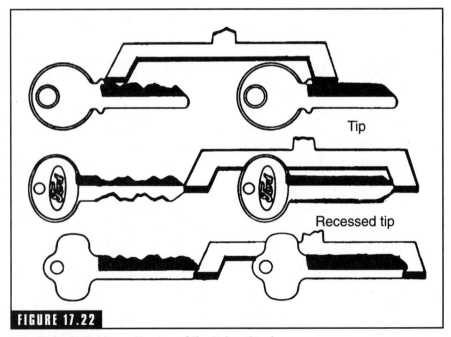

Tip

Recessed tip

FIGURE 17.22

Irregularly shaped keys. *(Courtesy of Ilco Unican Corp.)*

Duplicating Chicago double-sided keys:

1. Set the jaws to Wide or another position that provides a secure grip. Some of the less popular Chicago keys (41N, 41FD, etc.) can be secured firmly in the A or W jaw position.

2. Proceed as for regular keys by using the shoulder guide to gauge the shoulders, although the jaws provide a secure grip.

Duplicating Chicago double-sided keys (Wide):

1. Set the jaws to Wide or another position as needed to provide a secure grip.

2. Proceed as for regular keys by using the shoulder guide to gauge the shoulders.

3. Duplicate as for regular keys. Turn over to duplicate the reverse side.

4. Remove the finished key and deburr.

Duplicating Schlage double-sided keys:

1. Rotate the jaw to position A or W as required.

2. When inserting the key in the jaws, the shoulder of the key should abut the jaw (Figure 17.23), because the shoulder guide cannot be used in this case.

3. After cutting one side, turn the key and blank over to cut the other side.

Maintenance

Clean out the vises continually. They must be kept free of cuttings, dirt, or any foreign matter at all times. Keep a small paint brush handy for this purpose. Occasionally lubricate with grease the wing nut studs and the four inner surfaces of the vise clamps that align the top and bottom portions. Wipe the carriage spindle with 3-in-1 or light oil to clean and lubricate.

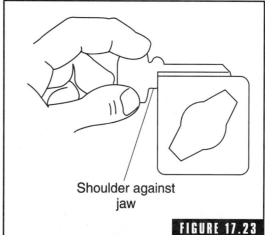

Shoulder against jaw

FIGURE 17.23

Abut shoulder of key against jaw. *(Courtesy of Ilco Unican Corp.)*

A few drops of medium lubricating oil once a month are sufficient for the oil cup in the cutter shaft. One or two drops of 3-in-1 or light machine oil once a month are sufficient for the oil cups on the motor.

Belt tension is automatically maintained by the freely suspended motor. Under normal conditions it needs no attention. To replace the belt, simply lift up the motor; the belt will be free to remove from the pulleys. After replacing the belt, make sure that the motor mounting bracket is free to move on its pivot.

Cutter replacement is necessary when the blank is being worn, rather than cut, away. The copying dog requires frequent adjustment when inaccurate cutting occurs. New cutters are available for prompt supply. It is wise to keep one or two extra cutters on hand at all times. As each is put on the machine, order a replacement.

The copying dog is set and adjusted perfectly before the machine leaves the factory, and no further adjustments should be necessary. However, as a cutter becomes worn or is replaced by a new cutter, it will be necessary to reset the copying dog.

To reset the copying dog, loosen the top screw and place a blank key into each of the jaws. Use two identical blanks. Turn the cutter by hand in the cutting direction. If the rotary cutter bites into the blank, turn the adjusting screw in front to advance the copying dog and move the carriage away from the cutter. If the milling cutter does not touch the blank, turn the adjusting screw in the opposite direction. Properly adjusted, the milling cutter should just graze the key blank. After adjusting, tighten the set screws. The spacing adjustment is fixed and requires no attention.

Power supply

The solid state power supply, located within the machine base, normally doesn't need servicing. If, however, an electrical failure should occur or the machine power supply is greater than required, a self-resetting circuit breaker located in the power supply will trip the ac circuit to protect the power transformer. The breaker will self-reset after a few seconds and start the motor unless the start switch is turned off immediately. Do not touch any rotating parts while the current is tripped.

Suspected defects in the power supply should be inspected only by qualified service people. Machines under warranty should be returned to the factory for examination and corrective action.

Ilco Unican 018 Lever-Operated Key Machine

Manufactured by Ilco Unican Corporation, the model 018 Lever-Operated key machine is a precision-crafted, semi-automatic machine designed to duplicate a wide variety of cylinder keys.

The machine comes with an accessory pack that consists of test keys, Allen wrenches, straight wires, a Ford shoulder adapter, and a screwdriver (Figure 17.24). The test keys are used for adjusting cutter to stylus. Allen wrenches are used for making adjustments on the machine and for performing periodic maintenance. Straight wires raise narrow keys requiring deep cuts in the vise and keep special keys from tilting in the vise. The Ford shoulder adapter allows use of gooseneck gauge on Ford keys.

Some features of the 018 include a manual switch to activate the cutting wheel and the wire brush, reversible vises for accommodating various kinds of keys and blanks, and a gooseneck gauge for aligning

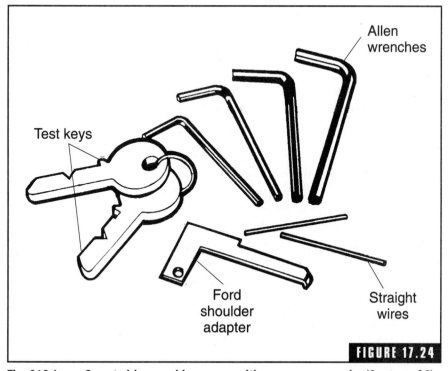

Allen wrenches

Test keys

Ford shoulder adapter

Straight wires

FIGURE 17.24

The 018 Lever-Operated key machine comes with an accessory pack. *(Courtesy of Ilco Unican Corp.)*

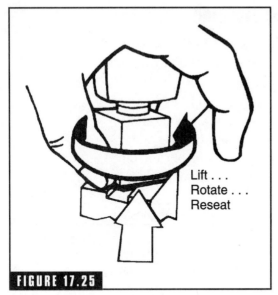

Lift . . .
Rotate . . .
Reseat

FIGURE 17.25

Set the reversible vises. *(Courtesy of Ilco Unican Corp.)*

the key with the blank. It is also equipped with a safety switch that must be disengaged for the machine to operate.

Operating Instructions

1. To duplicate keys with the 018, first select the proper key blank.

2. Set the reversible vises to the proper positions. The vise assemblies rotate to accommodate various types of keys. To rotate a vise, loosen the wing nut three or four turns from the closed position. Using the thumb and forefinger, grasp the bottom section of the vise. Lift this section up and free of the carriage. Rotate the vise assembly one-half turn and reseat lower section into groove of carriage (Figure 17.25).

   Notice the arrow on the top of each vise. Both arrows should always be pointing in the same direction, either toward or away from the machine. Do not cycle the machine without a key and blank in the vise jaws.

3. Position the key and blank in the vises. The upper vise holds the blank, and the lower vise holds the key. A key or blank is always placed in the vise with the bow to the left.

   To position single-sided keys, raise the protective shield to allow access to the wing nuts for loading keys. Loosen the wing nut on the lower vise. Insert the key to be duplicated with the bow to the left and cuts facing the stylus. Leave approximately $\frac{1}{4}$ inch between the shoulder of the key and the left side of the vise. Tighten the wing nut just enough to hold the key in place. Repeat this procedure on the key blank in the upper vise. The thin edge of the blank should be facing the cutter (Figure 17.26).

   To position a double-sided key, clamp the center edge of the blade against the face of the vise. Insert the key with the bow to the left, leaving a $\frac{1}{4}$-inch margin between the bow and the left side of the vise. Tighten the wing nut just enough to hold the key in place.

Repeat this procedure on the blank in the upper vise (Figure 17.27).

To position a double-sided corrugated key, clamp the key in the vise in the center groove. Position the key with the bow to the left, leaving a $\frac{1}{4}$-inch margin between the shoulder and the left side of the vise. Tighten the wing nut just enough to hold the key in place. Repeat this procedure on the key blank in the upper vise.

To position other keys: Narrow keys with deep cuts, such as General Motors, sometimes require the straight wire to be placed under the key and blank. This raises the key in the vise, enabling the cutter to reach full depths.

Some keys with rounded or wide millings are difficult to clamp firmly in the vises. Such keys have a tendency to tilt and roll during the cutting cycle. To get a good gripping surface, place a straight wire into the milling closest to the bottom of the key and blank and insert both into position. Straight wires must be used on both the key and blank.

4. Lock the gooseneck gauge in place. Pull the carriage toward you with your right hand using the lower wing nut. At the same time, pull the gooseneck gauge forward with your left hand until the pin on the carriage locks in the groove on the gooseneck gauge (Figure 17.28).

5. Align the key and blank in vises. The key and blank are aligned by using the gooseneck gauge as a common point of reference. The object is to have the shoulder of both the key and blank butted firmly against the gooseneck gauge. When they are in this position, they are aligned. Aligning the key and blank in the vises is critical. Take time to be sure they are aligned properly.

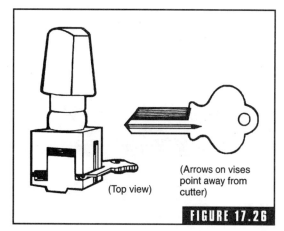

FIGURE 17.26

Properly position the key. *(Courtesy of Ilco Unican Corp.)*

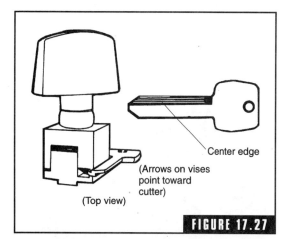

FIGURE 17.27

Clamp double-sided keys with the center edge against the face of the vise. *(Courtesy of Ilco Unican Corp.)*

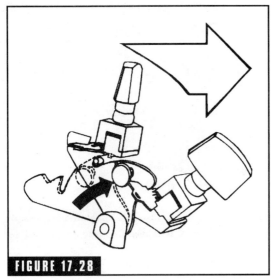

FIGURE 17.28

Pull the carriage toward you. *(Courtesy of Ilco Unican Corp.)*

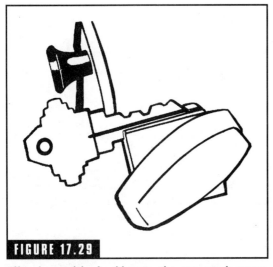

FIGURE 17.29

Align keys with shoulders to the gooseneck gauge. *(Courtesy of Ilco Unican Corp.)*

To align a key with a top shoulder, loosen the wing nut on the bottom vise assembly and slide the key to the right until the shoulder touches the gooseneck gauge. Holding the blade firmly in place (Figure 17.29), tighten the wing nut. Repeat this procedure on the blank.

To align Ford keys from the tip, place the adapter over the key with the bent ear over the tip of the key. Hold the bow of the key and the adapter between the thumb and middle finger on the edge of both the key and adapter.

6. Loosen the wing nut and push the key and adapter to the right. This abuts the adapter to the gooseneck. Keep the bottom edge of the key blade and the adapter pressed firmly against the face of the vise. Tighten the wing nut and remove the adapter. Repeat this procedure with the key blank in the top vise.

When aligning keys or blanks in the vises, use your index finger to force the blade of the key or blank down into the vise. Hold the bow of the key with your thumb and middle finger. This method of holding the key or blank keeps the edge of the blade flush against the inside of the vise and keeps the shoulder of the key butted against the gooseneck gauge (Figure 17.30).

When aligning a double-sided key, the center thickness of the key is forced down against the face of the vise in the same manner.

7. Return the carriage and gooseneck gauge to the starting position. Place your right hand on the carriage at the wing nut. Your left hand

should be on the gooseneck knob. Pull the carriage toward you slightly to relieve the tension on the gooseneck gauge, and push the gooseneck gauge down. As you lower the gooseneck gauge, make certain it is in contact with the safety switch. The gooseneck gauge must be in the down position or the machine will not operate.

8. Begin the cutting cycle by activating the starter switch. Pull down on the operating lever slowly, until the lever bottoms out. Push the lever upward to the starting position. When the lever is returned to the starting position, the cutting cycle is complete. Shut the switch off and remove the key from the vise. If you are cutting a double-sided key, remove the blank and flip it over. Go back to Step 3 and begin positioning the key blank with the uncut edge facing the cutter. Repeat Steps 3 through 7.

9. The duplicate key will have small burrs on the blade. Remove the burrs. Turn the manual switch on and hold the key gently against the face of the spinning brush. Turn the manual switch off and the job is complete (Figure 17.31).

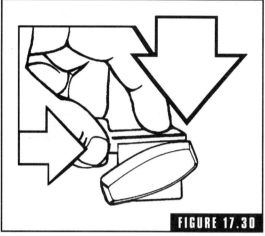

FIGURE 17.30

Use your index finger to force the blade of the key or blank into the vise. *(Courtesy of Ilco Unican Corp.)*

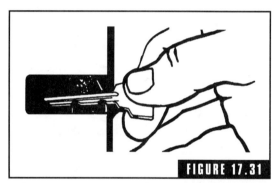

FIGURE 17.31

Hold the key against the face of the spinning brush. *(Courtesy of Ilco Unican Corp.)*

Adjustments

After considerable usage or when replacing a cutter, the machine might require adjustment. There are two basic adjustments: spacing and depth. Both spacing and depth refer to the alignment of the stylus and the cutter. Proper spacing assures that cuts copied from the key are the proper distance from the shoulder. Proper depth adjustment assures that cuts made on the blank match the depth of those on the key. Depth adjustment should be correct before attempting to adjust spacing.

Caution: Before making any adjustments, unplug the machine.

To adjust for depth of cuts, proceed as follows.

1. Remove the hood by releasing the screws on both sides of the machine.

2. Insert and align two identical, uncut key blanks in the vises.

3. Pull the plunger knob out and rotate it one-quarter turn in either direction to lock the plunger away from the cam follower plate. Remove the carriage tension spring to free the carriage. Move the carriage to the right so that the stylus is centered on the blade of the blank.

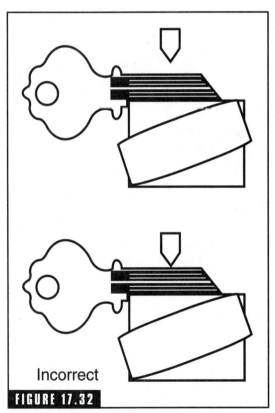

Incorrect

FIGURE 17.32

The cuts will be too shallow if the stylus touches the blank in the lower vise, but the cutter doesn't touch the blank in the upper vise. *(Courtesy of Ilco Unican Corp.)*

4. If the cutter and stylus are both touching the blanks, the machine is properly adjusted for depth of cut. The key should be touching the cutter only slightly. To check, turn the pulley that rotates the cutter a few turns by hand. The cutter should only nick the blank for only a small part of one full rotation. This occurs because no cutter is perfectly round. Make adjustments on the high point of the cutter.

5. If the stylus touches the key blank in the lower vise but does not touch the blank in the upper vise, the cuts will be too shallow (Figure 17.32). To make the proper adjustment, loosen the depth locking screw slightly by turning it counterclockwise. Turn the depth adjusting screw clockwise until the cutter, which should be rotated by hand, nicks the blank in the upper vise. Tighten the depth locking screw securely.

6. If the cutter touches the blank in the upper vise but the stylus does not touch

the blank in the lower vise, the cuts will be too deep. Loosen the depth locking screw slightly. Turn the depth adjusting screw until you are able to rotate the cutter so that it barely nicks the blank. Check the adjustment at another point and tighten the depth locking screw securely.

To adjust for spacing of cuts, proceed as follows.

1. Remove the hood by releasing the screws on both sides of the machine.

2. Locate the matching pair of test keys from the accessory pack supplied with the 018. Rotate each vise assembly to point arrow away from the cutter. Insert and align one test key in each vise.

3. Pull the plunger knob out and rotate it one-quarter turn in either direction to lock the plunger away from the cam follower plate. Remove the carriage tension spring to free the carriage (Figure 17.33).

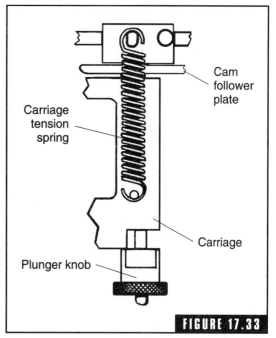

FIGURE 17.33

Remove the carriage tension spring to free the carriage. *(Courtesy of Ilco Unican Corp.)*

4. Slide the carriage to the right until the cutter and guide are centered in the grooves of their respective test keys. When the cutter is centered in the groove of the upper test key and the stylus is centered in the groove of the lower test key (Figure 17.34), the machine is properly adjusted for spacing. *Caution:* Never rotate the cutter when adjusting the machine for spacing. Rotating the cutter will damage the test key in the upper vise.

5. If the cutter touches only the right side of the groove and the stylus touches only the left side of the groove, cuts in the keys you duplicate will be too far from the shoulder (Figure 17.35). To make proper adjustment, loosen space locking screw slightly by turning it counterclockwise. Then turn the space adjusting screw counterclockwise until cutter and guide are centered in the grooves. Tighten space locking screw securely (Figure 17.36).

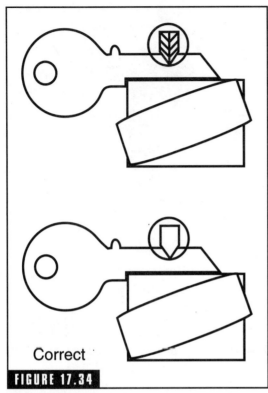

Correct

FIGURE 17.34

The machine is properly adjusted for spacing when the cutter is centered in the groove of the upper test key and the stylus is centered in the groove of the lower test key. *(Courtesy of Ilco Unican Corp.)*

6. If the cutter touches only the left side of the groove and the stylus touches only the right side of the groove, cuts in the duplicate key will be too close to the shoulder. To make proper adjustment, loosen space locking screw slightly and turn space adjusting screw clockwise until cutter and guide are centered in the grooves. Tighten the space locking screw securely.

7. After the spacing has been checked or adjusted, remove the test keys from the vises. Unlock the plunger. Slide the carriage to the left until plunger drops into the cam follower plate. Return carriage tension spring to the proper post.

Changing the Cutter

To change the cutter for a 018 key machine, proceed as follows.

1. Remove the hood by releasing the screws on both sides of the machine.

2. Remove the cutter shaft nut and cutter shaft spacer. When removing the cutter shaft nut, hold the cutter shaft with a ⅜₆-inch open-end wrench in the flats provided.

3. Remove the worn cutter and replace with a new one. *Note:* Be sure to install the cutter with the arrow pointing in the same direction as the rotation of the cutter shaft.

4. Check for depth of cut. Adjust if necessary.

Minimizing Cutter Shaft End Play

To minimize cutter shaft end play, proceed as follows.

1. Remove the hood by releasing the screws on both sides of the machine and linkage screw.

2. Remove the machine screw and washers at the right end of the cutter shaft. When removing the screw and washer, hold the cutter shaft secure with the wrench in flats provided.

3. Remove the deburring brush.

4. Loosen the two Allen screws that secure the machine pulley to the main cutter shaft.

5. Tighten the hex nut gradually, by hand, until all end play is eliminated. Then tighten the hex nut an additional one-eighth turn.

6. Tighten the two Allen screws in the machine pulley.

7. Replace the washer and screw. Hold the cutter shaft with the wrench in flats provided. *Caution:* Do not over-tighten the hex nut.

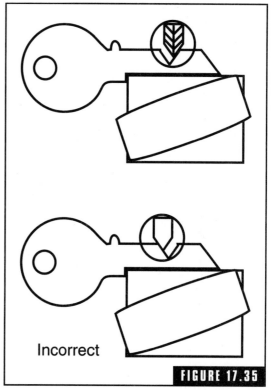

Incorrect

FIGURE 17.35

Cuts will be too far from the shoulder if the cutter touches only the right side of the groove and the stylus touches only the left side of the groove. *(Courtesy of Ilco Unican Corp.)*

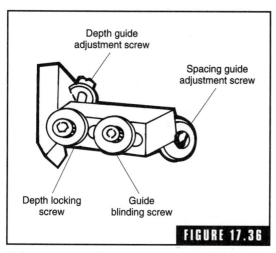

FIGURE 17.36

Tighten space locking screw. *(Courtesy of Ilco Unican Corp.)*

Key Coding Machines

A key coding machine lets you make keys to a lock when no key is available to copy. That's possible because lock makers often stamp a code on their locks and keys that tells locksmiths what they need to know to turn a blank into a working key.

Once you have the code, you can make a key by hand using the proper blank, a file, and a caliper. But a key coding machine can do the job faster. Some key coding machines can also duplicate keys.

Theory of Code Key Cutting

A code may be direct or indirect. A direct code makes no attempt to disguise the combination of the lock. With a direct code, anyone can use charts such as those in a pinning kit or in Appendix E to make a key by code. Low-cost locks sold in home improvement centers and department stores often have direct codes on their keys. Better locks have indirect codes, which must first be translated to a direct code with a code book or code software that is sold to locksmiths.

For example, a 1986 Chevrolet automobile uses code number 1V89. The V indicates the series of numbers for these cars. Refer to the V Series lists and locate 1V89. Adjacent to 1V89 is the number 322135, which represents the actual cuts in the key.

Spacing and Depth of Cuts

There are two critical dimensions in code cutting: spacing and depth of the cuts. *Spacing* is where the cuts are placed on the key and actually represents the distances between the centers of adjacent cuts (Figure 18.1). The key coding machine component that sets the spacing dimension is the *spacing plate.*

Note: Spacing is determined from left to right, also expressed as the bow or shoulder of the key (left) to the tip (right).

Depth refers to how deeply the cut is made into the blade of the key. Each depth has a definite dimension, which is measured from the bottom of the cut to the bottom of the key blade.

To simplify the code numbers, each depth is identified by a single number. For example, in the V Series there are five depths, identified as 1, 2, 3, 4, and 5. For key number 1V89, the cuts are 322135—the key does not use depth 4.

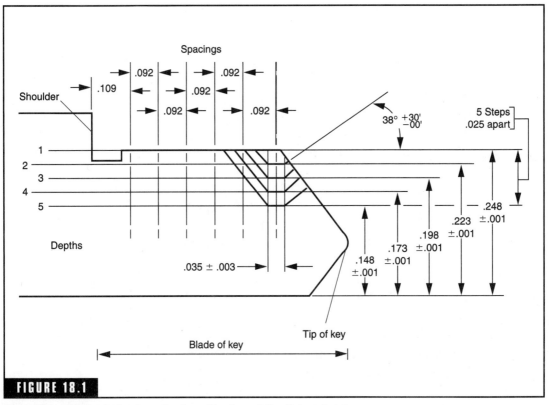

FIGURE 18.1

Dimensions of a typical automotive key. *(Courtesy of Ilco Unican Corp.)*

In a key coding machine, the component that sets the depths is the *depth knob* (Figure 18.2). When the knob is turned so that a 4 centers over the index mark, a 4 depth will be cut into a key. Turning the knob to 5 will produce a 5 depth, etc.

When reading the key cuts, pay attention to the order in which the cuts appear. In the example of key 1V89, the key cuts are 322135. The first number is 3, so a 3 depth must be cut in the first spacing, which is the spacing nearest the shoulder or bow of the key. The second number is 2, so a 2 depth must be cut in the second spacing from the shoulder or bow of the key. The last number in 322135 is a 5, so a 5 depth must be cut in the sixth spacing, which is the spacing closest to the tip of the key.

Some code charts are based on the reverse sequence of cuts—that is, the spacings start at the tip of the key and run from right to left. With these charts, the first number of a key combination must be cut in the first spacing nearest the tip of the key. The following cuts are then made in succession from that point.

Suppose you cut a key from bow to tip and it doesn't operate the lock. Try another blank, this time reversing the direction of cutting. Use the same numbers, but cut from tip to bow. The key might work. If not, the code charts do not apply to the lock or someone has changed the combination of the lock, or the lock is malfunctioning.

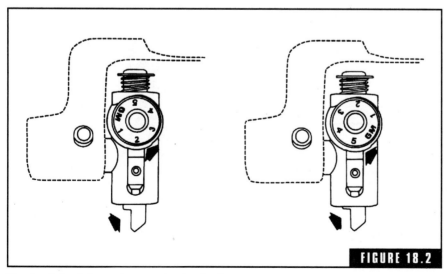

FIGURE 18.2

The depth knob is used to set the depth of a cut. *(Courtesy of Ilco Unican Corp.)*

KD80 Code Cutting Key Machine

Manufactured by Ilco Unican Corporation, the KD80 (Figure 18.3) has the dual capabilities of cutting keys by code and duplicating keys. Because code cutting is primarily centered around car keys, the KD80 is available with optional kits to cut keys for vehicles manufactured by General Motors, Ford, and Chrysler. The model numbers for the various kits are, for the basic machine, KD80; basic machine with Chrysler kit, AVCE-KD80; basic machine with Ford 5 and 10 code kit, 011-00147; basic machine with GM kit, 074-00010.

The KD80 is never used as-is. It must be equipped with the components in a specific kit to permit code cutting of a specific brand of car key. For example, the KD80 to cut General Motors keys is provided with the components to specifically cut GM keys. These components are a key guide assembly, a spacing plate, a depth knob, and a cutter.

When installed, these components set the KD80 to cut keys by code for GM vehicles, using original factory dimensions. Keys cut by code will be like the original keys supplied with the lock.

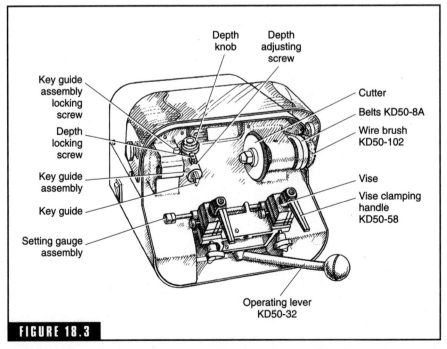

Depth knob
Depth adjusting screw
Key guide assembly locking screw
Cutter
Belts KD50-8A
Wire brush KD50-102
Depth locking screw
Key guide assembly
Vise
Vise clamping handle KD50-58
Key guide
Setting gauge assembly
Operating lever KD50-32

FIGURE 18.3

The KD80 can cut keys by code and by duplication. *(Courtesy of Ilco Unican Corp.)*

Setting Up

After unpacking the KD80, set it on a sturdy work bench. It's not necessary to bolt down the unit because its 70-pound weight makes it rigid enough for normal use. Attach the lever handle and the safety shield. Then locate the parts identified in Figure 18.3.

Plug the electric cord into an outlet and depress the on-off switch to make sure that the machine operates. Turn it off.

Cutting a Key

Before cutting a key with the KD80, be sure that the machine is provided with the proper components for cutting the brand of key you want to cut. If making a GM key, you should have the GM depth knob installed on the GM key guide, the GM cutting wheel and key guide assembly on the machine, and the GM spacing plate. You should also have the key cuts written down on paper, in proper sequence.

The procedure for cutting the key is as follows.

1. Clamp the spacing plate into the left vise jaw in any random position. Then, rotate the key gauge up and set the left finger in contact with the shoulder of the spacing plate.

2. Clamp the key blank into the right vise. Make sure that the blade of the blank is resting flat against the key rest surface of the vise and that the shoulder of the blank is touching the right finger of the setting gauge.

3. Determine the first depth cut of the key combination.

4. Turn the depth knob to set the number corresponding to the first depth cut at the index mark.

5. Depress the On-Off switch to turn on the machine.

6. Move the carriage lever so that the first notch of the spacing plate is under the key guide. Line up the point of the key guide with the center line of the first space in the spacing plate.

7. Raise the carriage (lift the lever). Continue lifting until the center line of the first space touches the tip of the key guide. At this point, the cutter will be cutting the key blank. Move the carriage carefully from side to side to widen the cut. Don't let the guide move away from the bottom of the cut, or it might jump into the

adjacent space in error. When the cut has been widened, lower the carriage lever.

8. Turn the depth knob to set the number corresponding to the second depth cut at the index mark.

9. Move the carriage lever so that the second notch of the spacing plate lines up with the key guide. Proceed exactly as you did with the first cut.

10. Raise the carriage and continue lifting the lever until the center line of the second space touches the tip of the key guide. Move the carriage from side to side to widen the cut. At this point, the cutter is cutting the blank.

11. Continue the same procedure for each successive depth cut. That is, rotate the depth knob to the appropriate depth number and move the carriage to the appropriate spacing position.

12. After making the last depth cut, remove the notched key from the right vise jaw.

13. Deburr the new key by running the underside of the key against the wire brush. Do not over-brush, and do not turn the notches of the key into the brush. If you over-brush, you could take away more metal and reduce the accuracy to which the key was cut.

Cutting Other Car Keys

The KD80 code cutter can be converted to cut keys for other vehicles, such as Chrysler or Ford. Generally, the procedure is the same. The numbers of Chrysler and Ford keys are also code numbers that are arranged in a series. The series translate into actual key combinations, which represent the depths of the cuts. The cuts are made according to the depths and spacings.

Major differences occur, however, with the actual values of the depth and spacing dimensions. The GM spacing measurements are not the same as Ford. The Chrysler depth and spacing measurements aren't the same as GM and Ford. They're all different. As a result, different spacing plates, depth knobs, and cutters are needed for each brand of vehicle. The setting gauge is used to position keys with shoulders.

If you have a KD80 set to cut GM keys and you want to cut Chrysler keys, you must replace the GM key guide assembly and depth knob with the Chrysler key guide assembly and depth knob.

You must also use the Chrysler spacing plate and install the Chrysler cutter. Once the proper parts are installed, you can cut the Chrysler key using the procedure described earlier.

Clamping Ford Double-Sided Keys

Ford keys are cut on both sides of the key blade and are called double-sided keys because they first must be cut on one side, then turned over and cut on the other side. The key cuts are the same on both sides.

To clamp the Ford double-sided key in its vise jaw, lay the center ridge of the key on top of the jaw surface. Then, tighten the vise jaw. After cutting, loosen the vise jaw and turn over the key blank for reclamping. Again, rest the center ridge of the key on the top surface of the vise jaw, as for the first cuts.

Because Ford keys don't have shoulders, it is not accurate to use the key gauge for aligning the keys in the vise jaws. On the Ford key, the tip of the key is the shoulder, so Ford keys are aligned by the tips.

On the KD80, there are two ways to align the tips of Ford keys. Use the service bar in one of the vise jaw slots to serve as a stop (use the same slot in both jaws), or use the special key gauge set on the right side of each vise jaw. Remove the service bar, or drop the key gauge before cutting.

Cutting Ford Five-Cut Keys

Ford vehicles from 1965 through 1984 used pin tumbler locks that had five pin tumblers and five depths. Key numbers were listed in the code charts running from FA000 to FA1863 (ignition) and FB000 to FB1863 (glove and trunk).

Cutting Ford Ten-Cut Keys

Selected 1985 and 1986 models in the Ford line use a key that has ignition and door cuts in one side of the key. The blank needed for the ten-cut system is slightly longer and wider than the previous five-cut blank. Even though the ten-cut blank looks like the five-cut blank, the two are different and cannot be used interchangeably.

A quick way to measure the key blanks is to line up the tips and check the lengths of the blades. The ten-cut key contains ten cuts (Figure 18.4).

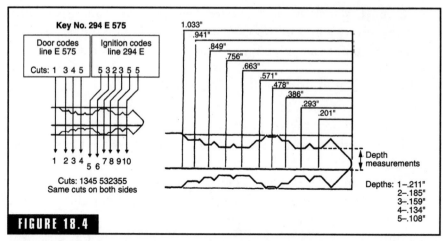

FIGURE 18.4

Depths and spaces of a key code. *(Courtesy of Ilco Unican Corp.)*

The ten cuts operate either one of two disc tumbler cylinders—one for the door and the other for the ignition lock. The ignition cylinder uses six tumblers, in positions 5, 6, 7, 8, 9, and 10. These are the positions closest to the tip of the key.

The door lock also has six tumblers, but these are placed in positions 1, 2, 3, 4, 5, and 6, which are the positions closest to the bow of the key. Note that the tumblers in the fifth and sixth positions are the same in both locks.

The ten-cut system uses the new FC series of code charts, which runs from FC100 to 344 (for the ignition lock codes) and FC501 to 624 (for the door lock codes). The charts contain five columns, identified as A, B, C, D, and E. The letter designation carries over to the key combination, which has three numbers, a letter, and then three more numbers. The cuts of the key are located by referring to the charts and using both the numbers and letters of the key combination.

To illustrate how key cuts are determined, assume there is a key with the number 294E575. Because E is in the combination, you must refer to the E column in the charts for both numbers 294 and 575. After locating 294 in the charts, go across the columns to the E column and find the number 532355, which represents the combination of the ignition lock, or the actual key depths.

After locating 575 in the charts, go across to column E to number 1345; this represents the combination of the door lock, or the actual key depths. Both groups of numbers together give a key combination of 1345532355 (Figure 18.4).

Next, determine whether you are going to cut from bow to tip (left to right) or from tip to bow (right to left). This depends on how the code charts are set up. Factory charts are set up so that spacings run from tip to bow. With these charts, the first number of the ignition combination is cut in the first spacing (which is the spacing closest to the tip of the key). The other cuts are then made in sequence. The first number of the door combination is cut into the seventh spacing, and the remaining cuts are made in sequence.

According to the factory charts, therefore, the combination for key 294E575 reads as 5431553235. In essence, both numbers produce the same cuts in the key, but it depends on the direction in which the key is cut (either right to left or left to right).

Align the key in the same manner. Raise the small key gauge at the right side of the vise jaw and push the tip of the key against the key gauge.

The spacing plate and the depth control knob must be changed when switching from a five- to ten-code key. Do not use one set of components for the other style of key.

Cutting Merkur Keys

Keys for the Merkur can be cut on the KD80 machine using FM components. That is, the spacing plate, the key guide assembly, the cutter, and the depth knob all marked FM. The change in components is necessary because the dimensions of the Merkur lock are different from other Ford locks.

The Merkur key is double-sided, but it does not have a shoulder. As a result, alignment of the original key and the blank can be made with the setting gauge. The Merkur key blanks are imprinted "TX" on the blades.

When clamping the key or blank in the vise jaw, set it so its bottom rests against the bottom of the vise. The key blank should not rest on the top surface of the vise jaw.

Because of the wide groove on each side of the Merkur key, the key may rotate or tilt toward the cutter. A tilted position of the key is not acceptable because the cuts will be inaccurate. To prevent the key from tilting, insert the 1.2 mm service pin into the back groove of the key (Figure 18.5). The tip of the service pin should be about ⅛ inch away from the shoulder of the key.

With the pin inserted, clamp the key in the vise jaw, making sure that the bottom of the key rests against the bottom of the vise. The service pin should remain in the groove during the actual cutting, in both the original pattern key and the key blank.

When turning the keys over to make the second side cuts, take extra care that the keys do not tilt fore and aft. The bottom-most points of the cut side should rest against the bottom of the vise, and the horizontal lines of the key should match the horizontal lines of the vise.

Duplicating Keys

To set the KD80 code cutter to duplicate a key, simply turn the depth knob to its neutral setting. This neutral setting is at the two letters that identify the knob.

On the GM depth knob, there are five numbers (1, 2, 3, 4, and 5) and two letters (GM) on its surface. When the knob is turned so that the GM is pointing to the index mark, the knob is at its neutral setting. In this position, the tip of the key guide is in the same plane as the tip of the cutter, having been preset at the factory.

The alignment of the key guide tip and the cutter is commonly referred to as the *adjustment*. Check the adjustment in the conventional manner. Clamp two key blanks in the left and right vise jaws. Then, lift the carriage so the left key blank touches the tip of the key guide. At

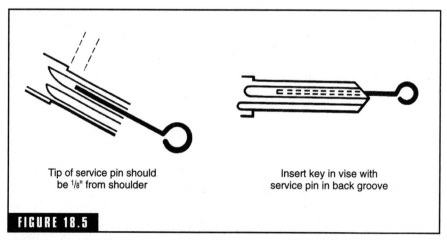

Tip of service pin should
be ⅛" from shoulder

Insert key in vise with
service pin in back groove

FIGURE 18.5

Insert service pin into back groove of the key. *(Courtesy of Ilco Unican Corp.)*

this point, the right key blank should also touch the cutter. If the right blank does not touch, move the key guide in or out until both blanks touch (Figure 18.6).

To adjust the key guide, loosen the depth locking screw (slotted screw) and turn the depth adjusting screw one-eighth turn or less, as needed. Then, tighten the depth locking screw.

When the adjustment is correct and the depth knob is at the neutral setting, the KD80 machine is ready for duplicating a key. Clamp the pattern key in the left vise and the key blank in the right vise. Use the setting gauge to properly line up the shoulders of both keys. Swing the setting gauge away, turn the machine on, and move the carriage with the lever to cut the duplicate key. When moving the lever sideways, use a steady, even motion. Avoid rapid or jerky movements because they could damage the cutter.

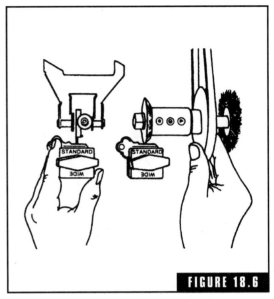

FIGURE 18.6

Check the adjustment of the key guide to the cutter.
(Courtesy of Ilco Unican Corp.)

When cutting the Merkur double-sided key, use the key gauge to align the shoulder of the pattern key with the key blank. Keep the service pins inserted in the keys. When turning the keys over to make the second side cuts, make sure the keys do not tilt fore and aft. The bottom-most points of the cut side should rest against the bottom of the vise, and the horizontal lines of the keys should match the horizontal lines of the vise.

The Cutter

Like all cutting instruments, cutters should be treated with care. Harsh and abusive treatment will ruin a good cutter quickly. Let the cutter do its work by applying a steady, moderate pressure and cutting only those materials it's designed to cut (brass, brass nickel-plated, or nickel silver keys).

In normal operation, the cutter should rotate downward (when looking at the machine from the operator's position). Do not alter the direction of the rotation of the cutter.

To replace the cutter, insert the stabilizing rod into the hole of the cutter shaft and use a wrench to unscrew the cutter nut (Figure 18.7).

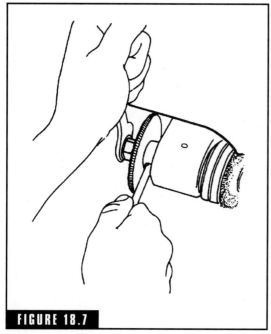

FIGURE 18.7

Insert the stabilizing rod into the hole of the cutter shaft. *(Courtesy of Ilco Unican Corp.)*

The cutter nut has a left-hand thread and must be turned clockwise to loosen. Be sure that the nut is tight after the new cutter has been installed on the shaft.

Exacta Code Key Cutter

Manufactured by Ilco Unican Corporation, the Exacta Code key cutter is a mechanical type of key coding machine called a *key bitting punch*. It stamps or punches cuts into a key rather than grinding them. Because a key bitting punch is mechanical, it's very useful to take on outside service calls.

The Exacta requires a minimum of care; the only danger to the machine is dirt and the only maintenance necessary is keeping the machine clean. Use a soft brush to make sure the key insert slot, key insert, and punch die assembly in particular are kept free of chips and dust. Empty the plastic chip box occasionally. Lubrication should be unnecessary because all moving parts are treated with a permanent lubrication.

Setting Up

Set up the Exacta Code key cutter in the following way (refer to the parts numbers in Figure 18.8).

1. Select proper depth knob (P-10), spacing plate (P-11), key insert (P-12), and key blank from your code book.

2. Assemble the depth knob by sliding it on the shaft over the pin, keying it to the shaft. Insert the screw and tighten it until the knob is resting against the shoulder.

3. Install the spacing plate by placing the dowel pin and swing into position where it will be held by detent.

4. Slide the key insert into the slot of the carriage from the right or left side of carriage, according to the instruction in your code book.

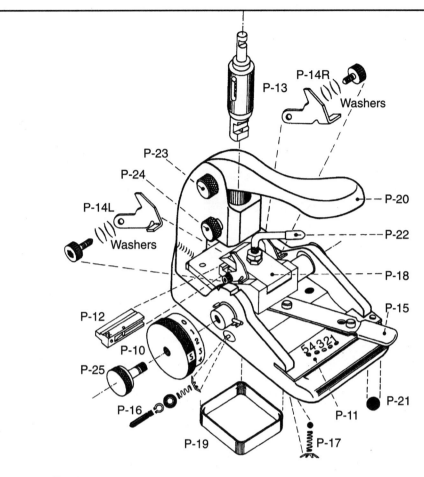

Spare parts list

P-10	Depth knob (knobs for different makes are identified by letters A, B, etc.)	P-17	Detent assembly for spacing plate
		P-18	Carriage assembly
P-11	Spacing plate (plates for different makes are identified by numbers 100, 101, etc.)	P-19	Plastic box
P-12	Key insert (inserts for different makes are identified by numbers 1, 2, etc.)	P-20	Lever
		P-21	Felt pads (set of 4)
P-13	Punch and die assembly	P-22	Carriage lever
P-14R	Shoulder guide assembly—Right side	P-23	Lever screw
P-14L	Shoulder guide assembly—Left side	P-24	Knob set screw
P-15	Spacing lever assembly	P-25	Depth knob screw
P-16	Detent assembly for depth knob		

FIGURE 18.8

An exploded view of the Exacta key bitting punch. *(Courtesy of Ilco Unican Corp.)*

5. To cut some keys, the punch and die assembly (P-13) must be replaced. Select the proper punch and die from the code book. Remove the lever (P-20) by unfastening and removing the hand lever (P-23) and die screw (P-24). Pull out the punch and die assembly. Slide the proper punch and die assembly into position, making sure that the frontal flat portion of the die is lined parallel to the carriage. Tighten the screw (P-24). Replace the lever and lever screw (P-23).

Operating Instructions

To operate the Exacta Code key cutter, proceed as follows.

1. Place the spacing lever (P-15) into the extreme left hole of the spacing plate (P-11).

2. Set the depth knob (P-10) to the extreme C.W. position.

3. Insert the key blank on the carriage (P-18) from the same side that the key insert (P-12) was installed, or according to code book instruction.

4. Locate the key blank with the right-hand shoulder guide, or by the left-hand shoulder guide; tip of key against stop on insert; or shoulder of key against insert, according to the instructions in the code book.

5. Lock the key blank of the carriage by tightening the carriage lever. Be sure that the blank is level and straight with the insert (P-12). Do not over-tighten the lever, or carriage could be hard to move.

6. Return the shoulder guide to the rest position against the side of the carriage.

7. Set the spacing lever (P-15) in position 1 on the spacing plate.

8. Set the depth knob to the required depth.

9. Press the lever (P-20) firmly to complete the cut.

10. Return the depth knob to the extreme C.W. position before attempting to advance the spacing lever to the next position.

11. Set the spacing lever in subsequent positions and repeat the procedure for all cuts.

12. When all cuts have been made, return the spacing lever to the extreme left position of spacing plate.

13. Loosen the carriage lever and remove the key.

14. For keys cut on two sides, repeat the procedure on second side.

15. For keys inserted from the right-hand side only: When the key is inserted from the left side, the spacing lever (P-15) is moved to the extreme right hole in the spacing plate (P-11).

Framon DC-300 Duplicating Code Machine

Manufactured by Framon Manufacturing Co., Inc., the DC-300 (Figure 18.9) is designed primarily to cut automotive keys by code and to duplicate keys. The machine uses depth cams and spacing keys.

The basic machine at the time of purchase includes one cam and five spacing keys. The No. 1 cam is furnished and has depths for cutting the five-pin Ford, the ten-wafer Ford, American Motors, Chrysler, and General Motors keys. Each of the five spacing keys is numbered both for identification and with the number of spaces for each manufacturer. Also included are an adjusting Allen wrench and instruction/service manual.

The machine can be purchased with either 100-volt ac or 12-volt dc power.

Cutter Head

The DC-300 cutter head is mounted on precision-grade, sealed bearings for accuracy and long life. The cutter is precision ground of M3 tool steel and is the precise configuration for most automotive keys.

Yoke

The yoke has two vises. The left vise is used for the blank. The right vise holds the spacing key when cutting by code and holds the pattern key when duplicating (Figures 18.10 and 18.11).

All spacing keys are used in the right-hand or guide-side vise, and keys to be cut by code or duplicated are used in the left-hand or cutter-side vise.

FIGURE 18.9

The Framon DC-300 is designed to cut automotive keys by code and by duplication. *(Courtesy of Framon Manufacturing Co., Inc.)*

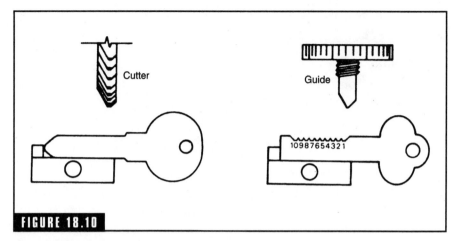

FIGURE 18.10

Typical set-up to cut keys by code using spacing key and blank. *(Courtesy of Framon Manufacturing Co., Inc.)*

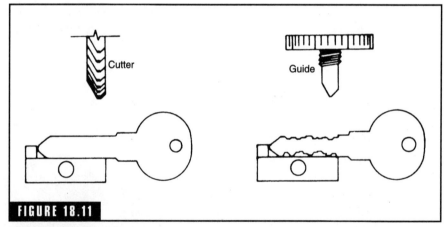

FIGURE 18.11

Typical set-up to cut duplicate keys using a pattern key and blank. *(Courtesy of Framon Manufacturing Co., Inc.)*

Key Blank Information

Most automotive key blanks are made without bottom shoulders and should be inserted into the guide-side vise with the tip of the key against the built-in stop in the vise. Key blanks that have a bottom shoulder must be inserted with the bottom shoulder against the right-hand side of the guide vise (Figure 18.12). The spacing key will always be inserted with the tip of the key against the stop in the guide vise.

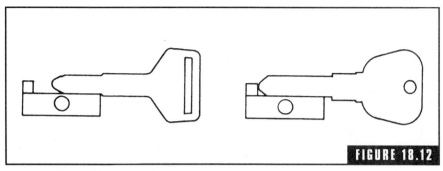

FIGURE 18.12

Insert keys that have a bottom shoulder with the bottom shoulder against the right-hand side of the guide vise. *(Courtesy of Framon Manufacturing Co., Inc.)*

Cams and Cam Post

As previously mentioned, the Framon DC-300 comes furnished with the No. 1 cam. This cam will handle all domestic automobile locks, including the Ford ten-wafer, Ford five-pin, American Motors, Chrysler, and General Motors.

Six other cams are available, with depth increments from .0138 to .040 inches. Each cam is numbered on the rear surface. The No. 1 depth is common to all cams, and this depth on any cam is used for duplicating keys.

To change cams, loosen the cam lock knob at the right rear of the cam post, withdraw the cam pin, and slide the cam out. Slide the new cam into the slot, push the cam pin into place, and tighten the cam lock knob.

Note: The counterbore at the rear of the cam is set to hold a wavy washer. Be sure to replace this washer each time cams are changed (Figure 18.13).

Cam Post and Guide

The key guide in the cam post is spring-loaded to allow the guide to enter cuts in either the spacing key (when cutting by code) or in a pattern key (when duplicating). This system is used to allow straight cuts.

The adjusting ring on the guide shaft controls the depth of each cut. If keys are cut too high, rotate the adjusting ring counterclockwise to change the depth. If keys are cut too deep, rotate the adjusting ring clockwise to change depth. To rotate the adjusting ring, loosen the set

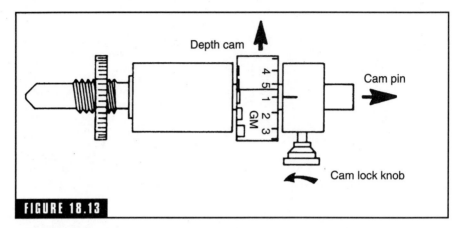

FIGURE 18.13

Loosen the cam knob lock to change cams. *(Courtesy of Framon Manufacturing Co., Inc.)*

screw in the edge of ring and tighten when the adjustment is made. Do not over-tighten the set screw.

Cutting Keys by Code

To cut a General Motors key, code 3V86, with cuts of 133545, proceed as follows.

1. Insert the key blank in the left-hand vise with the tip against the tip stop in the vise.

2. Insert spacing key No. 14 in the right-hand vise with the tip against the tip stop in the right-hand vise (Figure 18.14).

3. Insert No. 1 cam in the cam post and rotate the cam so GM No. 1 cut is aligned with the guide mark at the top of the cam post (Figure 18.15).

4. Lift the yoke so the guide engages the No. 1 cut on the spacing key, then continue lifting the yoke until the cutter engages the key and the cut is made.

5. Rotate the cam to the No. 3 cut and, following same procedure, make the next two cuts.

6. Rotate the cam to the No. 5 cut and make cuts in the No. 4 and No. 6 spacing positions.

7. Rotate the cam to the No. 4 cut and make cut in the No. 5 position on the spacing key. The key is now complete.

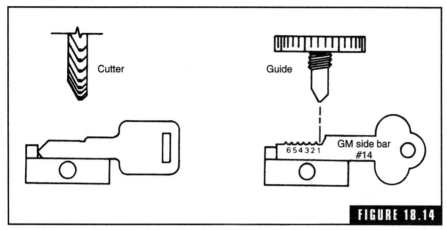

Insert the spacing key in the right-hand vise. *(Courtesy of Framon Manufacturing Co., Inc.)*

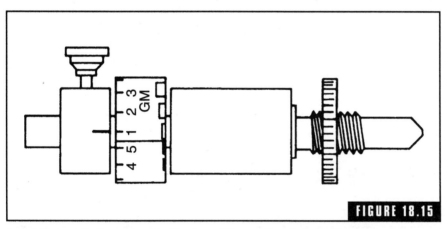

Insert the cam in the cam post. *(Courtesy of Framon Manufacturing Co., Inc.)*

Spacing Keys

On the spacing keys, each cut is numbered from bow to tip. This allows the operator to make cuts of the same depth anywhere on any key without changing the cam settings.

Each spacing key is numbered according to the provided chart. Framon can furnish spacing keys for any code series needed; over 250 spacing keys are available.

Duplicating Keys

To duplicate a key with the DC-300, proceed as follows.

1. Insert the key blank in the left-hand vise with the tip against the stop in the vise.

2. Insert the pattern key in the right-hand vise with the tip stop.

3. Rotate the cam to the No. 1 cut (No. 1 cut on any cam can be used for duplicating).

4. Set the guide in each cut on the pattern key. Make each cut by lifting the yoke until it comes to a complete stop at each cut, and the key is complete (Figure 18.16).

If the blank and pattern keys have a bottom shoulder, keys should be inserted in the vises with the bottom shoulder against the right-hand side of the vise. Otherwise, use the tip stop.

Lubrication

A small amount of fine oil can be used on the yoke slide rod. Wipe off all excess oil. If the guide needs lubrication, remove the cam, push the guide rearward, remove the snap ring at the rear of the guide shaft, and slide the shaft out. Lubricate as needed and reverse the procedure to replace.

The depth plunger under the guide shaft is spring-loaded and will eject itself when the guide shaft is removed. This rod can be lubricated. Replace all parts.

Borkey 989 Top-Cut

Distributed by DiMark International, the Borkey 989 Top-Cut (Figure

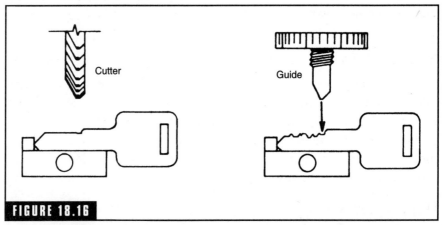

FIGURE 18.16

Set the guide in each cut on the pattern key. *(Courtesy of Framon Manufacturing Co., Inc.)*

18.17) cuts straight and curved track, as well as drill-type keys, to pattern or to code.

Changing the Cutter

To release the cutter, insert the pin punch provided into the hole over the cutter chuck. Hold the pin punch (Figure 18.18) securely and loosen the lower nut, turning to the left with the wrench provided. The cutter will drop out of the bottom. Insert the new cutter in the chuck and push it right up to the top, as far as it will go. Tighten by turning the nut to the right. Be sure it is firmly tightened in the collet.

Removing the Guide

Use the same wrench to loosen the nut above the guide, turning the nut to the left about one-half turn. The guide will drop out of the bottom. Insert the new guide into the collet-chuck as far as it will go, and tighten the nut firmly.

The locking nut that is above and on the right side of the casting has been preset at the factory, so it is not necessary to make adjustments to it. This controls a concentric adjustment and should not be adjusted by the operator, except with special instructions from factory representatives.

Cutting Drilled Keys

Install the drilled key and guide, following the instructions given previously.

Remove the key disc holders from the top of both jaws and put them in a safe place. Put blank keys in both vises.

Referring to Figure 18.19, loosen the lower knob (6) and turn the upper knob (5) counterclockwise two to three turns to release the previous settings. Turn knob (7) clockwise two to three turns to raise the guide higher than the cutter. Lower the cutter/guide assembly so the cutter lightly touches the blank. Securely tighten the left thumb turn (4) so that the cutter still lightly touches the key. Turn knob (7) until the guide just touches the left key, then stop turning.

FIGURE 18.17

The Borkey 989 Top-Cut is designed to cut a variety of key types by code and by duplication. *(Courtesy of DiMark International)*

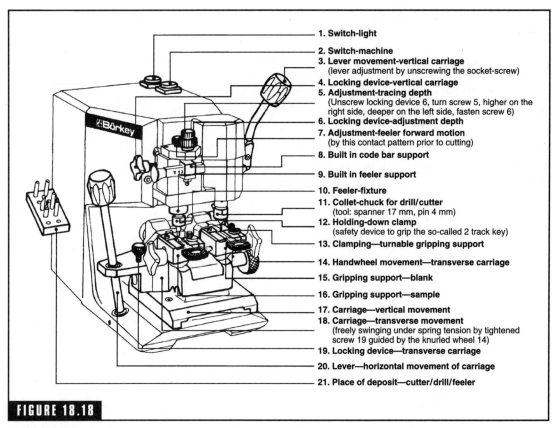

1. **Switch-light**
2. **Switch-machine**
3. **Lever movement-vertical carriage**
   (lever adjustment by unscrewing the socket-screw)
4. **Locking device-vertical carriage**
5. **Adjustment-tracing depth**
   (Unscrew locking device 6, turn screw 5, higher on the
   right side, deeper on the left side, fasten screw 6)
6. **Locking device-adjustment depth**
7. **Adjustment-feeler forward motion**
   (by this contact pattern prior to cutting)
8. **Built in code bar support**
9. **Built in feeler support**
10. **Feeler-fixture**
11. **Collet-chuck for drill/cutter**
    (tool: spanner 17 mm, pin 4 mm)
12. **Holding-down clamp**
    (safety device to grip the so-called 2 track key)
13. **Clamping—turnable gripping support**
14. **Handwheel movement—transverse carriage**
15. **Gripping support—blank**
16. **Gripping support—sample**
17. **Carriage—vertical movement**
18. **Carriage—transverse movement**
    (freely swinging under spring tension by tightened
    screw 19 guided by the knurled wheel 14)
19. **Locking device—transverse carriage**
20. **Lever—horizontal movement of carriage**
21. **Place of deposit—cutter/drill/feeler**

FIGURE 18.18

Nomenclature for parts of the Borkey 989 Top-Cut. *(Courtesy of DiMark International)*

Hold knob (6) stationary and turn knob (5) clockwise so it is lightly finger tight. Turn knob (6) clockwise to lock in the calibration. Release the cutter/guide assembly so it goes back up.

Turn on the machine to test the depth. The cutter should just touch the right key blank when the cutter/guide assembly is lowered. It should make a small mark, but no actual cut. If the depth is too high or low, repeat the complete instructions.

Once the depth is correctly set, you can put the guide in the spring-loaded mode by turning knob (7) counterclockwise several turns. If the spring-loaded mode is not desired, adjust knob (7) at this time.

Check the angle of the jaws to be sure they are in the right position for the key you are cutting.

They are normally set in the 0 position. To tilt the jaws, loosen the large thumb turn at the right rear. The jaws tilt in unison. The detent will index at 0.

Proceed to cut the key by sample or by depth keys. Using the large knurled knob on the right of the carriage, adjust the carriage assembly so that the cutter is near the cutting line on either the left or right side of the keys. Because the carriage is somewhat self-centering, it will find the center of the cut as each cut is placed on the key. You might want to pull all cuts to the left of center on one side, then turn the key over and do all the left cuts on the opposite side before adjusting the carriage to do all the right cuts.

To lock the left-right travel of the carriage so that shallow cuts can be centered in line, hold the guide and cutter in a deep cut on that side of the key and lock the carriage with the round black screw that is to the right of the main carriage handle.

Adjusting Depth of Cutter Guide for High-Security Automotive Keys

Referring to Figure 18.19, upper knob (5) controls the maximum depth of cuts.

Lower knob (6) is a locking nut to hold depth settings accurately. Rear knob (7) allows the guide to operate spring-loaded or fixed.

Put two key blanks in the vises. Four-track keys or the sides of flat safe keys work well. Two-track keys do not work well.

Loosen front knobs (5) and (6) counterclockwise two to three turns. Lower the cutter/guide assembly and turn knob (7) until it is just above the surface of the left key when the cutter touches the surface of the right key. Lock the cutter/guide assembly in position, using the thumb knob at the left (4).

With the cutter touching the surface of the right key, turn knob (7) until the guide is off the surface of the left key only enough to allow a piece of normal bond paper to pass between the guide and key. Holding lower knob (6) from turning, adjust upper knob (5) clockwise until it just stops. Lock it in place using lower knob (6).

Caution: At this time the cutter is lower than the guide and will be able to cut into parts of the machine. Do not turn the machine on at this point.

Remove the keys. Release the cutter/guide assembly so it is free, and position the cutter and guide over the face of the key vises. Put a business card on top of the right vise. Lower the cutter/guide assembly so the cutter lightly touches the business card, and lock the assembly

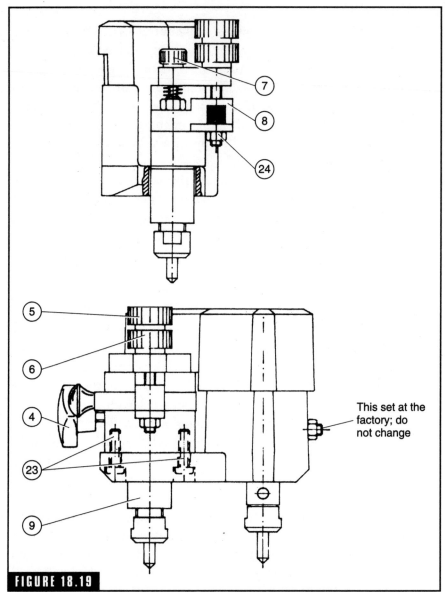

FIGURE 18.19

Adjustable parts of the Borkey 989 Top-Cut. *(Courtesy of DiMark International)*

into position using the left knob. When the depth is correctly set, the business card will catch a little as it is removed.

Before turning the machine on, move the carriage in all directions to make sure the cutter does not touch the face of the jaw on both sides of the key. Make sure the cutter is firmly tightened so that it won't slip down during cutting. Otherwise, damage might result.

Cutting Two-Track Keys

Secure the sample key in the left vise and the blank in the right vise, tip-stopping the keys. Move the straight side of the key disc clamps over the keys to keep them from tipping.

Tighten down using the round top knobs. It is not necessary to move these again while inserting or removing keys.

Use the knurled knob at the right of the carriage to position the carriage. The spring-loaded feature is controlled by turning this knob. To cut deeper on the left side of the key, turn the knob away from you. To cut deeper on the right side of the key, turn the knob toward you.

Position the cutter/guide assembly so the guide and cutter rest next to the first cut, closest to the bow of the key. Turn the machine on. Cuts will be made from bow to tip. Cutting should be accomplished in stages, especially if there are deep cuts on the key. As the deeper cuts are made into the key, the guide might bind against the high cuts. In that case, adjust the knurled knob to allow for passing those high cuts, then readjust to allow for cutting the deeper cuts individually.

This might seem awkward at first, but with practice this motion will become automatic.

Automotive Lock Servicing

This chapter provides the information a locksmith needs to enter the lucrative field of automotive lock servicing. Some of the topics covered include understanding differences among automotive locks; removing and servicing locks from vehicles; and opening locked automobiles.

Basics

Automotive lock servicing is a specialty field of locksmithing and can be very profitable. To be proficient in this field, you must stay informed of the constant changes that are made to automotive locks and locking systems. Most of the changes are made to increase vehicle security and make systems more convenient for owners to use.

Locksmiths are frequently called on to service automobiles that have lock-related problems. Such problems include foreign objects (such as a broken piece of key) that become lodged in the lock cylinder, keys that turn very hard in the cylinder, and keys that won't operate the lock.

A broken piece of key can be removed from an automobile lock in the same way it can be removed from other locks. A key that is stuck in a door lock can usually be removed by first turning the key to the upright position (the position the key is in when it's first inserted into the lock), then clamping locking pliers to the bow and pulling the key straight out.

When a key turns hard in a cylinder, it's often the result of a bent rod between the walls of the car door. A bent rod can be caused by the improper use of automobile opening tools. To solve the problem, remove the inside trim panel from the vehicle, then locate and straighten the improperly bent rod.

When the key turns smoothly but won't operate the door, the problem could be with the cylinder. Solve the problem by repairing or replacing the cylinder. More often, however, a disconnected rod within the walls of the door is the cause of a key not operating a lock. If this is the case, you must remove the inside trim panel from the vehicle, locate the disconnected rod, and reconnect it. This often requires a new retainer clip. Figure 19.1 illustrates a tool that can be used to help you replace retainer clips in hard-to-reach areas.

The procedure for removing an inside trim panel is different for different vehicles. In general, however, you need to do the following:

1. Wind the door window all the way up.

2. Remove the door handle. Sometimes it's held on by a screw, other times by a retainer clip. If the handle is held on by a clip, use a door handle clip tool to quickly remove it (Figure 19.2).

3. Remove the arm rest from the door. It is usually secured by screws and clips.

4. Remove all the screws located around the edge of the trim panel and carefully pull the panel from the door.

When replacing the trim panel, you may need to replace some of the retainer clips that hold the trip panel to the door. Those clips often break when the trim panel is being removed.

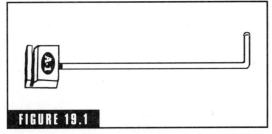

FIGURE 19.1

A retainer clip tool can be helpful for removing and replacing hard-to-reach retainer clips. *(Courtesy of A-1 Security Manufacturing Corp.)*

Automotive Lock Differences

From the outside, most automotive locks appear similar to one another, but the internal constructions often differ. The internal construction of an automotive lock depends on the purpose of the lock (ignition, door, trunk, etc.) and the manufacturer, model, and year of the vehicle for which the lock was made.

In most cases, two keys are used to operate the locks on a vehicle. The *primary key* usually operates the vehicle's ignition and doors, while the *secondary key* usually operates a vehicle's trunk and glove compartment. This two-key system allows the vehicle's owner to have someone (such as a parking lot attendant) drive the car without being able to open sensitive areas such as the trunk and glove compartment.

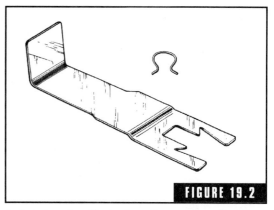

FIGURE 19.2

A door handle clip tool easily removes clips from Ford and GM vehicles. *(Courtesy of A-1 Security Manufacturing Corp.)*

Vehicle Identification Numbers

Every car in the United States is supposed to have a vehicle identification number (VIN) on a plate that's attached to the instrument panel near the vehicle's windshield on the left side. The plate should be visible from outside the vehicle. You can use a VIN to determine several things about the vehicle, including its model year. (In many cases, you need the model year to choose the right lock or car opening tool.)

Some VIN positions vary depending on the manufacturer and year of manufacture. However, the letters and numbers in positions 1, 2, and 10 (reading from left to right) are codes that show the vehicle's country of origin, make, and model year, respectively. Table 19.1 shows what the various numbers mean.

American Motors Corporation

All locks for American Motors Corporation (AMC) vehicles up to model year 1967 are standard five-disc tumbler locks. They are easy to pick. In 1968 AMC began using side bar disc tumbler locks as ignition locks on all its new vehicles, but the company continued using standard five-disc tumbler locks for most other areas, such as doors and trunk. The 1975 to 1980 Gremlin and Pacer models use side bar disc tumbler locks for their rear compartments.

TABLE 19.1 Reading a Vehicle Identification Number (VIN)

Position	Meaning	Code options
1	Country of origin	1=U.S.
		2=Canada
		3=Mexico
		J=Japan
2	Make	B=Dodge
		F=Ford
		1=Chevrolet
10	Model Year*	A=1980
		B=1981
		C=1982
		D=1983
		E=1984
		F=1985
		G=1986
		H=1987
		J=1988
		K=1989
		L=1990
		M=1991
		N=1992
		P=1993
		R=1994
		S=1995

*The letters I, O, and Q are not used to show model year.

The ignition and door of an AMC vehicle are usually keyed alike. The original key code can be found on the ignition lock after the lock has been removed from the vehicle. The trunk and glove compartment locks are also keyed alike. The glove compartment lock has four disc tumblers, which are identical to the last four tumblers used in the vehicle's trunk lock. A side bar disc tumbler lock used on an AMC vehicle's rear compartment has the code number stamped on the tailpiece.

It's usually easy to impression a key to one of the door locks. The blank should be twisted very lightly, however, because the dust shutter can break. When replacing ignition locks for AMC models manufactured after 1986, use General Motors locks and keyways.

Fitting a Key

Usually key impressioning is the fastest way to fit a key for an AMC vehicle.

Another method is to remove the door lock and lock pawl and read the bitting numbers stamped on the back of the tumblers. You can also remove the ignition lock by disassembling the steering wheel column, then cut a key by the code on the cylinder.

To fit a secondary key, cut a key for the glove compartment and cut one depth at a time in space No. 1 (the space closest to the bow) until you've cut that space to the depth that opens the trunk. After cutting to each depth, insert the key into the trunk lock to see if it operates the lock.

You can use depth and space charts to learn the proper spacing and depth increments for the lock.

Removing an AMC Ignition Lock

Ignition locks for AMC vehicles through the 1978 model year can be pulled out of the steering wheel column without first disassembling the column.

Locksmithing supply houses offer tools for that purpose; most are modified versions of a dent puller. Beginning in 1979, the ignition locks for new models were bolted in; these shouldn't be removed without first disassembling the steering wheel column.

Because of the potential danger that can result from improperly reassembling a steering wheel column, you shouldn't attempt to disassemble one until you've seen the procedure done several times on the vehicle model you're planning to service. To be on the safe side, you should have an experienced locksmith help you disassemble and reassemble a few steering wheel columns before you do it alone.

Audi

Most Audi vehicles made after 1971 use either eight- or ten-disc tumbler locks.

Usually all the locks in such a vehicle are keyed alike; in some cases, a primary key is used to operate the doors and ignition.

To fit a primary key for an Audi, use the code number found on the door lock after the lock has been removed from the vehicle. For a secondary key, use the code number on the glove compartment lock.

BMW

Most locks used on BMWs have ten-disc tumblers and are difficult to pick. All of the locks on a BMW are keyed alike, but sometimes a secondary key is used. Many BMWs are operated with dimple keys. Some late models have a high-security deadlocking system that should be worked on only by a BMW dealer or an authorized service center. A BMW deadlocking system allows a person to lock the car only by using a key; that makes it virtually impossible to be locked out of the car.

To fit a key on a BMW, cut the key by code from the number on the door lock, or disassemble the door lock and use the tumblers to visually fit a key. The door handle is usually held on by a Phillips head screw under the weatherstripping, or by a screw and bolt.

Chrysler

In most cases, Chrysler vehicles use pin tumbler locks on the ignition, doors, and trunk. The glove compartment locks have either three- or four-disc tumblers. The tilt/telescoping steering wheel columns found on some vehicles use a side bar disc tumbler lock.

The doors and ignition locks of a Chrysler are keyed alike and are operated by the primary key. The code number for these locks can be found on the ignition lock. Occasionally, the code number can be found on a door lock. Table 19.2 shows the various code series used for Chrysler locks.

TABLE 19.2 Chrysler Lock Code Series Information

Code series	Years	Locks	Tumbler	Depths	Spaces
EP 1-3000	1988–1990	Ign./door	Pin	6	5
ES 1-3000	1988–1990	Deck/glove	Pin	6	5
F0001-1394	1988½	All	Wafer	4	Varies
G0001-1394	1989–1992	All	Wafer	4	Varies
J0001-3580	1993	All	Wafer	4	Varies
L0001-3580	1994/95	All	Wafer	4	Varies

The secondary key operates the trunk and glove compartment locks. When the glove compartment lock has three-disc tumblers, they correspond to the three middle tumblers of the vehicle's trunk lock. When the glove compartment lock has four-disc tumblers, they correspond to the last four tumblers of the trunk lock. Many times you can find the code number for a secondary key on a trunk lock. See Table 19.3 for a comprehensive list that compares various Chrysler tumbler combinations.

Beginning in 1989, some Chrysler vehicles, such as Plymouth Acclaim and Dodge Spirit, began using disc tumbler locks that are operated with double-sided convenience keys. These locks are designed to resist picking.

Fitting a Key

To fit a primary key for a Chrysler vehicle that uses pin tumbler locks, remove and disassemble a door lock and measure the bottom pins with a caliper. The measurements for Chrysler bottom pins are: No. 1—.148; No. 2—.168; No. 3— .188; No. 4—.208; No. 5—.228; and No. 6—.248. If a pin is worn, these measurements might not hold out. In this case, replace the pin with one that is the proper size. The new pin will be a little longer than the one it is replacing.

To fit a secondary key, fit the key to the glove compartment lock. If the key has four cuts, find the first cut of the trunk lock by cutting the key's first space one depth at a time until the key operates the trunk. If the glove compartment lock has three cuts, you can impression the first and last cuts. When impressioning a key for a Chrysler pin tumbler lock, remember that the locks shouldn't have a No. 5 or 6 pin in the first

TABLE 19.3 Chrysler Wafer Lock Tumbler Arrangements (from Tip to Bow)

Lock	Space positions for 1988½ through 1992						
	1	2	3	4	5	6	7
Ignition	X	X	X	X	X	X	
Door	X	X	X	X	X		
Deck			X	X	X	X	X
Compartment					X	X	X

Lock	Space positions for 1993/1994						
	1	2	3	4	5	6	7
Ignition	X	X	X	X	X	X	X
Door*			X	X	X	X	X
Deck			X	X	X	X	X
Compartment					X	X	X
Seat back					X	X	X

*1994 Neons have a six-tumbler door lock, spaces 2–7.

Lock	Space positions for 1995 "wide body" wafer locks						
	1	2	3	4	5	6	7
Ignition	X	X	X	X	X	X	X
Door	X	X	X	X	X	X	X
Deck	X	X	X	X	X	X	X
Compartment					X	X	X

lower pin chamber and shouldn't have a No. 6 pin in the second lower pin chamber. When a No. 5 pin is found in the first or second lower pin chamber or a No. 6 pin is found in the second lower pin chamber, the lock was probably improperly rekeyed.

The depth and spaces for Chrysler locks that use key blank P19A/P1770U (1969–1989 ignition and doors) are as follows: Spacing No. 1—.146; No. 2—.286; No. 3—.426; No. 4—.566; and No. 5—.706 (spacing from center of one cut to center of next cut is .140). Depth No. 1—.246; No. 2—.226; No. 3—.206; No. 4—.186; No. 5—.166; and No. 6—.146. (Depth drop is .020 between depths.)

The depth and spacing for Chrysler locks that use key blank S19/S1770CH (1969–1989 trunk) are as follows: Spacing No. 1—.146; No. 2—.286; No. 3—.426; No. 4—.566; and No. 5—.706 (spacing from center of one cut to center of next cut is .140). Depth No. 1—.246; No. 2—.226; No. 3—.206; No. 4—.186; No. 5—.166; and No. 6—.146 (depth drop from cut depth to the next is .020).

The spacing and depth for Chrysler locks that use key blank P1789 (1989 and later Acclaim/Spirit) are as follows: Spacing No. 1—.757; No. 2—.665; No. 3—.573; No. 4—.481; No. 5—.389; No. 6—.297; and No. 7—.205 (spacing from one space to the next is .108). Depth No. 1—.340; No. 2—.315; No. 3—.290; and No. 4—.265 (depth drop from one depth to the next is .025).

Table 19.4 shows other spaces and depths used by Chrysler keys. For a list of key blanks used by Chrysler, see Table 19.5.

Datsun

Most locks used on Datsuns have six-disc tumblers and are easy to pick. All of the locks on a Datsun are keyed alike. They are operated by a double-sided convenience key.

Both sides of the key are cut, but either side can operate a lock because Datsun locks have only one set of tumblers.

A key can be fitted for Datsun locks by cutting a key by the code that's written on a piece of paper glued to the glove compartment lid. The code can also be found on a door lock. A door lock can also be used to impression a key.

TABLE 19.4 Spaces and Depths for Chrysler Keys (Cuts Are from Tip to Bow)

	19881/2–1992 F0001-1394/ G0001-1394	1993–95 J0001-3580/ L0001-3580
Depth 1	.340"	.340"
Depth 2	.315"	.315"
Depth 3	.290"	.290"
Depth 4	.265"	.265"
Space 1	.757"	.849"
Space 2	.665"	.757"
Space 3	.573"	.665"
Space 4	.481"	.573"
Space 5	.389"	.481"
Space 6	.297"	.389"
Space 7	.205"	.297"
	Cut-to-cut is .092" MAC-2	

Honda

Most locks used on Hondas have six-disc tumblers. These are operated with a double-sided convenience key and are easy to pick. All of the six-disc tumbler locks on a Honda are keyed alike. A lot of pre-1976 Hondas use locks that have eight-disc tumblers.

Impressioning is usually the fastest way to fit a key for a post-1976 Honda. Another way is to use the code number found on the door lock.

A key used for a Honda manufactured in 1989 or later is 4 mm (.175 inch) longer from the shoulder to the bow than is a key for an older model Honda. For pre-1989 Honda Accords, Preludes (from 1982), and Civics, use key blank HD83. For Honda Accords and Preludes made in or after 1989, use key blank HD90. Key blank HD91 can be used for

TABLE 19.5 Chrysler Key Blank Chart

Years	Code series	Key type	Briggs & Stratton	Ilco	Star
1988–89	F/G001-1394	Master	594145	P1789	HPL89
		Valet	321566	—	—
1991	G0001-1394	Master	594145	P1789	HPL89
		Valet	321566	—	—
1992	G0001-1394	Master	594145	P1789	HPL89
		Valet	321566	—	—
1993	J0001-1394	Master	595895	P1793V	—
		Valet	322140	1793V	—
1994	L0001-3580	Master	596504	P1794	CHR94
		Valet	322236	1794V	—
1995	L0001-3580	Master	596504	P1794	CHR94
		Valet	322236	1794V	—

Honda Civics made in or after 1989. If you use the HD83 blank to cut a key for a Honda model made in or after 1989, you might have difficulty removing the key from the ignition lock.

Ford

Up to the 1984 model year, pin tumbler locks with five sets of tumblers were used for all Ford ignitions, doors, and trunks. Glove compartment locks were either pin tumbler or disc tumbler. (Since 1981 only four-disc tumbler locks have been used on glove compartments.) In late 1984, many Ford vehicles began using only disc tumbler locks.

On pre-1982 Ford models, the ignition and doors are keyed alike and operated by the primary key; the glove compartment and trunk are keyed alike and operated by the secondary key.

On pre-1977 models, the code for the primary key can be found on one of the door locks, usually a passenger side. On pre-1980 models, the secondary key code can be found on the glove compartment lock latch housing. Beginning in 1980, codes were no longer stamped on Ford glove compartment locks.

The primary key for a post-1980 Ford fits only the ignition lock; the secondary key operates all the other locks. Many of those locks don't have key code numbers stamped on them, but the tumblers have bitting numbers stamped on them. Those bitting numbers can be seen when a lock is disassembled.

Fitting Keys to Pre-1984 Ford

You can fit a primary key to a pre-1981 Ford lock by removing the door lock and measuring the bottom pins. The measurements for Ford bottom pins are as follows: No. 1—.145; No. 2—.165; No. 3—.185; No. 4—.205; and No. 5—.225. To fit a primary key for a 1981 to 1984 Ford, either use the ignition lock to impression a key or remove the lock and read the bitting numbers on the tumblers.

Fit a secondary key to a pre-1981 Ford lock by cutting according to the code number on the glove compartment lock. To fit a secondary key for a 1981 to 1984 model, remove the disc tumbler lock and read the bitting numbers on the tumblers.

Fitting Keys to Post-1984 Fords

There are two basic locking systems for post-1984 Fords. The newer system uses only disc tumbler locks (a side bar disc tumbler lock is used for the ignition). The older system uses pin tumbler locks.

During mid-year production of the 1984 Mercury Cougar and the Ford T-Bird, Ford Motor Company began using a side bar disc tumbler ignition lock (similar to the one used by General Motors Corporation) and disc tumbler door locks. A convenience key is used to operate the locks. Either side of the key blade can be used.

With the new system, one convenience key is used to operate a vehicle's ignition and door locks.

The double-sided key (Ilco blank 1184FD), sometimes called "the 10-cut key," has 10 cuts on each side. The first six cuts (starting from the bow) are for the doors; the last six cuts (spaces 5 through 10) operate the ignition lock. Spaces 5 and 6 on the key correspond to the tumbler depths that the ignition and doors have in common. When the key is inserted into a door, the first six cuts are aligned with the tumblers;

TABLE 19.6 Ford 10-Cut Tumbler Positions

	Standard 84½ Ford 10-cut system									
Position	1	2	3	4	5	6	7	8	9	10
Door	X	X	X	X	X	X				
Ignition					X	X	X	X	X	X
Trunk	(Standard 5-pin Ford system, uses secondary blank)									

	1991 Ford Escort/Mercury Tracer									
Position	1	2	3	4	5	6	7	8	9	10
Door				X	X	X	X	X	X	
Ignition				X	X	X	X	X	X	X
Deck lid				X	X	X	X	X	X	

	1993 Ford Escort/Mercury Tracer									
Position	1	2	3	4	5	6	7	8	9	10
Door				X	X	X	X	X		
Ignition					X	X	X	X	X	X
Deck lid				X	X	X	X	X		

	1993 Mercury Villager/Nissan Escort									
Position	1	2	3	4	5	6	7	8	9	10
Door				X	X	X	X	X		
Ignition					X	X	X	X	X	X
Glove box								X		X

when inserted into an ignition, the last six cuts are aligned with the tumblers. See Table 19.6 for a comprehensive comparison of various Ford lock tumbler positions.

The older locking system uses two keys to operate all the locks of a vehicle; each double-sided convenience key has only five cuts on each side. (The primary blank is Ilco 1167FD; the secondary blank is Ilco S1167FD.) In the older system, all the locks except the ignition lock are keyed alike and use the secondary key; the primary key operates only the ignition lock.

Post-1984 Ford Disk Tumbler Locks

Neither the ignition nor door locks of post-1984 Fords with disc tumbler locks have key codes stamped on them. The easiest way to fit a key to those vehicles is to cut a key by code, if the code is available. The codes are stamped on key tags given to the purchaser of the vehicle. If no code is available, you can impression a key at one of the doors. If you need a key for the ignition, use the cuts of the key you made for the door to help you impression the key.

Remember, the last two tumblers of the door lock have the same depth as the first two tumblers of the ignition lock. Another option is to remove and disassemble the lock.

The ignition lock must be rotated about 30 degrees to the right (to the On position) before it can be removed. This allows the retaining pin to be depressed and the pilot shaft to bypass an obstruction in the column so the lock can slide out.

You can rotate the cylinder by using a drilling jig (available from locksmith supply houses) to drill out the side bar. The jig is held in place by a setscrew; insert a key blank into the lock to align the jig, and the jig aligns your drill bit. The jig allows you to drill easily through the roller bearings on either side of the lock's keyway. After drilling through the lock, rotate and remove it.

Now you can rekey an uncoded ignition lock, and use that as a replacement lock. Or, use the service kit supplied to Ford dealerships to replace the lock.

PATS Ignition Locks

Ford's Passive Anti-theft System (PATS) relies on low frequency radio transmissions to identify the correct key for starting the vehicle. The system was first available in Europe on 1993 Ford vehicles. It was introduced in the United States on the 1996 Ford Taurus SHO and LS and the Mercury Sable LX.

The system uses a transponder (a glass vial about the size of a car fuse) sealed in the head of each ignition key. The transponder has 72 million billion possible electronic codes. When the properly coded key is inserted in the ignition of a PATS equipped vehicle, the proper code is transmitted to the vehicle's control module, allowing the vehicle to be started. If a key with no code or the wrong code is used, the engine will be disabled.

Until 1998, the PATS system was easy for locksmiths to service. In 1998, Ford modified the system. The new version isn't locksmith-friendly, and is commonly referred to by locksmiths as PATS 2.

Vehicles equipped with the original PATS (or "PATS 1") include: Ford Contour, 1998; Ford Expedition, 1997–98; Ford Mustang, 1996–97; Ford Taurus, 1996–97; Lincoln Navigator, 1998; Mercury Sable, 1996–97; and Mercury Mystique, 1997–98.

Models equipped with PATS 2 in 1998 include the following: Ford Crown Victoria; Ford Explorer; Ford Mustang; Ford Taurus; Lincoln Mark VIII; Lincoln Town Car; Lincoln Continental; Mercury Sable; Mountaineer; and Mercury Grand Marquis. The 1999 model year Mercury Cougar is also equipped with PATS 2.

General Motors

A General Motors (GM) vehicle ordinarily uses side bar disc tumbler locks for the ignition, door, and trunk, and standard disc tumbler locks for the glove compartment and utility compartments. Some top-of-the-line GMs have side bar disc tumbler locks on the glove compartments.

A pre-1974 GM has its ignition and door locks keyed alike, and all of those locks are operated by the primary key. The code for the primary key can be found on the ignition lock.

Pre-1970 models have the code for the primary lock stamped on the door locks.

A post-1973 GM uses a primary key that fits only the ignition lock; its secondary key operates the other locks. Until the late 1970s, the secondary key code number could be found on the vehicle's glove compartment lock. The glove compartment lock has four tumblers, which correspond to the last four tumblers of the trunk lock (the trunk lock has six tumblers).

Fitting a Key

Fit a primary key for a pre-1970 GM by removing the door lock and using the code number stamped on it. To fit a primary key for a 1970 to 1973 model, remove, disassemble, and decode the door lock. Lock decoders are available from locksmith supply houses for this purpose (Figure 19.3). For a 1974 to 1978 model GM, save time by just pulling the ignition lock and installing a new one. Otherwise, you must disassemble the steering wheel column. A primary key can be fitted to a post-1978 GM model (not including vehicles with VATS or PASSKey) by disassembling the steering wheel column, removing the lock, and using the code stamped on the lock.

To fit a key for a secondary GM lock, remove the glove compartment plug and cut the key by code. Some GM glove compartment locks are tricky to remove without using a bezel nut wrench (Figure 19.4). The plug can be removed as follows: pick the lock open if it's locked, open the door, then pick it back to the locked position. Insert an ice pick or similar instrument in the small poke hole and depress the retaining pin. You should be able to easily remove the plug. If no code is available, fit a key to the glove compartment lock and use the following GM progression method to find the remaining two cuts.

The GM Progression Method

Since 1967, GM has adhered to the following three rules for making a factory original key:

- The sum total of the cut depths must equal an even number.

- There cannot be a more than two cut-depth difference between any adjacent cuts.

- There can never be more than three of the same cut depths in a row.

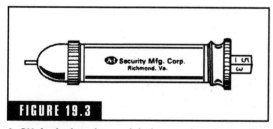

FIGURE 19.3

A GM lock decoder tool helps to decode tumbler combinations of GM locks. *(Courtesy of A-1 Security Manufacturing Corp.)*

The GM progression method is based on logically using these rules to progressively decrease the possible key cut combinations until the proper combination is determined. The first rule refers to the fact that whenever the cut depth numbers of a GM key are added together, the sum should be an even number. A GM key might have the cut depth numbers 3-2-4-3-2 (which equals 14), for example, but not 3-2-4-3-3, because the sum of the latter is an odd number.

Suppose you obtained four cut depths from a glove compartment lock and need to find the remaining two cuts for operating the trunk lock. If the sum of the four cut depths is an odd number, the two unknown depths must also equal an odd number, because any odd number plus any other odd number always equals an even number. If the sum of the four cut depths is an even number, the remaining two must equal an even number because any even number plus any other even number always equals an even number. Likewise, any odd number plus any even number equals an odd number.

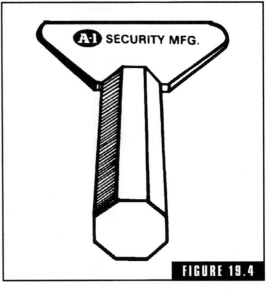

FIGURE 19.4

A bezel nut wrench is used to remove locks from GM glove compartments. *(Courtesy of A-1 Security Manufacturing Corp.)*

The second of the three rules refers to the fact that cuts directly next to each other should never differ by more than two cut depths. For example, a number 1 cut should not directly precede or follow a number 4 cut depth.

The third of the three rules means no GM key should have three consecutive cuts of the same depth. A key bitting of 2-2-2-3-1, for example, is forbidden.

Using these three rules, it's easy to use the four cut depths found on a glove compartment lock to figure out the remaining two cuts for the trunk lock. First, make a key with those four cuts; the first and second spaces on the key should be left uncut. There are only 25 possibilities for the first two cuts (five possible depths for two spaces equals 5 squared, or 25). The 25 possible depths for the two remaining spaces are 1,1; 1,2; 1,3; 1,4; 1,5; 2,1; 2,2; 2,3; 2,4; 2,5; 3,1; 3,2; 3,3; 3,4; 3,5; 4,1; 4,2; 4,3; 4,4; 4,5; 5,1; 5,2; 5,3; 5,4; 5,5.

Based on the second GM keying rule, six of those 25 possible depths can be ignored because they have more than two depth increments between them. They are: 1,4; 1,5; 2,5; 4,1; 5,1; 5,2. That leaves only 19 possible depth combinations in any instance where the first two depth cuts must be found for a GM.

Based on the first GM keying rule, you can immediately eliminate about half of those 19 possibilities. You would eliminate either all the odd pairs or all the even pairs, depending on whether you need a pair that equals an even number or a pair that equals an odd number. If you need a pair that equals an even number, you would have only the following 11 choices: 1,1; 2,2; 3,3; 4,4; 5,5; 3,1; 4,2; 5,3; 1,3; 2,4; 3,5. If you need a pair that equals an odd number, you would have only the following seven choices: 2,1; 1,2; 3,2; 2,3; 4,3; 5,4; 4,5.

The second GM rule would then allow you to eliminate several more of those pairs. If your four glove compartment lock cut depths are 1-1-2-3, for example, then rule two would be violated by preceding those cuts with the cuts 3,4; 5,4; or 4,5. If a 4 or 5 depth cut was next to a 1 cut on a key, the key would have adjacent cuts with more than 2 depth differences. That means only five possible cuts would be available. They are: 1,2; 2,3; 2,1; 3,2; and 4,3.

Using the same glove compartment lock cut depths as the example, you would then take the key and cut a 2 depth in the first space and a 1 depth in the second space; then try the key in the lock.

If the key doesn't work, you would then progress to cutting a 3 depth in the first space and a 2 depth in the second space (both spaces would be cut a little deeper). After cutting three of the five possibilities, you would then need to use another key with the four cuts from the glove compartment on it to cut the remaining two pairs of depths on that key, beginning with the shallowest pair. One of them will operate the lock.

By using the GM progression method, you should never have to waste more than one key blank if you're searching for an odd combination for the two cuts. You should never have to waste more than two keys if you're searching for an even number for the two cuts.

There are only two reasons this method can fail: the factory made an error in keying the lock; or someone rekeyed the lock without adhering to GM's rules.

Servicing General Motors Vehicles with VATS

The General Motors Vehicle Anti-Theft System (VATS), also called Personalized Automotive Security System (PASSKey), has been used in select GM models since 1986. The system has proven helpful in preventing automobile thefts. Table 19.7 shows a list of GM vehicles that are equipped with the system.

TABLE 19.7 General Motors Cars Equipped with VATS or PASSKey

Car/model	Model years	Ignition lock		
		Standard	Pushbutton	48-pin connector
Buick Electra	1991, 1992 (disc)	701286	—	No
Buick Reatta	1989, 1990, 1991, 1992 (disc)	700754	—	No
Buick Regal	1994, 1995	700754	700938	No
Buick Riviera	1990, 1991, 1992, 1993, 1994, 1995	701286	—	Yes 1991
Buick LeSabre	1992, 1993, 1994 1995	701286	—	Yes 1992
Buick Park Avenue	1991, 1992, 1993, 1994, 1995	701286	—	Yes 1991
Cadillac Allante	1989, 1990, 1991, 1993, 1994 (disc)	700930	—	No
Cadillac Brougham	1988, 1989, 1990, 1991, 1992, 1993, 1994, 1995	700930	—	No
Cadillac Eldorado	1988, 1989, 1990, 1991, 1992, 1993, 1994, 1995	701286	—	Yes 1992
Cadillac DeVille/Concour	1990, 1991, 1992, 1993, 1994, 1995	701286	—	Yes 1990
Cadillac Fleetwood	1990, 1991, 1992, 1993, 1994, 1995	701286	—	Yes 1995
Cadillac Seville	1988, 1989, 1990, 1991, 1992, 1993, 1994, 1995	701286	—	Yes 1992

TABLE 19.7 *(Continued)*

Car/model	Model years	Ignition lock		
		Standard	Pushbutton	48-pin connector
Chevrolet Camaro	1988, 1989, 1990, 1991, 1992, 1993, 1994, 1995	700754	700938	No
Chevrolet Corvette	1986, 1987, 1988, 1989, 1990, 1991, 1992, 1993, 1994, 1995	700754	700938	No
Chevrolet Lumina	1994, 1995	700754	700938	No
Chevrolet Monte Carlo	1994, 1995	700754	—	No
Oldsmobile Cutlass Supreme	1994, 1995	700754	700938	No
Oldsmobile Toronada	1991, 1992, 1993 (disc)	700754	—	No
Oldsmobile 88	1992, 1993, 1994, 1995	701286	—	Yes 1992
Oldsmobile 98	1991, 1992, 1993, 1994, 1995	701286	—	Yes 1992
Pontiac Bonneville	1992, 1993, 1994, 1995	701286	—	Yes 1992
Pontiac Firebird	1989, 1990, 1991, 1992, 1993, 1994, 1995	700754	700938	No
Pontiac Firebird GTA	1989, 1990 (disc)	700754	—	No
Pontiac Grand Prix	1994, 1995	700754	700938	No

VATS is an electromechanical system that consists of the following basic components: a computer module, keys that each have a resistor pellet embedded in them, an ignition cylinder, and a wire harness that connects the ignition cylinder to the computer module.

When a properly cut VATS key is inserted into the ignition cylinder, the cylinder will turn. The resistor pellet in the key will neither hinder nor aid the mechanical action of the ignition cylinder.

If the key is embedded with an incorrect resistor pellet or has no resistor pellet, the computer module shuts down the vehicle's electric fuel pump, starter, and power train management system for about four minutes.

This happens because vehicles with VATS are designed to operate only when one of 15 levels of resistance is present. The 15 levels are represented in 15 different resistor pellets. A VATS key is a standard GM key with one of 15 resistor pellets embedded in its bow. See Table 19.8 for a list of VATS keys.

When a VATS key is inserted into a VATS ignition cylinder, contacts within the cylinder touch the resistor pellet in the key and the resistor pellet's resistance value is transmitted to the VATS computer module by the wire harness connecting the cylinder to the computer module. Only if the resistance value is the right level can the vehicle be started.

It's important to remember that the turning of the ignition cylinder is a mechanical process that is independent of the system's electronics. Any properly cut key that fits the ignition cylinder can be used to turn the cylinder to the start position. However, unless the VATS control module also receives the correct resistor information, the vehicle won't start.

VATS keys look similar to other late-model GM keys, but come with a black rubber bow and contain a resistor pellet. They use standard GM depths and spacings and fit into an A keyway. All VATS key blanks are cut the same way other GM blanks are cut.

When cutting a key for a VATS vehicle, however, it is first necessary to determine which of 15 VATS blanks to use. That can be determined by measuring the resistor value of the pattern key (the one the customer wants duplicated) with an ohmmeter or multimeter and comparing the reading to the VATS pellet's resistor values. Table 19.9 shows the resistor values currently being used.

When VATS was used in the 1986 Corvette, each module had a pre-designated resistor pellet value. That system was used through 1988.

TABLE 19.8 VATS/PASSKey Blank Information

Key blank	*6 wafer	*10 wafer	Resistance value
Key blank w/pellet #1	594201	—	.402 kohms
Key blank w/pellet #2	594202	596772	.522 kohms
Key blank w/pellet #3	594203	596773	.681 kohms
Key blank w/pellet #4	594204	596774	.887 kohms
Key blank w/pellet #5	594205	596775	1.13 kohms
Key blank w/pellet #6	594206	596776	1.47 kohms
Key blank w/pellet #7	594207	596777	1.87 kohms
Key blank w/pellet #8	594208	596778	2.37 kohms
Key blank w/pellet #9	594209	596779	3.01 kohms
Key blank w/pellet #10	594210	596780	3.74 kohms
Key blank w/pellet #11	594211	596781	4.75 kohms
Key blank w/pellet #12	594212	596782	6.04 kohms
Key blank w/pellet #13	594213	596783	7.50 kohms
Key blank w/pellet #14	594214	596784	9.53 kohms
Key blank w/pellet #15	594215	596785	11.8 kohms

*Briggs & Stratton (Strattec) blank numbers

Starting with the 1988 Pontiac Trans AM GTA, General Motors began using a modified VATS. The new VATS was named the Personalized Automotive Security System. All GM vehicles with VATS manufactured after 1989 use this new system.

For locksmiths, there are two major differences between the two systems. First, the keys used with the new system are 3 mm longer than the keys used with the old system (Figure 19.5). The old key blanks have to be modified before they can be used to operate the new VATS ignition locks.

The other big difference between the two systems is that the older system had stickers on the VATS modules showing the modules' resistor number; the new system doesn't have the stickers.

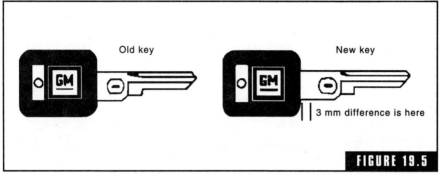

FIGURE 19.5

New VATS keys are longer than the older keys.

TABLE 19.9

VATS pellet	Resistance in ohms	B&S part # 1986, 1987	B&S part # 1988, 1989
1	400	593581	594201
2	500	593582	594202
3	679	593583	594203
4	885	593584	594204
5	1,128	593585	594205
6	1,468	593586	594206
7	1,871	593587	594207
8	2,369	593588	594208
9	3,101	593589	594209
10	3,728	593590	594210
11	4,750	593591	594211
12	6,038	593592	594212
13	7,485	593591	594213
14	9,531	593594	594214
15	11,769	535595	594215

Making a VATS First Key

When no pattern VATS key is available for you to duplicate, you can make a VATS key by first determining the proper bitting in the same way that you would determine the bitting for non-VATS late-model GM vehicles. Then, determine the VATS key blank to which to transfer the cuts.

The most expensive way to determine the correct blank is to cut and try a different VATS key blank until you find one that starts the vehicle. The high costs of VATS blanks make this method impractical. A less costly method involves using an ohmmeter or multimeter, an extra VATS ignition cylinder, and 15 different VATS blanks.

Disconnect the wire harness connecting the control module to the cylinder, and connect that wire to the extra VATS cylinder. Insert one of the VATS key blanks into the extra cylinder and attempt to start the vehicle by using the correctly cut mechanical key to turn the vehicle's ignition cylinder to the start position. If the vehicle shuts down, you'll need to wait four minutes, then repeat the procedure with another VATS key blank in the extra ignition cylinder until the vehicle starts. After the vehicle starts, transfer the cuts from the correctly cut mechanical key to the VATS key blank that allowed you to start the vehicle. Then disconnect the wire harness from your extra ignition cylinder and reconnect it to the vehicle's ignition cylinder.

USING A VATS DECODER

A VATS decoder can be very helpful for servicing vehicles with VATS. Several companies manufacture this device. A popular model is the All-Lock A-7000, manufactured by the All-Lock Company (Figure 19.6).

The A-7000 can be used to perform four functions: identify the correct VATS key blank from the customer's original; decode the correct VATS blank from the vehicle; diagnose steering column connection problems; and diagnose VATS computer problems.

With the A-7000, the resistor value of a VATS key can be determined simply by inserting the key into a slot in the decoder (Figure 19.7). This feature can be useful for quickly finding the right VATS key blank to use to duplicate a VATS key.

The decoder can also help determine which VATS blank to use when no VATS key is available.

First, you need to cut a correct mechanical key that will turn the vehicle's ignition cylinder to the start position. Then connect the decoder's two tester connectors to the mating VATS connectors at the base of the steering column under the dash. After turning the decoder's key code switch to 1, try to start the engine with your properly cut mechanical key. If the engine doesn't start, press the four-minute timer on the decoder (Figure 19.8). After four minutes, the timer light will go out.

That lets you know the vehicle should be ready to try another key code number. Then, turn the decoder's key code switch to the next number and try the mechanical key again. Follow this procedure until the vehicle starts. When the vehicle starts, transfer the cuts from your mechanically correct key to the VATS blank that corresponds to the number of the key code shown on the VATS decoder.

Many locksmiths don't appreciate VATS. They don't like having to stock 15 different expensive key blanks or having to take so much time making a first key for a vehicle. However, it's likely that VATS will be used in General Motors' vehicles for many years. Anyone who wants to service automotive locks should be prepared to handle vehicles with VATS. This means obtaining the proper tools and staying informed of changes in VATS.

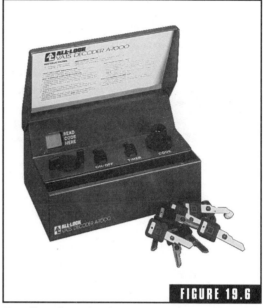

FIGURE 19.6

The All-Lock A-7000 is used to service vehicles with VATS. *(Courtesy of A-1 Security Manufacturing Corp.)*

FIGURE 19.7

The resistor value of a VATS key can be determined by inserting the key into the All-Lock A-7000. *(Courtesy of A-1 Security Manufacturing Corp.)*

Opening Locked Vehicles

Not long ago, virtually any locked vehicle could be opened by inserting a flat metal tool about 3 inches long and 1 inch wide into the door

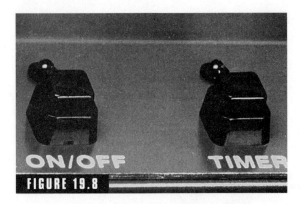

FIGURE 19.8

A light comes on whenever the All-Lock 7000's timer switch button is pushed. *(Courtesy of All-Lock Company*

between the window and the weather-stripping, then moving it up and down and from side to side until it caught something that unlocked the door. To reduce thefts, automobile manufacturers are now making vehicles increasingly difficult to open. The flat metal tool isn't nearly as effective an automobile-opening tool as it used to be. In many cases, using it can damage a vehicle's locking system in a way that prevents the operation of the locks by the key. In response to those changes, locksmiths have developed new tools and opening techniques.

To understand how to open a vehicle properly, you need to understand how vehicle locks work. When you're standing outside of a vehicle, you only see the face of the lock cylinder and the lock button on the door. For vehicle opening purposes, however, there are four important parts of a door's locking system: the lock cylinder; the cylinder cam; lock rods or connecting rods; and the lock button.

The cylinder cam, or pawl, is attached to the back of the cylinder. A lock rod is connected to the pawl. The lock rod or connecting rod is attached to the door's lock button. When the proper key is turned in the lock cylinder, the pawl is moved up or down, depending on the direction the key is being turned. The lock rod moves with the pawl, and the lock button moves with the lock rod.

Usually when any one of the parts is moved to its unlocked position, all the other parts are also moved to their unlocked positions. To open a locked vehicle, you need to use a tool to move one of those parts to its unlocked position.

In most cases, a locked vehicle can be opened by lifting up or pushing down on the lock pawl, pulling the lock rod up, pushing the lock rod forward, lifting the lock rod button, or picking the lock. The lock pawl can usually be manipulated with an L-shaped tool. You can make such a tool by bending a 39-inch length of ⁵⁄₁₆-inch-diameter steel to the dimensions shown in Figure 19.9.

Some door locks, such as those used on vehicles made by Ford Motor Company, have rigid or fixed pawls that cannot be lifted or

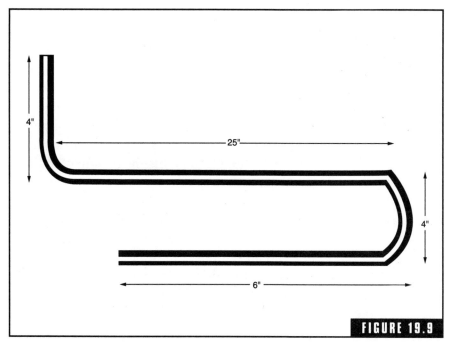

FIGURE 19.9

By properly bending a 39-inch piece of steel, you can make a very useful automobile opening tool.

pushed down. You can usually open a door with that type of lock by moving the lock rod.

The lock rod is connected to the pawl and is within the walls of a door. Some lock rods are vertical, and some are horizontal. In general, if a button on the door pops up when the door is being unlocked with a key, the door has a vertical lock rod. If the door is opened from the inside by sliding a button to the left or right (horizontally), the door probably has a horizontal lock rod.

Doors with vertical lock rods can usually be opened by using a tool to hook the lock rod and pull it up. Doors with horizontal lock rods can usually be opened by using a tool to hook the rod and pull it forward.

The lock rod button is on top of a lock rod that pops up or slides when the lock is opened. In older model automobiles, the vertical lock rod button often had a wide head that could be hooked and lifted with a wire such as a coat hanger. Most late-model automobiles that have vertical lock rods use lock buttons that are either tapered or that sit flush with the door when the door is locked. These are difficult to hook from the top with a piece of wire; you will have better success with the tool shown in Figure 19.9.

To use this tool to lift up a lock button, use the L end of the tool as a handle and place a wedge between the window and weatherstripping near the center of the door. This provides a gap into which you can insert your tool. Lower the U end of the tool below the rubber weatherstripping, and position the tip of the tool directly beneath the lock button. When the tip of the tool is touching the bottom of the lock button, lift the tool upward to unlock the door.

Wedges can be purchased from any locksmith supply house, but they are also easy to make. Use a smooth piece of plastic or wood that's about 4 or 5 inches long and tapered to about ½ inch thick. (Don't use metal because it can scrape paint off a vehicle.) You must be able to push the narrow side of the wedge partially into the door between the window and the rubber weatherstripping; that provides the gap for the automobile opening tool. In some cases, such as when searching for a lock rod within the walls of a door, you might want to insert a thin, flexible light into the gap before you insert the automobile opening tool. This can help you avoid haphazardly probing inside the door with your tool, which not only looks amateurish, but can also cause you to break a pawl, bend a rod in the door, or otherwise damage the vehicle.

Several companies publish and update manuals that provide lock opening information for hundreds of different automobile models. By using those manuals, you can quickly find out which opening methods are most efficient for the vehicle you're working on. Most publishers of those manuals, however, also sell a lot of automobile opening tools along with the manuals. In most cases, knowledge is much more important for opening vehicles than are a wide assortment of tools.

A typical multi-tool automobile opening kit will contain several L tools of different sizes, several different sizes of tools for lifting a lock button rod, several different sizes of tools for pulling a lock rod, etc. However, the tool shown in Figure 19.9 can be used to quickly open virtually any vehicle you are likely to encounter.

Many publishers of automobile opening manuals sell the manuals and tools separately. Some sell their products only to locksmiths; others also sell to other security professionals, such as law enforcement officers. All-Lock Company, High Tech Tools, Pro-Lok, and Slide Lock Tool Company are publishers of some very popular automobile-opening manuals.

Slide Lock Tool Company's compact manual (Figure 19.10) shows how to open over 620 vehicles with the company's Z-tool (Figure 19.11). The tempered spring steel tool has a long end for wide, paneled doors, such as are found on large luxury cars, and a shorter end to be used on the thin-walled doors of compact and subcompact cars. The tool is very versatile because it can be bent into different configurations and then bent back into its original shape. Slide Lock Tool Company's manual has many drawings that illustrate step-by-step directions for using the tool to open many vehicles.

The tool has three numbers stamped along its shaft to aid with linkage depth

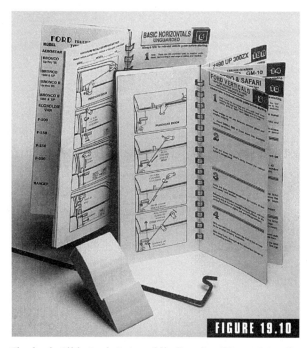

FIGURE 19.10

The basic Slide Lock Automobile Opening Kit consists of a manual, a wedge, and a Z-tool. *(Courtesy of Slide Lock Company)*

locations. It is designed to hook both vertical and horizontal lock rods quickly. Because it is so thin and can be bent, the tool can also bypass most anti-theft shield guards some automobile manufacturers use to protect lock rods. Figure 19-12 shows how the Z-tool is used.

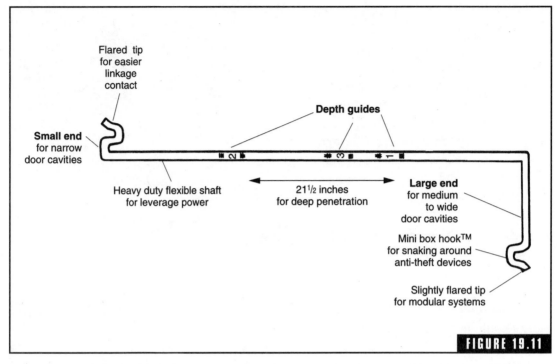

Flared tip
for easier
linkage
contact

Depth guides

Small end
for narrow
door cavities

Heavy duty flexible shaft
for leverage power

21½ inches
for deep penetration

Large end
for medium
to wide
door cavities

Mini box hook™
for snaking around
anti-theft devices

Slightly flared tip
for modular systems

FIGURE 19.11

The Z-tool has depth guide marks that can be helpful when opening automobiles. *(Courtesy of Slide Lock Tool Company)*

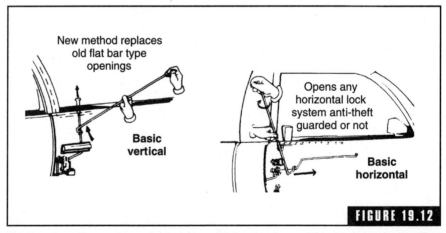

New method replaces
old flat bar type
openings

**Basic
vertical**

Opens any
horizontal lock
system anti-theft
guarded or not

**Basic
horizontal**

FIGURE 19.12

The Z-tool can be used to quickly open vehicles that have either horizontal or vertical lock rods. *(Courtesy of Slide Lock Tool Company)*

Closed Circuit Television Systems

Locks and other physical security devices can be more effective when used in conjunction with a closed circuit television (or CCTV) system. Such a system can allow several areas, such as elevators, entrances and exits, parking lots, lobbies, and cash handling areas, to be monitored constantly. Such monitoring can deter crime and reduce a company's security costs.

This chapter looks at the various components that make up a system and shows various ways that such a system can be used.

Basics

To begin selling and installing CCTV systems, you don't need to have a strong background in electronics. Although few locksmiths can handle the large multiplex systems used in airports and banks, most CCTV systems used in small offices, stores, and apartments are easy to install. Many CCTV systems come preconfigured as a complete package.

However, it's still important for you, the security professional, to have a basic understanding of each of the components you may be working with. That allows you to be more helpful to your customer—which can mean more profits for you. The major parts of a CCTV system are the cameras, housings, monitors, video recorders, and pan-and-tilt drives.

A black-and-white CCD camera responds well to low light conditions. *(Courtesy of CCTV Corp.)*

Some modern cameras are designed to attractively blend into a home or office environment. *(Courtesy of CCTV Corp.)*

Cameras

There are two main types of CCTV cameras: vacuum tube, or tube, and solid state CCD, or chip. Tube cameras are inexpensive, but have a short lifespan. CCD cameras not only last much longer, they also provide better resolution and adapt better to varying light conditions. As a rule, CCD cameras are a much better value than their tube counterparts (see Figure 20.1).

Cameras come in color or black-and-white. Black-and-white models are less expensive and are better for outdoor and low-light applications.

Cameras can be overt or covert. Overt models are designed to let people know that they may be being watched. Some are stylishly designed to fit various decor (see Figure 20.2). Covert models are designed to be unnoticed. Some covert models have been innocuously built into common items like wall clocks, radios, smoke detectors, and exit signs. Some popular covert models are shown in Figures 20.3, 20.4, 20.5, and 20.6.

Housings

Special housings are available to protect cameras from vandalism, weather, and environmental conditions such as dust. Accessories incorporated into housings include heaters, hoods, and lens-cover wipers. Housings are generally made of metal or high impact plastic.

Monitors

Like cameras, monitors are available in color and black-and-white. Unless you use a color camera, there's no need to use a color monitor.

(To view a scene in color, both the camera and monitor have to be color models.) Some monitors include a built-in switcher, which allows you to automatically or manually view scenes from multiple cameras. Monitors range in size from 5-inch to over 23-inch-diameter diagonal, but it's best not to use one with a screen smaller than 9 inches.

Video Recorders

A CCTV system has limited value if it can't record select events. Two basic types of video recorders are video tape and video cassette. Reel-to-reel video tape recorders (VTRs) can provide both real time and time lapse recording. However, video cassette recorders (VCRs) are easier to use and are becoming very popular for security applications. Standard video tape recorders can record continuously for up to six hours. Time lapse models can record up to 200 hours. Tape cost can be kept low by periodically erasing and reusing tapes.

Pan-and-Tilt Drives

A pan-and-tilt, or pan/tilt, drive is a motor-driven device that holds a camera.

The device allows you to remotely move the camera to various positions.

FIGURE 20.3

A CCD camera built into a battery-operated quartz clock. *(Courtesy of CCTV Corp.)*

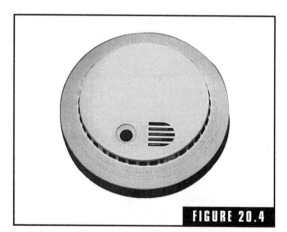

FIGURE 20.4

A camera built into a real smoke detector. *(Courtesy of CCTV Corp.)*

Pan-and-Tilt Technology

Jerry L. Jacobson, Ph.D.

By now everyone knows how sophisticated the front end of a security system can be, with the multitude of functions and the clever on-screen controls operated by mouse or by touch-screen. Out at the far

FIGURE 20.5

An exit sign with an inconspicuous camera. *(Courtesy of CCTV Corp.)*

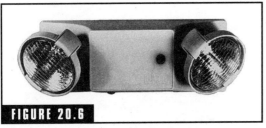

FIGURE 20.6

An exit sign with an inconspicuous camera. *(Courtesy of CCTV Corp.)*

end of the system things are changing too, including the old stand-by of CCTV systems, the pan-and-tilt drive.

The basic function of a pan-and-tilt is simple and straightforward: the pan-and-tilt swivels horizontally (panning) and vertically (tilting) to bring the camera to bear on a subject within its viewing area. Some units are designed to only bear on a subject within its viewing area. Some units are designed only to pan and do not offer motorized tilt action; these are called *scanners*. Scanners offer a manually adjustable tilt head. In its simplest form, control of a pan-and-tilt motion is carried out by an operator pressing buttons or a joystick that routes power to the motors in the pan-and-tilt. In its earliest incarnations, this was the full extent of pan-and-tilt operation.

Today, much more is expected of a pan-and-tilt, resulting in a proliferation of types and features.

The current capabilities of these devices must be well understood by the system designer and end user so that the system, once installed, does what is expected. On the other hand, some of the uses to which pan-and-tilts were put in the earlier days of CCTV have become obsolete, but the thinking associated with those functions still influences users' expectations and, to some extent, limits the overall effectiveness of their CCTV systems. In this chapter, we will look at pan-and-tilt drives and what they can do in a well-designed, modern system, and we will examine some of the misuses.

A third type of motor, called a stepping motor, has begun to appear in pan-and-tilt drives.

Stepping motors can provide variable speed operation with less expensive control circuits than those required by variable speed ac motors, and they do not have the radio frequency (RF) noise problem nor the brush replacement problem of dc motors.

Range of Motion

Each pan-and-tilt is designed with a certain range of horizontal movement and a certain range of vertical movement, and the range of each function is determined by a combination of practical design considerations and application requirements. For example, most pan-and-tilts are general-purpose units, suitable for use in most CCTV camera applications. In these units, a wide range of motion is desirable. In units designed for special purposes such as teleconferencing, however, only limited tilt is required, and the wider tilt range of the general-purpose unit is sacrificed in the interest of a lower profile.

Panning

The majority of drives can pan over a range of 350 to 355 degrees, and this meets most system requirements. These units all have a permanent pan limit stop that prevents movement beyond this range. This limited rotation is imposed by wiring that brings electrical power up to the tilt motors in the upper mobile part of the drive (the "head"). This is usually achieved by means of a coil cord, which looks like a coiled telephone handset cord. A coil cord can be flexed many times over a limited range without breaking, but as can be seen by the many knotted telephone coil cords, it can't be turned continuously in one direction without knotting up and tearing loose.

This mechanical arrangement has a drawback in some applications. If a subject who is being tracked moves through the dead zone created by the permanent limit stop, the pan-and-tilt has to be reversed through almost a full circle to pick up the subject again. During the reverse, the subject will be out of view for a considerable amount of time and can easily be lost from view.

This problem can be eliminated by a drive that can pan continuously in either direction without being impeded by the permanent limit stop.

Operating Speeds

No matter how many bells and whistles are added to a pan-and-tilt, pointing the camera remains its basic function. Most models move at a fixed, relatively slow speed that allows the scene to remain in reasonably good focus while the camera moves. These speeds, in the range of 5 to 8 degrees per second, also assure more accurate final positioning with fewer readjustments, but a faster-moving subject might get away from a camera mounted on such a pan-and-tilt.

Variable speed drives address this requirement by providing a range of operating speeds, allowing the operator to follow a fast-moving subject or to move slowly when needed. Currently, the speeds of variable speed drives range from under 1 degree/second to over 100 degrees/second. Higher speeds are useful primarily in variable speed drives; drives with fixed high speeds have less value, since the images deteriorate at higher speeds. Speeds above, say, 20 degrees/second produce an unintelligible image, so they are most useful for fast preset-position acquisition, which will be discussed more fully.

The effect of fast pan-speeds can be demonstrated dramatically by recording an image from a camera on a fast panning drive. If the image is played back in the still-frame or freeze-frame mode, most of the scene will be blurred out. The only part of the scene that might be sharp will be the objects moving at a speed close to the speed of the pan-and-tilt.

Variable speed is achieved with either ac motors, dc motors, or stepping motors. The three types have some important differences. The dc units require less expensive controls; basically, the speed is proportional to the load and to the input voltage level. Lowering the input voltage slows the speed and vice versa. However, dc motors generate radio frequency (RF) noise that can affect video signal quality. Also, they have an additional problem: the contact brushes that provide current to the rotation armature of the motor wear out and have to be replaced periodically.

The ac motors don't have the RF noise problem or the brush problem associated with dc motors, which is why today most constant speed pan-and-tilt drives use ac motors. However, to make a variable speed ac motor requires an electronic control interface that adds considerably to the cost.

Such pan-and-tilt drives are available, and they use a device called a slip ring assembly to achieve continuous rotation. To visualize a slip ring, place your right forefinger on your wedding ring (or any other ring on your left hand). Imagine that your forefinger is a spring-loaded contact that slides on the ring. If your finger could rotate continuously, the electrical connection between ring and contact would remain unbroken, no matter how many revolutions are made.

The slip ring assembly can transfer motor power, camera power, lens control signals, preset feedback, and video between the moving head and the fixed base of the drive. This can require over twenty contact rings and fingers in the slip ring assembly and, since slip ring assemblies are expensive, continuous rotation pan-and-tilts cost significantly more than limited rotation versions.

Tilting

The range of tilt motion is a simpler issue. Many units offer a tilt range of ±90 degrees, from straight up to straight down. Drives with the heaviest load capacity are often limited to ±60 degrees or a similar figure, and a few specialized units, such as teleconferencing pan-and-tilts, may offer less.

The range of tilt motion is a simple issue, but it has one unique additional consideration, which is the torque effect of gravity on the pan-and-tilt's load. (The force of gravity is exerted uniformly in the pan function and doesn't require special attention.) If the load on a pan-and-tilt is well balanced, gravity pulls evenly on the load and there's no unbalanced torque as long as the tilt head is at its extreme tilt position.

Well-designed medium- and heavy-duty drives include springs, counterweights, or both to reduce the torque effects of tilting. The effects of counterbalancing with springs and counterweights can be dramatic. Both remain neutral when the tilt platform is level, and their compensating effect increases as the tilt angle increases. Light-duty or inexpensive medium- or heavy-duty units may not have these features. All other things being equal, it is reasonable to expect a longer service life from pan-and-tilts with such features, because the forces on the tilt drive are better balanced.

Autopan and Random Pan

Most pan-and-tilt drives currently manufactured offer autopanning, and a few specialized scanners offer what is called random panning. *Autopanning* is easy to define: The head of the pan-and-tilt (or scanner) pans continuously back and forth over an angle selected by the system owner. Generally, the autopan range is set by positioning two moveable pan limit stops, although in more sophisticated units the limits may be set electronically.

Autopanning is something of an anachronism or dinosaur. In the earlier days of CCTV, the camera/lens assembly was a very expensive part of the system, and one camera had to cover as much area as possible to be economically effective. Thus, the need for autopan. Even then, however, there were some powerful factors that reduced the effectiveness of surveillance using autopan.

When the camera is in motion, the entire scene or background appears to the operator observing the monitor to be in motion. An object, such as a person, moving against a moving background is much less likely to be noticed, especially if the person is moving slowly. If this is combined with the dulling of the operator's senses that develops as the duty period wears on, there is a high likelihood that some important security breach may go unnoticed. Charlie Pierce, in his videotape training program on CCTV, tells of two large, agricultural machines (combines) being stolen from an equipment yard that was under observation by two autopanning cameras.

Pierce's training tapes also demonstrate another weakness of autopanning: if a person moves at the same rate as the camera, an illusion of nonmovement is created, regardless of the fact that the background is moving. Anyone can demonstrate this for himself with a camera in the autopan mode, a VCR, and a monitor. Just walk at a speed that matches the pan speed of the camera; then look at the tape.

Today, because camera prices have dropped drastically, it makes more sense to put two or three cameras on fixed mounts to oversee the same area that would formerly have been covered by a single autopanning camera. The overall effectiveness of the surveillance is greatly increased.

Random panning has one obvious feature in common with autopanning, which is that the motion of the drive unit is automatic. The similarity ends there. In *random panning*, the drive unit moves a random distance in one direction, stops, and moves again. For the person watching the monitor, the problems are similar to those for autopanning; the main advantage of random panning isn't at the monitor end of the system, but at the other end, in front of the camera. The random movement of the camera is supposed to be interpreted by an intruder as indicating that the camera is under the active control of a security person. If this ruse works, the "perp" may be dissuaded from whatever he or she is up to.

Presets and Alarms

Today, more use is being made of preset-position operation. What is it? *Preset-position operation* is the ability of a pan-and-tilt drive to return automatically to a specific scene within its overall field of view. To achieve this, the drive unit must be united with a control device, usually digital, that "remembers" a programmed combination of pan angle and tilt angle. The position information may be provided either electrically by potentiometers (specialized variable resistors) or optically. Whichever method is used, the specific pan and tilt angles of each programmed scene are retained in memory.

Preset operation places special demands on the mechanical components of the pan-and-tilt drive. For accurate acquisition of a preset scene, the drive train of the pan-and-tilt must have precise gearing with a minimum of play or backlash. A sloppier unit may be adequate for manual operation, but if a given preset recall repeatedly displays a slightly different scene, the preset function loses some of its effectiveness.

Since a camera on a pan-and-tilt nearly always has a motorized zoom lens, it follows that a lens on a pan-and-tilt with preset capability will also have preset capability. The lens will have potentiometers ("pots") or optical encoders for the zoom and focus settings, which allow the exact angle of view of the scene to be programmed, as well as the focus setting for the specific subject of interest. The iris mechanism is usually controlled independently by an auto-iris circuit or by a combination manual and auto-iris arrangement.

A preset position may be recalled manually by an operator, or automatically. In the manual mode, the operator decides he wants to view some scene, presses one or two buttons, and the camera automatically moves to the scene. Although this is a manual recall, the process is more precise and faster than if the operator had panned and tilted and zoomed and focused manually to produce the same scene on his monitor. However, the full advantages of preset operation are obtained in conjunction with alarm operation and in camera touring.

Let's say that within the viewing area of a pan-and-tilt are two alarmed doors, a couple of alarmed windows, and a driveway exit. Each of these subjects has been programmed into the control central processing unit (CPU) as a preset position for the drive unit and for the zoom and focus settings of the lens. The alarm device on each subject is connected to the CPU via an alarm interface or a host computer. The CPU is programmed to associate each alarm device with a specific preset, so that when an alarm goes active, the camera is automatically directed to view that scene. At the same time, a VCR will start recording the video output from the camera, probably in the real-time two-hour mode. With the latest technology, the CPU can be programmed to display on the monitor screen a title specific to the selected preset, in addition to the usual camera identification.

If the installation is very sophisticated, combining alarms, presets, and a variable speed drive, the drive will move at a high speed to acquire the preset scene and then will slow down for the last few degrees of movement before it locks on its target. At the same time that the pan-and-tilt is solving the preset command, various auxiliary equipment, such as lighting and locks, can be programmed to go active. The most advanced control systems also provide an acknowledged preset, which is a preset position to which the camera returns after the alarm is acknowledged. Such controllers also allow auxiliary, or aux, functions to be programmed to activate or deactivate on acknowledgment.

Preset position capability is also required for "guard-tour" operation of a CCTV security system. A CCTV guard tour simulates its namesake by displaying on a monitor a succession of scenes that represents the locations that a walking guard might visit on his rounds. CCTV touring takes two forms, one of which is merely a new term for an old function, and the other of which makes good use of the capabilities of modern CPU-based controllers and pan-and-tilt drives. The former type of guard tour is in fact merely a variety of sequential switching. It is called video touring and consists of the display on the monitor of different scenes from different cameras.

The other type of CCTV touring is camera touring, and it requires cameras on pan-and-tilt drives with preset positioning and motorized zoom lenses with presets, combined with a digital controller. A fully programmed camera tour can include a variety of different preset scenes from one or more cameras, interspersed with each other with variable dwell time (duration of the scene on the monitor) and individual preset scene tilting. The sequence of the tour has complete flexibility in programming with regard to the scene viewed, duration, and frequency of repetition in the overall tour plan.

Mechanical Issues

The basic pan-and-tilt drive hasn't changed much over the years, but there have been some changes in materials and in what one might call style. Recent pan-and-tilt designs are taking more advantage of modern polymers (plastics), which are remarkable materials. The tendency to associate "plastic" with "cheap" and "inadequate" can mislead us in making judgments about modern products using today's polymers. It isn't unusual for these materials to outwear equivalents, and they don't corrode.

On the other hand, we are currently seeing the introduction of pan-and-tilts with new shapes and configurations, but as attractive as these new designs are, in most cases they don't represent new engineering, just new packaging. The basic functions, panning and tilting, remain unchanged. In short, some of the newest units have an exotic-looking molded exterior with nothing new inside. The overriding factors in choosing a pan-and-tilt must remain the functional considerations: "Will it do what I want it to do, and will it last?"

Teleconferencing Pan-and-Tilt Drives

One new type of pan-and-tilt for which there is a growing market is the teleconferencing pan-and-tilt drive. All of these units have presets. Because they are used in environments where audio is also being transmitted or recorded, noise must be kept to a minimum in these units. Also, extreme smoothness of motion and precise gearing with the smallest possible backlash are necessary for teleconferencing. Lastly, many teleconferencing drives are designed to have a very low profile. These units are typically used with a preset-position controller with a large preset capacity.

Conclusion

The major changes in pan-and-tilt drives in recent years have been more in the area of control systems than in the drives themselves. The basic function, which is to point a camera in a certain direction, has not changed, but modern controllers have made this pointing function a much more versatile part of modern surveillance systems. New materials, including polymers and stepping motors, can probably be expected to improve performance and longevity.

The pan-and-tilt drive will have a secure place in CCTV for a long time to come.

Consider the Big Picture before Installing a CCTV System

Charlie Pierce

Deciding when, where, and how to use video in any given security situation has no simple solution. Despite what you may think or have been taught, no one form of security, including CCTV, is the answer to most problems. You must consider the entire situation to reach the complete solution. First, we'll look at CCTV in some simple applications that don't always have simple answers.

A clothier sells goods that demand personal intervention. Customers must try on an outfit to see if it fits. But, some clothes are stuffed into bags or coats and carried out. Other pieces are put on in the changing room under street clothes. And, there is "sweetheart selling," where a cashier rings up a $2 sale for a $20 item. All three situations demand specific security measures.

In the retail world, incorrect security causes losses that are beyond acceptability and lead to higher prices.

Stopping merchandise from leaving the store has been simplified by using electronic tags. Passing an exit barrier with a tag attached to an item trips an audio alarm. A camera can also be placed at the exit to record the incident. Since witnesses cannot be trusted to remember details, a time/date recording of the incident is useful. A shoplifter who gets away often returns during a different shift and tries again. Hard copy video images of the earlier recorded thefts, passed out to employees, security staff, and adjoining stores, give the clothier the advantage of multiple eyes. The camera is not the solution, but an enhancement to an associated security device.

The changing room problem calls for security in a place where a camera is unacceptable. Again, several different security tactics should be put into effect. One is to use stain tags, which squirt a permanent dye on the clothing and person if they are removed without the proper tool. Signs placed in the changing room tend to discourage shoplifting; no one wants to steal something that will be ruined. A second method is to lock changing room doors. Keys are issued to employees at the beginning of the shift. When a customer wants to try something on, he must ask for assistance.

All clothes taken into the room are either marked or counted prior to entrance and again upon leaving. A camera is placed outside the changing room and left in the time lapse mode to prevent "sweetheart changing." Once again, the camera was the secondary security measure.

Sweetheart selling is also becoming easier to stop. The best system today is to bar code the merchandise. This makes it harder to short the cash register and gives the retailer the ability to control inventory more effectively. If the clerk has to input information manually, a camera, placed with the cash register in sight and running on an event recorder, allows the complete recording of all transactions. Installing a compatible Point of Sale (POS) system in conjunction with the camera guarantees the honesty of all transactions. POS systems interface with the cash register and video recorder. If a $20 sweater is seen on the screen during playback and a $2 charge scrolls up the screen, you have an employee problem. Regular inventory checks of the store and proper sales tag processing are the main security in this case. Once again, the camera is used to provide hard copy evidence of right or wrong. Keep in mind that the camera can prove an employee innocent as well as guilty.

Another retail problem is the back door. Garbage bins are usually outside and are often used by employees to store goods to be picked up after hours. Having the manager check all garbage going out the door is not feasible. Putting a buzzer on the back door that must have a key override is a definite first step. A camera watching the garbage containers, tripped by video motion detection or lid contacts, will record employee activity. On one covert restaurant job, a camera at the back door trained on the garbage bin recorded three different employees stealing food and coming back for it later. Implementation of simple security measures is the first step; the camera is a back-up.

Shoplifting gangs are groups of highly organized, paid, and motivated individuals who cost stores hundreds of thousands of dollars annually. The process is simple. Three to four people enter the store— two or three keep security and clerks busy while the other individual is stealing. These groups are run by professionals who know the security staff, sometimes personally, and use methods ranging from force to bribery to get what they want.

A high-ranking officer who oversaw security at six major retail outlets in one city was offered, by a shoplifting gang organizer, several thousand dollars on an ongoing basis to look the other way. The only thing that saved this chain from major loss was the man's integrity. Security is not known for its high pay, so these situations happen. To stop these efforts, a number of security measures must be installed, including extensive CCTV coverage. Verify the design and layout of the store. How are the aisles laid out? How easy is it to exit without walking past a checkout counter? What type of training does the sales staff get? Are there set procedures for assistance? Is valuable merchandise marked or locked up? Which way do the counters face? Can cashiers see down the aisles at any given time? Is it possible to request assistance in such a way that the clerk would turn his back on the main store?

A chain jewelry store had several thefts from inside glass counters. The thieves waited until the clerk's back was turned, then rolled under a counter to the shop side. There they would sit, out of sight, helping themselves to whatever they wanted. At the last minute, they would roll back out and leave the store. The store stopped the crimes with two measures that cost very little. First, they trained their employees to look for people casing the store and to qualify customers with simple, key questions. Second, a carpenter built bottoms for the cases to prevent anyone from rolling under them.

Cameras were already installed in eight different key points, but were the only line of defense prior to the discovery of the thefts. Because the cameras were on a video switcher, the thief was caught by accident on two video frames rolling under the counter. Installing a video multiplexer ensured high-speed switching between cameras and prevented missed evidence in the future.

Finally, the store was redesigned. Originally, the counter where the clerk stood was a circle of glass counters in the back of the store. If the client had been properly advised by a security professional during the design of the store, the counter would have been one-sided at the front of the store. This would prevent anyone from entering or leaving the store without passing the clerk and would have saved thousands of dollars in renovation costs.

Proper security measures across the board decrease merchant losses each year. As a security professional, you need to keep abreast of the methods that have been tried and found effective. You need to be able to recommend a list of measures that can be implemented to stop theft.

Common sense is usually the best security method and doesn't cost anything. In most cases, cameras play a strong supporting role. They gather evidence, faces, actions, and methods of perpetrators. All this information is important and should be set up in some sort of exchange among the various branches of a corporation. Gangs usually hit all stores owned by one group, because they tend to have the same layout and security staff throughout a city. All videotapes made in these stores should be reviewed off-site by a secondary team not attached to the store that is trained to look for specific routines and/or actions. Routine reviews help to ensure the integrity of the on-site security force as well. This policy also helps the security director, since he or she knows that everything is double-checked outside of his or her jurisdiction.

Total response plans must be worked out in conjunction with security measures. Providing the police with hard copy pictures of the people involved in shoplifting gangs allows them to respond better with quicker and more accurate results. You should also ensure that the employees are trained properly. Nothing is more dangerous than an employee confronting a shoplifter or gang. The criminal often can be dangerous and may be armed and react out of panic and/or anger.

You must learn to use your imagination. As important as CCTV is to security, it is just as important to our daily routines. Knowing the when, where, and how of CCTV will open doors to your business that you never realized existed. One of the strongest markets you will develop over the next few years is the personal home. Electronic burglar and fire alarms have become a common appliance in the average home and are growing daily. CCTV, working with these systems and apart from them, is where the world is going fast.

Access Control, Alarms, and System Integration

To provide locksmithing services to businesses and institutions, you need to understand how various electronic systems work and how all of them can be integrated. As a locksmith, you probably won't be called on to design and install a full-blown integrated security, fire, and access control system. However, you may be asked to participate in creating such a system. Only by understanding the various systems will you be able to suggest the best ways to include locks and other physical security devices in the integrated system.

This chapter consists of contributions from renowned experts in access control, burglar, and fire alarm systems.

Plan Component Design Prior to Installing System

Lars R. Suneborn

Clarifying access control systems for the installer and service technician is critical because they have to make it work, often by matching parts and pieces not originally designed to work together or for the application at hand. Basic egress and ingress functions are the same regardless of access point, which is now simply considered a controlled opening through a barrier. To gain access, a user must identify himself to the system, which then scans its database to verify access privilege at this door and time and unlocks the opening.

The first necessary component to make this system operational is the access control panel (ACP), which contains the processor, the memory in which the user database is stored, and the relay that activates when access is granted. The ACP should have 110 Vac directly hardwired into the controller, preferably on a dedicated circuit. Ensure the cabinet is grounded if necessary. This eliminates electrical noise on the power line and ensures that the plug is not accidentally disconnected.

The next component, the card reader or keypad, is mostly powered from the ACP by an extra pair of wires in the data cable that connects the reader and ACP. Voltage levels are usually less than five volts, but should be verified. Do not exceed the manufacturer's distance limitation. Levels that are too low will cause the reader to misread or not read at all. The exception is where the ACP and reader are manufactured by different companies. In that case, power is supplied to both the ACP and reader, which will have a separate, independent power supply. Consequently, the reader will always have the correct voltage and distances can be extended.

Most ACP manufacturers offer battery back-up for their panels. If the reader is powered by the ACP, it also will continue to operate during a power failure. A reader powered by a separate supply will not function unless it too has battery back-up.

The last component of the access point is the locking device. The electric strike, available in a wide variety of electrical and mechanical configurations, is the most common type of locking device [among those integrated within access control systems]. Door strikes are divided into two categories: fail-safe and fail-secure. A fail-secure strike in the normal, locked state is not energized. Power is required to unlock this type of strike. Always use a separate power supply for locking hardware. When the controller is equipped with battery back-up, the locking device also should have back-up power.

Even basic ACPs can allow a door to be unlocked continuously during business hours and require a user to identify himself to the system by card or code during nonbusiness hours. When access is granted, the ACP will unlock the door hardware for a few seconds, with strikes designed for specific related purposes. A fail-secure strike intended for intermittent operation is often less costly than one designed for continuous operation. The intermittent strike usually operates on 12 or 24 volts ac and is less expensive to manufacture than the continuous duty strike, which operates on dc power. Additionally, a simple transformer is a sufficient power source for an ac strike.

The other side is that an ac strike is always noisy and not intended to keep a door unlocked all day. If used this way, the solenoid eventually will burn out, and often also ruin the transformer.

The dc strike runs silently, operates more efficiently, and can stay energized all day without heat buildup. It also can be used with a simple UPS power supply, enabling both the controller and door lock to be fully operational during a power failure.

Some manufacturers offer an ACP that powers both the reader and locking device. Verify that the locking hardware is of correct voltage before starting the installation.

The last related item is noise suppression. When a coil is de-energized, an inductive voltage spike is generated which can reach levels of 10 to 15,000 volts. There is no danger, but it can cause system problems. What at first seems to be an unexplainable system lock-up is likely caused by a spike reaching the controller which could, in severe cases, halt the ACP processor. Powering the unit down for a few seconds and then reapplying power usually will make the unit operational again.

To protect these products, most systems manufacturers today equip their circuit boards with suppression devices. Intended to remove any noise generated in the field wiring, these components are located near the wiring connectors and around the relays. The best place for a suppression device, however, is at the source right at the door strike.

The problem can affect all devices with a coil, but can be easily resolved. First, confirm that there are spikes generated by the lock. Remove the lock wire connected to the "common" terminal of the relay connector strip. Leave the other wire connected. Hold the wire by the insulation and let the strands touch the screw head of the terminal where the remaining wire is connected. With a fail-safe lock, this will be the NC terminal; with a fail-secure lock, it will be the NO terminal.

Tap the wire against the screw head several times. If you are near the lock, you will hear it click as you do. Watch the screw head carefully, and you will see small, inconsistent sparks. Now remove the locking device. Locate the connector that fastens the lock wires to the lock. Install a Metal Oxide Varistor (MOV) parallel with the load. The MOV is not polarity sensitive, and will work with ac and dc locks. The voltage rating of the MOV is inconsequential; any voltage higher than rated will be shorted and not find its way back to the ACP. On dc circuits, a reverse biased diode can be used; 1N4001–1N4007 works well. Test for sparks again; they should be gone. If there is still minor sparking, install one more MOV parallel with the first. Repeat this procedure on all doors.

Good, clean ac, good ground, and separate power for the door hardware are basic and very important for proper system operation. Do not cut corners in this area. It will cost time, money, and perhaps a good customer. Next: We will add a door contact to the access point. This will result in a dramatic increase in security, but also will present interesting challenges for the installer and service technician.

A New Breed of Standalone Readers: The High-Security Alternative

Bud Toye

There was a time when "standalone" meant dumb—no intelligence, no features, just basic security. Those were the days when the only readers that could make a smart decision had to be connected to a central processor. Today, some standalone readers are smarter then many central processor-based systems. They do more, cost less, and don't require communication wiring. Some even have an actual built-in personal computer (PC) processor, making them just as smart as a real PC.

The latest standalones can be all things to all people, including the ability not to stand alone. It can be a fully independent standalone, but still be able to talk to a PC or other reader just in case there is ever a need to be online. None of this versatility adds additional cost to the reader because its processor is so powerful that there aren't enough functions to exhaust its capacity.

Microprocessors Bring Simplicity

Perhaps you're beginning to think that we've lost sight of the simple objective of the standalone reader by making it too powerful and complicated; the opposite is actually the case. The power and low cost of the microprocessor enable manufacturers to program simplicity into their designs.

Microprocessors have injected new life into the standalone reader market and opened opportunities for both installers and end-users. Locksmiths and security dealers who are not interested in handling high-end, online systems now can enter the world of electronic locksmithing without needing much technical expertise. End-users now can provide high-level security to facilities that couldn't be served by an online system, or where the cost of an online system couldn't be justified.

A Standalone That Brings Home the Bacon

One of the world's largest pig farms uses smart standalone readers at scores of remote facilities in the Midwest to ensure that disease is not inadvertently carried from one facility to another. No one gets near a Premium Standard Farms facility without having a valid access card. Immediately upon entering, people must shower and don sterilized garments to enter the biohazard-sensitive areas.

All of these entry points are controlled by standalone readers that can receive their programming instructions via dial-up phone lines. The readers can be told who may enter; what time, dates, and days; and factor in holidays as well. They must use an exit reader to leave so that all activity is logged for reference.

General Telephone Company uses standalone readers to control more than 400 remote buildings. Because many are unstaffed, they require nothing less than the highest level of security to guard invaluable digital switching equipment. Trying to keep 400 remote sites updated with current card programming seems like an awesome job, but it isn't. It's all done automatically at night from a central database. When a change is made to the cardholder database, software in a central PC knows which remote sites are affected by that change and calls only those sites with the updated information.

Security personnel can grant access to any remote site instantly in case someone without an access card needs entry. That person can use a cellular phone or an outside courtesy phone to call GTE security; if authorized, the software will automatically call back to the site, unlock the door, and log the occurrence. The standalone reader can store all the access transactions, which can be transmitted back to headquarters for reporting and archiving.

Most smart standalone readers also have a "no-brainer" mode. If a local manager needs to eliminate a cardholder instantly, it can be done at the reader.

The Multi-Purpose Solution

In the old days, if an end-user wanted to control a parking lot using an existing ID badge with a bar code on it, there was no way to do it. A second card using a different technology had to be issued. Today, almost any existing badge and coding format can be used for access control. Standalone reader processors can be programmed to decode the specific formatting of each end-user's card. Thus, today's standalone readers are available for any type of encoding and can be customized to read any format within that encoding. Popular formats include differential optics, magnetic stripe, bar code, barium ferrite, proximity, Wiegand, fingerprint, and radio frequency.

How to Program Them

The biggest challenge that access control manufacturers face in standalone reader design is how to program them. To talk to a processor, you usually need another processor or some kind of input device, such as a keypad. Peripheral programming devices add cost—sometimes enough that the economy of a standalone is lost.

The industry's first intelligent standalone reader used a hand-held, calculator-style programmer to validate and void cards. It retailed for $500 in 1975, or about half the price of the reader it was supposed to program. Nevertheless, the reader was a big success because one programmer could be used to program any reader, and at $500 it was a lot less expensive than a central processor, the only other alternative at the time.

Next came standalone readers with built-in keypads used for programming, but now every reader needed a keypad and supporting electronics, which increased the unit cost. Twenty years after the development of the first intelligent standalone, everything imaginable has been used to solve the programming dilemma. Here is a review of some common programming techniques used today.

PLUG-IN PROGRAMMER

The plug-in programmer is still very popular, although the capabilities have been expanded, giving the programmer the ability to alter the reader's security parameters and extract stored transaction data for future reports.

BUILT-IN KEYPAD

The keypad, once used just for programming, now doubles as an input for a PIN code.

The keypad now can be used for card plus PIN code, card or PIN code, or for cardholder programming.

CARD DECK PROGRAMMING

By far the least expensive and most effective solution, card deck programming adds nothing to the cost of the reader and requires no special training or skills. Instead of a built-in keypad, you talk to the processor through the reader using specially coded programming cards.

To void card 1234, for example, you simply insert the four cards numbered 1, 2, 3, and 4, in that order. You complete the process by using the VOID card. To revalidate that card, you do the same thing, only conclude with the VALIDATE card.

TV REMOTE CONTROL

One manufacturer has utilized TV remote control technology to program its standalone card readers.

REMOVABLE MEMORY CARTRIDGE

The removable memory cartridge technique uses an inexpensive plug-in memory cartridge that can be taken to a PC or laptop for programming. It plugs into the serial port of the PC, and a software program allows the user to change card status and to extract transaction activity from the cartridge. Spare cartridges are cycled so the reader is never without memory. For users who want to archive transaction data generated from remote security points, shuttling memory cartridges back and forth to a PC is often the only way to do it.

Some manufacturers equip their standalone readers with an optional built-in modem so they can be connected to a standard dial-up phone line. A software program is provided for the host site that can dial out to the standalone reader to reprogram its memory and download transaction data. Some dial-up programs can automatically call multiple sites at night.

Standalone Reader Design Philosophies

Manufacturers usually design standalone readers using the one technology in which they specialize. A standalone produced by a company that makes magnetic stripe cards will only read magnetic stripe cards, and usually only the ones produced by that manufacturer. Many access control dealers like this philosophy because it restricts the bidding process and ensures ongoing card orders.

Other standalone reader manufacturers use a dual-component design philosophy. The reader consists of two basic components: an electronic control board and a separate read head.

The control board is identical for all technologies; only the read head is unique. This design offers the additional advantage that the two components can be separate, putting the vital electronics in a secure area and out of the weather.

The two-component philosophy also makes generic card reading possible because virtually any type of read head can be used, even read heads designed to recognize a proprietary encoding format. This gives dealers and end-users tremendous range when it comes to extending access control to a card that might have been designed for a time-keeping system.

Many standalone readers can perform more functions than anyone ever needs, but many of the functions have to be part of the basic design because every end-user has different requirements.

Here are some features offered by many standalone reader manufacturers.

- Built-in time-clock/calendar that allows the user to program multiple time zones, providing different levels of access by day and time, with holiday exceptions for specific individuals.

- The ability to program certain cards for access during a specific date range for short-term visitors.

- This feature also allows for automatic card voiding at a predetermined date and time.

- Time- and date-stamped activity storage.

- Printed activity reports.

- Five-figure card capacities.

- The option to require a supervisor to be the first to be allowed entry each day.

- The option to connect entrance and exit readers together for true anti-passback when there is no exit reader.

- The ability to monitor door contacts and trigger central station alarm reporting during off-hours.

- The ability to provide floor-specific elevator control so that each cardholder may be programmed for access to specific floors.

- The option to include a keypad for PIN codes that may be activated by time schedules. This feature requires the use of a card plus PIN code during off-hours, but will permit access using only the card during business hours.

- The option to provide keypad-only access.

- The ability to accept cards encoded with virtually any technology and any format, including standard credit cards.

- The ability to download a customer's existing personnel database into the standalone reader for programming purposes. This is, of course, a high-end feature that requires the reader to be equipped with a serial I/O port.

Standalone readers have evolved to become an excellent alternative to PC-based systems because many can perform most of the same functions. There is no compromise in security, especially when a keypad option is selected. By programming the reader to require the use of a unique PIN code during off-hours, there is no vulnerability to unreported lost or stolen cards, since the finder would not know the number.

Modern standalone readers offer basic security with attractive price tags. The best way to locate the standalone reader that's right for your application is to watch the ads and request information.

All major manufacturers use security media advertising to keep the industry up to date on what's new.

Design and Integration of Alarm Systems into Access Control Systems

Lionel Silverman, PE

Shelly Smith of ABC Burglar Alarm Co. sat across from Jose Perez and listened to what he wanted to do with his new burglar alarm system. Perez was vice president of a large high-tech distribution company with a number of locations and was a significant client of the ABC Burglar Alarm Co. Perez also had just spent a considerable amount of money on the installation of a PC-based access control system to control and monitor the movement of employees within the company.

Over the past three weeks, authorized employees had inadvertently set off the burglar alarm several times; in each case the police were dispatched, only to find it was a false alarm. The problem appeared to be that if an employee arrived at work and entered the building before a supervisor or manager turned off the burglar alarm system, the alarm would be inadvertently set off. This occurred despite the fact that the employee was authorized to enter the door during regular working hours.

Perez said, "I want you to connect the burglar alarm and controlled access together so that employees cannot enter the building until the alarm is shut off. But at the same time," he continued, "I need total flexibility to select who can operate the system and not be tied to preset time schedules."

The above scenario and many more are common in our fast-moving world. In many cases, the solution to these problems is the integration of the burglar alarm and access control systems. In many cases, the solution also requires the cooperation of both system suppliers, especially when there is more than one installation company involved.

The traditional approach would be to change access classes in the access control system, but that is normally related to a time schedule.

Today's flexible working schedules demand a total integration approach that allows for the arming/disarming of the burglar alarm system via the access control system; or using the burglar alarm system to secure the affected doors and prevent users from authorized access when the alarm is set.

The burglar alarm must signal the access control system when it is set, and the access control system then must restrict who can enter the building. At the same time, the access control system must operate in a normal manner during working hours. After hours, the reverse must take place; setting the burglar alarm system must protect the building as well as secure it from unauthorized entry.

To determine the best possible solutions, the systems integrator of ABC Burglar Alarm Co. takes a large piece of paper and carefully plots out the existing relationships between burglar alarm and access control systems, as follows:

1. Arriving at premises in the morning: Disarm the alarm system and then access control system must allow all employees, including supervisors and managers, to enter and exit the facility.

2. Normal day operation: Access control system allows all authorized employees, including supervisors and managers, to enter and exit the facility.

3. Leaving premises at night: Set alarm, then access control system must not allow employees except supervisors and managers to enter the facility.

The central issue with access control systems today is their ability to identify, control, and record the movement of authorized people into a building and the keeping of unauthorized people out of the building. With the arrangement detailed above, the question of access levels for cardholders arriving when the building is secured remains, since their access card will give them access unless another level of cardholders is created in the system.

For the sake of this discussion, a new class of badge holders, called super-users, could be created to allow selected badge holders access to the facility even when it was secure at night (i.e., employees who are burglar alarm code-holders). The super-user concept allows one to create a level of users that can secure the facility and disarm it at will. When secure, it will not allow regular cardholders access to the facility.

The systems integrator now adds the super-users to the concept to bring the full solution into play.

1. Arriving at premises in the morning: Super-user enters the building and disarms the alarm system. The access control system only allows supervisors and managers to enter and exit the facility at this time.

2. Normal day operation: With the burglar alarm system disarmed, the access control system allows all employees, including supervisors and managers, to enter and exit the facility.

3. Leaving premises at night: Super-user sets alarm, then access control system will not allow employees, except supervisors and managers, to enter and exit the facility at this time.

In deciding who is going to be a super-user, the following two questions must be asked: (1) Does the person to whom I am going to grant super-user status know how to arm/disarm the burglar alarm system? (2) Is that person in a responsible position within the company to be able to liaise with the monitoring company's central station in the event of a problem?

To determine if the super-user concept will work on a given situation, ask these questions:

- Does the plant work on a flexible schedule whereby the burglar alarm system is armed at the end of the shifts for that day and disarmed the following day at the start of the next operational shift?

- Will super-users have to be set up at a moment's notice?

- Are there multiple doors affected by this requirement and are they all constrained by the same criteria?

- How easy is it to schedule door locking/unlocking? Is it necessary for the controller to record all activity?

- If so, does it have sufficient capacity?

- Is the super-user access level easily programmed from the computer?

- What are the requirements for this programming?

- Can the access control system interface with the existing burglar alarm system?

Once the decision has been made, it is time to start the implementation of the system.

Remember that this change could have a significant effect on the organization, since it affects the ability of personnel to access areas they are allowed in during regular working hours. This pre-work that must be done prior to the implementation of the system will pay off with the smooth transition to the new access levels, and includes:

- Determining exactly how the current burglar alarm system works and ensuring that it has the required inputs and outputs to do the job. This may sound simple, but if the burglar alarm panel does not have the correct inputs/outputs available, the resultant installation and subsequent maintenance could be very costly. Ask the installation company whether the panel has a relay output when it is armed.

- Determining exactly how the current access control system works and ensuring that it has the required inputs and outputs to do the job. If the access control system and field controller do not have the correct inputs and outputs available, installation and subsequent maintenance could be expensive. Ask the installation company whether the access control system has the ability to change "access level of the user" on a given input and whether an output relay can be operated when the change of access level is activated.

- Ensuring that door-locking hardware meets life safety and ADA requirements. It is important to ensure that the fire alarm is in working order, and that when it works, the door will unlock. ADA interface must be included in the installation so that after-hours access to the building by people using the ADA option will be possible with the new system.

- Planning the access levels and door schedule. Discuss the proposed changes with the users of the system to ensure that it will do what is expected of it.

- Issuing a timely notice to all employees affected by this move to ensure that all users know what the changes are and how they will be affected.

Burglar alarm and access control systems operation can be successfully integrated today to provide an easy-to-use method to prevent unnecessary false alarms, while maintaining totally controlled access to the facility and keeping accurate historical recording of who enters/exits the building.

Integrated Fire Alarm and Security Systems

Michael Swiecicki

With advancing technology and electronic systems entering the software driven arena, systems integration is the goal of many designers. The prospect of adding and consolidating system functions to create a bigger and better product has excited many but, unfortunately, disappointed most. System integrators have been plagued with unforeseen circumstances (usually due to lack of expertise in some of the "lesser" system functions) and the fact that many system integration designs can inadvertently sacrifice the integrity of the subsystems.

When a fire alarm system is integrated with other systems, there is a tendency to forget that it is primarily a monitoring system only when things are normal; in the event of a fire it becomes a control station for fighting fires at a location away from the primary integrated system controls, by people other than those who normally control the integrated system. Additionally, the fire alarm system and all components tied to it must become functionally independent.

To understand the integration of fire alarm and security operations, you must first define the individual aspects of each function and its relationship to other functions. Second, you must outline how that cause and effect sequence is going to occur (manual or automatic, priority, sequence of operations). Finally, you must review what you have done and compare the integrated system operations with your original purpose for integrating these systems. Therefore, before integrating anything, you must state the mission for integration.

To properly analyze a system, it is important to choose a specific application that has multiple system functions and is large enough to justify integration. Colleges and universities provide the perfect scenario. Since the campus police center is typically the only 24-hour, manned central location for receiving and reacting to alarm emergencies, it is advantageous for uniformity and ease of training for all alarm conditions to be displayed on a single screen and be acknowledged on a common control panel.

Since both systems can control common items, such as doors and elevators, the sequence and priority of controls can be managed via common programming. Modern systems are designed for software-generated maintenance and diagnostics, such as changing access control cardholder status, that can be facilitated from remote locations, and it is beneficial to perform these operations from a common terminal. The Crime Awareness and Campus Security Act of 1990, which mandates certification of a campus security policy and disclosure of all security and criminal activities, shows the advantages for a single, consolidated incident logging system across campus.

Concurrently, there are several reasons not to integrate the fire alarm and security systems. Strict codes regulating response to a fire alarm make it undesirable for a campus security officer to have control of that system. Because fire alarm systems traditionally have been viewed as passive and security systems as active, merging the two may be considered mutually contradictory. The fire alarm system also has certain survivability restrictions, and the complete integration of fire and security systems at each location may have an undesirable economic impact on the security components.

Note that fire alarm and security systems are, in themselves, already integrated systems. Each performs a variety of monitoring functions, compares the status of each to a predetermined setting, processes the results of this comparison, analyzes the importance of those results, decides on appropriate control operation, and displays all appropriate conditions. Many components of this operation are not part of the fire alarm system, which typically consists of separate manual and automatic signaling, sprinkler supervisory, and proprietary reporting subsystems.

It is easiest to define fire alarm system functions by looking at the purpose of fire alarm systems.

- To detect (by recognition of a manual operation or management of a variety of automatic sensors) that there is a fire condition

- To notify the occupants (by activation of audible and visible devices within the protected area) and responding personnel (by use of a remote panel or screen at the constantly monitored location) of the condition so that appropriate action can be taken

- To automatically activate emergency control functions (e.g., capturing elevators so occupants cannot accidentally enter the fire area, closing normally held open doors so the spread of smoke can be hindered, or unlocking egress doors so that the occupant can evacuate) to make the protected premises safer

It also is important to remember that fire alarm systems generally protect an entire structure, as opposed to security systems that generally are designed for protection of specific high-risk areas and objects.

Fire alarm systems accomplish the above duties by integrating the following functions:

- Monitoring all manual pull stations

- Monitoring water movement, water shutoff, and condition of pumping equipment in sprinkler systems

- Monitoring smoke and heat presence in open areas

- Monitoring fire conditions within HVAC systems

- Monitoring specialized subsystems engineered for protection of hazardous areas and/or objects

- Controlling alarm notification devices

- Controlling elevators, smoke doors, smoke ventilation, fire extinguishing equipment, and power shutoff to selected systems

- Annunciating all critical conditions

- Supervising power and wiring to all monitoring and control circuits with automatic switchover to standby provisions in the event of failure

Security systems, on the other hand, have traditionally comprised independent subsystems that have attempted to integrate

- Monitoring intrusion detection devices

- Monitoring and processing card access devices and data

- Displaying, recording, and controlling CCTV cameras

- Recording, retrieving, and displaying personal identification video images

- Controlling, processing, recording, and displaying guard tour activities

- Recording, archiving, and displaying incident tracking logs

- Annunciating and processing intercom operation

- Controlling elevators, door locks, and lighting

- Annunciating all critical conditions

- Supervising wiring to intrusion detection devices

When security systems incorporate access control and video imaging operations, there is an entire second level of data that deals with the system cardholder information. The access control data (which contains a minimum of name, ID number, optional PIN, access level, and expiration information) must interact with the video data (which includes the electronically stored image, name, and ID number) and other information that may be useful to the system operators.

When these systems are installed on college campuses, this combined cardholder data must be integrated with the institutional computer databases for purposes of uploading and downloading massive amounts of student and personnel data.

Proper integration of both systems should allow for complete interactivity to allow, at a minimum, the following operations to occur.

- All combined systems activities can be simultaneously displayed and archived so that an overall evaluation can be made at the time of emergency for determination of appropriate response.

- All combined (alarm and diagnostic) system activities can be categorized and organized into a relational database for purposes of system and facility management.

- All combined controls can be cross-matrixed to any incoming monitored condition, regardless of their assignment to either fire alarm or security and without compromise to life safety. For example, a CCTV camera can be called up by activation of a fire alarm manual pull station or a remote intercom station. Whenever there is a conflict between fire alarm and security, the code-mandated fire alarm operation must take precedence.

- All system activities can be viewed from any integrated system control station regardless of its primary purpose.

- All system controls are layered within a multi-access level scheme, whereby code-regulated fire alarm operations cannot be compromised by routine or even high-level security operations.

- The security system components employ the noncentralized distributed processing architecture and nonvolatile firmware that modern fire alarm systems use so there is no one Achilles' heel in the combined system or any of its offshoots. Larger, multiplexed fire alarm systems today are designed to be networked, whereby all panels are standalone and share equally in system management. If any system components fail, the system can heal itself by isolating the failed unit and continuing all operations without resorting to degraded operations.

- The combined system software, even though individual portions may be protected from both view and edit rights, follows the same format and programming techniques for ease of operations.

Generally, there are three methods of hardware integration, and most system schemes will not be limited to any one. The first method uses a common communications protocol between subpanels, whereby a remote access control panel, intrusion detection panel, or fire alarm panel can communicate with the balance of the system using common systems wiring. This type of integration is very common when site-wide fire alarm systems (often referred to as proprietary systems) are an integrated combination of separate manual signaling, automatic signaling, and sprinkler supervisory systems.

The advantage of this layout is that all remote panels can communicate with each other without the interaction of a central CPU that acts as a translator from one system to another. This is especially advantageous when the network concept that is used in fire alarm communications also can be integrated with its self-healing and distributive processing properties. Overall, the system will operate faster, the software will be leaner and simpler, and the system will be free of bottlenecks during high-activity periods. Another key ingredient of this design is that it utilizes a manufactured standard of integration, as opposed to a unique software-driven handshake. This will have the long-term effect of lower life cycle costs by using standard components. The disadvantage is that if the wrong manufacturer is selected from the onset, the flexibility and modularity of an integrated system may be limited.

Another method of hardware integration is to use the personal computers that are so common in the various subsystems to communicate with each other using separate communication techniques. This generally requires using common software operating systems and calls for all intersystem communications to be routed through these computer gateways and be transformed to a format that can be recognized by the other interlinked systems.

The advantage of this layout is that it is much more open to subsystems by various manufacturers, and at least theoretically, there is very little limitation as to the capabilities of intersystem interaction. The disadvantages are that it is very difficult to come up with one system operating environment (although DOS is fairly standard in small systems, larger systems may use UNIX, VMS, OS2, QNX, etc.); most of the handshake software is custom and will, in the long run, be more costly to maintain and service; and, because the various subsystems generally use different programming software, the overall integrated system will be complex and more difficult to manage.

The third method uses an in-panel modular approach, whereby a single remote control panel is capable of accommodating various plug-in modules (usually printed circuit boards) that are preconfigured for discrete functions. For example, individual modules may be designated for intrusion detection monitoring, fire alarm monitoring, card reader interface, etc.

The advantages of this design are that each panel is custom-configured for the location, and additional hardware (with supporting software) is not necessitated by a one-size-fits-all configuration of remote panels; the overall system reflects the cumulative integrity of all combined systems (for example, the communications between panels may provide the redundancy required by fire alarm standards, and the panel may provide tamper monitoring operation that is standard with intrusion detection systems); and the system software is simple, uniform, and less costly to operate and maintain. The disadvantage is that this level of integration forces the system to be the product of a single manufacturer, and if the wrong manufacturer is chosen, the future of the system may be restricted.

In actuality, fully integrated systems use all three methods depending on the features and functions desired, the subsystems selected, and the capability of each subsystem to integrate to the next.

One of the last evaluations of a good design is what percentage of integration is standard versus custom software and an analysis of the life cycle costs that may be incurred by the customization.

Any attempt at systems integration requires a careful selection of the players (designer, manufacturer, integrator, and installer). This selection process should include scrutiny of the long-term goals, the financial health, the experience level, and an evaluation of their products and services. The corporation selected will determine the success and future of your system as well as who will operate, program, and maintain it.

The Art of Integrating Fire and Security Systems

Wayne D. Moore

The horror stories are many. A colleague just spent thousands of dollars to install a state-of-the-art, integrated fire and security packaged system in their facility. The systems installation is complete, but apparently they were not packaged as thought because over half the system is not operational. In addition, fire authorities will not issue an acceptance for the fire alarm portion of the system. Now the two manufacturers are accusing each other, trying to place blame rather than correct the problems.

The typical ensuing scenario is that the installer will attempt to splice and tape connections anywhere in the system to make it work somehow. His only goal is to get out of the facility, get paid, and hopefully, never have to return. The salesman for the project has stopped returning phone calls because he can't figure out what's wrong and the manufacturers have stopped returning his calls. Your colleague is trying to explain to the boss the rationale behind integrating two apparently different systems and why the corporation now is spending more money for a system that doesn't work. What caused this to happen? The security director had researched the reputation of both manufacturers and the background of the installer. The salesman assured them that he could integrate the two systems. Obviously, he was wrong. Now the company is paying for his failure to understand fire alarm code requirements and his inability to properly integrate the systems.

Later, your colleague analyzes what went wrong. She remembers the advice she didn't follow about hiring engineers skilled in security and fire alarm systems applications (it wasn't in the budget). She failed to develop goals for how she wanted the integrated systems to operate. She chose not to contact the local fire department for their input. And she didn't ask key questions, such as, "Have these proposed manufacturers worked together before?" "Is there a written contract between manufacturers for integration of their products?" and "Who maintains a spare-parts inventory for the equipment as it is integrated?"

The lack of codes and standards in the security industry leads to many abuses in systems application, design, and installation. Many security salespeople only want to satisfy their customer's needs at a price that will get them to sign the contract. A high percentage of security salespeople are uneducated in fire alarm codes and standards, a fact that also may pertain to the security director. Thus, the first step your colleague should have taken was to hire both a fire protection engineer and a security design professional to map out the requirements of both systems and how the system-to-system and human-to-system interfaces would work.

These same design professionals should have the responsibility not only for developing the technical requirements of the systems, but also for developing the budget for what needs to be done (not the other way around, as is most often the case).

Development of the fire alarm system should be the first priority because of the need to deal with the fire authority having jurisdiction and with codes and standards. Many security directors are unaware of the requirements of gaining approvals from the local fire authority, but they are necessary to avoid future liabilities or delayed occupancy of new or recently renovated facilities.

The National Fire Alarm Code, NFPA 72-1993, was adopted by the NFPA membership and describes the minimum acceptable requirements for all fire alarm systems. Chapter 1 of the code covers fundamental requirements such as primary and secondary power, monitoring components and circuits for integrity, and compatibility of equipment. The code allows combination systems to be used as long as the fire alarm system takes precedence. Chapter 3 covers "Protected Premises Fire Alarm Systems" and Section 3-8.14 provides the minimum requirements for combination systems.

Where common wiring is employed for combination systems, the equipment for other than fire alarm systems shall be permitted to be connected to the common wiring of the system. Short circuits, open circuits or grounds in this equipment or between the equipment and the fire alarm system wiring shall not interfere with the supervision of the fire alarm system or prevent alarm or supervisory signal transmission.

We are allowed, though not required, to use common wiring with some restrictions.

Security system wiring generally is covered under the National Electric Code, Article 725. Fire alarm system wiring is covered under the NEC, Article 760. There are subtle differences between the two articles, but design professionals will manage that concern. In addition, monitoring the integrity of the wiring is an important part of NFPA 72-1993 Chapter 1 requirements. The requirement of Subsection 3-8.14.3 is a little more restrictive.

To maintain the integrity of fire alarm system functions, the removal, replacement, failure or maintenance procedure on any hardware, software or circuit not required to perform any of the fire alarm system functions shall not cause loss of any of these functions. Exception: Where the hardware, software and circuits are listed for fire alarm use.

Obviously, if two separate manufacturers are involved in this integration process, there is a strong possibility of noncompliance with the referenced code subsection. This is especially true if both manufacturers are planning to provide software-driven equipment, which requires an interface software program so that the two systems are able to talk with each other and still comply with minimum code requirements. This is extremely important because the security system is subject to daily activity, while the fire alarm system is designed to sit quietly until called upon in a fire emergency.

It is the responsibility of the fire protection engineer to verify compliance of the packaged system with Subsection 3-8.14.3. There are also many other fire safety control functions that are controlled by or activated by the fire alarm system. Section 3-9 of the NFAC deals with these other interfaced systems, with Subsection 3-9.2.5 guiding the fire authority having jurisdiction.

"The interfaced systems shall be acceptance tested together in the presence of the authority having jurisdiction to ensure proper operation of the fire alarm system and the interfaced system(s)."

Obviously, more outside direction will be involved in what the security director thought was a simple marriage of two electronic systems. The local fire authority will be involved early on in the design discussions. The fire alarm system design must take into account your security measures for fire department access during inspections and fire fighting efforts. The security director will utilize the fire protection engineer for negotiations with fire officials if a conflict develops between fire protection requirements and access to secure areas.

The fire protection engineer also will work closely with the security design professional to ensure that all integrated operational and testing procedures are understood and accepted prior to systems installation. An important consideration when testing the fire alarm system is the impact it might have on the security system and whether or not a security system test will adversely affect the fire alarm system. Verification of the ability of the two manufacturers to work together is the responsibility of both design professionals.

Finally, the security director will conclude that although integration of fire and security systems makes sense, they should not and cannot be interdependent. Unilateral decision making when trying to integrate fire and security systems doesn't end with the decision to integrate. Making what seems an inconsequential decision more than doubles the scope of work effort and the background needed to accomplish the integration. As with any technical field, as it progresses it becomes more specialized. Understand the complications that can arise from fire and security systems integration and plan accordingly.

Systems Integration: More Than the Sum of Its Parts

Stephen F. Nelson

The operation and protection of your building has a lot to do with the success or failure of your business. Success is more likely when the building's operating systems contribute to your organizational objectives and provide your employees a safe, healthy, and productive work environment. Traditionally, the systems that control comfort and safeguard life and property have been mutually exclusive. Now that they share a common technology base, building planners have the opportunity to combine system functionality for enhanced performance at a lower price. A systems integration investment's payoff can be greater than the sum of its parts.

Building control and protection systems on the market today are remarkably similar in their architectures. They all have a central processor, typically a personal computer with an operator's terminal and printer. The PC is connected to microprocessor-based remote panels, which communicate with nearby sensors and actuators. The functional elements also have similar operating systems, time/day schedules, alarm processing logic, input monitoring, output control, archiving, and reporting capabilities. It is the feature of intelligence at the local level, however, that distributes the workload and makes a multi-functional architecture practical.

This has not always been the case. In earlier systems, all local data was sent to the central computer for processing. Command actions then were sent back for local execution. As systems grew larger and functionality expanded, the performance of such systems tended to slow down under the weight of heavy information traffic and an overworked central processor. The added load imposed by integration only made matters worse. Now that architectures have become decentralized, local panels carry the burden of collecting and processing information without taxing communication links or the central computer.

At the same time that decision-making moved downstream in the architecture, the central man-machine interface became a bit more friendly. Cryptic alphanumeric commands and displays gave way to an interactive, menu-driven operator interface. In today's control systems, information appears in easy-to-understand graphic formats that are site specific, showing exactly what and where things are happening.

These evolutionary steps, which occurred in the span of just a few years, have drastically changed the character of the control system. Decision-making has moved from central to local computers.

System architectures, influenced by digital PC technology to which they migrated, no longer need to be dedicated to one function. The user-friendly central operator interface, no longer a computational workhorse, is free to assume a broader role. The scene is set for the integration of functions in a single, multi-tasking building management system. This is to say, integration is beckoning. But is it welcome?

Combining the functions of several control systems into one common system can be a way to optimize the cost and operation of these systems. Starting with initial cost, you can expect to get more aggregate functionality for the same or lower cost, in part because you have eliminated redundant hardware, software, communication paths, and terminals.

If the integrated system comes from a single supplier, you can expect a unified design and a single point of responsibility during all phases of design, installation, and commissioning. Although the advent of standard communications protocols makes it possible for the systems of several suppliers to share the same communication system, there usually is some loss of functionality that may degrade integrated performance.

Since fire, security, and environmental signals come together in a single operator interface, all such terminals will be of a common design, making them easier to learn, operate, and maintain.

Workstations will no longer be cluttered with multiple display units and printers. Uniform operating procedures eliminate errors and make it easier to become proficient. In almost every case, the universal operator interface with its sophisticated interactive graphics will be more advanced and informative than equivalent standalone systems, even those with graphic displays of their own.

An integrated system gives you greater flexibility in the way you manage a building. It can be operated from several locations, each segregated to monitor and control over a single geographic area, such as one building in a complex, or in the case of security, to restrict alarms received at a particular guard station to that guard's area of responsibility. In similar fashion, data segregation can be applied to restrict the activities of an operator. For example, a guard may be permitted to receive and acknowledge security alarms, but prevented from accessing reader-controlled doors since that would disable the accounting of who entered each door at what time.

Security systems typically are manned 24 hours a day, while other systems, such as environmental control, are manned only during work hours. An integrated system can easily transport functions from other systems to a manned security terminal during off hours so that emergency alarms can be received. In addition, a guard receiving a door intrusion alarm may acquire evidence of arson if he subsequently receives a fire alarm from the same area, causing him to respond differently than if the two alarms were not linked in his mind.

Access control has become a major element in most security systems. Because it automatically monitors, controls, and records the movement of people into and within a facility, it has a pervasive role in systems integration.

In such a system, the individual is identified by a unique credential, such as an access card, when it is presented to card readers located at entrances and other controlled doors within the building.

Access is controlled for each reader location by the individual's ID number encrypted on the card, and by time of day, day of week, and other conditions that the system may impose. Before admitting the person, the card reader verifies that all the conditions for admittance have been met, then releases the door strike and allows the cardholder to enter.

Some systems are more sophisticated, requiring a personal identification number (PIN) to be entered as the credential is used. It is also possible to measure a biometric characteristic as a further means of identification.

Access control, with its ability to trace the movements of specific cardholders through various areas of the facility, offers many opportunities to serve as a resource to other departments within the organization. This capability is enhanced when biographical information is stored in the system database. Here are a few examples.

- A chemical spill occurs in a special assembly area and the safety department needs a list of those in the working area to make sure all are accounted for.

- The medical department wants to know when certain doctors and other key medical personnel are on the premises.

- The payroll department suspects that an employee is falsifying time card entries and wants verification of the parking ramp arrival and departure times.

- The production department wants a list of workers with certain skill classifications to assist in restaffing an assembly line when illness or weather has left them shorthanded.

Integrated Applications

The functional elements in an integrated building management system can pool resources and perform interactive tasks that are otherwise impossible, thus adding value to your investment in systems integration. There is more potential for systems integration with the access control function than with any other. Because cardholders go everywhere and do everything, many consider access control the universal integrator. As a consequence, security directors are in a position to play a key role in optimizing the cost and operation of building control systems throughout the organization.

Although there are many opportunities to combine access control with other protection and control functions to form integrated applications, not all are appropriate for every building type and operating style. Following are some of the more popular opportunities for office building complexes.

ELEVATOR CONTROL

The elevator control application controls the floor(s) that a cardholder can access.

Presentation of the credential to a card reader installed in the elevator cab activates the floor buttons authorized for that individual and locks out other buttons. Most systems keep the ground floor button active so all may exit the building. In most cases, the elevator readers are active during off-hours only. The elevator control function can be implemented using contacts in series with the floor selection buttons or by a direct data exchange between the elevator access control subsystem and the elevator control computer.

TENANT METERING

Tenant metering involves integration of the access control and environmental control systems in a tenant-occupied building. It allows the building operator to optimize off-hours energy use by applying it only when and where needed for after-hours tenants, and to recover the extra energy costs from the user. Presentation of an access credential by a late-working tenant causes the system to activate lighting and heating/air conditioning in the zone containing the individual's workstation. Exiting reverses the process. A stored record of metered energy consumption is used for monthly billing.

PARKING LOT CONTROL

Parking lot control has many variations and levels of sophistication. All applications use the standard access credential with card readers to control motorized gates at parking lot/ramp entrances and exits. In the simplest form, the system admits cardholders in their autos with an anti-passback feature to prevent a second entry without an intervening exit. The system can track the number of cars inside the lot and prevent entry when all parking spaces are filled. More sophisticated versions allow a means for fee collection for: (1) those who pay a monthly fee for a reserved space, (2) those who pay a monthly fee based on metered usage, and (3) the general public, paying a fee upon exiting.

FIRE MANAGEMENT

Linking access control and fire alarm systems allows reader-controlled doors to be released in a fire emergency to facilitate evacuation of the area. The system advises central security operators that door control has been deliberately breached. It also can inform fire fighters how many people are in the fire area so all can be accounted for. If environmental control is included in this integration, the system automatically can adjust fans and dampers to purge smoke from the fire area.

ENVIRONMENTAL CONTROL/ENERGY MANAGEMENT

ASHRAE codes now require that ventilation be based on occupancy. In an integrated system, access control can be used to initiate, terminate, or rest various elements of the environmental control system, thus minimizing energy consumption while meeting code-mandated ventilation requirements based on measured occupancy.

TIME AND ATTENDANCE

The time and attendance application uses the access credential as a time card to log employees in and out of the facility for payroll purposes. In a simple application where only a small number of employees are involved, the system may use the same computer as the access control system. In larger, more complex applications, a dedicated time/attendance processor may be required to expedite the higher traffic load and capture necessary data. Although the basic operation of all time and attendance systems is similar, the system designer must exercise a variety of operational choices to accommodate user needs.

Other integration opportunities for office buildings include point of sale, executive protection, video imaging, equipment checkout control, cafeteria meal billing, computer access, lighting control, and guard tour.

Designing the "Right" Integrated System

Obtaining an integrated system that is right for your facility takes careful planning in a process that keeps the right people involved and informed. The following guidelines may be helpful:

- Carefully examine and exploit the opportunities for integration that are appropriate for your building use and style of operation.

- Be sure top management is fully aware of integration opportunities and the benefits they can deliver, including the role of the system database as a resource for retrieving selected information and preparing customized reports.

- Involve participating department heads in the planning process. Their input is necessary to ensure they receive maximum benefit from the integration and will ensure their continued support throughout the project.

- Be aware of applicable codes in your area to make certain that applications you develop are allowable.

- Select an experienced consultant with a proven track record and a strong background in integrated systems. Check with clients to assess their satisfaction.

- Base the specification on realistic expectations of performance. State what you require in simple terms, avoiding detailed hardware descriptions that tend to make their specification proprietary and add unnecessary costs.

- Be sure the specification is developed specifically for your facility and describes your desired applications. It should not be a new version of another project.

- When sizing the system, allow adequate capacity for future growth.

- Select a responsible supplier with integrated system experience. As before, verify performance and satisfaction with several recent customers. Be wary of extremely low bids—performance may match price.

- Select systems that have the required approvals in your locale. Failure to do so can result in permit and start-up delays and problems with your underwriter and local authorities.

By following this advice, you can take full advantage of the operational benefits and financial rewards that systems integration has to offer.

Integrated Systems: The Whole-Building Approach

Kevin J. Haughey

Benefiting from sophisticated technological advances of the past decade, the methods of accessing buildings and security facilities have changed dramatically. Access control systems have grown from lock and key to affordable PC-based management systems. Security systems have evolved into sophisticated alarm monitoring equipment and often are integrated with CCTV camera controllers and video switching systems.

The advent of the microprocessor and the software written to manage these systems has enabled security managers to install integrated systems, which, in turn, have reduced manpower overhead and optimized security management.

Systems integration is an outgrowth of building and facility managers' desires to obtain systems that offer the lowest cost and the greatest benefit, while reducing the installation and operating costs of the independent systems. A typical integrated security system only incorporates physical security of the building, including CCTV, access control, and badging systems. Several systems also integrate fire alarm monitoring.

Before considering an integrated security system, look beyond the traditional security-related functions, consider the facility as a whole, and identify all the major systems which can be integrated or interfaced. A typical facility may have security (alarm, elevator, and environmental) control. Traditional integrated security systems usually carry a hefty price tag, and the expense may be difficult to justify. However, if a single system can manage all these functions, the potential cost savings can make the system affordable.

One of the largest systems in any facility is the environmental control system. Since the mid-1970s energy crisis, the technology involved in maintaining indoor environmental conditions has paralled the strides made in the security industry. Systems once were totally controlled by pneumatic air pressure devices and required a large engineering staff to ensure proper operation. These systems have matured.

During the 1960s, many of the large facilities and multi-tenant office buildings were equipped with computer-based energy management systems. They comprised electronic control interfaces to the existing pneumatic systems tied together by a single mainframe or microcomputer for centralized processing and control. These systems suffered from three major drawbacks: (1) They were expensive; (2) due to centralized processing and control, they suffered from single point of failure problems; (3) the degree of software maturity could not enable the systems to save energy reliably while maintaining comfort levels.

Technological advances in the late 1980s and early 1990s have been incorporated into the environmental control systems to the extent that they are now commonly referred to as Building Automation Systems (BASs). Featuring sophisticated microprocessor-based, distributed controllers and PC front ends, BASs have become more affordable and more reliable. Many systems feature operator-level programming capabilities and Graphical User Interfaces (GUIs). Although most control only lighting and heating, ventilation, and air conditioning (HVAC) subsystems, some BASs include or provide an interface to an automated Maintenance Management System (MMS).

If properly designed and installed, these systems usually pay for themselves within two to five years through reduced energy and equipment maintenance costs.

BAS manufacturers realize that the market is moving toward the totally integrated building concept. A handful of these vendors have moved beyond their traditional rules and have developed products which integrate several of the component systems of a modern building or facility. These combined systems can handle a range of building sizes, from small buildings to large-scale multi-building sites or multi-site systems such as university campuses. These systems now usually are referred to as Facility Management Systems (FMSs). Before discussing FMS features, you must understand the other non-security-related component systems incorporated by the vendor.

These systems provide effective control of facility heating, ventilation, and air conditioning. Systems exist at various levels within the facility. Central plant systems include boilers, chilled water systems, and related auxiliary equipment. Primary subsystems include primary fans, air conditioning/heating components, and lighting controllers which are distributed throughout the facility, each responsible for a large area such as a group of floors. Unit control systems are responsible for local control nearest the personnel, usually controlling single-office or common open floor plan areas. Operating time for each piece of equipment is collected by the BAS and shared with the MMS, which schedules routine maintenance.

Life safety equipment must be able to override the operation of access control and HVAC equipment. Building codes nearly always require electrical interlocks controlled by the fire alarm system to ensure that personnel have unencumbered egress from the building and that ventilation equipment is secured to reduce the spread of fire and smoke. Newer alarm systems offer intelligent interfaces which can be monitored by the BAS.

Elevator systems usually limit floor access control functions to individuals or groups. Many large multi-tenant buildings are beginning to install sophisticated elevator management systems to optimize elevator use and minimize user wait times. These intelligent systems may require a communications interface instead of the more traditional relay interfaces. Access control of main elevators is usually, but not always, limited to after-hours implementation.

Facility management systems, and their predecessor building automation systems, have been designed to meet two major guiding principles: (1) the architecture of the system must be flexible enough to adapt to a large variety of applications; (2) fast and reliable communication is paramount. Many of the controllers used in the system must share globalized tenets and easily lend themselves to alarm monitoring and access control applications.

FMS and BAS system architectures usually differ from that of a typical security or access control system in that they usually are point-based. Points are the individual monitored input and controlled output signals, and are the framework or supporting structure of the system. Each point is identified with a unique address and signal type identifier which describes its function and location within the entire system. Text descriptors allow the operator to recognize easily the point's purpose or significance. All application programming then is structured around the individual points as required.

FMS and BAS commonly utilize a three-tiered or layered architecture to maximize communication efficiency. Points may be defined at the lowest or unit control level and at the primary control level.

In an FMS system, access controlled portals and security/alarm devices exist at the unit control tier. Level 1 of the architecture comprises limited-purpose or application-specific controllers which monitor or control a group of 20 or fewer inputs and/or outputs. Unit controllers typically exist on a reliable high-speed RS-485 or RS-422 polling network and are serviced by a master controller which controls communication, event/transaction handling, and time functions.

Each level 1 controller maintains a database which has been configured by the system front end, and, in the case of access controllers, each will contain a master copy of the portal user authorization data. Since the number of points or portals assigned to each controller is relatively small, single controller failures do not affect the operation of the system as a whole.

Primary control functionality exists at level 2 of the FMS architecture. The majority of the control functions reside at this level. In BAS, level 2 controllers service families of unit controllers or provide control to primary lighting, heating, and air conditioning equipment. These controllers have greatly increased point capacities and are fully capable of standalone operation in event of a communication failure.

Communication at this level depends on the vendor. Some vendors have chosen to integrate a PC chassis into the controller and communicate with other primary controllers and the front end through IEEE802.2 Ethernet hardware. Others use high-speed RS-422 or RS-485 polling networks.

Peer-to-peer communication is preferable in that the network integrity does not rely on a single device to poll all others. Although polling networks can service their systems very efficiently, time and communication resources are degraded slightly since the master will continue to poll for missing devices. Peer-to-peer networks can be accomplished through Ethernet, RS-422, or RS-485.

At level 2 of the architecture, a wide variety of alternate communication methods are available. Nearly every vendor has incorporated an auto-dial/auto-answer modem communication technique, which allows the central site to monitor and update programming at remote sites through existing phone lines. A few vendors offer optional equipment to utilize leased telephone lines, fiber optics, and microwave and radio transceivers to avoid the distance limitation of hard-wired installations.

Level 2 of the architecture is where vendors often choose to provide their interfaces with other building systems. Fire alarm, camera controllers, and video switches are commonly built-up programmable logic controllers (PLCs) and include a proprietary communications interface to RS-232, RS-422, or RS-485 equipment. Communications between FMS and the PLC are accomplished through events passed via a custom communication protocol converter normally codeveloped by the FMS manufacturer and the third-party system manufacturer.

Level 3 of the FMS is a PC-based front end. BAS and FMS manufacturers have used a simplified GUI for years to make the building controls easier for building engineers and operators to use. The ease of use and quality of graphics vary widely from vendor to vendor and are based upon a full range of operating systems and hardware platforms.

The front-end platform is much the same as integrated security systems in that it provides the user with an interface for event, reader transaction, and alarm history reporting and handling. Other features include system status summaries, manual/override control of portals and other output devices, program modification, data entry, and audit trail review. Access to these functions is password-protected to ensure system integrity.

The largest development in FMS is the use of computer networks. A handful of FMS manufacturers have front ends which can exist on an IEEE 802.3 Ethernet system. This has enabled system owners to install multiple level 3 workstations throughout their facilities. By using simple password-controlled configuration screens and password-protected controllers, the owner can route events and transactions to designated workstations over a single network. Some of the FMS front ends can operate on more than one network operating system, usually at the peer-to-peer level.

Use of the Ethernet systems within office and manufacturing environments now is quite commonplace and offers high-speed PC-to-PC data sharing. A major advantage to using peer-to-peer methods is the distributed data environment. Security managers and building managers are no longer forced to buy expensive backup and redundant equipment to ensure against system downtime.

Password authorization data and the entire access control database can be equalized among all workstations. If desired, secure workstations can be dedicated to automatic backup of event history and programming entered at any operator workstation. Badging and maintenance management systems are most often integrated at this level, where they can share common databases. Ethernet systems may even allow you to install access control workstations in tenant offices so that the systems can manage their own subsystems. Programming and monitoring can be limited to only their portals.

The single, greatest advantage of the fully integrated building is reader transaction initiated control. In an integrated security access system, this is limited to control of the information presented at the monitoring station. For example, when a user presents his or her credential at an access control reader, cameras are controlled to preset positions, and video presentations at the monitoring stations are switched to the view of interest. Badge information can be displayed simultaneously for comparison.

A facility management system can take this several steps further by providing the link to the BAS and elevator systems. As individuals present their credentials at an entry point, the system can turn on the lights in their offices, and adjust the setpoint for the individual space temperature for occupied conditions. When the same individuals present their credentials at an exit point, the system can turn off office lighting and return the temperature control of the office to unoccupied settings automatically. If an exit reader is located in the office area, an elevator cab can be called to the floor and await the arrival of the user.

Working as a Locksmith

As was explained in Chapter 1, there are many money-making opportunities for a person who has locksmithing skills. Most people begin their locksmithing career by working for a locksmithing shop. This allows someone to gain a great deal of experience while being paid.

Other people prefer to begin their own locksmithing business without first working for another locksmithing shop. Running your own business can give you many learning experiences and allow you to earn a lot of money.

This chapter explains how to find a job as a locksmith and how to start and run a successful locksmithing business. Many related issues are also discussed, including the pros and cons of joining locksmithing associations, getting certified and licensed, and legal and ethical issues every locksmith needs to understand.

Locksmithing Associations

Belonging to a locksmithing association can help you improve your credibility among other locksmiths and in your community. Most of the associations offer trade journals, technical bulletins, classes, discounts on books and supplies, locksmith bonds, insurance, etc. They provide membership certificates you can display in your shop and logos you can use in your advertisements.

Many successful locksmiths, however, don't belong to a locksmithing association. Some don't join because they believe the membership dues exceed the value of the services such groups provide. Other locksmiths refuse to join because they disagree with the policies or legislative activities of such organizations. The criteria for becoming a member differs among them, as do the policies, legislative activities, and membership dues. You'll need to decide for yourself whether or not joining one will be beneficial for you. Appendix H lists the addresses of many locksmithing organizations. Contact them to obtain membership information.

Whether or not you decide to join an association, it's a good idea to subscribe to physical and electronic security trade journals and newspapers. Some are distributed free to qualified security professionals. Such publications can help you stay abreast of new products, trends, and legislation related to the security industry. For addresses of some popular trade periodicals, see Appendix B.

Certifications

A locksmith certification signifies that a person has demonstrated a level of knowledge or proficiency that meets a school or association's criteria for being certified. The significance of a certification depends on the integrity of the organization issuing it. Some of the better known certifications are granted by the Associated Locksmiths of America (ALOA), the American Society of Industrial Security (ASIS), and the International Association of Home Safety and Security Professionals (IAHSSP). A sample certification test, based on IAHSSP's Registered Professional Locksmith test, is provided in Chapter 23.

Locksmiths are divided about the need for certifications. Many feel they shouldn't have to meet the approval of a specific school or organization. They prefer to allow the free market determine the competency of a locksmith. An incompetent locksmith, they argue, won't be able to successfully compete against a competent one.

Others feel that locksmith certifications can benefit the locksmith industry by raising the competency level of all locksmiths and by improving the public perception of locksmiths.

Locksmiths have similar disagreements on the issue of licensing.

Licensing

A license differs from a certification in that a license is issued by a municipality rather than by a school or an association. Most cities and states don't offer or require locksmith licenses. In those places, locksmiths are required only to abide by laws that apply to all businesses—zoning, taxes, building codes, etc. (However, because the alarm industry is heavily regulated, a locksmith who wants to install alarms will probably first need to obtain an alarm systems installers license.)

A few places, such as New York City, Las Vegas, Dade County in Florida, and the state of California, require a person to get a locksmith license before offering locksmithing services.

Contact your city, county, and state licensing bureaus to find out if you need to have a locksmith (or other) license. Some places levy stiff fines on people who practice locksmithing without a license. In Dade County, for instance, you can be fined up to $10,000.

The criteria for obtaining a locksmithing license vary from place to place. Some require an applicant to take a competency test, be fingerprinted, provide photographs, submit to a background check, and pay an annual fee of $200 or more. Other places simply require applicants to register their name and address and pay a few dollars annually.

Locksmiths are divided on three major issues concerning licensing: whether or not licensing is necessary, what criteria should be required to obtain a license, and whether or not a national locksmith association should have an integral part in qualifying locksmiths for licensing.

Some locksmiths feel that licensing is needed to protect consumers from unskilled locksmiths and to improve the image of the profession. Other locksmiths feel that the free market does a good job of separating good locksmiths from the bad.

Proposed criteria for licensing—such as the fees, liability insurance, and competency testing—are also of concern to many locksmiths. The primary arguments about such matters center around whether or not a specific criterion is unnecessary, too costly, or too burdensome for locksmiths.

Some proposed licensing bills include provisions to allow certification tests offered by national locksmith trade associations to satisfy the locksmith competency criteria. In other words, according to some bills, a person who gets certified by a national locksmith association is to be considered competent to do locksmithing work. People in favor of such a provision believe it is in the best interest of all locksmiths for locksmith trade associations to play an integral part in the licensing process. Those who disagree with such a provision feel that bills authorizing an association to test applicants for a license would not benefit locksmiths who don't want to join one and would give too much power to associations.

Some locksmith trade associations are actively working to enact new locksmithing laws throughout the United States. Bills are being proposed constantly, but because only a small minority of locksmiths belong to associations, most locksmiths are unaware of such bills until they become law. If you're a locksmith or plan to become one, you should take an interest in the current bills related to locksmiths in your area.

Write or call your local, county, state, and federal representatives and ask to be kept informed of proposed bills related to locksmiths. When licensing bills are proposed, ask your representative to mail a copy to you. In addition to letting your representatives know what you think of the bills, you can send letters to the editors of your local newspapers and to state, regional, and national locksmith associations.

Planning Your Job Search

Locksmithing jobs are plentiful; you should have little difficulty finding the one you want. Your job search will be most productive if you approach it in a professional manner. In a sense, when you're seeking a job you're a salesperson—you're selling yourself. You need to convince a prospective employer to hire you, whether or not the employer is currently seeking a new employee.

There are five steps you should consider when planning a job search: decide where you want to work, locate potential employers, convince potential employers to meet with you, meet with potential employers, and make an employment agreement.

Deciding Where You Want to Work

Before contacting prospective employers, decide what type of shop you want to work in, where you want to work, and what kind of employer you want to work for.

Which cities are you willing to work in? Do you prefer to work in a large, mid-size, or small shop? Do you prefer to work for a highly experienced shop owner or for an owner who knows little about locksmithing?

You can answer those questions by considering your reasons for seeking employment. If you're primarily seeking an immediate, short-term source of income, for example, your answers might be different than if you were more concerned about job security or gaining useful locksmithing experience.

In a small shop you might be given a lot of responsibility and be able to get a great deal of experience quickly. A large shop might make you feel like the lowest head on a totem pole, and you are more likely to get a lot of pressure and little respect. However, a large shop might be better able to offer you more job security and a lot of opportunities for advancement.

A highly experienced locksmith can teach you a lot, but you will probably have to work a long time to learn much. Experienced locksmiths place a lot of value on their knowledge and rarely share much of it with new employees. Often, experienced locksmiths worry that if a new employee learns a lot very quickly, the employee might quit and start a competing company.

Some shop owners know very little about locksmithing. Working for them can be difficult because they often use outdated tools, supplies, and locksmithing methods. Sometimes such an owner is a retired or wealthy person who does locksmithing as a hobby. You won't gain much useful experience working for such a person; instead, you'll probably pick up a lot of bad habits.

Locating Prospective Employers

You can find prospective employers by looking through the yellow pages of telephone directories under locksmiths and by looking through the help-wanted ads in newspapers and locksmithing trade journals. You might also want to place "job wanted" ads in some locksmithing trade journals.

When creating an ad, briefly state the cities in which you would like to work, your most significant qualifications (bondable, good driving record, have own tools, etc.), your name, mailing address, and telephone number. Blind advertisements—those that don't include your name, address, or any direct contact information—won't get many responses. Few locksmith shop owners are that desperate for help.

QUICK»TIP If you're working as a locksmith and your employer doesn't know you're looking for another job, be cautious about answering "blind" help-wanted ads (those with no company name or traceable address). Such ads are sometimes placed by employers who are checking on their employees.

Prompting Prospective Employers to Meet with You

It's usually better for you to set up a meeting with a prospective employer than to just walk into the shop unscheduled. You might come in when the owner is very busy, which could give the person a negative impression of you. Also, it might be hard to interest the shop owner in hiring you without any prior knowledge about you.

One way to prompt a prospective employer to meet with you is send a resumé and a cover letter. It isn't always necessary to have a resumé to get a locksmithing job, but it can be a highly effective selling tool. A resumé allows you to project a good image of yourself to a prospective employer, and it sets the stage for your interview.

The resumé is an informative document designed to help an employer know you better. When writing it, view your resumé as a document designed to promote you. Don't include everything there is to know about yourself, only information that will help an employer decide to hire you. Don't include, for example, information about being fired from a previous job. It's best to wait until you're face to face with a person before you try to explain past problems.

The resumé should be neatly typed in black ink on 20-pound bond, 8½-×-11-inch white paper. If you can't type, have someone else type it. Don't use graphics or fancy typestyles (remember, you're seeking work as a locksmith—and not as a graphic artist). A resumé should be kept to one page; few prospective employers like wading through long resumés.

Figure 22.1 is a sample resumé. Use it as a guideline, but don't be afraid to organize yours differently. There is no perfect structure for a resumé; organize it in the way that allows the employer to quickly see reasons for hiring you. If your education is your strongest selling point, for example, include that information first. If your work history is your strongest selling point, include your work history first (Figure 22.1a).

Include a short cover letter with your resumé (Figure 22.2). The cover letter should be directed to an owner, manager, or supervisor by name and should prompt him or her to review your resumé. Your local library should have books on writing resumés and cover letters, which contain more samples.

John A. Smith
123 Any Street
Any Town, Any State 01234
(012)345-6789

Job Objective
Entry level position as a locksmith in a progressive shop.

Special Capabilities
- Can quickly open locked automobiles
- Can use key cutting and code machines
- Can install, rekey and service many types of locks
- Can pick locks and impression keys
- Can install and service emergency exit door hardware
- Can operate cash registers

Special Qualities
Dependable (missed work only 2 days over the past 5 years), good driver (no accidents), bondable (no arrests), good health, fast learner, and self-starter.

Education/Training
BA degree in Business Administration from ABC College in Quincy, CA.
Self-study with *Locksmithing,* by Bill Phillips; and *The Complete Book of Locks & Locksmithing, 4th Edition,* by Bill Phillips.

Memberships
Member of the International Association of Home Safety & Security Professionals.

Work Highlights
OFFICE ASSOCIATE
SEARS IN QUINCY, CA FROM JANUARY 1997 TO PRESENT
Mann the switchboard; handle complaints; accept money; balance money taken from the safe, registers and other areas of the store; train other associates; and work with all of the office equipment.

ASSISTANT MANAGER
MCDONALD'S IN QUINCY, CA FROM JUNE 1995 TO JANUARY 1997.

References Available Upon Request

FIGURE 22.1A

If you have little formal training or experience, don't emphasize those things on your resumé.

John A. Smith
123 Any Street
Any Town, Any State 01234
Phone: (012)345-6789

Job Objective
Seeking position as a locksmith/access control systems technician in a University.

Work Experience
April 1995 - Present, Manager of ABC Locksmith Shop in Quincy, CA. Supervisor of 6 locksmiths. Duties include: training apprentices; designing and maintaining masterkey systems; installing and servicing emergency exit door devices, electromagnetic locks, electric locks, electric strikes, and a variety of high security locks; and manipulating, drilling, and recombinating safes.

January 1992-April 1995, Locksmith at DEF Locksmith Shop in Brookdale, CO. Duties included: opening locked automobiles; rekeying, master keying, impressioning, and servicing a variety of basic and high-security locks; manipulating, drilling, and recombinating safes; installing and servicing emergency exit door devices and other door hardware; servicing foreign and domestic automobile locks; installing a wide variety of electric and electronic security devices; operating the cash registers.

December 1989-January 1992, Key Cutter/Apprentice locksmith at The Key Shop in Brookdale, CO. Cutting keys and assisting three locksmiths. Worked exclusively inside the shop during the first year, but did outside work about half the time thereafter.

June 1985-December 1989, Key Cutter/Salesperson at Building Supply Hardware in Brookdale, CO.

Licenses/Certificates
Have a current California Locksmith Permit
Certified as a Residential Protection Specialist (RPS)
Certified as a Certified Protection Professional (CPP)
Member of the International Association of Home Safety and Security Professionals

References Available Upon Request

FIGURE 22.1B

If you have little formal training or experience, don't emphasize those things on your resumé.

123 Any Street
Any Town, Any State 01234
Phone: (012)345-6789

Today's Date

Ms. Janet L. Griffin, owner
The Lock & Key Shop
321 Another Street
Another Town, Another State 43210

Dear Ms. Griffin:

I can perform most basic locksmithing tasks, and especially enjoy doing foreign and domestic automobile work. Please look over my enclosed resume. I'd like to meet with you to see if we might be able to work together.

Please call me at your earliest convenience to let me know when I can come by your shop.

Sincerely yours,

John A. Smith

John A. Smith

FIGURE 22.2

A brief cover letter should be sent along with a resumé.

Meeting With Prospective Employers

After reviewing your resumé, a prospective employer will probably either call you on the telephone or write a letter. If you're not contacted within two weeks after mailing your resumé, call the person you addressed it to and ask if your letter was received. If it was received, request a meeting. You might be told there are no job openings there. In that case, ask if you could still arrange a meeting so you two can get to know each other.

Before going to a meeting, be sure you are well rested, have a positive attitude, and are fully prepared. A positive attitude requires seeing yourself as a valuable commodity. Project this image to the person you want to work for. Do not tell an employer you "really need a job," even if the statement is true. Few people will hire you simply because you need a job. If you seem too needy, people will think you are incompetent.

Don't go to a meeting with the feeling that the only reason you're there is so a prospective employer can look you over to decide if you are hireable. You both have something to offer that the other needs. You have your time, personality, knowledge, and skills to offer—all of which can help the prospective employer make more money. The employer, in turn, has knowledge, experience, and money to offer you. The purpose of the meeting is to allow both of you to get to know each other better and to decide if you want to work together. It might also lead to an employment agreement.

Before going to the meeting, honestly assess your strengths and weaknesses. Consider which locksmithing tasks you're able to perform well. Also consider how well you can perform other tasks a prospective employer might want you to do, such as selling products, working a cash register, etc. Then write a list of all your strengths and a list of the last four places you've worked. Include dates, salaries, and the names of supervisors.

At this point, prepare explanations for any negative questions the prospective employer might ask you during the interview. If there is a gap of more than three months between your jobs, for example, decide how to explain that gap. If you were fired from one of your jobs or if you quit one, figure out the best way to explain difficult situations to a prospective employer. Your explanations should put you in the best light possible.

Never blame other people, such as former supervisors, for problems in past jobs; this will make you seem like a crybaby or a back-stabber. If there is no good explanation for your firing, it might be in your best interest to simply not mention that job unless the employer is likely to find out about it anyway. Don't lie about problems you've had because a prospective employer, if he learns the truth, will probably not hire you and might tell other locksmiths about you. The locksmithing industry is fairly small and word gets around quickly.

Before the meeting, learn all you can about the prospective employer and his or her shop. Stop by the shop to find out what products the company sells and what special services it offers. Call the local Better Business Bureau and Chamber of Commerce to find out how long the business has been established and how many consumer complaints have been filed against the company. Contact local, state, and national locksmithing trade associations to find out if the owner belongs to any of them.

Before the meeting also read the most current issue of a locksmithing trade journal. Study the issue to find out about major news related to the trade. Be prepared to confidently speak about such matters.

When you go to the interview, wear clean clothes and be well groomed. Arrive a few minutes early. When you shake hands with the prospective employer, use a firm (but not tight) grip, look into his or her eyes, and smile. The person will probably give you a tour of the shop. That will help you assess whether or not it's a place you want to work. Allow the prospective employer to guide the meeting. If he or she offers you a cup of coffee, decline it unless the prospective employer also has one. Don't ask if you may smoke; and don't smoke if invited to.

In the meeting, sit in a relaxed position and look directly at the person. Constantly looking away will make you appear insecure or dishonest. Listen intently while the employer is talking; don't interrupt. Smile a few times during the meeting. Be sure you understand a question before attempting to answer it. Whenever you have the opportunity, emphasize your strengths and what you have to offer, but don't be boastful when doing so.

If you're asked a question you feel uncomfortable answering, keep your body in a relaxed position, continue looking into the person's eyes, and answer it in the way you had planned to answer it. Don't immediately begin talking about another topic after answering the question; this will seem as if you're trying to hide something. Instead, pause after answering the question and smile at the person; he or she will then either ask you a follow-up question or move on to another topic. Don't give an audible sigh of relief when you move to a new topic.

If asked about your salary requirements, don't give a figure. Instead say something like: "I don't have a salary in mind, but I'm sure we could agree on one if we decide to work together." Salary is usually discussed at a second meeting. However, if the prospective employer insists on discussing salary during the first meeting, let him or her state a figure first. Ask what the employer believes is a fair salary. When discussing salary always speak about "fairness to both of us."

Making an Employment Agreement

The prospective employer's first salary offer will almost always be less than the amount the company is willing to pay. You might be told that the employer doesn't know much about how well you work, so you will start at a certain salary and will be reviewed after a short time.

That might sound good, but the salary you start out with has a lot to do with how much you'll earn from the company later. You want to begin working for the highest salary possible.

If the prospective employer's salary offer is too low, you can reply that you would like to devote your full attention to the job and work hard for the company, but don't know if you could afford to do that with the salary offered. Explain that you simply want a fair salary. Pushing for the highest salary possible (within reason) will not only allow you to earn more money, but will also give the prospective employer confidence in you. You will be proving to the person that you're a good salesperson.

If the employer refuses to agree to an acceptable salary, tell him or her you need to think about the offer. Then smile, stand up, shake hands, and leave. If the person demands an immediate answer, say you want to discuss the matter with someone else, such as your spouse.

Don't get pressured into accepting an unreasonable employment agreement. It's in your best interest to give yourself time to think the matter over and to meet with other prospective employers. If no one is willing to make a reasonable employment agreement with you, consider starting your own business.

Starting Your Own Business

As explained in Chapter 1, there are two basic types of locksmithing shops: store-front and mobile. Usually it's less expensive to begin a mobile shop than it is to establish a store-front shop. For either type to be successful, you need to have sufficient working capital, obtain the tools and supplies you need, and make good marketing decisions.

Before starting a business, you should seek professional assistance. Business mistakes are easy to make and can be very costly to you. First, meet with an attorney who can help you decide which organizational structure (sole proprietorship, corporation, etc.) is best for your business. An attorney can also inform you about zoning, licensing, and other legal matters.

After you've drawn up a business plan—which should include estimates of how much money you need to begin your business and how much money you anticipate earning—meet with an accountant to review it. He or she can objectively assess your plan and offer suggestions for improving it. The accountant can also show you how to keep accurate business records.

You'll also need to meet with an insurance agent to figure out how much and which types of insurance you need. You'll probably want fire and theft insurance for your inventory and equipment. You might also want product and liability insurance.

Tools

Chapter 6 provides a list of the tools and supplies you'll need to perform most locksmithing services. If you plan to offer limited services, you won't need to obtain all of them.

Before purchasing tools, carefully decide which ones you need and where you can get them at the best prices. Look through several catalogs to compare prices and quality.

Telephones

Whether you have a mobile shop or a store-front shop, you'll need at least one telephone. People who are locked out of their homes or cars don't walk to a locksmithing shop; they use the telephone. If they get a busy signal, they usually call another shop. That's why the telephone you use for your business should usually be free to accept incoming calls. If you're using a single telephone for both business and personal purposes, you might want to get call-waiting service.

You could miss important calls unless someone is available to answer the telephone 24 hours a day. Some people use an answering machine. However, an answering service is a better alternative. A person in an emergency situation probably won't leave a message on a machine; they will just call another locksmith.

Advertising

Most locksmithing shops don't spend a lot of money on advertising. You might want to test various forms of advertising (newspapers, magazines, radio, etc.) to find the one that works best for your shop. The yellow pages of a local telephone directory and word of mouth are usually the most cost-effective forms of advertising for locksmiths. Contact the telephone company to find out the deadline for placing an advertisement in the next directory.

Look through the "Locksmiths" heading in the telephone directory to see the advertisements of other shops. That will give you an idea of how you should organize your ad and how large it should be. Unless you live in a large city, you probably won't need to have a full-page advertisement.

Pricing

A common mistake made by people who begin locksmithing businesses is to charge too little for their products and services. They believe low prices will provide a competitive edge over other locksmithing businesses. What usually happens is that a new locksmithing business fails because it doesn't make enough profit.

Don't be afraid to charge fair prices for your products and services. Compete with other locksmiths on the basis of superior service and better customer relations, not on the basis of prices.

Service Vehicle

Whether you have a store-front shop or a mobile shop, you'll need a service vehicle. Most locksmiths use a van for that purpose, but a truck or a car can also be used. You'll need to properly organize your service vehicle so you can work efficiently in it. Several companies manufacture interior units to help you better use the space in a service vehicle.

If you don't want to have your shop's name, telephone number, and address painted on the service vehicle, get a magnetic sign with that information and use it when you are out on calls.

Store-Front Location

If you decide to operate from a store-front, location will be very important. A building that many people regularly pass by will provide you with the opportunity to attract a lot of walk-in customers. People often walk into locksmithing shops on impulse, but they seldom spend much time trying to locate a particular shop.

Keep the shop clean and organize it in such a way that people will want to come in and browse. Good lighting, comfortable air temperature, and attractive displays (Figure 22.3) prompt people to come into a shop.

Laws about Duplicating Keys

Some people have "Do Not Duplicate," "Do Not Copy," "Master Key," or a similar phrase stamped on their house keys to help prevent key duplication by unauthorized people. However, in most jurisdictions such phrases don't automatically make the key illegal for you to duplicate. Generally, only keys made with restricted key blanks, such as United States Post Office keys, are illegal to copy. (It's against federal law to duplicate U. S. Post Office keys. They use the following blanks:

Attractive displays prompt people to come into a store-front shop to browse. *(Courtesy of Master Lock Company)*

Ilco Y2R/9RA; Orion YAL15L; Silca YA5R; and Borkey 206.5L.) Los Angeles and New York City are two of the few cities that have ordinances restricting the duplication of keys that are stamped with "Do Not Duplicate" or a similar phrase.

Even if it isn't illegal for you to copy a key stamped "Do Not Duplicate," it's generally safer not to copy such a key for anyone you don't know. If you copy the key for someone who isn't supposed to have a copy, you might face a lawsuit. To avoid a confrontation, you could just say that you don't have the right blank in stock.

If you decide to copy the key, ask for identification. To reduce the risk of a lawsuit, develop a strict policy regarding the duplication of such keys. Your policy might be, for example, to copy nonrestricted keys stamped "Do Not Duplicate" only after seeing the customer's identification. You and all the locksmiths in your shop should always follow the policy.

Sue Yourself . . . Before Someone Else Does

Charles A. Sennewald, CMC, CPP, CPO

There was a time when tort litigation in the United States rarely focused on security-related issues; the few lawsuits involving security tended to address acts of commission, as opposed to omission.

In 1965, the first significant award for inadequate security was reported to be $25,000. As the 1970s progressed, crime increased and the public became outraged over the criminal justice system's liberal view of the criminal and criminal rights. From this outrage came an increase in lawsuits against land owners and business operators. Victims of crimes, dissatisfied with the results of the criminal justice process, bypassed available civil action against the perpetrator of the crime. Instead, they asserted their rights of action against third parties whose negligence had put the criminal in a position to victimize or who had failed to deter or prevent the victimization.

Criminal Assault

One particular crime gave impetus to the victim's rights movement and tort litigation involving security. Connie Francis, an internationally known recording artist, was criminally assaulted in her second floor hotel room in a motor lodge on Long Island, New York. The assailant entered through a sliding glass door off the balcony outside her room. She sued the hotel for negligence in failing to provide adequate security. More specifically, she alleged the hotel was negligent because they knew of the defective condition of the glass doors on the balconies. Indeed, the doors were defective, as testified to by an expert.

The legal theory of the Francis suit was that innkeepers owe a special duty of security to guests, that this duty was breached through the negligence of not repairing or replacing defective door locks, and this negligence was the cause of her injury. The $2.5 million award, subsequently reduced to $1.5 million, opened the gates to security lawsuits.

Since that case, there has been a cascade of lawsuits alleging security negligence. With the threat of multi-million dollar awards, security executives, corporate attorneys, risk managers, and consultants now also must include another element in the security assessment process: How does this affect our exposure to liability and litigation?

Avoiding Litigation

Not uncommon today is the term "litigation avoidance," which simply means designing, planning, budgeting, and operating a security program or project in such a fashion as to actually prevent a future lawsuit. The irony is that security practitioners today have more clout, more of a voice than ever before, caused by this fear of the consequences of being found deficient by a civil jury.

Abduction and Murder

Here is a prime example. A young nurse was abducted from the hospital's multi-story parking ramp one evening. There was only one security officer on duty in the large hospital. Following her abduction, she was raped and strangled. The culprit was subsequently caught and imprisoned. Her relatives filed a suit alleging the hospital was negligent in its duties to provide protection, and its security was inadequate.

The following deficiencies were identified by a security consultant/expert:

- Only one security officer on duty for a large, complex site was insufficient.

- The officer was supposed to patrol the entire area once each hour; there was no record or evidence that patrols actually occurred.

- The security chief was responsible to, and reported to, the maintenance engineer, who didn't understand security needs or problems and refused to listen to the security chief's expressed concerns.

- Records revealed that the on-duty security officer was required to do nonsecurity tasks, such as moving television sets from one patient's room to another.

- The parking ramp from which the woman was abducted had a history of thefts from cars, vandalism, and suspicious circumstances, yet no security measures, such as access control or CCTV, were considered.

- Security officers were all moonlighting from the local police department, following their normal police shift. Hence they were not fresh and not necessarily dedicated to the job. One reason for selecting these off-duty officers was the cost; they were less expensive than permanent staff members because no benefits were provided.

When the lawsuit was filed, the security chief was quoted as saying, "I knew this was going to happen, but they wouldn't listen to me." However, the jury listened and handed down a staggering award for the family against the hospital. It would have been less expensive to provide first-class security, in terms of not only dollars, but also reputation and goodwill in the community.

Negligent Hiring

A national security guard company obtained the contract to provide uniformed security officers at a major airport. The security officers were to augment the airport police. Specifically, the contract guards were assigned to patrol and monitor the parking lots.

On the day prior to a major holiday, a woman arrived just before noon. She parked her expensive car and was getting out when she was accosted by a uniformed security officer who sexually assaulted her and attempted to choke her to death. She attracted the attention of a passer-by, causing the guard to flee.

It was subsequently discovered that the guard's application had not been screened, nor had he been subjected to a background check. The guard had a criminal history and had falsified his application for employment. Had the security company exercised reasonable care in examining and verifying information contained in the application, he would not have been hired.

Inadequate Supervision

A major telecommunications company had a remote mountain site. Three security officers were assigned to patrol duties at that site. An older guard was the sergeant and worked the day shift. Two younger men worked the swing and graveyard shifts. The two night officers were required to clock in every hour and telephone the main security desk in the valley several times each shift.

The sergeant complained to the main office about the conduct of the two younger men. He reported that he had found a can of beer in the jacket of one guard and an alarm clock in the pocket of the other. He also complained the two men weren't regularly clocking in, and their explanations were not valid. His complaints and suspicions were ignored.

One night the graveyard officer came to the site early and, contrary to rules, patrolled with the swing officer. They drank beer and smoked marijuana. During their patrolling they came upon a young man and woman parked in a car near the site. They killed the man and pushed his car over a cliff. They took the woman to one of the buildings on the site and raped her. Later they stabbed her and threw her over a cliff. She survived and spent hours crawling to the road, reaching it at daylight. The guards saw her, stabbed her many more times, and again threw her over the side. At the end of their shifts they went to their homes, unaware that the woman refused to die and had again made her way to the road, where she was found and rushed to the hospital.

The lawsuit's theory of liability was that the conduct of the officers was the result of inadequate supervision. It was determined that not only did the security management fail to investigate the sergeant's complaints, they failed to make unannounced and periodic inspection visits to the site. Consequently, the two young officers had no concern about being observed during their working hours or being discovered performing an unauthorized or illegal activity.

Negligent Performance of Duties

The management of an exclusive private community of mobile homes retained the services of a guard company to control access to the development. Uniformed officers were stationed at the guard house located at the park's entrance. Residents and authorized guests came and went freely, but visitors were denied access until the officer received approval and verbal authorization from a resident. If authorization was not obtained, the officers were instructed to deny entry.

On the day in question, three juveniles decided to visit the park to purchase a small amount of drugs from another juvenile who lived there with his parents. After several hours of drinking beer and using drugs, they were high. They drove to the park and were stopped at the main gate by the security officer. They told the officer they wanted to see their friend and identified him by name. The officer called the home but there was no answer. The officer advised them there was no one home and they could not enter the complex. The youths persuaded the officer to let them in nonetheless.

All roads inside the community had a posted 10 mph speed limit. The intoxicated youths ignored the signs and drove in a dangerous and reckless manner. One resident was sitting on the lawn in front of his home with his wife and two children. When he saw the vehicle make a dangerous turn at his corner, he shouted at the juveniles to "slow it down." They stopped and backed up. One of the youths shot the man in the head with a handgun. The innocent victim died in front of his family. The three youths sped out of the complex and later were apprehended.

The successful litigation against the guard company was based on the fact that the officer failed to deny access to unauthorized persons who were obviously intoxicated. Had the officer performed his duties as required, the youths would never have been able to shoot and kill the resident.

Inadequate Training

In another exclusive community, security officers controlled access at three separate gatehouses. Only authorized vehicles were allowed to enter. Each resident provided the security staff with a list of friends and relatives who could enter at any time without the need to obtain approval by phone. If an individual was not on the list, the officer was required to contact the resident.

One of the residents was separated from her husband, who recently had been released from prison. The woman was engaged in a custody battle over their son. The boy's mother was concerned by threats made by the father and telephoned the security officer to have his name removed from the authorized list and request that a special warning be posted at all gatehouses. The warning described the boy's father and his vehicle and stated the man should not be allowed into the community under any circumstances.

Some days later, the boy's grandmother also called security with a second request to deny entry to the father and again described the yellow sports car he probably would be driving. Two weeks later, the man was allowed to enter the complex at 1:30 in the morning; he later shot and killed the boy's mother and aunt.

It was subsequently discovered that the security officers who had been requested to post a warning and remove the father's name from the guest list had never been instructed how to handle such requests. Indeed, they had not received any training in a number of operating procedures, other than how to call the police or other emergency services.

As a direct result of the officer's lack of training and direction, the assailant's name was not removed from the list, nor was a warning posted. His unauthorized entry and crimes were directly related to that failure.

Protective Measures

What can a security firm do to protect against such lawsuits? In my view, the answer is simple: Manage the security in a responsible and professional manner.

- Screen and investigate applicants.

- Supervise security employees. Monitor their work and share with them your assessment of their performance. Remember, employees do what you inspect, not what you expect.

- Ensure security employees know what their duties are and how to properly perform them.

- Provide employees with a structured new-employee orientation, which includes the objective of security's role and initial training on what to do, and not do, on the assignment. Follow up with periodic training sessions to ensure the employee is still current and knowledgeable about his or her duties. Document every training session, recording the topic covered, the time devoted to the training, and who performed the training.

These four action points are certainly not the only steps available to reduce liability exposure, but do address the problems reflected in the examples of security failures mentioned previously.

Finally . . .

Not all lawsuits filed are meritorious. As a forensic consultant, it is not uncommon for me to be retained to assess the facts in a pending litigation, only to report to the legal firm that I find no fault with the security firm, nor did I find a security failure or negligence, and consequently cannot testify in support of their theory of liability.

Contrary to popular belief, this explosion of litigation has, in many ways, benefited our industry. The lack of professionalism, sloppy workmanship, and poor management practices of some have placed us center stage in the judicial system. When you realize that you might be next on stage in the limelight, you tend to clean up your act.

The security industry is better today than 10 years ago, thanks to the potential for litigation. Reviewing your security operation in the context of the potential for litigation helps reduce the likelihood of being sued and increases the professional level of the protection.

Ethics of Locksmithing

To develop and maintain good relationships with other locksmiths and local law enforcement agents, you should strictly adhere to the following rules of ethics:

- Always safeguard your locksmithing tools.

- Never duplicate a master key or a key stamped "Do Not Duplicate" for anyone without first obtaining written permission from a person who has legal control of the key.

- Never unlock a vehicle or building without first assuring yourself that the person hiring you to unlock it is authorized to do so.

- Keep a written record of the model, year, and license plate number of every vehicle you are hired to unlock. Also, keep a written record of the name and driver's license number of every person who hires you to unlock a vehicle.

- Keep a written record of the address of every building you have been hired to unlock. Also, keep a written record of the name and driver's license (or number from other positive identification) of every person who hires you to unlock a building.

- Don't perform locksmithing services that you're not qualified to perform.

- Perform each locksmithing job to the best of your ability, regardless of the price you're charging the customer.

Test Your Knowledge

This test is based on the general knowledge section of the International Association of Home Safety and Security Professionals' Registered Professional Locksmith (RPL) certification program. If you pass this test, you should be able to pass the RPL test and many other locksmithing certification and licensing examinations.

For accurate results, when taking the test don't search through the book for answers (it isn't an open book test). Choose the one best answer for each question. If you choose more than one answer for any question, you receive no credit for answering that question.

1. Which are basic parts of a standard key cutting machine?

    a. a pair of vises, key stop, and grinding stylus

    b. two cutter wheels, a pair of vises, and key shaper

    c. a pair of vises, a key stylus, and a cutter wheel

    d. a pair of styluses, a cutter wheel, and a key shaper

2. Which pin tumbler cylinder is likely to be easier to pick with a standard lock pick and torque wrench?

    a. a new Medeco 6-pin

    b. a worn Kwikset 5-pin with worn and broken springs

    c. a worn Kwikset 5-pin with good springs

    d. a worn Medeco 6-pin with worn and broken springs

3. Most locks used on Datsuns are 5-pin tumblers.

    a. true

    b. false

4. What are two critical dimensions for code cutting cylinder keys?

    a. spacing and depth

    b. bow size and blade thickness

    c. blade width and keyhole radius

    d. shoulder width and bow size

5. Ford began using wafer side bar locks in their automobiles in which year?

    a. 1967

    b. 1994

    c. 1984

    d. 1974

6. Typically the lock on a car's driver side will be harder to pick open than other less often used locks on the car.

    a. true

    b. false

7. Which manufacturer is best known for its residential key-in-knob locks?

    a. Best Locks

    b. Medeco Security Locks

    c. The Key-in Knob Corporation

    d. Kwikset Corporation

8. The most popular mechanical lock brands in the United States include:

    a. Yale, Master, Corby, and Gardall

    b. Yale, Kwikset, Master, and TuffLock

    c. Master, Corby, Gardall, and TuffLock

    d. Master, Yale, Kwikset, and Schlage

9. A standard electromagnetic lock includes a rectangular electromagnet and a rectangular wood and glass strike plate.

    a. true

    b. false

10. A mechanical lock that is operated mainly by a pin tumbler cylinder is commonly called a:

    a. disc tumbler pinned lock

    b. cylinder pin lock

    c. mechanical cylinder pin lock

    d. pin tumbler cylinder lock

11. A key-in-knob lock whose default position is inside knob unlocked and whose outside knob can be locked or unlocked with a key is:

    a. a classroom lock

    b. an institution lock

    c. a function lock

    d. a school lock

12. One difference between a bit key and barrel key is the bit key has a hollow shank.

    a. true

    b. false

13. A key-in-knob lock whose default position is that both knobs are locked and require that a key be used for unlocking is:

    a. a classroom lock

    b. a function lock

    c. an institution lock

    d. a school lock

14. Four basic types of keys are:

    a. barrel, flat, bow, and tumbler

    b. cylinder, flat, tubular, and barrel

    c. dimple, angularly bitted, corrugated, and blade

    d. cylinder, flat, warded, and V-cut

15. Parts of a flat key include the bow, blade, and throat cut.

    a. true

    b. false

16. The two most common key stops are:

    a. blade and V-cut

    b. keyway grooves and bittings

    c. bow and blade

    d. shoulder and tip

17. Bit keys are mostly commonly made of:

    a. brass, copper, and silver

    b. aluminum, iron, and silver

    c. copper, silver, and aluminum

    d. iron, brass, and aluminum

18. The Egyptians are credited with inventing the first lock to be based on the locking principle of today's pin tumbler lock.

    a. true

    b. false

19. Which of the following key combinations provides the most security?

    a. 55555

    b. 33333

    c. 35353

    d. 243535

20. Which of the following key combinations provides the least security?

    a. 243535

    b. 35353

    c. 321231

    d. 33333

21. Before impressioning a pin tumbler cylinder, it's usually helpful to lubricate the pin chambers thoroughly.

    a. true

    b. false

22. A blank is basically just:

    a. a change key with cuts on one side only

    b. an uncut or uncombinated key

    c. any key with no words or numbers on the bow

    d. a master key with no words or numbers on the bow

23. You can often determine the number of pin stacks or tumblers in a cylinder by:

    a. its key blade length

    b. its key blade thickness

    c. the key blank manufacturer's name on the bow

    d. the material of the key

24. When you are picking a pin tumbler cylinder, sometimes spraying a little lubrication into the keyway can be helpful.

    a. true

    b. false

25. Spool and mushroom pins:

    a. make keys easier to duplicate

b. make a lock harder to pick

c. make a lock easier to pick

d. make keys harder to duplicate

26. As a general rule, General Motors' 10-cut wafer side bar locks have:

    a. up to four of the same depth cut in the 7, 8, 9, and 10 spaces

    b. no number 4 depth in the first space (closest to the shoulder)

    c. a maximum of five number 1 depths in a code combination

    d. at least one 4-1 or 1-4 adjacent cuts

27. The electromagnetic lock was invented in the United States.

    a. true

    b. false

28. When drilling open a standard pin tumbler cylinder, position the drill bit:

    a. at the first letter of the cylinder

    b. at the shear line in alignment with the top and bottom pins

    c. directly below the bottom pins

    d. directly above the top pins

29. When viewed from the exterior side, a door that opens inward and has hinges on the right side is a:

    a. left-hand door

    b. right-hand door

    c. left-hand reverse bevel door

    d. right-hand reverse bevel door

30. Most locks used on Honda automobiles are 5-pin tumblers.

    a. true

    b. false

31. A utility patent:

    a. relates to a product's appearance, is granted for 14 years, and is renewable

    b. relates to a product's function, is granted for 17 years, and is nonrenewable

    c. relates to a product's appearance, is granted for 17 years, and is renewable

    d. relates to a product's function, is granted for 35 years, and is nonrenewable

32. To earn a UL-437 rating, a lock must:

    a. pass a performance test

    b. use a patented key

    c. use hardened steel mounting screws and mushroom and spool pins

    d. pass an attack test using common hand and electric tools, such as drills, saw blades, puller mechanisms, and picking tools

33. It's illegal to duplicate a U.S. post office box key at the request of the box renter, even if the box renter shows a current driver's license.

    a. true

    b. false

34. Tumblers are:

    a. small metal objects that protrude from a lock's cam to operate the bolt

    b. fixed projections on a lock's case

    c. small pins, usually made of metal, that move within a lock's case to prevent unauthorized keys from entering the keyhole

    d. small objects, usually made of metal, that move within a lock cylinder in ways that obstruct a lock's operation until an authorized key or combination moves them into alignment

35. Electric switch locks are:

    a. mechanical locks that have been modified to operate with battery power

    b. complete and break an electric current when an authorized key is inserted and turned

    c. installed in metal doors to give electric shocks to intruders

    d. mechanical locks that have been modified to operate with alternating current (AC) electricity instead of with a key

36. Based on ANSI A156 standards, Grade 2 locks are for heavy-duty commercial applications.

    a. true

    b. false

37. A popular type of lock used on GM cars is:

    a. a Medeco pin tumbler

    b. an automotive bit-key

    c. a side bar wafer

    d. an automotive tubular key

38. When cutting a lever tumbler key by hand, the first cut should be the:

    a. lever cut

    b. stop cut

    c. throat cut

    d. tip cut

39. A typical disk tumbler lock allows over 1500 possible key changes.

    a. true

    b. false

40. Which manufacturer is best known for its interchangeable core locks?

    a. Best Lock

    b. Kwikset Corporation

    c. Ilco/Unican Corporation

    d. Interchangeable Core Corporation

41. James Sargent is famous for:

    a. inventing the Sargent key-in-knob lock

    b. inventing the time lock for banks

    c. inventing the double-acting lever tumbler lock

    d. being the first person to pick open a Medeco cylinder

42. Fire-rated exit devices usually have dogging.

    a. true

    b. false

43. As a safety precaution, before servicing an ignition lock on an automobile, a locksmith should:

    a. disconnect the negative battery cable from the battery

    b. touch a plastic part of the vehicle to discharge static electricity

    c. insert the proper key into the ignition cylinder

    d. connect a ground cable to the car's battery

44. Which code series is commonly used by Ford glove compartment and trunk locks?

    a. FTC 001-1888

    b. FRD 1111-9999

    c. FB 0001-1863

    d. FMC 2223-9999

45. To pick open a pin tumbler cylinder, you need a pick and torque wrench.

    a. true

    b. false

46. General Motors' ignition lock codes can generally be found:

    a. on the ignition lock

    b. on the passenger side door

    c. below the Vehicle Identification Number (VIN) on the vehicle's engine

    d. under the vehicle's brake pedal

47. Which code series is commonly used on Chrysler door and ignition locks?

    a. EP 1-3000

    b. CHR 1-5000

    c. CRY 1-4000

    d. GM 001-6000

48. The Romans are credited with inventing the warded lock.

    a. true

    b. false

49. How many styles of lock pawls does General Motors use in its various car lines?

    a. one

    b. five

    c. over 20

    d. three

50. The double-sided (or "10-cut") Ford key:

    a. has five cuts on each side; one side operates the trunk and door while the other side operates the ignition

    b. has five cuts on each side; either side can operate all locks of a car

    c. has 10 cuts on each side; one side operates the trunk and door while the other side operates only the ignition

    d. has 10 cuts on each side

51. Five common keyway groove shapes are left angle, right angle, square, V, and round.

   a. true

   b. false

52. Usually the simplest way to change the combination of a double-bitted cam lock is to:

   a. rearrange the positions of two or more tumblers

   b. remove two tumblers and replace them with new tumblers

   c. remove the tumbler assembly and replace it with a new one

   d. connect a new tumbler assembly to the existing one

53. When shimming a cylinder open:

   a. use the key to insert the shim into the keyway

   b. insert the shim into the keyway without the key

   c. insert the shim along the left side of the cylinder housing

   d. insert the shim between the plug and cylinder housing between the top and bottom pins

54. A ¼-inch drill is generally the best all-purpose size for locksmiths.

   a. true

   b. false

55. In 1868 Henry R. Towne joined with:

   a. Linus Yale, Jr. to form the Yale Lock Manufacturing Company

   b. Linus Yale, Sr. to form the Yale and Towne Manufacturing Company

   c. Walter Schlage to form the Schlage Lock Company

   d. Stephen Bucknall to form the Master Lock Company

56. A *lock* is any:

   a. barrier or closure that restricts entry

    b. fastening device that allows a person to open and close a door, window, cabinet, drawer, or gate

    c. device that incorporates a bolt, cam, shackle, or switch to secure an object—such as a door, drawer, or machine—to a closed, locked, on, or off position, and that provides a restricted means—such as a key or combination--of releasing the object from that position

    d. device or object that restricts entry to a given premise

57. A ¼-inch single stage reduction gear drill can have chuck speed of over 1000 RPM.

    a. true

    b. false

58. Before duplicating a General Motors VATS key, you need to:

    a. remove the resistor pellet from the key being copied

    b. demagnetize the resistor pellet in the key being copied

    c. determine the resistance level of the pellet in the key, so you can choose the right blank

    d. use a ground strap to avoid transferring static electricity to the resistor pellets

59. Chicago Lock Company introduced:

    a. the first lever tumbler lock

    b. the Chicago knob lock

    c. the Chicago Ace lock

    d. the first double-acting lever tumbler lock

60. As a rule, a ½-inch electric drill has more power than does a 1/4-inch cordless drill.

    a. true

    b. false

Answers to the Test

When scoring the test, give yourself two points for each correctly answered multiple choice question and one point for each correctly answered true/false question. In each case where you gave no answer to a question, and in each case where you gave two or more answers to a question, give yourself no credit.

Scoring Key: 75% is minimum for passing; 85% is very good; 95% or better is excellent.

1. c	16. d	31. b	46. a
2. c	17. d	32. d	47. a
3. b	18. a	33. a	48. a
4. a	19. d	34. d	49. c
5. c	20. d	35. b	50. d
6. b	21. b	36. b	51. a
7. d	22. b	37. c	52. c
8. d	23. a	38. c	53. d
9. b	24. a	39. a	54. b
10. d	25. b	40. a	55. a
11. a	26. b	41. b	56. c
12. b	27. a	42. b	57. a
13. c	28. b	43 a	58. c
14. b	29. b	44. c	59. c
15. a	30. b	45. a	60. a

Frequently Asked Questions

Q What's the difference between a cylindrical lockset, a tubular lockset, and a key-in-knob lock?

A Cylindrical and tubular locksets are types of key-in-knob locks. When such locks are installed on a door, you may not notice how they differ from each other. If you take a cylindrical lock off of a door, you'll notice that the lock has a cylindrical chassis (or housing) that fits in the lock hole and connects to the latch. A tubular lockset connects to the latch by a spindle with "legs" that passes through holes in the latch.

Q Is there a masterkey that can open any lock?

A There can be masterkeys for certain buildings and for certain building complexes that use locks with the same keyway. But there is no key that can open all locks, because the keyway sizes and shapes are too varied and because there are too many different internal configurations among locks and lock cylinders.

Q **Are deadbolt locks hard to pick?**

A The term *deadbolt* refers to a lock that relies on a rigid bolt for security, but says nothing about how easy or hard it is to pick open. That depends on the type of cylinder the deadbolt has. Most low-cost deadbolts (under about $20) come with standard 5-pin cylinders and are easy to pick open. Cylinders with six or more sets of pins are harder to pick open. High-security cylinders can be virtually impossible to pick open without intimate knowledge of the lock and without specially designed equipment. By adding a couple of mushroom or serrated pins, you can make most any pin tumbler cylinder harder to pick.

Q **Can every lock be picked?**

A In theory, any lock that's operated with a mechanical key can be picked open, because "picking" refers to using a tool to simulate the action of a key. (But many locks that don't use a manual key can be easily bypassed in ways other than picking.) There are locks that have never been picked open, because doing so would take a long time and would require specially designed tools and intimate knowledge of the lock's construction. Most locks that use patented or UL-listed cylinders are impractical to pick open.

Q **Where can I get lockpicks?**

A You can buy lockpicks and other locksmithing tools from a locksmith supply house. To find a local supplier, look in your Yellow Pages under "Locksmiths' Equipment & Supplies." See Appendix G for an international list of suppliers. In some cases, you may be required to supply a copy of your business license, driver's license, letterhead, or newspaper or telephone book advertisement to show that you work as a locksmith (usually you'll have the option of choosing among several things to send). Another option is to buy lockpicks that are advertised in personal safety, detective, and survival magazines. They don't require identification, but offer few choices and charge much more for the picks than do locksmith supply houses.

Q **Are pick guns worth the money?**

A Contrary to movies and television shows, pick guns don't quickly open most any lock. They work on a very simple principle that applies to many common locks. A pick gun is somewhat like training wheels for locksmiths. Although it takes more practice to use standard picks, they allow the locksmith to open far more locks. It isn't unprofessional to use a pick gun, but it shouldn't be used as a substitute for learning to use standard lockpicks.

Q **Can "The Club" steering wheel be picked open when locked?**

A The Club can be easily picked open. Picking is a good way for the locksmith to open it quickly. Car thieves rarely pick open a steering wheel lock, however. They're much more likely to saw the steering wheel and slip the lock off.

Q **Is it legal to carry lockpicks?**

A In many places, whether or not carrying lockpicks is a crime depends on the intent of the person carrying them. A locksmithing student taking them to school might be fine, for instance, but someone carrying them while committing a burglary may be charged with possessing "burglary tools." In some places, the only people who may legally carry lockpicks are those mentioned by statute (which typically include bona fide locksmiths, repossessors, and law enforcement officers). In such cases, unmentioned persons who have a legitimate need to carry lockpicks (such as building maintenance persons) may have to get a locksmith license. Places that have (or have had) fairly strict laws about carrying lockpicks include Canada, California, Illinois, Maryland, New Jersey, New York State, and Washington, D.C. Talk with an attorney to find out which laws apply to your situation.

Q **What's the best drill for locksmiths?**

A A ½-inch electric drill is most useful for locksmithing. When looking for a drill, don't compare them based on price alone, because better drills usually cost several times more than the low-cost models sold in department stores. Look for a ½-inch electric drill with the following features: at least a 5 amp motor, variable speed reversing (VSR), 600 RPM (or faster), three-stage reduction gearing, and all ball and needle bearings. Popular brands among locksmiths include Bosch, Makita, Milwaukee, Porter-Cable, and Ryobi (see Appendix I for drill manufacturer Website addresses).

Q **Which lubrication is best for servicing locks?**

A WD-40, Tri-Flow, and KeyLube 2 are popular lubricants among locksmiths.

Q **What can I do to prevent other locksmiths and key cutters from duplicating a key?**

A A knowledgeable locksmith can copy any key for which he or she has a blank, but there are things you can do to make it less likely that anyone will duplicate a key. Use a neuter bow blank—one with a bow that gives no information about the key it copied. That alone will stump most key cutters, because they don't know how to identify blanks by keyway grooves. Then stamp "Do Not Duplicate" on the bow. Many people won't duplicate a key with such a phrase stamped on it. Another thing you can do is, after duplicating the key, use your key machine cutter to lightly shave the length of the new key along its bottom. That will make the new key seem to be its normal width, but it will sit too low in a key machine vise so that any new key made from it will be miscut.

Q **Is it illegal to duplicate a key marked "Do Not Duplicate"?**

A In some places it is illegal to duplicate a key marked "Do Not Duplicate" without getting positive identification and keeping a written record of the work on file. In most places, however, such a phrase stamped on a key is merely a request, and doesn't create any legal restrictions or obligations on locksmiths or key cutters. Anyone can have any key marked "Do Not Duplicate." I've had many customers ask to have that phrase stamped on their keys, because it at least causes eyebrows to be raised when someone tries to get copies. As a legal matter, however, the type of key is usually more significant than a stamping with respect to which keys may be copied. Whether required or not, for your protection, it's best to have a policy of not duplicating any key marked "Do Not Duplicate" unless you know you can legally copy it, and the key holder shows positive identification. You should also maintain a log of all such keys you duplicate.

Q **Which keys are illegal for locksmiths to copy?**

A It's almost always illegal (or foolish) for a locksmith to duplicate a key that he or she knows or reasonably suspects is being copied without the consent of the owner, or used for criminal activity. That isn't to say, however, that every time someone wants a key made that the locksmith must track down the owner of the key and figure out the keyholder's intentions. But in unusual situations, you could be found negligent for not looking further into a matter before duplicating the key.

Here's a situation that happened to me. A woman came into my shop with a clay mold of a Medeco key, and wanted me to make that key. She explained that she made the mold because her husband wouldn't let her have a key to their house. The woman was acting nervous, and wouldn't show me any identification. Nor would she tell me where she lived. I declined to make the key. I think if I had made the key and she used it to break into a home or business, I could have faced criminal and civil charges because I would have been negligent under that unique circumstance.

It's also illegal to duplicate post office boxes without permission of the postmaster or post office superintendent.

Q **May locksmiths fit keys to U.S. Navy and U.S. Army locks?**

A Because thousands of war surplus locks marked "U.S. Navy" and "U.S. Army" have been sold to the general public, such a marking isn't in itself a reason for locksmiths not to fit keys to a lock.

Q Is it legal to duplicate safe deposit box keys?

A It's common for locksmiths to duplicate safe deposit box keys. Such keys aren't restricted because safe deposit box security isn't primarily based on a box holder's key. (It's also dependent on a second key, personnel, and building security.) Unless there's something suspicious surrounding a request to copy a safe deposit box key, there's generally no problem with making copies.

Q If I rekeyed a lock on a home and later learned that the person who ordered the work wasn't authorized to do so, would I be liable?

A You might be liable for doing unauthorized work, especially if you messed up a landlord's masterkey system or if your actions prevented someone from gaining lawful entry during an emergency. Anytime you do work on location, you need to be especially careful about being properly authorized to do the work. Before rekeying a lock on a home, ask to see a driver's license or other positive identification. Then ask the person why he or she wants the lock rekeyed, and ask who is the owner of the home. If the person is going through a divorce or separation and wants to lock out a spouse or partner, it's safer to decline the job (even though the locksmith may be legally allowed to do the work without the consent of the other spouse or partner). If the person doesn't own the home, get permission to call the landlord and ask if it's all right for you to rekey the lock. Generally, a locksmith isn't obligated to call a landlord. But that phone call could help you avoid a lawsuit.

Q If a tenant wants me to install a new lock or other hardware on the door, do I need to get permission from the landlord?

A Many locksmiths simply have the tenant sign an authorization form, and have had no problems with that practice. In most cases, unless the locksmith has to drill holes or otherwise permanently alter the door, there's no requirement for the locksmith to get a landlord's permission to install a lock. However, it's a good idea to get a landlord's permission whether you drill or not. If you don't seek the landlord's permission, at least leave all the locks and hardware you remove with the tenant (but if you still get sued, don't blame me).

Q **If I mistakenly opened an automobile or house door for a thief, would I be held liable?**

A You would if it were my house or car. When unlocking doors, you have to act in good faith and exercise due care. Generally, that means checking a driver's license or car registration. It might also mean asking neighbors to verify the identity of the person who wants you to unlock the door. But acting in good faith and exercising due care may not help you avoid civil liability (losing a lawsuit), especially if someone is harmed or his or her property is stolen as a result of your actions. It isn't enough just to come up with excuses for why you were tricked; you just have to not open doors for unauthorized persons.

Establish and consistently follow a policy that minimizes your risk. For instance, when someone asks you to open a door, immediately fill out a work order that includes all relevant information, such as the customer's name, address, telephone number (get that even if the caller isn't at home), driver's license number, license plate number, and the make, model, and year of the car. If the customer wants you to open a car, ask for the name and phone number of someone you can call to confirm the customer's identity. If the situation seems suspicious, decline to do the job. Be sure you're making consistent decisions based on a clear written policy that's reasonable; otherwise, you may end up facing a lawsuit (or bad press) for discriminatory practices.

Q **If I install a lock and the customer refuses to pay, may I take my locks back?**

A Once a lock is installed on a door, it becomes part of that door and is the property of the door owner. The proper remedy would be to file a lawsuit. If the lock were on an apartment and you had gotten the landlord's consent to install it, you might want to include the landlord in your lawsuit.

Q If I finish a job in someone's home and the customer refuses to pay me, would I be within my rights to refuse to leave until I'm paid?

A Not being paid doesn't give a locksmith the right to be in someone's home. Staying after being asked to leave could quickly become criminal trespassing. The proper remedy to not being paid is to file a lawsuit promptly (usually with small claims court or with a district justice).

Q If I go to someone's home or car to unlock a door and find the door already open when I get there, can I still charge for my time?

A It isn't uncommon that after a customer calls a locksmith to open a lock on a home or car, the customer gains entry before the locksmith arrives. Sometimes to get faster service, people call several locksmiths for the same job. To charge for your time even if the door has already been opened, you need to clearly make such an agreement before you leave for the job. When the customer is requesting the work, you have to tell the customer of your minimum service charge and that it is payable upon your arrival. Then you'll be able to collect that fee (either before you leave the job or later in court).

Q How can I make sure of getting paid after opening a car?

A It isn't unusual for customers to renege after the locksmith performs the service. That's why you need to be vigilant during that critical period between opening the door and closing your hands around the payment. When I open a car door, I stand close to the door. If the person gives me any reason to believe that I'm not getting paid, I quickly close the door. Then I tell him he has to pay an additional fee in advance for me to open the door again.

If a customer doesn't have cash, I ask him to postdate a check. Or I'll ask to hold something as collateral. I also have the person sign an IOU. I consider these steps necessary because the customer knew of my fee before I arrived, and knew that it was to be paid in full upon completion of the work. Because the person has already reneged on our agreement, I need to deal with him differently if I'm to be paid.

Q **What are the best ways to continue learning about locksmithing?**

A Books, videotapes, correspondence courses, residential training programs, and talking with other locksmiths are good ways to continue learning about locksmithing. Sometimes online forums, newsgroups, and mailing lists can be helpful (or entertaining). But much of the information posted on them is misleading or wrong. Because people are able to post messages anonymously, most everyone online instantly becomes a "master locksmith" with all the answers. The best way to continue your learning is by doing. Practice installing, servicing, disassembling, and reassembling all types of locks and locking devices.

Q **Which is the best book for learning locksmithing?**

A There are a lot of good general books on locksmithing. Joseph E. Rathjen's *Locksmithing: From Apprentice to Master* (McGraw-Hill) is one of them. My *The Complete Book of Locks and Locksmithing*, 4th Edition (McGraw-Hill) is the world's best-selling locksmithing book, and is used as a textbook in many trade schools. For comprehensive information on a specific lock or security device, contact the manufacturer for technical manuals.

Q **What's the best locksmithing school?**

A There are too many locksmithing programs to pick one as being best for all people. The best would depend on where you live, how much money you want to spend, and how much time you can devote to the program. When choosing a residential program, contact several schools, speak to their instructors, and ask for names of former students or of employers who have hired former students. The better schools will provide you with all that information. Before enrolling, visit the school to evaluate the facilities. Choosing a correspondence program is mostly a matter of comparing the course offerings, supplies, and prices. You may also want to post messages on the Internet asking people to share their feelings about certain schools you're considering. Two good places to start are http://www.locksmithing.org and the alt.locksmithing newsgroup.

Security Training Programs

Abram Friedman Occupational Center
  1646 S. Olive St.
  Los Angeles, CA 90015
  213-742-7657
  website:
  http://www.otan.dni.us/webfarm/afoc/
  A full-time Regional Occupational Center
  operated by the Los Angeles Unified School
  District's Division of Adult and Career
  Education. AFOC offers several low-cost,
  one-year locksmithng programs.

Academy of Locksmithing, Inc.
  2220 Midland Ave. Unit 106
  Scarborough, ON MlP 3E6 Canada
  416-321-2220
  A registered private vocational school.

Acme School—Locksmithing Division
  11350 S. Harlem Ave.
  Worth, IL 60482-2000
  708-361-3750, Fax: 708-448-9306

American Locksmith Institute of Nevada
  875 S. Boulder Hwy.
  Henderson, NV 89015
  702-565-8811, Fax: 702-565-7017

California Alarm and Lock Institute
  430 N. 16th St.
  Sacramento, CA 95814
  916-498-1150, 800-804-0505
  Fax: 916-498-1152
  email: cali@cwo.com
  website:
  http://www.cwo.com/~cali/home.htm
  Offers a residential program and
  correspondence course in Lock Technology
  and Electronic Alarm Security Technology.
  Approved by the Council for Private Post-
  Secondary and Vocational Education of the
  California State Department of Education.

California Institute of Locksmithing
   14721 Oxnard St.
   Van Nuys, CA 91411
   818-994-7426
   website:
   http://home.earthlink.net~lockschool/
   Founded in 1972. Private/proprietary
   school. Offers a 12-week residential course.
   Accredited by the Accrediting Commission
   for Career Schools/Colleges of Technology.
   Charles Hasekian, President.

Charles Stuart School
   1420 Kings Hwy., 2nd Floor
   Brooklyn, NY 11229
   718-339-2640, Fax: 718-339-7901

Colorado Locksmith College, Inc.
   4991 W. 80th Ave.
   Westminster, CO
   303-427-7773, 800-304-4414

Commercial Technical Institute
   116 Fairfield Rd.
   Fairfield, NJ 07004-2491
   973-575-5225, 800-526-0890

Foley-Belsaw Institute
   6301 Equitable Rd.
   Kansas City, MO 64120
   800-821-3452
   website: http://www.foley-belsaw.com/
   Founded in 1926. Offers home study
   courses.

Golden Gate School of Locksmithing
   3722 San Pablo Ave.
   Oakland, CA 94608
   510-654-2677

Granton Institute of Technology
   263 Adelaide St.
   West Toronto, ON M5H 1Y3 Canada
   416-977-3929, 800-950-1972
   Fax: 416-977-5612
   email: info@grantoninstitute.com
   website: http://www.grantoninstitute.com

Greater Regional Technical College
   6830 Burlington Ave.
   Burnaby, BC V5J 4H1 Canada

HPC Learning Center
   3999 N. 25th Ave.
   Schiller Park, IL 60176-2195
   847-671-6280

Lock and Safe Institute of Technology, Inc.
   1650 N. Federal Hwy.
   Pompano Beach, FL 33062
   954-785-0444, 800-457-LOCK
   website:
   http://www.thelocksmithschool.com/

Lockmasters
   5085 Danville Rd.
   Nicholasville, KY 40356-9531
   606-885-6041, 800-654-0637
   Fax: 606-885-7093

Locksmith Business Management School
   P.O. Box 8525
   Emeryville, CA 94662
   510-654-2677

Locksmith School
   51 Beverly Hills Drive
   Toronto, ON M3L 1A2 Canada
   416-960-9999

Locksmith School, Inc.
   3901 S. Meridian St.
   Indianapolis, IN 46217-3343
   317-632-3979

Locksmithing Institute of America, Inc.
   116 Fairfield Road
   Fairfield, NJ 07004
   201-575-5225, 800-526-0890
   Fax: 201-808-1948

L.T.C. Training Center
   P.O. Box 3583
   Davenport, IA 52808-3583
   319-322-6669, 800-358-9396
   Fax: 319-324-7938

Master Locksmith Training Courses
Units 4/5 The Business Park
Woodford Halse Daventry
Northants NN22 6PZ England
(44) 01327 262255
Fax: (44) 01327 262539

Messick Vo-Technical Center
703 South Greer
Memphis, TN 38111
901-325-4840, Fax: 901-325-4842

North Bennet Street School
39 N. Bennet St.
Boston, MA 02113-1914
617-227-0155, Fax: 617-227-9292
Founded in 1885. Private/proprietary
school. Two-year programs offered. Cynthia
Stone, Executive Director.

Northern Metropolitan College of TAFE—
Security Technology Section
Waterdale Rd. and Bell St.
Heidelberg, Vic. 3081 Australia
(61) 3 242-8687, Fax: (61) 3 242-8673

NRI School of Locksmithing
4401 Connecticut Ave.
NW Washington, D.C. 20008-2322
202-244-1600
Home study courses.

Pine Technical College
1000 Fourth St.
Pine City, MN 55063-2198
320-629-6764, 800-521-7463
Fax: 320-629-7603
email: information@ptc.tec.mn.us
website: http://www.ptc.tec.mn.us/
A Minnesota state college. Accredited by
the North Central Association of Colleges
and Schools.

Prince George's Community College
301 Largo Rd., Room K-205
Largo, MD 20772-2199
301-322-0871, Fax: 301-808-0960

Quintilian Institute Services (Q.I.S.)
5001-A Lee Hwy., Suite 101
Arlington, VA 22207
703-525-7525

Red Deer College
P.O. Box 5005
Red Deer, AB T4N 5H5 Canada
403-342-3300, Fax: 403-340-8940

San Francisco Lock School
4002 Irving St.
San Francisco, CA 94122
415-566-5545, 415-347-2222

School of Lock Technology
1049 Island Ave.
San Diego, CA 92101-7228
619-234-4512, Fax: 619-234-5937

School of Lock Technology
302 W. Katella Ave.
Orange, CA 92667-4705
714-633-1366, Fax: 714-525-1364

Security Education Plus
400-B Etter Drive
P.O. Box 497
Nicholasville, KY 40356
606-887-6027, Fax: 606-887-6087

Security Systems Management Schools
116 Fairfield Rd.
Fairfield, NJ 07004
201-575-5225, 800-526-0890

Southern Locksmith Training Institute
1387 Airline Drive
Bossier City, LA 71112
318-227-9458, Fax: 318-746-1734

South Metropolitan College of TAFE
  Security Technology Section
  15 Grosvenor St.
  Beaconsfield, Western Australia 6162
  (61) 09-239-8386, Fax: (61) 09-239-8555
  e-mail: Tissa@newton.dialix.com.au

Stotts Correspondence College
  Australian College of Locksmithing
  140 Flinders St.
  Melbourne, VIC 3000 Australia

Stratford Career Institute, Inc.
  233 Swanton Rd., Ste. 121
  St. Albans, VT 05478-9911
  800-363-0058
  Home study courses.

Sydney Institute of Technology/
  Ultimo Campus
  Locksmithing Section
  Building M Mary Ann St.
  Ultimo, NSW 2007 Australia
  (61) 02-217 3449, Fax: (61) 02-217 4008
  website:
  http://www.sydneyit.nsw.edu.au/ultimo.htm

Universal School of Master Locksmithing
  3201 Fulton Ave.
  Sacramento, CA 95821
  916-482-4216

Universal Career Institute
  190 Graveline St.
  St. Laurent, Quebec H4T 1R7 Canada

Valley Technical Institute
  5408 N. Blackstone
  Fresno, CA 93710
  209-436-8501, Fax: 209-439-3814

Security Trade and Professional Journals

The Home Protector
  P.O. Box 2044
  Erie, PA 16512-2044
  email: webmaster@iahssp.org
  website: http://www.iahssp.org
  Technical & business newsletter
  Monthly; free to qualified professionals

Locksmith Ledger International
  850 Busse Hwy.
  Park Ridge, Il 60068
  "The Technical News Magazine for the
  Security Professional"
  Monthly, plus annual Directory issue in
  January

The National Locksmith
  1533 Burgundy Parkway
  Streamwood, IL 60107
  Monthly; includes annual Directory issue

Security
  P.O. Box 5080
  Des Plaine, IL 60018
  "For Buyers of Products, Systems and
  Services"
  Monthly; free to qualified professionals

Security Dealer
  445 Broad Hollow Rd.
  Melville, NY 11747
  "The News Source for Integrated Systems
  Installations"
  Monthly, includes annual Directory issue;
  free to qualified professionals

Security Distributing & Marketing (SDM)
  P.O. Box 7594
  Highlands Ranch, CO 80126-9394
  Monthly; free to qualified professionals

Security News
P.O. Box 460
Salamanca, NY 14779-0460
"The News Source for the Security
Industry"
Monthly; free to qualified
professionals

Security Technology & Design
850 Busse Hwy.
Park Ridge, IL 60068-2382
"The Publication for Total Systems
Integration"
Monthly; free to qualified
professionals

Lockset Function Charts

Non-Keyed Locks *ANSI A156.2 Series 4000*

Schlage Number	A.N.S.I. No.	Grade	
A10S D10S ∎ ▲ F10N	F75	2 1 2	

Passage Latch: Both knobs always unlocked.

D12D	F89	1	

Exit Lock: Unlocked by knob inside only. Outside knob always fixed.

A20S			

Closet Latch: Outside knob and inside thumbturn are always unlocked.

A25D D25D ∎			

Exit Lock: Blank plate outside. Inside knob always unlocked. (Specify door thickness, 1⅜" or 1¾".)

A30D D30D F30N	F77	2 1 2	

Patio Lock: Push-button locking. Turning inside knob releases button. Closing door on A & D Series also releases button.

A40S D40S ∎ ▲ F40N	F76	2 1 2	

Bath/Bedroom Privacy Lock: Push-button locking. Can be opened from outside with small screwdriver or flat narrow tool. Turning inside knob releases push-button. Closing door on A, C and D Series also releases button, preventing lock-out.

A43D	F79	2	

Communicating Lock: Turn button in outer knob locks and unlocks knob and inside thumbturn.

A44S D44S			

Hospital Privacy Lock: Push-button locking. Unlocked from outside by turning emergency turn-button. Rotating inside knob or closing door releases inside button.

A170 D170 ∎ F170N			

Single Dummy Trim: Single dummy trim for one side of door. Used for door pull or as matching inactive trim.

Keyed Locks

Schlage Number	A.N.S.I. No.	Grade	
F51N	F81	2	

Entrance Lock: Unlocked by key from outside when outer knob is locked by turn-button in inside knob. Inside knob always unlocked.

D50PD ∎ (ATH & OLY designs only)	F82	1	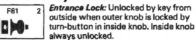

Entrance/Office Lock: Push button locking. Pushing button locks outside lever until unlocked with key or by turning inside lever.

Keyed Locks

Schlage Number	A.N.S.I. No.	Grade	
A53PD D53PD ▲	F81 F82	2 1	

Entrance Lock: Turn/Push button locking. Pushing and turning button locks outside knob requiring use of key until button is manually unlocked. Push button locking: Pushing button locks outside knob until unlocked by key or by turning inside knob.

A55PD D55PD	F92	2 1	

Service Station Lock: Unlocked by key from outside when outer knob is locked by universal button in inside knob. Closing door releases button. Outside knob may be fixed by rotating universal button.

D60PD ∎	F88	1	

Vestibule Lock: Unlocked by key from outside when outside knob is locked by key inside knob. Inside knob is always unlocked.

D66PD ∎†	F91	1	

Store Lock: Key in either knob locks or unlocks both knobs.

A70PD D70PD ∎ ▲	F84	2 1	

Classroom Lock: Outside knob locked and unlocked by key. Inside knob always unlocked.

D72PD†	F80	1	

Communicating Lock: Key in either knob locks or unlocks each knob independently.

A73PD D73PD ∎	F90	2 1	

Dormitory Lock: Locked or unlocked by key from outside. Push-button locking from inside. Turning inside knob or closing door releases button.

D76PD	F85	1	

Classroom Hold-Back Lock: Outside knob locked or unlocked by key. Inside knob always unlocked. Latch may be locked in retracted position by key.

A79PD			

Communicating Lock: Locked or unlocked by key from outside. Blank plate inside.

A80PD D80PD ∎ ▲ F80N	F86	2 1 2	

Storeroom Lock: Outside knob fixed. Entrance by key only. Inside knob always unlocked.

D82PD†	F87	1	

Institution Lock: Both knobs fixed. Entrance by key in either knob.

A85PD D85PD	F93	2 1	

Hotel-Motel Lock: Outside knob fixed. Entrance by key only. Push-button in inside knob activates visual occupancy indicator, allowing only emergency masterkey to operate. Rotation of inside spanner-button provides lockout feature by keeping indicator thrown.

∎ Available functions for Athens and Olympiad designs.
▲ Available functions for "C" Series non-ferrous locks.

FIGURE C.1

Schlage Number	A. N. S. I. No.	Grade	

Deadbolt Locks *ANSI A156.5*

B160N E2151 2
B460P 1
B560 1

Single Cylinder Deadbolt Lock: Deadbolt thrown or retracted by key from outside or by inside turn unit. Bolt automatically deadlocks when fully thrown.

B162N† E2141 2
B462P† 1
B562† 1

Double Cylinder Deadbolt Lock: Deadbolt thrown or retracted by key from either side.

B461P E2161 1

One-Way Deadbolt Lock: Deadbolt thrown or retracted by key only. Blank plate inside.

B463P E2171 1

Classroom Deadbolt Lock: Deadbolt thrown or retracted by key outside. Inside turn unit will retract bolt only.

B464P

Cylinder Lock: Deadbolt thrown or retracted by key from one side. No inside trim.

B180 E2191 2
B480 1

Door Bolt: Deadbolt thrown or retracted by turn unit only. No outside trim.

Schlage Number	A. N. S. I. No.	Grade

Deadlatch Locks *ANSI A156.5*

B250PD E2121 1

Night Latch: Deadlocking latchbolt retracted by key from outside or by inside turn unit. Rotating turn unit and activating hold-back feature keeps latch retracted.

B252PD† E2111 1

Double Cylinder Deadlatch: Deadlocking latchbolt retracted by key from either side. No hold-back feature.

B270D E2181 1

Exit Latch: Deadlocking latchbolt retracted by inside turn unit only. No outside trim. Rotating turn unit and activating hold-back feature keeps latch retracted.

Schlage Number

Lever Functions

B245S

Lever Passage Latch: For use on passage, closet and doors that do not require locking. Rotating either lever retracts latchbolt. (Specify door hand.)

B281
B282

Single Dummy Trim–Double Dummy Trim: For use on single or pairs of doors when fixed trim is required. (Specify door hand.)

Schlage Number

Grip Handle Sets

E51PD

Entrance Lock: Unlocked by key from outside when thumb-piece is locked by inside turn-button.

Schlage Number

Grip Handle Sets

F160N

Entrance Lock: Deadbolt thrown or retracted by key from outside or by inside turn unit Latch retracted by thumbpiece from outside or by inside knob.

F162N†

Double Cylinder Entrance Lock: Deadbolt thrown or retracted by key from either side. Latch retracted by thumbpiece from outside or by inside knob.

E193

Outside and Inside Dummy Trim: For use as door pull or as dummy trim on an inactive pair of doors. Fixed thumbpiece and inside knob. Thru bolted dummy cylinder.

F193N

Outside and Inside Dummy Trim: For use as door pull or as dummy trim on inactive leaf of pair of doors. Fixed thumbpiece and inside knob. Dummy cylinder with inside plate.

Schlage Number	A. N. S. I. No.	Grade

Interconnected Locks *ANSI A156.12*

H110 F95 4

Entrance—Single Locking: Deadbolt thrown or retracted by key in upper lock from outside or by inside turn unit. Latchbolt retracted by knob from either side. Turning inside knob retracts deadbolt and latchbolt simultaneously for immediate exit.

H153 F97 4

Entrance—Double Locking: Deadbolt thrown or retracted by key in upper lock from outside or by inside turn unit. Deadlatch retracted by key in outer knob when locked by pushing turn-button in inner knob. Outer knob may be fixed in locked position by rotating turn-button. Inside knob retracts deadbolt and deadlatch simultaneously for immediate exit.

H160 F102 4

Entrance, Single Locking Decorative Grip Handle Trim Outside: Deadbolt thrown or retracted by key in upper lock from outside or by inside turn unit. Latchbolt retracted by grip outside or knob from inside. Turning inside knob retracts deadbolt and latchbolt simultaneously for immediate exit.

H180

Storeroom Lock: Bolt may be operated by key from outside or by turn unit from inside. Bolt automatically deadlocks when fully thrown. Lock may be opened by key from outside. Inside knob will retract both latch and deadbolt. Latch automatically deadlocks when door is closed, inside knob always free for immediate exit. Outer knob always fixed.

† Caution: Double cylinder locks on residences and any door in any structure which is used for egress are a safety hazard in times of emergency and their use is not recommended. Installation should be in accordance with existing codes only.

FIGURE C.1

Schlage Number	A. N. S. I. No.	Grade

Interconnected Locks
ANSI A156.12

H185	F100	4

Hotel-Motel Lock: Deadbolt thrown or retracted by key in upper lock from outside or by inside turn unit. Deadlatch retracted by key in outer fixed knob. Push-button in inner knob activates visual occupancy indicator, allowing only emergency masterkey to operate. Rotation of inside spanner-button provides lockout feature by keeping indicator thrown. Turning inside knob retracts deadbolt simultaneously for immediate exit.

H170		

Single Dummy Inside Trim: Snap-on rose and knob. Concealed mounting screws.

H172		

Dummy Trim Inside and Outside: Snap-on rose and knobs thru-bolted.

Schlage Number	A. N. S. I. No.	Grade

Mortise Locks Non-Keyed
ANSI A156.13 Series 1000

L9010	F01	1

Passage Latch: Latch bolt retracted by lever or knob from either side at all times.

L9040	F22	1

Bath/Bedroom Privacy Lock: Latchbolt retracted by lever or knob from either side unless outside is locked by inside turn piece. Operating inside lever or knob or closing door unlocks outside lever or knob. To unlock from outside, remove emergency button, insert turn piece (furnished) in access hole and rotate.

L0170		

Single Dummy Trim: Lever or knob on one side fixed by mounting bar.

L0172		

Pair Dummy Trim: Lever or knob on both sides fixed by mounting bar.

L9175*		

Single Dummy Trim: Lever or knob on one side fixed. Includes lock chassis and armor front.

L9176*▪		

Pair Dummy Trim: Lever or knob both sides fixed. Includes lock chassis and armor front.

*When armored front is required as strike for inactive door, specify L9177 for single or L9178 for pair of dummy trim. Specify door hand.

Schlage Number	A. N. S. I. No.	Grade

Keyed Locks

L9050 ●▪	F04	1

Office and Inner Entry Lock: Latchbolt retracted by lever or knob from either side unless outside is made inoperative by key outside or by rotating inside turn piece. When outside is locked, latchbolt is retracted by key outside or by lever or knob inside. Outside lever or knob remains locked until thumbturn is returned to vertical or by counter clockwise rotation of key. Auxiliary latch deadlocks latchbolt when door is closed.

L9060 ●	F09	1

Apartment Entrance Lock: Latchbolt retracted by lever or knob from either side unless outside is locked by key from inside. When locked, latchbolt retracted by key outside or lever or knob inside. Auxiliary latch deadlocks when door is closed.

L9070 ●▪	F05	1

Classroom Lock: Latchbolt retracted by lever or knob from either side unless outside is locked by key. Unlocked from outside by key. Inside lever or knob always free for immediate exit. Auxiliary latch deadlocks latchbolt when door is closed.

L9080 ●▪	F07	1

Storeroom Lock: Latchbolt retracted by key outside or by lever or knob inside. Outside lever or knob always inoperative. Auxiliary latch deadlocks latchbolt when door is closed.

L9080EL		

Storeroom Lock: Electrically locked. Outside lever or knob continuously locked by 24V AC or DC. Latchbolt retracted by key outside or by lever or knob inside. Switch or power failure allows outside lever or knob to retract latchbolt. Auxiliary latch deadlocks latchbolt when door is closed. Inside lever or knob always free for immediate exit.

L9080EU		

Storeroom Lock: Electrically unlocked. Outside lever or knob unlocked by 24V AC or DC. Latchbolt retracted by key outside or lever or knob inside. Auxiliary latch deadlocks latchbolt when door is closed. Inside lever or knob always free for immediate exit.

L9082		

Institution Lock: Latchbolt retracted by key from either side. Lever or knob on both sides always inoperative. Auxiliary latch deadlocks latchbolt when door is closed.

L9453 ●▪	F20	1

Entrance Lock: Latchbolt retracted by lever or knob from either side unless outside is locked by 20° rotation of thumbturn. Deadbolt thrown or retracted by 90° rotation of thumbturn. When locked, key outside or lever or knob inside retracts deadbolt and latchbolt simultaneously. Outside lever or knob remains locked until thumbturn is restored to vertical position. Throwing deadbolt automatically locks outside lever or knob. Auxiliary latch deadlocks latchbolt when door is closed.

FIGURE C.3

Keyed Locks

L9456 ● ▪ F12   1

Dormitory/Exit Lock: Latchbolt retracted by lever or knob from either side. Deadbolt thrown or retracted by key outside or inside thumbturn. Throwing deadbolt locks outside lever or knob. Rotating inside lever or knob simultaneously retracts deadbolt and latchbolt, and unlocks outside lever or knob.

L9465 ●   1

Closet/Storeroom Lock: Latchbolt retracted by lever or knob from either side. Deadbolt extended or retracted by key outside.

L9466   F14   1

Store/Utility Room Lock: Latchbolt retracted by knob or lever from either side. Deadbolt extended or retracted by key from either side.

L9473 ●   F21   1

Dormitory/Bedroom Lock: Latchbolt retracted by knob or lever from either side. Deadbolt extended or retracted by key outside or thumbturn inside.

L9485
(Spec-Rite Trim Only)

Hotel Lock: Latchbolt by key outside or by lever or knob inside. Outside lever or knob always fixed. Deadbolt thrown or retracted by inside thumbturn. When deadbolt is thrown, all keys become inoperative except emergency or display keys. Turning inside lever or knob retracts both deadbolt and latchbolt simultaneously. Auxiliary latch deadlocks latchbolt when door is closed.

L9486   F15   1

Hotel Lock: Latchbolt retracted by key outside or by lever or knob inside. Outside lever or knob always fixed. Deadbolt thrown or retracted by inside thumbturn. When deadbolt is thrown, "DO NOT DISTURB" plate is displayed —all keys become inoperative except emergency or display keys. Turning inside lever or knob retracts both deadbolt and latchbolt simultaneously. Auxiliary latch deadlocks latchbolt when door is closed.

Deadlocks

Schlage Number   A. N. S. I. No.   Grade

L9460   F17   1

Cylinder X Thumbturn: Deadbolt thrown or retracted by key outside or thumbturn inside.

L9462   F16   1

Double Cylinder: Deadbolt operated by key from either side.

● Available functions for Spec-Rite series.
▪ Available functions for grip handle sets.

Keyed Locks

Schlage Number   A. N. S. I. No.   Grade

L9463   1

Classroom Lock: Deadbolt thrown or retracted by key from outside. Inside cylinder turn retracts deadbolt but cannot project it.

L9464   F18   1

Cylinder Lock: Deadbolt thrown or retracted by key from one side. No trim on opposite side.

Intellis® Locks

Schlage Number

TH885   TL8485

Hotel Lock: Latchbolt unlocked by key card outside or by lever or knob inside. Outside lever or knob always rotates but does not retract latchbolt until activated by key card. Deadbolt thrown or retracted by inside thumbturn. When thrown, all key cards become inoperative except key cards encoded with the deadbolt override feature. Display light indicates that deadbolt is thrown when key card is passed through lock. Turning inside lever or knob retracts both deadbolt and latchbolt simultaneously. Auxiliary latch deadlocks latchbolt when door is closed.

TH880   TL8080

Storeroom Lock: Outside lever or knob always locked. Key card unlocks lever or knob for one entry. Inside lever or knob always free for immediate exit. Auxiliary latch deadlocks latchbolt when door is closed.

General Purpose/Classroom Lock*: Latchbolt retracted by lever or knob from either side unless outside is locked by key card. Unlocked from outside by key card. Inside lever or knob always free for immediate exit. Auxiliary latch deadlocks latchbolt when door is closed.

All "T" Series Locks

Passage Latch*: Latchbolt is retracted by lever or knob from either side at all times until reprogrammed with a key card.

Maximum Security Lock*: Outside knob or lever always locked. Two key cards necessary for entry. Inside lever or knob always free for immediate exit. Auxiliary latch deadlocks latchbolt when door is closed.

All "T" Series Locks When Suffix 5 Is Specified

"Smart" Lock*: Unlocks/relocks twice in a 24 hour period. Programmable for a 7 day cycle. Eliminates need for manually unlocking and relocking at specific times. Inside lever or knob always free for immediate exit. Auxiliary latch deadlocks latchbolt when door is closed.

*These functions are field programmable. Consult the Intellis "User Reference Manual," or contact your Intellis representative.

FIGURE C.4

Comparative Key Blank List

American	ESP
1J	AM1
2J	AM3

Arco	ESP
30	R30

Arrow	ESP
K2	AR1
K2C	AR5
K7	AR4

Best	ESP
1A1A1	BE2
1A1A1	BE2-A
1A1B1	BE2-B
1A1C1	BE2-C
1A1D1	BE2-D
1A1DD1	BE2-DD
1A1E1	BE2-E
1A1F1	BE2-F
1A1G1	BE2-G
1A1H1	BE2-H
1A1J1	BE2-J
1A1K1	BE2-K
1A1L1	BE2-L
1A1M1	BE2-M
1A1N1	BE2-N
1A1Q1	BE2-Q

Briggs & Stratton	ESP
32318	B10
32319	B11
32671	Y152
32725	Y152
32838	H27
32839	H26
32842	H27
32849	H26
32900	B24
32903	Y152
32915	Y152
42107	B4
75101	B1
75102	B2
320032	H26
320045	B5
320085	H26
320158	H50
320181	H27
320259	Y149
320296	B40
320297	B41
320321	H50
320368	B42
320369	B43
320380	Y152
320381	Y149
320404	B44
320405	B45
320433	Y149
320434	Y152
320509	RA4
320510	RA3
320588	B48
320589	B49
320652	B50
320653	B51
321355	B46
321356	B47
GAS	GAS

Chicago	ESP
K4	CG1
K4L	CG2
K4R	CG3
K4W	CG6
K5	CG16

Cole National	ESP
AM1	AM1
AM4	AM3
AR1	AR1
AR4	AR4
AR5	AR5
B1	B1
B2	B2
B4	B4
B5	B5
B10	B10
B11	B11
B24	B24
B40	B40
B41	B41
B42	B42

Cole National	ESP
B43D	B43
B44E	B44
B45H	B45
B46J	B46
B47K	B47
B48A	B48
B49B	B49
B50C	B50
B51D	B51
BE2	BE2
BN1	BN1
BN7	BN7

471

BO1	HL2	EN15	MG1	K2	K2	SC8	SC8
CG1	CG1	ER1	ER1	54KL	L37	SC9	SC9
CG2	CG2	FR2 (FO373)	FT36	KW1	KW1	SC10	SC10
CG4	CG3	FR2	PP10	L1	IN33	SC22	SC22
CG6	CG6	FR2	RN11	L1	L1	SE1	SE1
CG15	CG16	GE1 (FO417)	V26K	L4	L4	SK1	SK1
CO1	CO1	GE11 (FO466)	V28M	L5	L5	GW5 (FO418)	VL3
CO2	CO2	GE12 (FO467)	V29R	M1	M1	SW12	VL5
CO3	CO3	GE21	YS1	M2	M2	SW13	VL4
CO4	CO4	GE24 (FO460)	MB33	M3	M4	T4	T7
CO5	CO5	GE25 (FO461)	MB34	M10	M10	WE1	WE1
CO6	CO6	GE26	PA2	M11	M11	WK1	WK2
CO7	CO7	GE30 (FO468)	V30F	M12	M12	WR2	WR3
CO10	CO10	GE30 (FO468)	V30R	NA5	NA6	WR5	WR4
CO26	CO26	GE31 (FO394)	OP19	NA12	NA12	XL7	XL7
CO34	CO34	GE34	PA6	NA13	NA24	Y1	Y1
CO35	CO35	GE57 (FO383)	OP11	NH1	NH1	Y2	Y2
CO36	CO36	H7	FC2	RA3	RA3	Y3	Y3
CO44	CO44	H26	H26	RA4	RA4	Y4	Y4
CO45	CO45	H27	H27	RO1	RO1	Y11	Y11
CO62	CO62	H32	H50	RO4	RO4	Y12	Y12
CO65	CO87	H33	H51	RU1	RU1	Y14	Y14
CO66	CO66	HO3	HO3	RU2	RU2	Y52	Y52
CO67	CO97	IN1	IN1	RU4	RU4	Y54	Y54
CO68	CO68	IN3	IN3	RU16	RU16	Y103	Y103
CO89	CO89	IN8	IN8	RU18		Y104	Y104
CO90	CO90	IN8	ES8	RU181/2		Y107	DC2
CO91	CO91	IN10	IN28	RU19	RU19	Y145	Y220
CO92	CO92	IN21	IN18	RU20	RU45	Y149	Y149
CO94	CO94	IT3	FT37	RU21	RU46	Y152	Y152
CO95	CO95	IT4	FT38	S1	S1		
CO105	CO106	IT6	WS2	S3	S3	**Corbin**	**ESP**
CO105	HL1	JA1	GAS	S4	S4	X1-27-5	CO3
DE6	DE6	JA10	MZ12	S6	S6	X1-27-6	CO4
DE8	DE8	JA11 (FO469)	DA22	S16	S16	X1-57A1-6	CO35
EA1	EA1	JA11 (FO469)	SR1	S22	S22	X1-57A2-6	CO45
EA27	EA27	JA62 (FO444)	TR23	S31	S31	X1-57B1-6	CO44
EL3	EL3	JA63 (FO454)	TR20	S32	S32	X1-57B2-6	CO34
EL10	EL10	JA64	TR25	S43	S68	X1-57D1-6	CO57
EL11	EL11	JA65	MZ9	S44	S69	X1-57D2-6	CO58
EN1 (U2)	UN3	JA72	MZ10	SC1	SC1	Z1-59A1-6	CO91
EN2 (FO272)	UN18	JA73	DA21	SC4	SC4	Z1-59A2-6	CO92
EN11 (FO248)	UN16	JA77	HD69	SC6	SC6	Z1-59B1-6	CO94
EN13 (FO249)	YS2	JA79	FC5	SC7	SC7	Z1-59B2-6	CO95

Z1-59C1-6	CO98
Z1-59C2-6	CO99
Z1-59D1-6	CO51
Z1-59D2-6	CO52
Z1-059AB-5	CO90
Z1-059AB-6	CO89
Z1-60-5	CO87
Z1-60-6	CO66
X1-67-6	CO36
Z1-67-5	CO7
X1-77-6	CO62
Z1-80-5	CO97
X1-97-5	CO5
X1-97-6	CO6
X1-99-5	CO1
X1-99-6	CO2
5865 JVR	CO68
8658 JVR	CO26
8618C-CR	CO10
8618C-R14	CO106

Curtis	ESP
AA2	AA2
AM1	AM1
AM3	AM3
AR1	AR1
AR4	AR4
AR5	AR5
B1	B1
B2	B2
B4	B4
B5	B5
B10	B10
B11	B11
B24	B24
B40	B40
B41	B41
B42	B42
B43	B43
B44	B44
B45	B45
B46	B46
B47	B47
B48	B48

Curtis	ESP
B49	B49
B50	B50
B51	B51
BE2	BE2
BM3	BM3
BN1	BN1
BN7	BN7
BO1	HL2
CG1	CG1
CG2	CG2
CG4	CG3
CG6	CG6
CG16	CG16
CO1	CO1
CO2	CO2
CO3	CO3
CO4	CO4
CO5	CO5
CO6	CO6
CO7	CO7
CO10	CO10
CO26	CO26
CO35	CO35
CO36	CO36
CO44	CO44
CO45	CO45
CO62	CO62
CO68	CO68
CO87	CO87
CO89	CO89
CO91	CO91
CO92	CO92
CO94	CO94
CO95	CO95
CO97	CO97
CO98	CO98
CO102	CO99
CO106	CO106
CO106	HL1
DA21	DA21
DA22	DA22
DA23	DA23
DA24	DA24
DC2	DC2

DE6	DE6
DE8	DE8
EA1	EA1
EA27	EA27
EL3	EL3
EL3	EL10
EL11	EL11
ER1	ER1
FC2	FC2
FC5	FC5
FC6	FC6
FC7	FC7
FT36	FT36
FT37	FT37
FT38	FT38
H26	H26
H27	H27
H50	H50
H51	H51
H54	H54
HD69	HD69
HD70	HD70
HD70	HD71
HD71	HD70
HD71	HD71
HO3	HO3
IN1	İN1
IN3	IN3
IN8	IN8

Curtis	ESP
IN8	ES8
IN18	IN18
IN28	IN28
IN29	IN29
IN33	IN33
K2	K2
KW1	KW1
L1	L1
L4	L4
L5	L5
M1	M1
M2	M2
M4	M4

M10	M10
M11	M11
M12	M12
MB33	MB33
MB34	MB34
MG1	MG1
MZ9	MZ9
MZ10	MZ10
MZ12	MZ12
NA6	NA6
NA12	NA12
NA24	NA24
NH1	NH1
OP11	OP11
OP19	OP19
PA2	PA2
PA5	PA5
PA6	PA6
PA7	PA7
PP10	PP10
PP10	RN11
RA3	RA3
RA4	RA4
RN11	PP10
RN11	RN11
RO1	RO1
RO4	RO4
RU1	RU1
RU2	RU2
RU4	RU4
RU16	RU16
RU18	RU18
RU18½	
RU18½	
RU19	RU19
RU20	RU20
RU21	RU21
RU45	RU45
RU46	RU46
S1	S1
S3	S3
S4	S4
S6	S6
S16	S16

S22	S22	Y1	Y1	O1EA	CO4	O7RMB	S32
S221/2	S221/2	Y1E	Y1E	O1EB	CO3	U7E	Y54
S32	S31	Y2	Y2	O1EG	CO036	UO7LA	S22
S31	S32	Y3	Y3	O1EN	CO7	WT7	PA6
S68	S68	Y4	Y4	O1GM	CO090	8	Y4
S69	S69	Y11	Y11	O1GH	CO097	9	Y1
SB11	SB11	Y12	Y12	O1MA	CO044	9A	Y2
SC1	SC1	Y14	Y14	O1MB	CO045	9B	Y220
SC4	SC4	Y52	Y52	RO1ED	CO034	C9	Y3
SC6	SC6	Y54	Y54	RO1EE	CO035	CE9	FC7
SC7	SC7	Y103	Y103	RO1EG	CO062	DM9	WS2
SC8	SC8	Y104	Y104	RO1EN	SK1	K9	Y1E
SC9	SC9	Y149	Y149	UO1A1	CO091	MZ9	MZ9
SC10	SC10	Y152	Y152	UO1A2	CO092	NE9	FT36
SC22	SC22	Y220	Y220	UO1B1	CO094	O9	S1
SE1	SE1	YS1	YS1	UO1B2	CO095	SB9	SB11
SK1	SK1	YS2	YS2	UO1C1	CO098	10	S3
SR1	SR1			UO1C2	CO099	10N	S68
T7	T7	**Dexter**	**ESP**	UO1D1	CO051	A10N	S69
TR20	TR20	2	DE6	UO1D2	CO052	HF10	OP11
TR23	TR23	2L	DE8	UO1GM	CO089	MZ10	MZ10
TR25	TR25			AC2	R30	U10	S4
TR26 (disc)	TR25	**Dominion**	**ESP**	MA2	M11	11	RU1
TR29	TR29	00	CO1	UN2	MG1	11D1	RU45
UN3	UN3	00AB	CO2	O3M	CO106	11GH	RU19
UN16	UN16	00BH	HL2	O3M	HL1	11P	RU4
UN18	UN18	00G	CO010	MA4	M12	A11D1	RU46
V26	V26K	00V	CO026	MZ4	FC5	A11P	RU16
V28	V28M	00Z	CO087	O4	L1	12	RU2
V29	V29R	SO0V	CO068	O4A	L4	MZ12	MZ12
V30	V30F	UO0Z	CO066	O4AL	L5	NE12	VL3
V30	V30R	RUKM	RU18	O4KL	L37	TA13	TR23
V32	V32FB	RUKM		MZ5	FC6	14	EA1
VL3	VL3	RU181/2		SF5	FT37	U14T	EA27
VL4	VL4	CA1	V30F	BG6	BN1	TA17	TR20
VL5	VL5	CA1	V30R	KL6	FC2	DT18	DA22
WE1	WE1	EG1	EL10	SF6	FT38	DT18	SR1
WE3	WE3	GA1	GAS	WT6	PA5	DT19	DA21
WK2	WK2	MA1	M10	7E	Y52	HF19	V26K
WR3	WR3	MS12	DC2	BG7	BN7	TA20	TR25
WR4	WR4	OM1	JE1	O7KMA	S6	YM20	YS1
WS2	MZ12	XL1	XL7	O7KMB	S16	DT21	DA23
WS2	WS2	01	CO5	O7LA	S221/2	DT22	DA24
XL7	XL7	01AB	CO6	O7RMA	S31	NE21	AA2

22	SE1	62DR	UN18	127ES	H26	9432	H50
22EZ	NH1	U62VP	OP19	141GE	T7	9433	H27
22W	AR1	L64A	NA12	145	SC1	9524	H27
D22	AR5	L64BH	NA24	145E	SC8	9525	H26
HL22W	AR4	R64D	NA6	145F	SC7	9544	H27
NE22	PP10	69	RO01	A145	SC4	9545	H26
NE22	RN11	M69C	RO4	A145E	SC9	9546	H27
HF24	MB33	79B	K2	A145F	SC10	9547	H26
NE24	VL5	UN90	UN16	167FD	H51	9549	H26
HF25	MB34	92	M1	S167FD	H50		
NE25	VL4	92B	M2	170	HO3	**Ilco**	**ESP**
YM26	YS2	92V	M4	H175	WK2	BMW1	BM3
HF28	BM3	96L	EL3	176	KW1	DC1	DC2
TA28	TR29	E96LN	EL11	770U	Y152	MG1	MG1
HF30	PA2	98M	B1	S770U	Y149	YS1	YS1
HF31	PA7	98X	B4	707A	SC6	AA2	AA2
HF32	V29R	H98A	B40	707W	SC22	FC2	FC2
HF33	V28M	H98C	B42	970AM	RA4	YS2	YS2
HF36	V32FB	H98DB	B5	S970AM	RA3	MZ4	FC5
41C	AM1	H98LA	B10			MZ5	FC6
41E	CG16	H98M	B2	**Eagle**	**ESP**	PA5	PA5
41G	CG1	H98X	B24	11309	EA1	PO5	PA2
41GA	CG2	P98A	B48	11929B	EA27	PA6	PA6
41GR	CG3	P98C	B50			PO6	PA7
41N	CG6	P98E	B44	**Earle**	**ESP**	FC7	FC7
41X	AM3	P98J	B46	7000K	ER1	MZ9	MZ9
HD44	HD69	S98B	B49			MZ10	MZ10
54F	IN1	S98D	B51	**Harloc**	**ESP**	OM10	JE1
54UN	IN29	S98H	B45	700	EA27	OP11	OP11
H54KD	DE6					MZ12	MZ12
H54WA	WR3	**Dominion**	**ESP**	**Hollymade**	**ESP**	MZ12	WS2
HD54	HD70	S98K	B47	1015CA	HO3	MB15	MB34
HD54	HD71	U98B	B41			UN16	UN16
HL54KD	DE8	U98D	B43	**Hurd**	**ESP**	MB18	MB33
L54B	IN8	U98LA	B11	9124	H27	OP19	OP19
L54B	ES8	114A	BE2	9128	H50	TR26	TR25
L54WA	WR4	119	ER1	9129	H51	FT37	FT37
X54F	IN18	U122	Y11	9338	H50	FT38	FT38
X54FN	IN28	U122A	Y12	9422	H51	F44	FT36
X54K	IN3	U122AR	Y14	9423	H27	HO44	HD69
X54MT	IN33	U122B	Y103	9424	H50	RE61F	PP10
HD54	HD70	U122BR	Y104	9427	H51	RE61F	RN11
HD55	HD71	123	WE1	9428	H50	T61C	TR20
62DP	UN3	127DB	H27	9431	H51	T61F	TR23

62DP	UN3	A1001BH	CO94	1022	SE1	01098B	B41
62DT	DA22	A1001C1	CO98	1041C	AM1	01098D	B43
62DT	SR1	A1001C2	CO99	1041G	CG1	01098LA	B11
62DU	DA21	A1001D1	CO51	1041GA	CG2	P1098A	B48
62FS	UN18	A1001D2	CO52	1041GR	CG3	P1098C	B50
AB62C	AB1	A1001DH	CO95	1041N	CG6	P1098CV	B63-C
VO62	VL3	A1001EH	CO66	1041T	CG16	P1098E	B44
VW67	V26K	A1001FH	CO92	1046	AM3	P1098J	B46
HD70	HD70	R1001ED	CO34	1054F	IN1	S1098B	B49
HD70	HD71	R1001EE	CO35	1054FN	IN28	S1098D	B51
HD71	HD70	R1001EG	CO62	1054MT	IN33	S1098H	B45
HD71	HD71	R1001EN	SK1	1054UN	IN29	S1098K	B47
VW71	V28M	1003M	HL1	1054WB	WR3	P1098WC	B64-C
VW71A	V29R	1003M	CO106	A1054WB	WR4	1114A	BE2
73VB	V30F	R1003M	HL2	D1054K	DE6	1119	ER1
73VB	V30R	1004	L1	D1054KA	DE8	K1122D	BN1
VO73	VL5	1004A	L4	K1054B	BN7	01122	Y11
VO73S	VL4	1004AL	L5	L1054B	IN8	01122A	Y12
997E	Y52	1004KL	L37	L1054B	ES8	01122AR	Y14
0997E	Y54	1007LA	S221/2	X1054F	IN18	01122B	Y103
997X	Y6	N1007KMA	S6	X1054K	IN3	01122BR	Y104
998	Y4	N1007KMB	S16	R1064D	NA6	01122R	Y13
999	Y1	N1007RMA	S31	1069	RO1	1123	WE1
999A	Y2	N1007RMB	S32	1069FL	RO4	1123S	WE3
999B	Y220	01007LA	S22	1069LA	NA12	1127DP	H27
999N	Y1E	1009	S1	1069LC	NA24	1127ES	H26
C999	Y3	1010	S3	1079B	K2	1131R	R30
1000	CO1	1010N	S68	1092	M1	1141GE	T7
1000AB	CO2	L1010N	S69	1092B	M2	1145	SC1
1000G	CO010	01010	S4	1092D	M12	1145A	SC4
1000V	CO026	1011	RU1	1092H	M11	1145E	SC8
S1000V	CO068	1011D1	RU45	1092N	M10	1145F	SC7
1001	CO5	1011D41	RU19	1092V	M4	A1145E	SC9
1001AB	CO6	1011P	RU4	1096L	EL3	A1145F	SC10
1001ABM	CO090	1011PZ	RU18	C1096CN	EL10	1167FD	H51
1001EA	CO4	A1011D1	RU46	C1096LN	EL11	S1167FD	H50
1001EB	CO3	A1011D41	RU20	1098DB	B5	1170B	H03
1001EG	CO036	A1011M	RU21	1098GX	GAS	1175N	WK2
1001EH	CO087	A1011P	RU16	1098M	B1	1176	KW1
1001EN	CO7	A1011PZ		1098X	B4	1177N	NH1
1001GH	CO097	RU181/2		H1098A	B40	1179	AR1
1001MA	CO044	1012	RU2	H1098C	B42	1179A	AR4
1001MB	CO045	1014	EA1	H1098LA	B10	1179C	AR5
A1001ABM	CO089	1014C	HR1	H1098M	B2	1180	XL7
A1001AH	CO091	X1014F	EA27	H1098X	B24	1184FD	H54

1307A	SC6	64MA	CO44	122C	L5	A159WB	WR4
1307W	SC22	64N	CO90	125B	AR1	E159	SC8
S1770U	Y149	A64AH	CO91	125BA	AR4	E159A	SC9
P1770U	Y152	A64BH	CO94	125BC	AR5	F159	SC7
1970AM	RA4	A64C1	CO98	153GB	B41	F159A	SC10
S1970AM	RA3	A64C2	CO99	153GD	B43	X159AA	IN18
		A64D1	CO51	153GH	B45	D161VW	V26K
Keil	**ESP**	A64D2	CO52	153GK	B47	G161VW	V28M
2A	Y220	A64DH	CO95	153H	RO1	H161VW	V29R
2B	Y1	A64EH	CO66	153HA	B40	168B	EA1
2C	Y2	A64FH	CO92	153HE	B44	X168	EA27
2KK	K2	A64N	CO89	153HJ	B46	169FL	RO4
6P	Y11	65	CO5	153PG	B11	169LA	NA12
6S	Y12	65A	CO6	153PH	B10	170	HO3
6SS	Y14	65E	CO35	L153GB	B49	175N	WK2
6TB	BN1	66A	CO10	L153HA	B48	176	KW1
6V	Y103	66N	CO26	L153HC	B42	180AJ	AM3
6VV	Y104	66NS	CO68	N153GD	B51	180BC	CG16
7A	Y4	83	RU2	N153HC	B50	180E	AM1
8GL	Y149	84	RU1	154P	BE2	180FS	CG1
8HM	Y152	84A	SE1	H154NL	RA4	180GA	CG2
11	Y6	84AA	ER1	H154R	B24	180GR	CG3
12B	YS2	A87N	RU21	H154SS	B2	180S	CG6
12E	Y54	88	RU4	R154NL	RA3	181N	IN8
17N	NH1	88A	RU16	R154S	B5	181N	ES8
24F	Y3	88AZ		R154SS	B1	181NB	BN7
59D	H27	RU181/2		R154X	B4	202C	SC6
		88D1	RU45	155BN	EL10	202W	SC22
Keil	**ESP**	88D41	RU19	155F	WE1		
59E	H26	88Z	RU18	155FS	WE3	**Kwikset**	**ESP**
60D	CO1	A88D1	RU46	155GE	T7	1268	KW1
60E	CO2	A88D41	RU20	155S	M1		
62CG	H50	A96LA	S221/2	155W	EL3	**Lockwood**	**ESP**
62HG	H51	B96LA	S22	155WN	EL11	B308	L1
63M	CO106	99LN	S16	155X	M2	B310	L4
63M	HL1	N99RN	S32	D155K	DE6	B346	L5
63MR	HL2	100LN	S6	D155KA	DE8		
64	CO3	N100RN	S31	R155D	NA6	**Lori Corp.**	**ESP**
64A	CO4	102	S3	158N	M10	LOR27	EA27
64C	SK1	102N	S68	158V	M4		
64CA	CO62	102NA	S69	159AA	IN1	**Master**	**ESP**
64D	CO7	A102	S4	159H	SC1	1K	M1
64EH	CO87	103	S1	159J	SC4	7K	M2
64G	CO36	122	L1	159K	IN3	15K	M10
64GH	CO97	122A	L4	159WB	WR3	17K	M11

81KR	M4	**Schlage**	**ESP**	HBR5M	B42	LDC1	DC2
150K	M12	100C	SC1	OBR7	B43	5DE3	DE6
		100E	SC8	HBR9E	B44	6DE3	DE8
National	**ESP**	100F	SC7	OBR9H	B45	5EA1	EA27
(EZ)		101C	SC4	HBR10J	B46	5EA2	EA1
9407	NH1	101E	SC9	OBR10K	B47	5EL1	EL3
		101F	SC10	HBR11	RA4	5EL3	EL11
National	**ESP**	180	SC6	OBR11	RA3	5EL4	EL10
(Rockford)		200	SC22	HBR12A	B48	5ER1	ER1
68-619-1	RO4	920A	SC6	OBR12B	B49	HFD4	H27
68-635-1	RO1	923C	SC1	HBR14C	B50	OFD4	H26
68-676-11	NA24	923E	SC8	OBR14D	B51	HFD10	H51
411-31	NA6	924C	SC4	CG1	CG1	OFD10	H50
676-1	NA12	924E	SC9	CG2	CG3	HFD12	H54
		924F	SC7	CG6	CG2	5FT1	FT36
Russwin	**ESP**	924F	SC10	5CG7	CG16	HN2	HD70
5D1R	RU45	927W	SC22	5CO1	CO7	HN2	HD71
6D1R	RU46			6CO1	CO036	HN3	HD70
5D41	RU19	**Segal**	**ESP**	5CO2	CO3	HN3	HD71
6D41	RU20	K9	SE1	6CO2	CO4	5HO1	HO3
752R	RU2			5CO3	CO1	5IL1	IN1
852R	RU1	**Skillman**	**ESP**	5CO4	CO5	7IL2	L37
960GGM		SK100	SK1	5CO5	SK1	5IL4	IN3
RU181/2				6CO5	CO62	IL5	IN8
961	RU16	**Star**	**ESP**	5CO6	CO010	IL5	ES8
980BGGM	RU18	AD1	PA6	CO7	CO068	5IL7	IN18
981B	RU4	5AR2	AR1	LCO7	CO026	51L9	IN28
59812	RU21	6AR2	AR4	5CO11	CO087	IL10UN	IN29
		5AU1	CO106	6CO11	CO066	5IL11	IN33
Safe	**ESP**	5AU1	HL1	5CO12	CO090		
7525	RU2	5AU2	NA12	6CO12	CO089	**Star**	**ESP**
		6BE1	BE2	5CO13	CO097	JU1	AM1
Sargent	**ESP**	BN1	BN1	6CO16	CO051	5JU2	AM3
265K	S3	5BO1	HL2	6CO16	CO052	5KE1	K2
265R	S1	HBR1	B2	6CO16	CO098	5KW1	KW1
265U	S4	OBR1	B1	6CO16	CO099	5LO1	L1
270LN	S16	OBR1DB	B5	CP1	FC2	6LO1	L4
270RN	S32	HBR2	B10	CP2	YS1	7LO1	L5
275LA	S221/2	OBR2	B11	CP3	YS2	MA1	M1
275S	S68	HBR3	B24	5DA2	MZ12	4MA2	M2
6270LN	S6	OBR3	B4	DA3	DA21	5MA3	M4
6270RN	S31	HBR5	B40	DA4	DA22	5MA5	M10
6275LA	S22	OBR5	B41	DA4	SR1	5MA6	M11
6275S	S69						

5MA7	M12	VW3	V28M	14A	Y2	X26	MZ9
MZ1	MZ9	VW4	V30F	14YM	Y3	P27	H51
MZ2	MZ10	VW4	V30R	E14	Y1E	S27	H50
5NA1	NH1	VW5	V29R	X14S	Y220	X27	MZ10
HPL68	Y152	5WE1	WE1	XL16	XL7	X29	VL5
OPL68	Y149	5WK1	WK2	P19	Y152	X30	VL4
RO1	RO1	5WR2	WR3	S19	Y149	31R	R30
RO3	RO4	6WR2	WR4	20	CO01	X32	PA7
5RO4	NA6	4YA1	Y220	20AB	CO02	35	L1
5RU1	RU1	5YA1	Y1	20G	CO010	35A	L4
5RU2	RU4	5YA1E	Y1E	20V	CO026	35AL	L5
6RU2	RU16	6YA1	Y2	20VS	CO068	40F	JE1
5RU5	RU18	5YA2	Y3	X20	FC2	41C	AM1
6RU5		6YA3	Y4	21A	CO4	41G	CG1
RU181/2		5YA6	Y52	21EB	CO3	41GA	CG2
5RU6	RU2	6YA6	Y54	21EG	CO36	41GR	CG3
5RU7	RU45	YJ1	Y12	21EN	CO7	41N	CG6
6RU7	RU46	YJ2	Y14	B21EF	CO35	41R	CG16
5RU8	RU19	YJ3	Y11	B21EG	CO44	41RB	IN29
6RU8	RU20	YJ4	Y103	B21EH	CO45	J41	AM3
6RU9	RU21			B21EJ	CO34	X44	HD69
5SA1	S4	**Taylor**	**ESP**	R21EG	CO62	43LA	S221/2
5SA2	S1	X1	MZ12	R21EN	SK1	043LA	S22
5SA3	S16	X4	FC5	X21	YS1	48	S1
6SA3	S6	X5	FC6	22B	HL2	48KM	S16
5SA5	S3	X6	DA22	22GM	CO90	48KMR	S32
5SA6	S32	X6	SR1	22Z2	CO87	048KM	S6
6SA6	S31	7E	Y52	A22A1	CO91	048KMR	S31
5SA7	S68	7NX	Y11	A22A2	CO92	50	S3
6SA7	S69	7X	Y6	A22B1	CO94	050	S4
5SE1	SE1	X7	DA21	A22B2	CO95	51S	S68
5SH1	SC1	07B	Y103	A22C1	CO98	51SA	S69
6SH1	SC4	07BR	Y104	A22C2	CO99	X51	AA2
SH2	SC6	07E	Y54	A22D1	CO51	X52	SB11
5SH4	SC8	07NX	Y12	A22D2	CO52	X53	V32FB
6SH4	SC9	RO7NX	Y14	A22GM	CO89	54DR	DE6
5SH5	SC7	R7NX	Y13	A22Z2	CO66	54F	IN1
6SH5	SC10	X9	V30F	K22	CO97	54FN	IN28
SH6	SC22	X9	V30R	R22B	CO106	54KL	L37
5TA4	T7	12GM	Y4	R22B	HL1	54KS	KW1
TO1	TR20	X12	PP10	X22	YS2	54WA	WR4
UN3	UN18	X12	RN11	23	CO5	54WB	WR3
VW2	V26K	14	Y1	23AB	CO6	A54DR	DE8

L54B	IN8	M81G	MG1	X123	DA25	307W	SC22
L54B	ES8	T81B	TR25	X123	SR5	**Weiser**	**ESP**
L54N	BN7	V81V	V29R	127DP	H27	1556	WR3
L54P	BN1	V81W	V28M	127ES	H26	1559	WR4
X54	DC2	X86	FC7	X128	HD79		
X54F	IN18	P91A	B48	X129	HD80	**Weslock**	**ESP**
X54K	IN3	P91C	B50	X130	HD81	4425	WK2
55	RU1	S91B	B49	X131	MZ13		
55P	RU4	S91D	B51	133	WE1	**Yale**	**ESP**
56	RU2	92	M1	133S	WE3	8	Y1
57M	RU18	92B	M2	135	AR1	E8	Y1E
57MA		92G	M12	135A	AR4	91/2	Y220
RU181/2		92N	M10	135C	AR5	11	Y2
57PA	RU16	92T	M11	X137	TR33	121/2	Y52
57R	RU19	U92A	M4	X143	B53	121/2	Y54
57-1D	RU45	96CN	EL10	145	SC1	111GMK	Y4
A57-1D	RU46	96L	EL3	145A	SC4	385	Y3
61	EA1	96LN	EL11	145E	SC9	9114	Y11
X61F	EA27	98M	B1	145ES	SC8	9278	Y12
X61FR	HR1	98X	B4	145F	SC10	9279	Y14
62	RO1	H98C	B42	145FS	SC7	9290	Y103
62DL	UN3	H98DB	B5	X145	B55	9882	Y104
62H	RO4	H98LA	B10	X146	B56		
F68XR	UN16	H98M	B2	X151	TR39		
S71B	UN18	H98X	B24	X159	TR37		
X71	HD70	O98B	B41	X160	HY2		
X71	HD71	O98D	B43	X165	HD84		
F74T	FT36	O98H	B45	170	HO3		
076R	OP11	O98K	B47	174BA	NA12		
V78JK	V26K	O98LA	B11	174BN	NA24		
79HK	K2	X98A	B40	R174D	NA6		
F79-1	FT37	X98E	B44	X174	TR40		
F79-3	FT38	X98J	B46	175W	WK2		
M79S	MB33	99A	RA4				
M79T	MB34	99B	RA3	**Taylor**	**ESP**		
079JB	OP19	102	SE1	X176	MIT1		
V79D	VL3	N102	NH1	X178	MZ16		
B80NR	BM3	111GE	T7	X181	HD90		
T80R	TR20	114A	BE2	X182	HD91		
T80V	TR23	X114	DA24	X183	HD92		
A81M	PA2	X115	DA23	X185	SUZ15		
A81R	PA5	X116	RN24	X186	SUZ17		
A81S	PA6	119	ER1	X192	B72		
F81E	WS2	X121	DC3	307A	SC6		

Depth and Space Charts

KEY: Cuts start at = to first cut; spacing = between cut centers (from one center cut to the next).

Manufacturer: Abus
Key Series: Padlocks
Key Blank No.: 244L & 2441R
No. of Steps: 5, 1–5
Drop: .025
Cuts Start At: .155
Spacing: .120
Depth No. 1: .260
Depth No. 2: .235
Depth No. 3: .210
Depth No. 4: .185
Depth No. 5: .160

Manufacturer: Abus
Key Series: Padlocks
Key Blank No.: 42
(Orig.)
No. of Steps: 5, 1–5
Drop: .025
Cuts Start At: .145

Spacing: .140
Depth No. 1: .260
Depth No. 2: .235
Depth No. 3: .210
Depth No. 4: .185
Depth No. 5: .160

Manufacturer: Abus
Key Series: Padlocks
Key Blank
No.: 5525
(Orig.)
No. of Steps: 3, 1–3
Drop: .030
Cuts Start At: .100
Spacing: .125
Depth No. 1: .180
Depth No. 2: .150
Depth No. 3: .120

Manufacturer: American
Key Series: Padlocks
Key Blank No.: 1046
No. of Steps: 8, 1–8
Drop: Var.
Cuts Start At: .156
Spacing: .125
Depth No. 1: .2840
Depth No. 2: .2684
Depth No. 3: .2523
Depth No. 4: .2372
Depth No. 5: .2215
Depth No. 6: .2059
Depth No. 7: .1903
Depth No. 8: .1747

Manufacturer: American
Key Series: P4–P6 Padlocks Key
Blank No.: 1046
No. of Steps: 5, 1–5
Drop: Var.
Cuts Start At: .155
Spacing: .130
Depth No. 1: .260
Depth No. 2: .235
Depth No. 3: .210
Depth No. 4: .185
Depth No. 5: .165

Manufacturer: Amerock
Key Series: All
Key Blank No.: 1179A
No. of Steps: 10, 0–9
Drop: .014
Cuts Start At: .265
Spacing: .155
Depth No. 0: .315
Depth No. 1: .301

Depth No. 2: .287
Depth No. 3: .273
Depth No. 4: .259
Depth No. 5: .245
Depth No. 6: .231
Depth No. 7: .217
Depth No. 8: .203
Depth No. 9: .189

Manufacturer: Arrow
Key Series: Standard
Key Blank No.: 1179
No. of Steps: 9, 1–9
Drop: .018
Cuts Start At: .230
Spacing: .160
Depth No. 1: .320
Depth No. 2: .302
Depth No. 3: .284
Depth No. 4: .266
Depth No. 5: .248
Depth No. 6: .230
Depth No. 7: .212
Depth No. 8: .194
Depth No. 9: .176

Manufacturer: Arrow
Key Series: New
Key Blank No.: 1179
No. of Steps: 10, 0–9
Drop: .014
Cuts Start At: .265
Spacing: .155
Depth No. 0: .335
Depth No. 1: .321
Depth No. 2: .307
Depth No. 3: .293
Depth No. 4: .279

Depth No. 5: .265
Depth No. 6: .251
Depth No. 7: .237
Depth No. 8: .223
Depth No. 9: .209

Manufacturer: Arrow
Key Series: Old
Key Blank No.: 1179
No. of Steps: 7, 0–6
Drop: .020
Cuts Start At: .265
Spacing: .155
Depth No. 0: .335
Depth No. 1: .315
Depth No. 2: .295
Depth No. 3: .275
Depth No. 4: .255
Depth No. 5: .235
Depth No. 6: .215

Manufacturer: Craftsman Key
Series: Key-in-knob
Key Blank No.: 1096CN
No. of Steps: 10, 0–9
Drop: .018
Cuts Start At: .160
Spacing: .156
Depth No. 0: .323
Depth No. 1: .305
Depth No. 2: .287
Depth No. 3: .269
Depth No. 4: .251
Depth No. 5: .233
Depth No. 6: .215
Depth No. 7: .197
Depth No. 8: .179
Depth No. 9: .161

Manufacturer: Dexter Key
Series: After 1969
Key Blank No.: D1054K
No. of Steps: 10, 0–9
Drop: .015
Cuts Start At: .216
Spacing: .155
Depth No. 0: .320
Depth No. 1: .305
Depth No. 2: .290
Depth No. 3: .275
Depth No. 4: .260
Depth No. 5: .245
Depth No. 6: .230
Depth No. 7: .215
Depth No. 8: .200
Depth No. 9: .185

Manufacturer: Dexter Key
Series: Close Pin
Key Blank No.: 1054KD
No. of Steps: 8, 0–7
Drop: .020
Cuts Start At: .180
Spacing: .125
Depth No. 0: .325
Depth No. 1: .305
Depth No. 2: .285
Depth No. 3: .265
Depth No. 4: .245
Depth No. 5: .225
Depth No. 6: .205
Depth No. 7: .185

Manufacturer: Falcon
Key Series: A,E,M,R,S,X
Key Blank No.: 1054WB
No. of Steps: 10, 0–9

Drop: .018
Cuts Start At: .237
(from tip to bow)
Spacing: .156
Depth No. 0: .315
Depth No. 1: .297
Depth No. 2: .279
Depth No. 3: .261
Depth No. 4: .243
Depth No. 5: .225
Depth No. 6: .207
Depth No. 7: .189
Depth No. 8: .171
Depth No. 9: .153

Manufacturer: Harloc
Key Series: Large Pin
Key Blank No.: X1014F
No. of Steps: 10, 1–0
Drop: .018
Cuts Start At: .216
Spacing: .155
Depth No. 1: .320
Depth No. 2: .302
Depth No. 3: .284
Depth No. 4: .266
Depth No. 5: .248
Depth No. 6: .230
Depth No. 7: .212
Depth No. 8: .194
Depth No. 9: .176
Depth No. 0: .158

Manufacturer: Ilco
Key Series: FN, XK, MT
Key Blank No.: 1054FN
No. of Steps: 10, 0–9
Drop: .018

Cuts Start At: .277
Spacing: .156
Depth No. 0: .320
Depth No. 1: .302
Depth No. 2: .284
Depth No. 3: .266
Depth No. 4: .248
Depth No. 5: .230
Depth No. 6: .212
Depth No. 7: .194
Depth No. 8: .176
Depth No. 9: .158

Manufacturer: Ilco
Key Series: XR
Key Blank No.: 1154G
No. of Steps: 7, 1–7
Drop: .018
Cuts Start At: .162
Spacing: .140
Depth No. 1: .270
Depth No. 2: .252
Depth No. 3: .234
Depth No. 4: .216
Depth No. 5: .198
Depth No. 6: .180
Depth No. 7: .162

Manufacturer: Ilco
Key Series: #308 Padlocks
Key Blank No.: K1054AX
No. of Steps: 7, 1–7
Drop: .018
Cuts Start At: .165
Spacing: .140
Depth No. 1: .270
Depth No. 2: .252
Depth No. 3: .234

Depth No. 4: .216
Depth No. 5: .198
Depth No. 6: .180
Depth No. 7: .162

Manufacturer: Ilco
Key Series: AH & F Small Pin
Key Blank No.: X1054A & JK
No. of Steps: 7, 1–7
Drop: .018
Cuts Start At: .162
Spacing: .125
Depth No. 1: .270
Depth No. 2: .252
Depth No. 3: .234
Depth No. 4: .216
Depth No. 5: .198
Depth No. 6: .180
Depth No. 7: .162

Manufacturer: Ilco
Key Series: Large Pin
Key Blank No.: X1054
No. of Steps: 10, 0–9
Drop: .018
Cuts Start At: .277
Spacing: .156
Depth No. 0: .320
Depth No. 1: .302
Depth No. 2: .284
Depth No. 3: .266
Depth No. 4: .248
Depth No. 5: .230
Depth No. 6: .212
Depth No. 7: .194
Depth No. 8: .176
Depth No. 9: .158

Manufacturer: Juncunc Key
Series: Pin Tumbler
Key Blank No.: 1046
No. of Steps: 8, 1–8
Drop: .015
Cuts Start At: .156
Spacing: .125
Depth No. 1: .285
Depth No. 2: .270
Depth No. 3: .255
Depth No. 4: .240
Depth No. 5: .225
Depth No. 6: .210
Depth No. 7: .195
Depth No. 8: .180

Manufacturer: Kwikset
Key Series: Old
Key Blank No.: 1176
No. of Steps: 4
Drop: .031
Cuts Start At: .247
Spacing: .150
Depth No. 1: .328
Depth No. 3: .297
Depth No. 5: .266
Depth No. 7: .235

Manufacturer: Kwikset Key
Series: New
Key Blank No.: 1176
No. of Steps: 7, 1–7
Drop: .023
Cuts Start At: .247
Spacing: .150
Depth No. 1: .328
Depth No. 2: .305
Depth No. 3: .282

Depth No. 4: .259
Depth No. 5: .236
Depth No. 6: .213
Depth No. 7: .190

Manufacturer: Lustre Line Key
Series: Key-in-knob
Key Blank No.: 1176
No. of Steps: 7, 1–7
Drop: .020
Cuts Start At: .170
Spacing: .190
Depth No. 1: .310
Depth No. 2: .290
Depth No. 3: .270
Depth No. 4: .250
Depth No. 5: .230
Depth No. 6: .210
Depth No. 7: .190

Manufacturer: Master
Key Series: 1K, 77K, 15, 17, 81
Key Blank No.: 1092, 1092V, etc.
No. of Steps: 8, 0–7
Drop: .015 Cuts
Start At: .185
Spacing: .125
Depth No. 0: .275
Depth No. 1: .260
Depth No. 2: .245
Depth No. 3: .230
Depth No. 4: .215
Depth No. 5: .200
Depth No. 6: .185
Depth No. 7: .170

Manufacturer: Master
Key Series: 7K

Key Blank
No.: 1092B
No. of Steps: 7, 0–6
Drop: .0155
Cuts Start At: .132
Spacing: .125
Depth No. 0: .212
Depth No. 1: .1965
Depth No. 2: .181
Depth No. 3: .1655
Depth No. 4: .150
Depth No. 5: .1345
Depth No. 6: .119

Manufacturer: Master Key
Series: #150 & #160 Large
Key Blank No.: 1092N & 1092NR
No. of Steps: 9, 0–8
Drop: .015
Cuts Start At: .150
Spacing: .129
Depth No. 0: .270
Depth No. 1: .255
Depth No. 2: .240
Depth No. 3: .225
Depth No. 4: .210
Depth No. 5: .195
Depth No. 6: .180
Depth No. 7: .165
Depth No. 8: .150

Manufacturer: Master
Key Series: #19 Padlocks
Key Blank No.: F76 (Orig.)
No. of Steps: 8, 0–7
Drop: .025
Cuts Start At: .213
Spacing: .156

Depth No. 0: .370
Depth No. 1: .345
Depth No. 2: .320
Depth No. 3: .295
Depth No. 4: .270
Depth No. 5: .245
Depth No. 6: .220
Depth No. 7: .195

Manufacturer: Schlage
Key Series: Pin Tumblers
Key Blank No.: 1145C, etc.
No. of Steps: 10, 0–9
Drop: .015
Cuts Start At: .231
Spacing: .156
Depth No. 0: .335
Depth No. 1: .320
Depth No. 2: .305
Depth No. 3: .290
Depth No. 4: .275
Depth No. 5: .260
Depth No. 6: .245
Depth No. 7: .230
Depth No. 8: .215
Depth No. 9: .200

Manufacturer: Weiser Key
Series: New
Key Blank No.: 1054WB
No. of Steps: 10, 0–9
Drop: .018
Cuts Start At: .237 (from top
  shoulder)
Spacing: .155
Depth No. 0: .315
Depth No. 1: .297
Depth No. 2: .279

Depth No. 3: .261
Depth No. 4: .243
Depth No. 5: .225
Depth No. 6: .207
Depth No. 7: .189
Depth No. 8: .171
Depth No. 9: .153

Manufacturer: Weiser
Key Series: Old
Key Blank No.: 1054WB
No. of Steps: 10, 0–9
Drop: .018
Cuts Start At: .237 (from top
  shoulder)
Spacing: .156
Depth No. 0: .320
Depth No. 1: .302
Depth No. 2: .284
Depth No. 3: .266
Depth No. 4: .248
Depth No. 5: .230
Depth No. 6: .212
Depth No. 7: .194
Depth No. 8: .176
Depth No. 9: .158

Manufacturer: Yale
Key Series: IN & AL Series
Key Blank No.: 01122, etc.
No. of Steps: 7, 1–7
Drop: .018
Cuts Start At: .175
Spacing: .135
Depth No. 1: .260
Depth No. 2: .242
Depth No. 3: .224
Depth No. 4: .206

Depth No. 5: .188

Depth No. 6: .170

Depth No. 7: .152

Manufacturer: Yale

Key Series: Standard #8

Key Blank No.: 999 (#8 Orig.)

No. of Steps: 10, 0–9

Drop: .019

Cuts Start At: .200

Spacing: .165

Depth No. 0: .320

Depth No. 1: .301

Depth No. 2: .282

Depth No. 3: .263

Depth No. 4: .244

Depth No. 5: .225

Depth No. 6: .206

Depth No. 7: .187

Depth No. 8: .168

Depth No. 9: .149

Manufacturer: Yale Key

Series: Large Sectional

Key Blank No.: 998, etc.

No. of Steps: 8, 0–7

Drop: .025

Cuts Start At: .200

Spacing: .165

Depth No. 0: .320

Depth No. 1: .295

Depth No. 2: .270

Depth No. 3: .245

Depth No. 4: .220

Depth No. 5: .195

Depth No. 6: .170

Depth No. 7: .145

ANSI/BHMA Finish Numbers

New No.	Description	Material	Old No.
600	primed for painting	steel	USP
601	bright japanned	steel	US1B
603	zinc plated	steel	US2G
604	zinc plated and dichromate sealed	brass	—
605	bright brass	brass	US3
606	satin brass	brass	US4
607	oxidized satin brass, oil rubbed	brass	—
608	oxidized satin brass, relieved	brass	—
609	satin brass, blackened, satin relieved	brass	US5
610	satin brass, blackened, bright relieved	brass	US7
611	bright bronze	bronze	US9
612	satin bronze	bronze	US10
613	dark oxidized satin bronze, oil rubbed	bronze	US10B
614	oxidized satin bronze, relieved	bronze	—
615	oxidized satin bronze, relieved, waxed	bronze	—
616	satin bronze, blackened, satin relieved	bronze	US11

New No.	Description	Material	Old No.
617	darkened oxidized satin bronze, bright relieved	bronze	US13
618	bright nickel plated	brass/bronze	US14
619	satin nickel plated	brass/bronze	US15
620	satin nickel plated, blackened, satin relieved	brass/bronze	US15A
621	nickel plated, blackened, relieved	brass/bronze	US17A
622	flat black coated	brass/bronze	US19
623	light oxidized statuary bronze	bronze	US20
624	dark oxidized statuary bronze	bronze	US20A
625	bright chromium plated	brass/bronze	US26
626	satin chromium plated	brass/bronze	US26D
627	satin aluminum	aluminum	US27
628	satin aluminum, clear anodized	aluminum	US28
629	bright stainless steel	stainless steel	US32
630	satin stainless steel	stainless steel	US32D
631	flat black coated	steel	US19
632	bright brass plated	steel	US3
633	satin brass plated	steel	US4
634	oxidized satin brass, oil rubbed	steel	—
635	oxidized satin brass, relieved	steel	—
636	satin brass plated, blackened, bright relieved	steel	US7
637	bright bronze plated	steel	US9
638	satin brass plated, blackened, satin relieved	steel	US5
639	satin bronze plated	steel	US10
640	oxidized satin bronze plated, oil rubbed	steel	US10B
641	oxidized satin bronze plated, relieved	steel	—
642	oxidized satin bronze plated, relieved, waxed	steel	—
643	satin bronze plated, blackened, satin relieved	steel	US11

New No.	Description	Material	Old No.
644	dark oxidized satin bronze plated, bright relieved	steel	US13
645	bright nickel plated	steel	US14
646	satin nickel plated	steel	US15
647	satin nickel plated, blackened, satin relieved	steel	US15A
648	nickel plated, blackened, relieved	steel	US17A
649	light oxidized bright bronze plated	steel	US20
650	dark oxidized statuary bronze plated, clear coated	steel	US20A
651	bright chrome plated	steel	US26
652	satin chromium plated	steel	US26D
653	bright stainless steel	stainless steel	—
654	satin stainless steel	stainless steel	—
655	light oxidized satin bronze, bright relieved, clear coated	bronze	US13
656	light oxidized satin bronze plated, bright relieved	steel	US13
657	dark oxidized copper plated, satin relieved	steel	—
658	dark oxidized copper plated, bright relieved	steel	—
659	light oxidized copper plated, satin relieved	steel	—
660	light oxidized copper plate, bright relieved	steel	—
661	oxidized satin copper, relieved	steel	—
662	satin brass plated, browned, satin relieved	steel	—
663	zinc plated with clear chromate seal	steel	—
664	cadmium plated with chromate seal	steel	—
665	cadmium plated with iridescent dichromate	steel	—
666	bright brass plated	aluminum	US3
667	satin brass plated	aluminum	US4
668	satin bronze plated	aluminum	US10
669	bright nickel plated	aluminum	US14
670	satin nickel plated	aluminum	US15

New No.	Description	Material	Old No.
671	flat black coated	aluminum	US19
672	bright chromium plated	aluminum	US26
673	aluminum clear coated	aluminum	—
674	primed for painting	zinc	USP
675	dichromate sealed	zinc	—
676	flat black coated	zinc	US19
677	bright brass plated	zinc	US3
678	satin brass plated	zinc	US4
679	bright bronze plated	zinc	US9
680	satin bronze plated	zinc	US10
681	bright chromium plated	zinc	US26
682	satin chromium plated	zinc	US26D
683	oxidized satin brass plated, oil rubbed	zinc	—
684	black chrome, bright	brass, bronze	—
685	black chrome, satin	brass, bronze	—
686	black chrome, bright	steel	—
687	black chrome, satin	steel	—
688	satin aluminum, gold anodized	aluminum	US4
689	aluminum plated	any	US28
690	dark bronze painted	any	US20
691	light bronze painted	any	US10
692	tan painted	any	—
693	black painted	any	—
694	medium bronze painted	any	—
695	dark bronze painted	any	—
696	satin brass painted	any	US4
697	bright brass plated	plastic	US3

New No.	Description	Material	Old No.
698	satin brass plated	plastic	US4
699	satin bronze plated	plastic	US10
700	bright chromium plated	plastic	US26
701	satin chromium plated	plastic	US26D
702	satin chromium plated	aluminum	US26D
703	oxidized satin bronze plated, oil rubbed	aluminum	US10B
704	oxidized satin bronze plated, oil rubbed	zinc	US10B

Courtesy of Builders Hardware Manufacturers Assn., Inc.

Locksmith Suppliers, Profiles/Addresses

Accredited Lock Supply Co.
1161 Paterson Plank Rd.
Secaucus, NJ 07094
800/652-2835
Fax: 201/865-5031
email: mail@lock-it.com
website: http://www.acclock.com
Complete line of locks and supplies; some access control and other electronic security supplies. 45,000-square-foot warehouse. Background: Founded in 1974 as a locksmith shop by Rudy Weaver and his son, Ron.

Acme Wholesale Distributors, Inc.
P. O. Drawer 13748
New Orleans, LA 70185
800/788-2263
Fax: 504/837-7321
Full line distributor of most major lock lines, supplies, safes, and access control devices. Has branch distribution centers in New Orleans, Houston, San Antonio, and Ft. Worth. Background: Founded in the early 1970s. Joined the LSDA Group in 1985.

American Lock & Supply, Inc.
4411 E. LaPalma Ave.
Anaheim, CA 92807
800/844-8545
714/996-0791
Fax: 714/579-3508
Full line distributor of most major lock lines. Over $20 million inventory at 11 locations throughout the U.S.

Aristo Sales Company, Inc.
27-24 Jackson Ave.
Long Island City, NY 11101
800/221-1322;
718/361-1040;
Fax: 718/937-5794
Supplier of automotive locks, alarms, safes, and supplies.

Arius
8259 Exchange Dr.
Orlando, FL 32809-7687
407/850-2625
800/292-7487
Fax: 407/850-2616
Wide range of electronic security products, including CCTVs, access control, and burglar/fire alarms.

Armstrong's Lock & Supply, Inc.
1440 Dutch Valley Place, NE
Atlanta, GA 30324
800/726-3332
404/875-0136
Fax: 404/888-0834
Full line distributor of locks, safes, supplies, and electronic security devices. Carries over 13,000 different products from over 250 manufacturers. Branches in Miami; Tampa; Norfolk, VA; and Jacksonville, FL.

Clark Security Products
4775 Viewridge Ave.
San Diego, CA 92123
Over 30,000 products from over 250 manufacturers. Branches in Chicago, Houston, Salt Lake City, San Diego, Denver, Phoenix, Sacramento, Seattle, Washington DC, Los Angeles, and New England. Background: Began in 1950 as the Key Department of the Wilson F. Clark Wholesale Hardware Co.

Fried Brothers, Inc.
467 N. 7th St.
Philadelphia, PA 19123
800/523-2924
Fax: 215/523-1255
Products from over 120 different manufacturers. Background: Established in 1922.

KingAlarm
35 Green St.
Hackensack, NJ 07601
800/526-0162
201/488-4990
Fax: 201/342-7097
Distributor of burglar/fire alarm systems, CCTV equipment, access control equipment, telephone systems, intercoms and related accessories and supplies. Stocks over 9000 products. Warehouse sales centers located in Elmsford, NY; Toms River, NJ; Kenilworth, NJ; Bellmawr, NJ; Anaheim, CA; Doraville, GA; Farmington Hills, MI; and Deerfield Beach, FL.

Maziuk & Company, Inc.
1251 W. Genesee St.
Syracuse, NY 13204
800/777-5945
315/474-3959
Fax: 315/472-3111
Stocks wide range of locks and supplies from over 135 manufacturers. Has a 5300-square-foot branch office and warehouse in the Buffalo, NY area. Background: Established in 1943.

McDonald Dash Locksmith Supply, Inc.
5767 East Shelby Dr.
P. O. Box 752506-2506
Memphis, TN 38175
901/797-8000
800/238-7541
Fax: 901/366-0005
Distributor of over 15,000 locks, tools, supplies, and related security products from 150 manufacturers. Background: Established in 1945.

M. Taylor Inc.
5635-45 Tulip St.
Philadelphia, PA 19124
800/233-3355
215/288-5588
Fax: 215/288-2511
Over 11,000 items from over 130 manufacturers. Background: Established in 1912.

Security Lock Distributors
59 Wexford St.
P. O. Box 815
Needham Heights, MA 02194
800/847-5625
617/444-1155
Fax: 800/878-6400
Sells electronic and mechanical locking devices.

Wilco Supply
5960 Telegraph Ave.
Oakland, CA 94609
800/745-5450
510/652-8522
Fax: 510/653-5397
Over 32,000 different locks, tools, supplies, and related products. 52 employees. Background: Founded in 1951.

Wm. B. Allen Supply Co., Inc.
Allen Square
301 North Rampart St.
New Orleans, LA 70112-3106
800/535-9593
504/525-8222
Fax: 800/444-1726
Sells burglar/fire alarm systems, equipment, and supplies. Stocks over 72,000 different products from more than 300 manufacturers. Background: Established in 1940.

Zipf Lock Co.
830 Harmon Ave.
Columbus, OH 43223
800/848-1577
614/228-3507
Fax: 800/228-6320
Stocks over 16,000 different locks, lock parts, tools, and supplies. Background: Established in 1908.

Security Organizations

American Society for Industrial Security
(ASIS)
1655 N. Ft. Meyer Dr., Suite 1200
Arlington, VA 22209

Associated Locksmiths of America, Inc.
(ALOA)
3003 Live Oak St.
Dallas, TX 75204

Associated Locksmiths of Ireland
P. O. Box 3599
Dublin 4
Ireland

Association of Ontario Locksmiths
2220 Midland Ave., Unit 106
Scarsborough, ON
Canada M1P 3E6

Belgium Locksmith Federation (BLF)
c/o Brussels Chamber of Commerce &
Industry
Industry Ave., Louise 500
Brussels B1050
Belgium

British Columbia Locksmith Association
349 W. Georgia St.
P.O. Box 2507
Vancouver, BC
Canada V6B 3W7

Builders Hardware Manufacturers
Association, Inc.
355 Lexington Ave., 17th Floor
New York, NY 10017

Canadian Alarm and Security Association
610 Alden Rd., Suite 201
Markham, ON
Canada L3R 9Z1

Door and Hardware Institute (DHI)
14170 Newbrook Dr.
Chantilly, VA 22021-0750

Institutional Locksmiths' Association
P.O. Box 810
Accokeek, MD 20607

International Association of Home Safety and
  Security Professionals (IAHSSP)
  P.O. Box 2044-P
  Erie, PA 16512-2044
  email: webmaster@iahssp.org
  website: http://www.iahssp.org

Locksmiths Guild of Australia, Inc.
  P.O. Box 82
  Ramsgate, NSW 2217
  Australia

Master Locksmiths Association
  Units 4/5, The Business Park
  Woodford Halse
  Daventry, Northants NN116PZ
  England

Master Locksmiths Association
  of Australia Ltd.
  P.O. Box 1195
  South Melbourne, Vic. 3205
  Australia

National Alarm Association of America
  P.O. Box 3409
  Dayton, OH 45401

National Burglar & Fire Alarm Association
  7101 Wisconsin Ave., Suite 901
  Bethesda, MD 20814-4805

National Locksmith Automobile Association
  1533 Burgundy Parkway
  Streamwood, IL 60107

National Locksmith Suppliers Association
  1900 Arch St.
  Philadelphia, PA 19103-1498

National Safeman's Organization (NSO)
  1533 Burgundy Parkway
  Streamwood, IL 60107

Professional Locksmith Association of Alberta
  Box 68060 Bonnie Doon PO
  Edmonton, AB
  Canada T6C 4N6

Safe & Vault Technician's Association
  (SAVTA)
  5083 Danville Rd.
  Nicholasville, KY 40356

Security Industry Association
  1801 K St., NW, Suite 1203L
  Washington, DC 20006-1301

Other Locksmithing-Related Internet Sites

ABLOY Home Page. ABLOY makes a wide range of advanced locking systems with large masterkeying possibilities. Brand names include ABLOY, AVA, and Primo. http://www.abloy.com/

Amateur Locksmith Discussion/Mailing List, publicly accessible. list-server@pylon.pillar.com (To join, write "JOIN LOCKSMITH" in the body of the message.)

Archive of GIF and JPEG images of picks. ftp://ftp.vigra.com/steve/locks/

Arrow Architectural Hardware website. A leading manufacturer of locking hardware, door controls, and key systems; a part of the ASSA ABLOY group. http://www.arrowlock.com

Bosch Power Tools website. http://www.npschtools.com

ClearStar. Online discussion forums for security professionals. Includes public areas and password-protected "professionals only" areas. http://www.clearstar.com/public/pubboard. htm

Home Systems Installer Magazine. News, trends, and installation advice. Includes a searchable product database. http://www.gohomesystems.com

ILCO UNICAN website. A world leader in the manufacture and sale of key blanks, key machines, mechanical pushbutton locks, and electronic access controls. http://www.ilcounican.com/

Locksmithing FAQ. http://www.indra.com/archives/ altlocksmithing

Locksmithing World. Information about locks, keys, safes, alarms, and access control systems. Includes links to related websites. http://www.locksmithing.com

Lostsoft website. Creators of commercial and custom software for locksmiths. http://www.locksoft.com/

MAG Security Online. Catalog of MAG Security's door reinforcers, strike plates, and other products. Includes dealer/retailer list and trade show listings. http://www.magsecurity.com/

Medeco High Security Locks website. http://www.medeco.com/sitenav.htm

Milwaukee Electric Tool website. A major manufacturer of drills and other electric tools for professionals. http://www.mil-electric-tool.com/

MIT Guide to Picking Locks. (Not affiliated with or endorsed by the Massachusetts Institute of Technology.) http://www.lysator.liu.se/mit-guide/mitguide.html

Steve Haehnichen's pick images. Useful guides for making your own picks. ftp://ftp.vigra.com/steve/locks/

Mul-T-Lock The Art of Locking. Mul-T-Lock is a worldwide leader in developing, manufacturing, and marketing high-security products for institutional, commercial, industrial, and residential applications. http://www.mul-t-lock.co.il/

Porter-Cable website. http://www.portercable.com

Ryobi North America Home Page. Powertool forum, tech support, and online catalog. http://www.ryobi.com

SDM Magazine Online. Electronic security, safety, and home systems information. http://www.sdmmag.com

Security Magazine on the Web. http://www.secmag.com/

GLOSSARY

Many locksmithing terms have popular synonyms and variant spellings. The entries in this glossary are based on a survey of locksmithing trade journals, reference books, technical manuals, supply catalogs, and trade association glossaries. When a main entry has two or more commonly used synonyms or spellings, they're listed in order of popularity. When two or more are equally popular, those are listed in order of age (from oldest usage to newest). In cases where two or more common locksmithing terms are spelled alike but have different meanings, each term is listed in a separate entry.

160 prep A standard door preparation that consists of a $2\frac{1}{8}$-inch cross-bore, a $2\frac{3}{8}$-inch backset, and a 1-inch edge-bore with a mortise 1-inch wide and $2\frac{1}{4}$-inch high.

161 prep A standard door preparation that consists of a $2\frac{1}{8}$-inch cross-bore, a $2\frac{3}{4}$-inch backset, and a 1-inch edge-bore with a mortise $1\frac{1}{8}$-inch wide and $2\frac{1}{4}$-inch high.

ac Alternating current. Electrical current that reverses its direction of flow at regular intervals. For practical purposes, alternating current is the type of electricity that flows throughout a person's house and is accessed by the use of wall sockets.

access code The symbolic data, usually in the form of numbers or letters, that allows entry into an access controlled area without prompting an alarm condition.

access control Procedures and devices designed to control or monitor entry into a protected area. Many times access control is used to refer to electronic and electromechanical devices that control or monitor access.

Ace lock A term sometimes used to refer to any tubular key lock. The term is more properly used to refer to the Chicago Ace Lock, the first brand name for a tubular key lock.

actuator A device, usually connected to a cylinder, which, when activated, causes a lock mechanism to operate.

adjustable mortise cylinder Any mortise cylinder whose length can be adjusted for a better fit in doors of varying thickness.

AFTE Association of Firearm and Toolmark Examiners.

AHC Architectural Hardware Consultant, as certified by the Door and Hardware Institute.

all-section key blank The key section that enters all keyways of a multiplex key system.

ALOA Associated Locksmiths of America.

Americans with Disabilities Act. A congressional act passed to ensure the rights of persons with various types of disabilities. Part of the act requires that buildings provide easy access to the physically disabled.

ampere (or amp) A unit of electrical current.

angularly bitted key A key that has cuts made into the blade at various degrees of rotation from the perpendicular.

annunciator A device, often used in an alarm system, that flashes lights, makes noises, or otherwise attracts attention.

ANSI American National Standards Institute.

anti-passback A feature in some electronic access control systems designed to make it difficult for a person who has just gained entry into a controlled area to allow another person to also use the card to gain entry.

antipick latch A spring latch fitted with a parallel bar that is depressed by the strike when the door is closed. When the bar is depressed it prevents the latch from responding to external pressure from lock picking tools.

architectural hardware Hardware used in building construction, especially that used in connection with doors.

armored front A plate covering the bolts or set screws holding a cylinder to its lock. These bolts are normally accessible when the door is ajar.

ASIS American Society for Industrial Security.

associated change key A change key that is related directly to particular master key(s) through the use of constant cuts.

associated master key A master key that has particular change keys related directly to its combination through the use of constant cuts.

ASTM American Society for Testing and Materials.

audit trail A record of each entry and exit within an access controlled area.

automatic deadbolt A deadbolt designed to extend itself fully when the door is closed.

automatic flush bolt A flush bolt designed to extend itself when both leaves of the pair of doors are in the closed position.

auxiliary code A secondary or temporary access code.

auxiliary lock Any lock installed in addition to the primary lockset.

back plate A thin piece of metal, usually with a concave portion, used with machine screws to fasten certain types of cylinders to a door.

backset The horizontal distance from the edge of a door to the center of an installed lock cylinder, keyhole, or knob hub. On locks with rabbeted fronts, it is measured from the upper step at the center of the lock face.

ball bearing 1. A metal ball used in the pin stack to accomplish some types of hotel or construction keying. 2. A ball, usually made of steel, used by some lock manufacturers as the bottom element in the pin stack in one or more pin chambers. 3. Any metal ball used as a tumbler's primary component.

ball locking A method of locking a padlock shackle into its case using ball bearing(s) as the bolt(s).

barrel key A key with a bit projecting from a hollow cylindrical shank. The hollow fits over a pin in a lock keyway and helps keep the key aligned. The key is also known as a hollow post key or pipe key.

bell crank or belcrank A flat metal plate attached to connecting rods within the walls of an automobile's doors. The bell crank converts movement from vertical to horizontal and vice versa.

bell key A key whose cuts are in the form of wavy grooves milled into the flat sides of the key blade. The grooves usually run the entire length of the blade.

bezel A threaded collar commonly used to secure certain cylinder or lock assemblies.

BHMA Builders Hardware Manufacturers Association.

bible That portion of the cylinder shell normally housing the pin chambers, especially those of key-in-knob cylinders or certain rim cylinders.

bicentric cylinder A cylinder that has two independent plugs, usually with different keyways. Both plugs are operable from the same face of the cylinder. It is designed for use in extensive master key systems.

bi-directional cylinder A cylinder that can be operated in a clockwise and counterclockwise direction with a single key.

binary cut key A key whose combination only allows for two possibilities in each bitting position: cut/no cut.

binary type cylinder or lock A cylinder or lock whose combination only allows for two bitting possibilities in each bitting position.

bit 1. The part of the key that serves as the blade, usually for use in a warded or lever tumbler lock. 2. To cut a key.

bit key or bit-key A key with a bit projecting from a solid cylindrical shank. The key is sometimes referred to as a "skeleton key." A bit key is used to operate a bit key lock.

bit key lock A lock operated by a bit key.

bitting 1. The number(s) representing the dimensions of the key cut(s). 2. The actual cut(s) or combination of a key.

bitting depth The depth of a cut that is made into the blade of a key.

bitting list A listing of all the key combinations used within a system. The combinations are usually arranged in order of the blind code, direct code, and/or key symbol.

bitting position The location of a key cut.

blade The portion of a key that contains the cuts and/or milling.

blank See key blank. Uncut key.

blind code A designation, unrelated to the bitting, assigned to a particular key combination for future reference when additional keys or cylinders are needed.

block master key (BM) The one pin master key for all combinations listed as a block in the standard progression format.

bored lock Any lock that is installed by cross-boring two holes in a door; one hole in the face of the door, and the other through the edge of the door. Common bored locks include deadbolt locks and key-in-knob locks.

boring jig A tool temporarily mounted to a door to act as a template and drill guide for installing hardware.

bottom of blade The portion of the blade opposite the cut edge of a single-bitted key.

bottom pin A tumbler, usually cylindrical (also may be conical, ball-shaped, or chisel-pointed), that makes contact with the key.

bow The portion of the key that serves as a grip or handle.

bow stop A type of stop located near the key bow.

box strike A strike equipped to line the bolt cavity for both aesthetic and protective purposes.

break-away padlock or frangible padlock A padlock with a shackle that's designed to be easily broken off. Break-away padlocks are commonly used on fire-safety equipment and on other items that must be readily accessible.

broach 1. A tool used to cut the keyway into the cylinder plug. 2. To cut the keyway into a cylinder plug with a broach.

building master key A master key that operates all or most masterkeyed locks in a given building.

burglar resistant A broad term used to describe locks, doors, or windows designed to resist attack by prowlers and thieves for a limited time.

bypass key The key that operates a key override cylinder.

cam A flat actuator or locking bolt attached to the rear of a cylinder perpendicular to its plug and rotated by the key.

cam 1. A lock or cylinder component that transfers the rotational motion of a key or cylinder plug to the bolt mechanism of a lock. 2. The bolt of a cam lock.

cam lock A complete locking assembly in the form of a cylinder whose cam is the actual locking bolt.

cap 1. A spring cover for a single-pin chamber. 2. A part that can serve as a plug retainer and/or a holder for the tailpiece. 3. To install a cap.

capping block A holding fixture for certain interchangeable cores that aids in the installation of the caps.

case The housing or body of a lock.

case (of a cylinder) See shell.

case (of a lock) The box that houses the lock-operating mechanism.

case ward 1. A ward directly attached to or projecting from a lock case. 2. A ward or obstruction integral to the case of a warded lock.

central processing unit (CPU) Also called a central processor; the section in a digital computer that contains the logic and internal memory units.

chamber Any cavity in a cylinder plug and/or shell that houses the tumblers.

changeable bit key A key that can be recombined by exchanging and/or rearranging portions of its bit or blade.

change key A key that operates only one cylinder or one group of keyed-alike cylinders in a keying system.

circuit A complete path through which electricity flows to perform work.

circuit breaker A device designed to protect a circuit by automatically breaking (or opening) the circuit when current flow becomes excessive.

CK 1. Change key. 2. Control key.

clutch The part of a profile cylinder that transfers rotational motion from the inside or outside element to a common cam or actuator.

CMC Certified Management Consultant, as certified by the Institute of Management Consultants.

code A designation assigned to a particular key combination for reference when additional keys or cylinders might be needed.

code key A key cut to a specific code rather than duplicated from a pattern key. It may or may not conform to the lock manufacturer's specifications.

code original key A code key that conforms to the lock manufacturer's specifications.

combinate To set a combination in a lock, cylinder, or key.

combination The group of numbers that represent the bitting of a key and/or the tumblers of a lock or cylinder.

combination lock A lock that may or may not be operated with a key, but can be operated by inserting a combination of numbers, letters, or other symbols by rotating a dial or by pushing buttons.

combination wafer A type of disc tumbler used in certain binary type disc tumbler key-in-knob locks. Its presence requires that a cut be made in that position of the operating key(s).

compensate drivers To select longer or shorter top pins, depending on the length of the rest of the pin stack, in order to achieve a uniform pin stack height.

complementary keyway Usually a disc tumbler keyway used in master keying. It accepts keys of different sections whose blades contact different bearing surfaces of the tumblers.

complex circuit A combination of series and parallel circuits.

composite keyway A keyway that has been enlarged to accept more than one key section, often key sections of more than one manufacturer.

concealed shell cylinder A specially constructed (usually mortise) cylinder. Only the plug face is visible when the lock trim is in place.

conductor Material, such as copper wire, used to direct current flow.

connecting bar A flat bar attached to the rear of the plug in a rim lock to operate the locking bar mechanism.

constant cut Any bitting(s) that are identical in corresponding positions from one key to another in a keying system. They usually serve to group these keys together within a given level of keying, and/or link them with keys of other levels.

construction breakout key A key used by some manufacturers to render all construction master keys permanently inoperative.

construction core An interchangeable or removable core designed for use during the construction phase of a building. The cores are normally keyed alike and, upon completion of construction, they are to be replaced by the permanent system's cores.

construction master key (CMK) A key normally used by construction personnel for a temporary period during building construction. It may be rendered permanently inoperative without disassembling the cylinder.

construction master keyed Of or pertaining to a cylinder that is operated temporarily by a construction master key.

control cut Any bitting that operates the retaining device of an interchangeable or removable core.

control key 1. A key whose only purpose is to remove and/or install an interchangeable or removable core. 2. A bypass key used to operate and/or reset some combination type locks. 3. A key that allows disassembly of some removable cylinder locks.

control lug The part of an interchangeable or removable core retaining device that locks the core into its housing.

control sleeve The part of an interchangeable core retaining device surrounding the plug.

controlled cross keying A condition in which two or more different keys of the same level of keying and under the same higher level key(s) operate one cylinder by design. For example, XAA1 can be operated by AA2 but not by AB1. This condition could severely limit the security of the cylinder and the maximum expansion of the system when more than a few of these different keys operate a cylinder, or when more than a few differently cross-keyed cylinders per system are required.

convenience key A key that has the same cuts on two sides of its blade, and can operate the lock with either side of the blade facing up in the keyway. A convenience key has cuts on two sides for convenience only, because only one side of the key manipulates the tumblers and other parts involved in locking and unlocking.

core A complete unit, often with a figure-8 shape, which usually consists of the plug, shell, tumblers, springs, plug retainer, and spring cover(s). It is primarily used in removable and interchangeable core cylinders and locks.

corrugated key A key with pressed longitudinal corrugations in its shank to correspond to a compatibly shaped keyway.

CPL Certified Professional Locksmith (as certified by Associated Locksmiths of America).

CPO Certified Protection Officer, as certified by the International Foundation for Protection Officers.

CPP Certified Protection Professional, as certified by American Society for Industrial Security.

crash bar See panic bar.

cross-bore A hole drilled into the face of a door where a bored or interconnected lockset is to be installed.

cross keying The deliberate process of combinating a cylinder (usually in a master key system) to two or more different keys that would not normally be expected to operate together. See also controlled cross keying and uncontrolled cross keying.

CSI Construction Specifiers Institute.

current The flow of electricity. Current is measured in amperes.

cut An indentation, notch, or cutout made in a key blank in order to make it operate a lock. See bitting.

cut To make cuts into a key blade.

cut angle A measurement, usually expressed in degrees, for the angle between the two sides of a key cut.

cut edge A key that has been bitted or combinated.

cut root The bottom of a key cut.

cut root shape The shape of the bottom of a key cut. It might have a flat or radius of a specific dimension, or be a perfect V.

cutter The part of a key machine that makes the cuts into the key blank.

cylinder A complete operating unit that usually consists of the plug, shell, tumblers, springs, plug retainer, a cam/tailpiece, or other actuating device, and all other necessary operating parts.

cylinder blank A dummy cylinder that has a solid face and no operating parts.

cylinder clip A spring steel device used to secure some types of cylinders.

cylinder collar A plate or ring installed under the head of a cylinder to improve appearance and/or security.

cylinder guard A protective cylinder mounting device.

cylinder key A broad generic term including virtually all pin and disc tumbler keys.

cylindrical lock See key-in-knob lock.

cylindrical lockset A bored lockset whose latch or bolt locking mechanism is contained in the portion installed through the cross-bore.

dc Direct current. Electric current that flows in one direction. For practical purposes, direct current is the type of electricity obtained from batteries.

deadbolt or dead bolt A lock bolt, usually rectangular, that has no spring action when in the locked position, and that becomes locked against end pressure when fully projected.

deadbolt lock or deadbolt, tubular deadbolt, tubular dead lock, cylindrical deadbolt A lock that projects a deadbolt.

deadlatch A lock with a beveled latchbolt that can be automatically or manually locked against end pressure when projected.

declining step key A key whose cuts are progressively deeper from bow to tip.

decode To determine a key combination by physical measurement of a key and/or cylinder parts.

degree of rotation A specification for the angle at which a cut is made into a key blade as referenced from the perpendicular.

department master key A master key that operates all or most masterkeyed locks of a given department.

depth key set A set of keys used to make a code original key on a key duplicating machine to a lock manufacturer's given set of key bitting specifications. Each key is cut with the correct spacing to one depth only in all bitting positions, with one key for each depth.

derived series A series of blind codes and bittings that are directly related to those of another bitting list.

DHI Door and Hardware Institute.

dimple A key cut in a dimple key.

dimple key A key that has cuts drilled or milled into its blade surfaces. The cuts normally do not change the blade silhouette.

direct code A designation assigned to a particular key that includes the actual combination of the key.

disc tumbler or wafer tumbler, disc-tumbler, disk tumbler 1. A flat tumbler that must be drawn into the cylinder plug by the proper key so that none of its extremities extends into the shell. 2. A flat, usually rectangular tumbler with a gate that must be aligned with a sidebar by the proper key.

display key A special change key in a hotel master key system that will allow access to one designated guest room, even if the lock is in the shut-out mode. It might also act as a shut-out key for that room.

dmm Digital multimeter. A device used to measure current, resistance, and voltage.

double acting hinge A hinge that allows movement of a door in either direction from the closed position.

double bitted key A key bitted on two opposite surfaces.

double pin To place more than one master pin in a single pin chamber.

drive-in latch A cylindrical latch with a cylindrical knurled ring around its face designed to grip the edge bore of a door. Drive-in latches are commonly used with deadbolt locks on metal doors.

driver or top pin, upper pin A cylindrical tumbler, usually flat on both ends, that is installed directly under the spring in the pin stack.

driver spring A spring placed on top of the pin stack to exert pressure on the pin tumblers.

drop A pivoting or swinging dust cover.

dummy cylinder 1. A nonfunctional facsimile of a rim or mortise cylinder used for appearance only, usually to conceal a cylinder hole. 2. A nonlocking device that looks like a cylinder, and is used to cover up a cylinder hole.

duplicate key Any key reproduced from a pattern key.

dust cover A device designed to prevent foreign matter from entering a mechanism through the keyway.

dustproof cylinder A cylinder designed to prevent foreign matter from entering either end of the keyway.

edge-bore A hole drilled into the edge of a door where a bored or interconnected lockset is to be installed.

effective plug diameter The dimension obtained by adding the root depth of a key cut to the length of its corresponding bottom pin, which establishes a perfect shear line. This will not necessarily be the same as the actual plug diameter.

ejector hole A hole found on the bottom of certain interchangeable cores under each pin chamber. It provides a path for the ejector pin.

ejector pin A tool used to drive all the elements of a pin chamber out of certain interchangeable cores.

electric strike An electrically controlled solenoid and mechanical latching device.

electrified lockset A lock which is controlled electrically.

electromagnetic lock A locking device that uses magnetism to keep it in a locked position.

emergency key The key that operates a privacy function lockset.

emergency master key A special master key that usually operates all guest room locks in a hotel master key system at all times, even in the shut-out mode. This key may also act as a shut-out key.

emf Electromotive force (also called voltage). The force needed to cause current to flow within a circuit.

EMK Emergency master key.

ENG Symbol for engineer's key.

escutcheon A surface-mounted trim that enhances the appearance and/or security of a lock installation.

extractor key A tool that normally removes a portion of a two-piece key or blocking device from a keyway.

face plate A mortise lock cover plate exposed in the edge of the door.

factory original key The cut key furnished by the lock manufacturer for a lock or cylinder.

fail safe lock A lock that automatically unlocks during a power failure.

fail secure lock A lock that automatically locks during a power failure.

fence A projection on a lock bolt that prevents movement of the bolt unless it can enter gates of properly aligned tumblers.

finish A material, coloring and/or texturing specification.

fireman's key A key used to override normal operation of elevators, bringing them to the ground floor.

first generation duplicate A key that was duplicated using a factory original key or a code original key as a pattern.

first key Any key produced without the use of a pattern key.

five-column progression A process wherein key bittings are obtained by using the cut possibilities in five columns of the key bitting array.

five-pin master key A master key for all combinations obtained by progressing five bitting positions.

flexible head mortise cylinder An adjustable mortise cylinder that can be extended against spring pressure to a slightly longer length.

floor master key A master key that operates all or most master keyed locks on a particular floor of a building.

following tool See plug follower.

four-column progression A process wherein key bittings are obtained by using the cut possibilities in four columns of the key bitting array.

four-pin master key A master key for all combinations obtained by progressing four bitting positions.

frangible shackle A padlock shackle designed to be broken easily.

gate A notch cut into the edge of a tumbler to accept a fence or side-bar.

graduated drivers A set of top pins of different lengths. Usage is based on the height of the rest of the pin stack, in order to achieve a uniform pin stack height.

grand master key (GMK) The key that operates two or more separate groups of locks, which are each operated by a different master key.

grand master key system A master key system that has exactly three levels of keying.

grand master keyed Of or pertaining to a lock or cylinder that is or is to be keyed into a grand master key system.

great grand master key (GGMK) The key that operates two or more separate groups of locks, which are each operated by a different grand master key.

great grand master key system A master key system that has exactly four levels of keying.

great grand master keyed Of or pertaining to a lock or cylinder that is or is to be keyed into a great grand master key system.

great great grand master key (GGGMK) The key that operates two or more separate groups of locks, which are each operated by different great grand master keys.

great great grand master key system A master key system that has five or more levels of keying.

great great grand master keyed Of or pertaining to a lock or cylinder which is or is to be keyed into a great great grand master key system.

ground An electrical connection to a metallic object that is either buried in the earth or is connected to a metallic object buried in the earth.

guard key A key that must be used in conjunction with a renter's key to unlock a safe deposit lock. It is usually the same for every lock within an installation.

guest key A key in a hotel master key system that is normally used to unlock only the one guest room for which it was intended, but will not operate the lock in the shut-out mode.

guide That part of a key machine that follows the cuts of a pattern key or template during duplication.

hardware schedule A listing of the door hardware used on a particular job. It includes the types of hardware, manufacturers, locations, finishes, and sizes. It should include a keying schedule specifying how each locking device is to be keyed.

hasp A hinged metal strap designed to be passed over a staple and secured in place.

heel & toe locking Refers to a padlock that has locking dogs at both the heel and toe of the shackle.

heel (of a padlock shackle) The part of a padlock shackle which is retained in the case.

high-security cylinder A cylinder that offers a greater degree of resistance to any or all of the following: picking, impressioning, key duplication, drilling, or other forms of forcible entry.

high-security key A key for a high-security cylinder.

hold open cylinder A cylinder provided with a special cam that will hold a latch bolt in the retracted position when so set by the key.

holding fixture   A device that holds cylinder plugs, cylinders, housings, and/or cores to facilitate the installation of tumblers, springs and/or spring covers.

hollow driver   A top pin hollowed out on one end to receive the spring, typically used in cylinders with extremely limited clearance in the pin chambers.

horizontal group master key (HGM)   The two-pin master key for all combinations listed in all blocks in a line across the page in the standard progression format.

housekeeper's key (HKP)   A selective master key in a hotel master key system that may operate all guest and linen rooms and other housekeeping areas.

housing   That part of a locking device designed to hold a core.

impression   1. The mark made by a tumbler on its key cut. 2. To fit a key by the impression technique.

IAHSSP   International Association of Home Safety and Security Professionals.

impression technique   A means of fitting a key directly to a locked cylinder by manipulating a blank in the keyway and cutting the blank where the tumblers have made marks.

incidental master key   A key cut to an unplanned shearline created when the cylinder is combinated to the top master key and a change key.

increment   A usually uniform increase or decrease in the successive depths of a key cut, which must be matched by a corresponding change in the tumblers.

indicator   A device that provides visual evidence that a deadbolt is extended or that a lock is in the shut-out mode.

individual key   An operating key for a lock or cylinder that is not part of a keying system.

insulator   Materials such as rubber and plastics that provide resistance to current flow. They are used to cover conductors and electrical devices to prevent unwanted current flow.

interchangeable core (IC)   A key removable core that can be used in all or most of the core manufacturer's product line. No tools other than the control key are required for removal of the core.

interlocking pin tumbler   A type of pin tumbler that is designed to be linked together with all other tumblers in its chamber when the cylinder plug is in the locked position.

International Association of Home Safety and Security Professionals A trade association.

jamb The vertical components of a door frame.

jimmy proof To provide a lock with a bolt which interlocks with its strike.

jumbo cylinder A rim or mortise cylinder 1½ inches in diameter.

k Symbol for "keys" used after a numerical designation of the quantity of the keys requested to be supplied with the cylinders: 1k, 2k, 3k, etc. It is usually found in hardware/keying schedules.

KA Keyed alike. This symbol indicates cylinders that are to be operated by the same key(s)—for example: KA1, KA2, etc. KA/2, KA/3, etc. is the symbol used to indicate the quantity of locks or cylinders in keyed alike groups. These groups are usually formed from a larger quantity.

KBA Key bitting array.

KD Keyed different.

keeper See strike plate.

key A properly combined device that is, or most closely resembles, the device specifically intended by the lock manufacturer to operate the corresponding lock.

key bitting array A matrix (graphic) of all possible bittings for change keys and master keys as related to the top master key.

key bitting punch A manually operated device that stamps or punches the cuts into the key blade, rather than grinding or milling them.

key bitting specifications The technical data required to bit a given key blank or family of key blanks to the lock manufacturer's dimensions.

key blank Any material manufactured to the proper size and configuration that allows its entry into the keyway of a specific locking device. A key blank has not yet been combined or cut.

key changeable Of or pertaining to a lock or cylinder that can be recombinated without disassembly, by use of a key. The use of a tool might also be required.

key coding machine A key machine designed for the production of code keys. It might or might not also serve as a duplicating machine.

key control 1. Any method or procedure that limits unauthorized acquisition of a key and/or controls distribution of authorized keys. 2. A systematic organization of keys and key records.

key cut(s)　The portion of the key blade that remains after being cut and that aligns the tumbler(s).

key cut profile　The shape of a key cut, including the cut angle and the cut root shape.

key duplicating machine　A key machine that is designed to make copies from a pattern key.

key gauge　A device (usually flat) with a cutaway portion indexed with a given set of depth or spacing specifications. Used to help determine the combination of a key.

key-in-knob cylinder　A cylinder used in a key-in-knob lock.

key-in-knob lock or cylindrical lock　A lock that uses one or two knobs, and has a lock cylinder in one or both knobs.

key interchange　An undesirable condition, usually in a master key system, whereby a key unintentionally operates a cylinder or lock.

key machine　Any machine designed to cut keys.

key manipulation　Manipulation of an incorrect key in order to operate a lock or cylinder.

key milling　The grooves machined into the length of the key blade to allow its entry into the keyway.

key override　A provision allowing interruption or circumvention of normal operation of a combination lock or electrical device.

key override cylinder　A lock cylinder installed in a device to provide a key override function.

key pull position　Any position of the cylinder plug at which the key can be removed.

key records　Records that typically include some or all of the following: bitting list, key bitting array, key system schematic, end user, number of keys/cylinders issued, names of persons to whom keys were issued, hardware/keying schedule.

key retaining　1. Of or pertaining to a lock that must be locked before its key can be removed. 2. Of or pertaining to a cylinder or lock that may prevent removal of a key without the use of an additional key and/or tool.

key section　The exact cross-sectional configuration of a key blade as viewed from the bow toward the tip.

keyswitch　A switch that is operated with a key.

key system schematic　A drawing with blocks utilizing keying symbols, usually illustrating the hierarchy of all keys within a master key system. It indicates the structure and total expansion of the system.

key trap core/cylinder A special core or cylinder designed to capture any key to which it is combinated, once that key is inserted and turned slightly.

keyed 1. Combinated. 2. Having provision for operation by key.

keyed alike Of or pertaining to two or more locks or cylinders that have the same combination. They may or may not be part of a keying system.

keyed random Of or pertaining to a cylinder or group of cylinders selected from a limited inventory of different key changes. Duplicate bittings may occur.

keying Any specification for how a cylinder or group of cylinders are combinated in order to control access.

keying conference A meeting of the end user and the keying system supplier at which the keying and levels of keying, including future expansion, are determined and specified.

keying kit A compartmented container that holds an assortment of tumblers, springs, and/or other parts.

keying schedule A detailed specification of the keying system listing how all cylinders are to be keyed and the quantities, markings, and shipping instructions of all keys and/or other parts.

keying symbol A designation used for a lock or cylinder combination in the standard key coding system: AA1, XAA1, X1X, etc.

keyway 1. The opening in a lock or cylinder shaped to accept a key bit or blade of a proper configuration. 2. The exact cross-sectional configuration of a keyway as viewed from the front. It is not necessarily the same as the key section.

keyway unit The plug of certain binary type disc tumbler key-in-knob locks.

KR 1. Keyed random. 2. Key retaining.

KWY Keyway.

layout tray A compartmented container used to organize cylinder parts during keying or servicing.

lazy cam/tailpiece A cam or tailpiece designed to remain stationary while the cylinder plug is partially rotated (or vice versa).

LCD Liquid crystal display.

levels of keying The divisions of a master key system into hierarchies of access, as shown in the table below. Note that the standard key coding system has been expanded to include key symbols for systems of more than four levels of keying.

TABLE G.1

Level of keying	Key name	Abb.	Key symbol
Two-level system			
Level II	Master key	MK	AA
Level I	Change key	CK	1AA, 2AA, etc.
Three-level system			
Level III	Grand master key	GMK	A
Level II	Master key	MK	AA, AB, etc.
Level I	Change key	CK	AA1, AA2, etc.
Four-level system			
Level IV	Great grand master key	GGMK	GGMK
Level III	Grand master key	GMK	A, B, etc.
Level II	Master key	MK	AA, AB, etc.
Level I	Change key	CK	AA1, AA2, etc.
Five-level system			
Level V	Great great grand master key	GGGMK	GGGMK
Level IV	Great grand master key	GGMK	A, B, etc.
Level III	Grand master key	GMK	AA, AB, etc.
Level II	Master key	MK	AAA, AAB, etc.
Level I	Change key	CK	AAA1, AAA2, etc.
Six-level system			
Level VI	Great great grand master key	GGGMK	GGGMK
Level V	Great grand master key	GGMK	A, B, etc.
Level IV	Grand master key	GMK	AA, AB, etc.
Level III	Master key	MK	AAA, AAB, etc.
Level II	Sub-master key	SMK	AAAA, AAAB, etc.
Level I	Change key	CK	AAAA1, AAAA2, etc.

Courtesy: Master Keying Study Group of the ALOA Sponsored National Task Group for Certified Training Programs.

lever lock or key in-lever lock, lever handle lock A lock that has a lever handle.

lever tumbler A flat, spring-loaded tumbler that pivots on a post. It contains a gate that must be aligned with a fence to allow movement of the bolt.

lever tumbler lock or lever lock, lever-tumbler lock A lock that has a lever tumbler cylinder.

loading tool A tool that aids installation of cylinder components into the cylinder shell.

lock A device that incorporates a bolt, cam, shackle, or switch to secure an object—such as a door, drawer, or machine—to a closed, locked, off or on position, and that provides a restricted means of releasing the object from that position.

lock plate compressor or lock plate remover A tool designed to depress the lock plate of an automobile steering column. The tool is used when disassembling automobile steering columns.

lockout Any situation in which the normal operation of a lock or cylinder is prevented.

lockout key A key made in two pieces. One piece is trapped in the keyway by the tumblers when inserted and blocks entry of any regular key. The second piece is used to remove the first piece.

lockset A locking device complete with trim mounting hardware and strike.

locksmith A person trained to install, service, and bypass locking devices.

mA Milliampere.

MACS Maximum adjacent cut specification.

maid's master key The master key in a hotel master key system given to the maid. It operates only cylinders of the guest rooms and linen closets in the maid's designated area.

maison key system A keying system in which one or more cylinders are operated by every key (or relatively large numbers of different keys) in the system—for example, main entrances of apartment buildings operated by all individual suite keys of the building.

manipulation key Any key other than a correct key that can be variably positioned and/or manipulated in a keyway to operate a lock or cylinder.

master disc A special disc tumbler with multiple gates to receive a sidebar.

master key (MK) 1. A key that operates all the master keyed locks or cylinders in a group, with each lock or cylinder operated by its own change key. 2. To combinate a group of locks or cylinders such that each is operated by its own change key as well as by a master key for the entire group.

master key changes The number of different usable change keys available under a given master key.

master key system 1. Any keying arrangement that has two or more levels of keying. 2. A keying arrangement that has exactly two levels of keying.

masterkeyed Of or pertaining to a cylinder or group of cylinders that are combinated so that all may be operated by their own change keys and by additional keys known as master keys.

masterkeyed only Of or pertaining to a lock or cylinder that is combinated only to a master key.

master lever A lever tumbler that can align some or all other levers in its lock so that lever gates are at the fence. It is typically used in locker locks.

master pin 1. Usually a cylindrical tumbler, flat on both ends, placed between the top and bottom pin to create an additional shear line. 2. A pin tumbler with multiple gates to accept a sidebar.

master ring A tube-shaped sleeve located between the plug and shell of certain cylinders to create a second shear line. Normally the plug shear line is used for change key combinations and the shell shear line is used for master key combinations.

master ring lock/cylinder A lock or cylinder equipped with a master ring.

master wafer A ward used in certain binary type disc tumbler key-in-knob locks.

maximum adjacent cut specification The maximum allowable depths to which opposing cuts can be made without breaking through the key blade. This is typically a consideration with dimple keys.

metal oxide varister A voltage-dependent resistor.

miscut Of or pertaining to a key that has been cut incorrectly.

MOCS Maximum opposing cut specification.

mogul cylinder A very large pin tumbler cylinder whose pins, springs, key, etc., are also proportionately increased in size. It is frequently used in prison locks.

mortise An opening made in a door to receive a lock or other hardware.

mortise cylinder A threaded cylinder typically used in mortise locks of American manufacture.

MOV Metal oxide varister.

mullion A vertical center post in the frame of a pair of doors.

multi-section key blank A key section that enters more than one, but not all, keyways in a multiplex key system.

multiple gating A means of master keying by providing a tumbler with more than one gate.

multiplex key blank Any key blank that is part of a multiplex key system.

multiplex key system 1. A series of different key sections that may be used to expand a master key system by repeating bittings on additional key sections. The keys of one section will not enter the keyway of another key section. This type of system always includes another key section which will enter more than one, or all of the keyways. 2. A keying system that uses such keyways and key sections.

multitester A device designed to measure current, resistance, and voltage. The VOM and the DMM are two types of multitesters.

mushroom pin A pin tumbler, usually a top pin, that resembles a mushroom. It is typically used to increase pick resistance.

NC (or N/C) Normally closed.

NCK No change key. This symbol is primarily used in hardware schedules.

negative locking Locking achieved solely by spring pressure or gravity, which prevents a key cut too deeply from operating a lock cylinder.

nickel-cadmium A long-life rechargeable battery or cell oftentimes used as a backup power supply.

night latch An auxiliary rim lock with a spring latchbolt.

NMK Not master keyed. This keying symbol is suffixed in parentheses to the regular key symbol. It indicates that the cylinder is not to be operated by the master key(s) specified in the regular key symbol—for example: AB6(NMK).

NO (or N/O) Normally open.

nonkey-retaining (NKR) Of or pertaining to a lock whose key can be removed in both the locked and unlocked positions.

nonkeyed Having no provision for key operation. Note: This term also includes privacy function locksets operated by an emergency key.

nonoriginal key blank Any key blank other than an original.

nonremovable pin A pin that cannot be removed from a hinge when the door is closed.

normally closed switch A switch whose contacts normally remain closed when electrical current isn't flowing through it.

normally open switch A switch whose contacts normally remain open when electrical current isn't flowing through it.

NSLA National Locksmith Suppliers Association.

odometer method A means of progressing key bittings using a progression sequence of right to left.

ohm A unit of measure of resistance to electrical current flow.

Ohm's Law The description of the relationship between voltage, current, and resistance in an electrical circuit. Ohm's Law states that a resistance of 1 ohm passes through a current of one ampere, in response to 1 volt. Mathematically expressed, $E = IR$, with E as voltage in volts, I as current in amperes, and R as resistance in ohms.

one-bitted Of or pertaining to a cylinder that is combinated to keys cut to the manufacturer's reference number one bitting.

one-column progression A process wherein key bittings are obtained by using the cut possibilities in one column of the bitting array.

one pin master key A master key for all combinations obtained by progressing only one bitting position.

operating key Any key that will properly operate a lock or cylinder to lock or unlock the lock mechanism, and is not a control key or reset key.

operating shear line Any shear line that allows normal operation of a cylinder or lock.

original key blank A key blank supplied by the lock manufacturer to fit that manufacturer's specific product.

padlock A detachable and portable lock with a shackle that locks into its case.

page master key The three-pin master key for all combinations listed on a page in the standard progression format.

panic bar A door-mounted exit bar designed to allow fast egress from the inside of the door and resistance to entry from the outside of the door.

paracentric Of or pertaining to a keyway with one or more wards on each side projecting beyond the vertical center line of the keyway to hinder picking.

parallel circuit An electrical circuit that provides more than one path for current to flow.

PASS-Key Personalized Automotive Security System. See VATS.

pass key A master key or skeleton key.

pattern key 1. A key kept on file to use in a key duplicating machine when additional keys are required. 2. Any key used in a key duplicating machine to create a duplicate key.

pawl A tailpiece or cam for an automobile door or deck lock.

peanut cylinder A mortise cylinder of ¾-inch diameter.

pick 1. A tool or instrument, other than the specifically designed key, made for the purpose of manipulating tumblers in a lock or cylinder into the locked or unlocked position through the keyway without obvious damage. 2. To manipulate tumblers in a keyed lock mechanism through the keyway without obvious damage, by means other than the specifically designed key.

pick key A type of manipulation key, cut or modified to operate a lock or cylinder.

pin To install pin tumblers into a cylinder and/or cylinder plug.

pin chamber The corresponding hole drilled into the cylinder shell and/or plug to accept the pin(s) and spring.

pin kit A type of keying kit for a pin tumbler mechanism.

pin stack All the tumblers in a given pin chamber.

pin stack height The measurement of a pin stack, often expressed in units of the lock manufacturer's increment or as an actual dimension.

pin tumbler Usually a cylindrical shaped tumbler. Three types are normally used: bottom pin, master pin, and top pin.

pin tweezers A tool used in handling tumblers and springs.

pinning block A holding fixture that assists in the loading of tumblers into a cylinder or cylinder plug.

pinning chart A numerical diagram that indicates the sizes and order of installation of the various pins into a cylinder. The sizes are usually indicated by a manufacturer's reference number, which equals the quantity of increments a tumbler represents.

plug The part of a cylinder containing the keyway, with tumbler chambers usually corresponding to those in the cylinder shell.

plug follower A tool used to allow removal of the cylinder plug while retaining the top pins, springs, and/or other components within the shell.

plug holder A holding fixture that assists in the loading of tumblers into a cylinder plug.

plug retainer The cylinder component that secures the plug in the shell.

plug spinner A tool designed to quickly spin a plug clockwise or counterclockwise into an unlocked position, when the lock has been picked, into a position that doesn't allow the lock to open.

positional master keying A method of master keying typical of certain binary type disc tumbler key-in-knob locks and of magnetic and dimple key cylinders. Of all possible tumbler positions within a cylinder, only a limited number contain active tumblers. The locations of these active tumblers are rotated among all possible positions to generate key changes. Higher level keys must have more cuts or magnets than lower level keys.

positive locking The condition brought about when a key cut that is too high forces its tumbler into the locking position. This type of locking does not rely on gravity or spring pressure.

post (of a key) The portion of a bit key between the tip and the shoulder to which the bit or bits are attached. **practical key changes** The total number of usable different combinations available for a specific cylinder or lock mechanism.

prep key A type of guard key for a safe deposit box lock with only one keyway. It must be turned once and withdrawn before the renter's key will unlock the unit.

privacy key A key that operates an SKD cylinder.

profile cylinder A cylinder with a uniform cross section that slides into place and is held by a mounting screw. It is typically used in mortise locks of non-U.S. manufacturers.

progress To select possible key bittings, usually in numerical order, from the key bitting array.

progression A logical sequence of selecting possible key bittings, usually in numerical order from the key bitting array.

progression column A listing of the key bitting possibilities available in one bitting position as displayed in a column of the key bitting array.

progression list A bitting list of change keys and master keys arranged in sequence of progression.

progressive Any bitting position that is progressed rather than held constant.

proprietary Of or pertaining to a keyway and key section assigned exclusively to one end user by the lock manufacturer. It may also be protected by law from duplication.

radiused blade bottom The bottom of a key blade that has been radiused to conform to the curvature of the cylinder plug it is designed to enter.

random master keying Any undesirable process of master keying that uses unrelated keys to create a system.

rap 1. To unlock a plug from its shell by striking sharp blows to the spring side of the cylinder while applying tension to the plug. 2. To unlock a padlock shackle from its case by striking sharp blows to the sides in order to disengage the locking dogs.

read key A key that allows access to the sales and/or customer data on certain types of cash control equipment, such as a cash register.

recombinate To change the combination of a lock, cylinder, or key.

recore To rekey by installing a different core.

register groove The reference point on the key blade from which some manufacturers locate the bitting depths.

register number 1. A reference number, typically assigned by the lock manufacturer to an entire master key system. 2. A blind code assigned by some lock manufacturers to higher level keys in a master key system.

rekey or re-key To change the existing combination of a cylinder or lock so that the lock can be operated by a different key.

relay A type of switching device, usually electronic or electro-mechanical.

removable core A key removable core that can only be installed in one type of cylinder housing—for example, rim cylinder or mortise cylinder or key-in-knob locks.

removable cylinder A cylinder that can be removed from a locking device by a key and/or tool.

removal key The part of a two-piece key that is used to remove its counterpart from a keyway.

renter's key A key that must be used together with a guard key, prep key, or electronic release to unlock a safe deposit lock. It is usually different for every unit within an installation.

repin To replace pin tumblers, with or without changing the existing combination.

reset key 1. A key used to set some types of cylinders to a new combination. Many of these cylinders require the additional use of tools and/or the new operating key to establish the new combination. 2. A key that allows the tabulations on various types of cash control equipment such as cash registers to be cleared from the records of the equipment.

resistance Opposition to electrical current flow.

resistor A component that resists electrical current flow in a dc circuit.

restricted Of or pertaining to a keyway and corresponding key blank whose sale and/or distribution is limited by the lock manufacturer in order to reduce unauthorized key proliferation.

retainer clip tool A tool designed to install or remove retainer clips from automobiles.

reversible key A symmetrical key that may be inserted either up or down to operate a lock.

reversible lock A lock in which the latchbolt can be turned over and adapted to doors of either hand, opening in or out.

rim cylinder A cylinder typically used with surface applied locks and attached with a back plate and machine screws. It has a tailpiece to actuate the lock mechanism.

RL Registered Locksmith (as certified by Associated Locksmiths of America).

RM Row master key.

root depth The dimension from the bottom of a cut on a key to the bottom of the blade.

rose A usually circular escutcheon.

rotary tumbler A circular tumbler with one or more gates. Rotation of the proper key aligns the tumbler gates at a sidebar, fence, or shackle slot.

rotating constant One or more cut(s) in a key of any level that remain constant throughout all levels and are identical to the top master key cuts in their corresponding positions. The positions where the top master key cuts are held constant may be moved, always in a logical sequence.

rotating constant method A method used to progress key bittings in a master key system, wherein at least one cut in each key is identical to the corresponding cut in the top master key. The identical cut is moved to different locations in a logical sequence until each possible planned position has been used.

row master key The one pin master key for all combinations listed on the same line across the page in the standard progression format.

RPL Registered Professional Locksmith, as certified by the International Association of Home Safety and Security Professionals.

S/A Sub-assembled.

SAVTA Safe and Vault Technicians Association.

scalp A thin piece of metal that is usually crimped or spun onto the front of a cylinder. It determines the cylinder's finish and may also serve as the plug retainer.

second generation duplicate A key reproduced from a first generation duplicate.

security collar A protective cylinder collar.

segmented follower A plug follower that is sliced into sections, which are introduced into the cylinder shell one at a time. It is typically used with profile cylinders.

selective key system A key system in which every key has the capacity of being a master key. It is normally used for applications requiring a limited number of keys and extensive cross keying.

selective master key An unassociated master key that can be made to operate any specific lock in the entire system, in addition to the regular master key and/or change key for the cylinder, without creating key interchange.

sequence of progression The order in which bitting positions are progressed to obtain change key combinations.

series circuit An electrical circuit that provides only one path for current flow.

series wafer A type of disc tumbler used in certain binary type disc tumbler key-in-knob locks. Its presence requires that no cut be made in that position on the operating key(s).

set-up key A key used to calibrate some types of key machines.

set-up plug A type of loading tool shaped like a plug follower. It contains pin chambers and is used with a shove knife to load springs and top pins into a cylinder shell.

seven-column progression A process wherein key bittings are obtained by using the cut possibilities in seven columns of the key bitting array.

seven-pin master key A master key for all combinations obtained by progressing seven bitting positions.

shackle The usually curved portion of a padlock that passes though a hasp and snaps into the padlock's body.

shackle spring The spring inside the body of a padlock that allows the shackle to pop out of the body when in the unlocked position.

shank The part of a bit key between the shoulder and the bow.

shear line A location in a cylinder at which specific tumbler surfaces must be aligned, removing obstruction(s) that prevent the plug from moving.

shell The part of the cylinder that surrounds the plug and that usually contains tumbler chambers corresponding to those in the plug.

shim 1. A thin piece of material used to unlock the cylinder plug from the shell by separating the pin tumblers at the shear line, one at a time. 2. To unlock a cylinder plug from its shell using a shim.

shoulder Any key stop other than a tip stop.

shouldered pin A bottom pin whose diameter is larger at the flat end to limit its penetration into a counter-bored chamber.

shove knife A tool used with a set-up plug that pushes the springs and pin tumblers into the cylinder shell.

shut-out key Usually used in hotel keying systems, a key that will make the lock inoperative to all other keys in the system, except the emergency master key, display key, and some types of shut-out keys.

shut-out mode The state of a hotel function lockset that prevents operation by all keys except the emergency master key, display key, and some types of shut-out keys.

sidebar A primary or secondary locking device in a cylinder. When locked, it extends along the plug beyond its circumference. It must enter gates in the tumblers in order to clear the shell and allow the plug to rotate.

simplex key section A single independent key section that cannot be used in a multiplex key section.

single-key section An individual key section that can be used in a multiplex key system.

single-step progression A progression using a one increment difference between bittings of a given position.

six-column progression A process wherein key bittings are obtained by using the cut possibilities in six columns of the key bitting array.

six pin master key A master key for all combinations obtained by progressing six bitting positions.

SKD Symbol for "single keyed," normally followed by a numerical designation in the standard key coding system—SKD1, SKD2, etc. It indicates that a cylinder or lock is not master keyed but is part of the keying system.

skeleton key A warded lock key cut especially thin to bypass the wards in several warded locks so the locks can be opened. The term is commonly used by laypersons to refer to any bit key.

spacing The dimensions from the stop to the center of the first cut and/or to the centers of successive cuts.

special application cylinder Any cylinder other than a mortise, rim, key-in-knob, or profile cylinder.

split pin master keying A method of master keying a pin tumbler cylinder by installing master pins into one or more pin chambers.

spool pin Usually a top pin that resembles a spool, typically used to increase pick resistance.

spring cover A device for sealing one or more pin chambers.

standard key coding system An industry standard and uniform method of designating all keys and/or cylinders in a master key system. The designation automatically indicates the exact function and keying level of each key and/or cylinder in the system, usually without further explanation.

standard progression format A systematic method of listing and relating all change key combinations in a master key system. The listing is divided into segments known as blocks, horizontal groups, vertical groups, rows, and pages, for levels of control.

step pin A spool or mushroom pin that has had a portion of its end machined to a smaller diameter than the opposite end. It is typically used as a top pin to improve pick resistance by some manufacturers of high-security cylinders.

stepped tumbler   A special (usually disc) tumbler used in master keying. It has multiple bearing surfaces for blades of different key sections.

stop (of a key)   The part of a key from which all cuts are indexed and which determines how far the key enters the keyway.

strike   See strike plate and strike box.

strike box or strike reinforcement   A strike plate that incorporates a metal or plastic box that encloses the lock's bolt or latch when in a locked position.

strike plate or strike, keeper   The part of a locking arrangement that receives the bolt, latch, or fastener, when the lock is in the locked position. The strike is usually recessed in a door frame.

sub-master key (SMK)   The master key level immediately below the master key in a system of six or more levels of keying.

switch   A device used for opening and closing a circuit.

tailpiece   An actuator attached to the rear of the cylinder, parallel to the plug, typically used on rim, key-in-knob, or special application cylinders.

tension wrench or turning tool, torque wrench, torsion wrench, turning wrench   A tool, usually made of spring steel, used in conjunction with a lock pick. While the pick is moving a lock's tumblers into a position that frees the plug to be rotated, the tension wrench places rotational force on the plug. Although "tension wrench" is older and more commonly used than any of its synonyms, a large minority of locksmiths think the term is technically inaccurate and shouldn't be used by locksmiths.

theoretical key changes   The total possible number of different combinations available for a specific cylinder or lock mechanism.

three-column progression   A process wherein key bittings are obtained by using the cut possibilities in three columns of the key bitting array.

three-pin master key   A master key for all combinations obtained by progressing three bitting positions.

thumb turn cylinder   A cylinder with a turn knob rather than a keyway and tumbler mechanism.

tip   The portion of the key that enters the keyway first.

tip stop   A type of stop located at or near the tip of the key.

tolerance   The deviation allowed from a given dimension.

top master key (TMK) The highest level master key in a master key system.

top of blade The bitted edge of a single bitted key.

top pin See driver.

torque wrench See tension wrench.

torsion wrench See tension wrench.

total position progression A process used to obtain key bittings in a master key system wherein bittings of change keys differ from those of the top master key in all bitting positions.

transformer A device that transfers electrical energy from one circuit to another without direct connection between them.

try-out key A manipulation key that is usually part of a set, used for a specific series, keyway, and/or brand of lock.

tubular key A key with a tubular blade. The key cuts are made into the end of the blade, around the circumference.

tubular key lock A type of lock with tumblers arranged in a circle, often used on vending machines and coin-operated washing machines.

tubular lock or key-in-knob lock, tubular key-in-knob lock A key-in-knob lock that has two screw posts, one on each side of the lock's central spindle.

tumbler A movable obstruction of varying size and configuration in a lock or cylinder that makes direct contact with the key or another tumbler, and prevents an incorrect key or torquing device from activating the lock or other mechanism.

tumbler spring Any spring that acts directly on a tumbler.

turning tool See tension wrench.

turning wrench See tension wrench.

two-column progression A process wherein key bittings are obtained by using the cut possibilities in two columns of the key bitting array.

two-pin master key A master key for all combinations obtained by progressing two bitting positions.

two-step progression A progression using a two increment difference between bittings of a given position.

UL Underwriters Laboratories.

unassociated change key A change key that is not related directly to a particular master key through the use of certain constant cuts.

unassociated master key A master key that does not have change keys related to its combination through the use of constant cuts.

uncombinated 1. Of or pertaining to a cylinder that is supplied without keys, tumblers, and springs. 2. Of or pertaining to a lock, cylinder, or key in which the combination has not been set.

uncontrolled cross keying A condition in which two or more different keys under different higher level keys operate one cylinder by design—for example: XAA1 operated by AB, AB1. Note: This condition severely limits the security of the cylinder and the maximum expansion of the system, and often leads to key interchange.

unidirectional cylinder A cylinder whose key can turn in only one direction from the key pull position, often not making a complete rotation.

upper pin See driver.

Vac ac volts.

VATS Vehicle Anti-Theft System.

VATS decoder A device designed for determining which VATS key blank to use to duplicate a VATS key or to make a VATS first key.

VATS key A key designed to operate a vehicle equipped with VATS.

Vdc dc volts.

vehicle anti-theft system An electromechanical system used in many General Motors vehicles to deter theft. Sometimes referred to as the PASSKey system.

vertical group master key (VGM) The two pin master key for all combinations listed in all blocks in a line down a page in the standard progression format.

visual key control (VKC) A specification that all keys and the visible portion of the front of all lock cylinders be stamped with standard keying symbols.

volt A unit of measure for voltage.

voltage The force that pushes electrical current. Voltage (or electromotive force) is measured in volts.

voltage drop The change in voltage across an electrical component (such as a resistor) in a circuit.

vom Volt-ohm-milliammeter. A type of multitester.

ward A usually stationary obstruction in a lock or cylinder that prevents the entry and/or operation of an incorrect key.

ward cut A modification of a key that allows it to bypass a ward.

warded lock A lock that relies primarily on wards to prevent unauthorized keys from operating the lock.

watt A unit of measure of electrical power.

X Symbol used in hardware schedules to indicate a cross-keyed condition for a particular cylinder—for example, XAA2, X1X (but not AX7).

zero bitted Of or pertaining to a cylinder that is combinated to keys cut to the manufacturer's reference number "0" bitting.

INDEX

Abus keys, depth and space guide, 473
access control integrated systems,
    375–410
  access control panel (ACP), 376–377
  alarm system integration with
      system, 384–388
  battery back-up supplies, 376
  card reader or keypad, 376, 378–384
  designing the system, 375–378,
      403–404
  electric strikes, 376–377
  elevator control, 401
  energy management systems, 402
  environmental control systems, 402
  fire alarm integrated with system,
      388–397, 402
  integrating all security systems,
      398–410
  liability, 426–432
  microprocessors in card readers, 379
  noise suppression devices, 377–378
  parking lot control systems, 402
  personal identification number (PIN)
      systems, 400
  programming card readers,
      380–382
  standalone card readers, 378–384
  tenant metering systems, 402
  time and attendance applications,
      403
  whole-building approach to design,
      404–410
access control panel (ACP), integrated
    access control systems, 376–377
Ace keys and locks, 12, 20

Adams Rite Manufacturing Co. electric
    strikes, 251–264, **260–271**
advertising your business, 424
Alarm Lock Model 715 exit device,
    213–217, **214**
Alarm Lock Models 250/250L/260/260L
    emergency exit doors, 202–204
Alarm Lock Models 700/700L/710/710L
    exit devices, 209–213, **212**
alarm system integration, integrated
    access control systems, 384–388
alarms, emergency exit doors, 187
alternating current (ac), 220, 222
American keys, 463
  depth and space guide, 474
American Motors Corporation (AMC)
    locks, 331, 333
American Society of Industrial
    Security (ASIS), 412
Amerock keys, depth and space guide,
    474
angularly bitted key, 17, 21 **22**
ANSI/BHMA finish numbers guide,
    481–485
Arco keys, 463
Arrow keys and locks, 10, **26**
  depth and space guide, 474–475
Associated Locksmiths of America
    (ALOA), 412
associations for locksmiths, 411–412
Audi locks, 334
automotive keys and locks, 329–358
  American Motors Corporation
      (AMC) locks, 331, 333
  Audi locks, 334

Note: Boldface numbers indicate illustrations.

automotive keys and locks (*Cont.*):
  BMW locks, 334
  broken key stuck in lock, 329
  Chrysler keys, Ilco Unican KD80 coding machine, 308
  Chrysler locks, 334–337, 339
  clip removal tool, 330, **330**, 331, **331**
  clips for door panels, 330
  Datsun locks, 337
  differences in automotive locks, 330–331
  door handle (automotive) clip remover, **78**
  Ford keys, Ilco Unican KD80 coding machine, 308–311
  Ford locks, 339–343
  GM decoder tool, **78**
  GM keys, Ilco Unican KD80 coding machine, 306–308
  GM locks, 343–353
  hard to turn keys, 330
  Honda locks, 338–339
  key coding machines, 303–327
  key won't work, 330
  Merkur keys, Ilco Unican KD80 coding machine, 311–312
  opening locked vehicles, 353–357, **355–358**
  opening tool, **76**
  Passive Anti-theft System (PATS) locks, Ford, 342–343
  Personalized Automotive Security System (PASSKey), GM, 346–348
  primary and secondary automotive keys, 331
  removing door panels, 330
  typical dimensions, **304**, 304
  Vehicle Anti-Theft System (VATS) locks, GM, 346–353, **353**
  vehicle identification numbers (VIN), 331, 332

ball-bearing butts, 173–174
barrel keys, 16, 18, 23, **25**
battery back-up supplies, integrated access control systems, 376
Best keys and locks, 10, 463
bezel nut wrench, **77**

biaxial cylinders, Medeco high-security, 128–129
bicycle locks, 10, **17**, 38
bit key locks, 10, 12
  cover plate, 46
  parts of, 46–47, **46**
  servicing tips, 47
  warded locks, 45
bit keys, 10, 16, 17, **20**, 23
blade or bit of key, 17
blank face or plain hinges, 172
BMW locks, 334
boat locks, keyways, 38
Borkey 954 Rexa 3/CD key duplicating machine, 280–282, **281**
Borkey 986 key duplicating machine, 276–280, **277**
Borkey 989 Top-Cut key code cutting machine, 322–327, **323**
bow of key, 17, 24–26
Briggs & Stratton keys, 463
broken-key extractors, 65, **66**
business of locksmithing, 1–8, 411–433
  advertising your business, 424
  associations for locksmiths, 411–412
  certifications, 412, 435
  contracts and employment agreements, 422
  demand for locksmiths, 1
  duplicating keys, laws concerning, 425–426
  earning potential, 1
  ethical code for locksmiths, 432–433
  in-house locksmiths, 7
  instructors of locksmithing, 7–8
  Internet web sites of interest, 493–494
  interviewing for a job, 419–422
  job search, 414–422
  lawsuits and liability, 426–432
  licensing, 413–414
  mobile shops, 5, **6**, 424
  number of locksmiths in U.S., 1
  on-call locksmithing, 7
  pricing your services, 424
  resume writing, 417–419
  scope of locksmithing, 2–3
  security organizations, 491–492
  security system design, 8
  security training programs, 449–452

business of locksmithing (*Cont.*):
  skills required, 3
  starting your own business, 5–6,
    422–425
  store-front shops, 5, **6**, 424–425
  telephones for locksmith business,
    423
  test for locksmith certification, 412,
    435–447
  tools, 423
  training and education, 3–5, 449–452
  vehicle for service calls, 424
  working for manufacturer/
    distributor, 7
  working in a shop, 6–7
butts, 171–172, **172**

cabinet locks, 10, 38
cameras, closed circuit TV, 360, **360,**
    361, 362
camper locks, keyways, 38
capacitors, 223
card reader or keypad, integrated
    access control systems, 376,
    378–384
certifications for locksmiths, 412, 435
change keys, **80,** 165
Chicago Ace Lock Company keys
    and locks, 20, 463
Chrysler keys, Ilco Unican KD80
    coding machine, 308
Chrysler locks, 334–337, 339
circuits, electrical, 220, **221,** 222
circular-hole cutter kit, **81**
classroom locks, 13
clear swing hinge, 173
clip removal tool, 330, **330,** 331, **331**
closed circuit TV (CCTV), 359–373
  alarms, 367–368
  autopan, 365–366
  cameras, 360, **360, 361, 362**
  housings, 360
  locations for system, 370–373
  mechanical quality, 369
  monitors, 360–361
  operating speeds, 363–365
  pan-and-tilt drives, 361–369
  panning, 363
  presets, 367–368

closed circuit TV (*Cont.*):
  random pan, 365–366
  range of motion, 363
  scanners, 362
  selecting the right system,
    370–373
  stepping motors, 362
  teleconferencing with pan-and-tilt
    drives, 369
  tilting motion, 365
  video recorders (VCRs), 361
Club, The, keyways, 38
code keys, 303–327
Cole National keys, 463–464
combination locks, 10
  pushbutton style, 137–149
concealed hinges, 174
conductors, 220
contracts and employment agreements,
    422
copier locks, keyways, 38
Corbin keys and locks, 10, 464, 465
cordless drills, 65, **66**
CorKey/CorKit high-security cylinder
    system, 113–119
  deadbolts, installation, 114–115, **115**
  key-in-knob lock, **115**
  Kwikset tubular deadbolts, 116–119,
    117–118
  Model 400K CorKit, **118**
  Model 485K CorKit, **118**
  operation, 115
  rim lock, **116**
corrugated keys, 16, 18–19, **21,** 24
cover plate, bit key lock, 46
Craftsman keys, depth and space
    guide, 475
crossbars, emergency exit doors,
    188–189
current, 220, 223–224, 255, 257
current limiters, 255–256
Curtis keys, 465–466
cylinder case, pin tumbler locks, 53
cylinder key mortise locks, 86, **102**
  changing lock handing, 109, **110–111**
  grip handle installation, 109–110, **111**
  installation, 100–111, **103–109**
cylinder keys, 16, 19, **21,** 24
cylinder removal tools, **73**

Datsun locks, 337
deadbolt locks, 10, **16**, 86, **99**
  CorKey/CorKit high-security
    cylinder, 114–115, **115**
  exploded view, **99**, **100**, **101**, **102**
  Kaba Gemini high-security cylinder,
    125, **127**
  parts list, 90–91
  tubular, CorKey/CorKit, 116–119,
    117–118
  warded locks, 46–47
deadlocks, **19**
deburring a new key, 275
depth and space charts, 473–480
desk locks, keyways, 38
Dexter keys and locks, 10, **26**, 466
  depth and space guide, 475
dial caliper, **71**
DiMark International, 276, 280, 322
dimple keys, 17, 21, **22**
  DOM IX KG high-security cylinder
    system, 119–121, **120–121**
direct current (dc), 220, 222
disassembling a lock, 47
disc grinder, **67**
disc tumbler locks, 12, 49–52, **50**,
  51, **52**
  masterkeying, 168
  parts, 49–52, **50**, **51**
  picking locks, 157
  plug, 52
  side bar wafer locks, 52
DOM IX KG high-security cylinder
  system, 119–121, **120–121**
  construction keys, 120
  split keys, 120–121, **121**
Dominion keys, 466–467
door handle (automotive)
  clip remover, **78**
doors and door hardware, 171–185
  Alarm Lock Model 715 exit device,
    213–217, **214**
  Alarm Lock Models
    250/250L/260/260L emergency
    exit doors, 202–204
  Alarm Lock Models
    700/700L/710/710L exit devices,
    209–213, **212**
  ball-bearing butts, 173–174

doors and door hardware (*Cont.*):
  blank face or plain hinges, 172
  butts, 171–172, **172**
  clear swing hinge, 173
  concealed hinges, 174
  door holders, 185, **185**
  door viewers, 185, **185**
  doorstops, **184**, 185
  double-acting hinges, 174, **174**
  drilling holes, 85, 101
  Electronic Exit Lock Model 265 exit
    device, 204–209, **205**, **206**
  emergency exit devices, 187–217, **188**
  Exitgard Models 35 and 70 emergency
    exit door, 200–202 **201**, **202**
  fast or rivet pins, 172
  finish numbers, ANSI/BHMA guide,
    481–485
  fire ratings, 194–195
  full-mortise butts, 172, **173**
  full-surface butts, 172
  gravity-pivot hinges, 174
  half-mortise butts, 172
  half-surface butts, 172, **173**
  handing of, 83, **84**
  hasps, 182, **184**
  high-security strike plates, 177–179,
    178
  hinges, 171–172, **172**
  Install-A-Lock door reinforcers,
    179–182, **180–183**
  J-U-5 replacement hinges, 174–177,
    175, **176**
  loose-pin butts, 173
  nontemplate hinges, 172
  Pilfergard Model PG-10 emergency
    exit door, 195–198, **196**, **197**, **198**
  Pilfergard Model PG-20 emergency
    exit door, 198–200, **199**
  pivot reinforced hinges, 174
  removable vs. nonremovable pins
    for hinges, 172
  rising butts, 173
  simple butts, 173
  spring-loaded hinges, 174, **174**
  template for hole drilling, **139**
  template hinges, 172
  Underwriters Laboratory (UL) tests,
    door strength, 190–194

doors and door hardware (*Cont.*):
    Uni-Force door reinforcer,
      181–182, **183**
door holders, 185, **185**
door reinforcers, **80**
door viewers, 185, **185**
doorstops, **184**, **185**
double-acting hinges, 174, **174**
drill rigs, **80**
drilling holes, 85, 101
    template for hole drilling, **139**
dummy plate, warded locks, 45
duplicating keys, laws concerning,
    425–426

Eagle keys, 467
Earle keys, 467
electric drill, 62–65, **63**, **64**
electric strike plates, 251–264, **252**,
    260–271
    Adams Rite Manufacturing Co.
      models, 251–264, **260–271**
    buzzing sound, 253, 255
    continuous locks, 253, 254
    continuous/reverse action locks, 253
    current checking, 257
    current draw, electrical use, 255
    current limiters, 255–256
    electrical considerations, 253–256
    fail-safe reverse action strikes, 253
    integrated access control systems,
      376–377
    intermittent locks, 253, 254
    line drop, 257
    overheating, 258–259
    schematics, **260–271**
    selection criteria, 251–252, **252**
    short circuits, 257–258
    strike inoperative after installation,
      258
    strike inoperative after use, 258
    surge current, 255
    transformers for low voltage,
      253–254
    troubleshooting, 256–259
    voltage checking, 256
    voltage sources, 254
    wiring, 254
electrical metallic tubing (EMT), 224

electricity for locksmiths, 219–224
    alternating current (ac), 220, 222
    capacitors, 223
    circuits, 220, **221**, 222
    conductors, 220
    controlling electricity, 222
    current, 220, 223–224, 255
    current checking, 257
    current limiters, 255–256
    direct current (dc), 220, 222
    electrical metallic tubing (EMT), 224
    insulation on wires, 224
    line drop, 257
    Ohm's law, 223–224
    polarity, 222
    positive and negative, 222
    resistance, 222
    resistors, 223
    running wires, 224
    safety, 224
    short circuits, 257–258
    surge current, 255
    switches, 220, **221**
    symbols used in electrical wiring,
      222
    transformers, 223, 253–254
    voltage, 222, 223–224
    voltage checking, 256
    voltage sources, 254
    wire gauge, 240–242
electromagnetic locks, 225–250
    aluminum frame glass doors, 232–234
    buzzing or humming noise, 246
    double doors, 234, 243–244, **244**, **245**
    electromagnet, 225
    electronic noise interference, 248–249
    emergency release, 245
    exterior gates, 236–239, **238**
    general electrical characteristics, 239
    in-swinging doors, position and
      installation, 231–232, 232
    indicator LEDs, 244–245
    installation kit, 227 **227**
    Magnalock L with indicator LED,
      244–245
    Magnalock Model 62 (Securitron),
      226–250, **227**
    Magnalock models, 249–250,
      249, **250**

electromagnetic locks (*Cont.*):
   magnet mounting, 229–231
   no magnetic attraction, 246
   out-swinging doors, position and
      installation, 227–228, **228**
   positioning the lock, 227–228, **228**
   power failure, 226
   reduced holding force, 246
   running wires, 226
   rusted locks, 248
   Senstat Magnalocks S and C, 242–243
   solid glass doors, 234, **235**
   split strike for double doors, 234
   standard locks, 240
   status reporting in error, 247
   status reporting, 243–244, **244**, **245**
   steel header filled with concrete,
      235–236
   strike plate mounting, 228–229
   strike plate, 225, **226**
   stuck lock, 247–248
   tamper-proofing, 239
   troubleshooting, 245–249
   wire gauge, 240–242
   wood frame doors, 235, **236**
Electronic Exit Lock Model 265 exit
   device, 204–209, **205**, **206**
elevator control, integrated access
   control systems, 401
emergency exit door devices,
   187–217, **188**
   Alarm Lock Model 715, 213–217, **214**
   Alarm Lock Models
      250/250L/260/260L exit doors,
      202–204
   Alarm Lock Models
      700/700L/710/710L exit devices,
      209–213
   alarms, 187
   axial load test, 192
   crossbars, 188–189
   cylinder test, 191
   Electronic Exit Lock Model 265 exit
      device, 204–209, **205**
   Exitgard Models 35 and 70 exit
      doors, 200–202, **201**, **202**
   fire ratings, 194–195
   force to latch door test, 191
   humidity test, 193

emergency exit door devices (*Cont.*):
   installation, 187, 195–198, 198–200,
      200–202
   locked outside knob torque test, 192
   locked outside thumbpiece test, 192
   outside knob or lever crush test,
      192–193
   outside rose and escutcheon dent
      test, 193
   outside rose and escutcheon
      deformation test, 193
   panic exit alarm, 209–213, **212**
   pencil hardness test, 193
   Pilfergard Model PG-10 emergency
      exit door, 195–198, **196**
   Pilfergard Model PG-20 exit door,
      198–200, **199**
   push test, 191
   pushbars, 188–189
   salt spray test, 193
   Tabor abrasion test, 193
   torque to retract latchbolt test, 191
   trim durability test, 191
   ultraviolet light and condensation
      test, 193
   Underwriters Laboratory (UL) tests,
      190–194
   unlocked outside knob or lever
      torque test, 191–192
   vertical load test, 192
emergency or on-call locksmithing, 7
energy management systems,
   integrated access control
   systems, 402
entrance locks, 13
environmental control systems,
   integrated access control
   systems, 402
ESP keys, 463–472
ethical code for locksmiths, 432–433
Exitgard Models 35 and 70 doors
   emergency exit door, 200–202,
   201, **202**

Falcon keys, depth and space guide,
   475–476
fast or rivet pins, 172
feel method, picking locks, 156
file cabinet locks, keyways, 39

files, **69**
finish numbers, ANSI/BHMA guide,
    481–485
fire alarm integrated with access
    control system, 388–397, 402
flat keys, 16, 18, **20**, 24, **25**
forced entry, 162–164
    drilling pin tumbler locks, 163
    high-security strike plates,
        177–179, **178**
    jimmying, 162–163
    loiding, 162
    padlocks, 163
    removing mortise cylinders, 163
Ford keys, Ilco Unican KD80 coding
    machine, 308–311
Ford locks, 339–343
Framon DBM-1 flat key duplicating
    machine, 283–285 **283**
Framon DC-300 duplicating code
    machine, 317–322, **317**
Framon Mfg. Co., Inc., 283, 317
freezer locks, keyways, 39
full-mortise butts, 172, **173**
full-surface butts, 172
function charts, locksets, 457–461
functions of locks, 13–14

garage door locks, keyways, 39
garage door opener locks, keyways, 39
gas cap locks, keyways, 39
gates, lever tumbler locks, 48
generic names for locks, keys, 10
GM decoder tool, **78**
GM keys, Ilco Unican KD80 coding
    machine, 306–308
GM locks, 343–353
gravity-pivot hinges, 174
gun locks, 10

half-mortise butts, 172
half-surface butts, 172, **173**
Half-Time key duplicating machine,
    273–276, **274**
hand tools, 61, **62**
hand-cutting keys, 37
handing:
    changing lock handing, 109, **110–111**
    door handing, 83, **84**

handlesets, 10
hard to turn keys, 101
Harloc keys, depth and space guide, 476
hasps, 182, **184**
Haughey, Kevin J., 404–410
Hazelton, key blanks, 30
high-security cylinders, 113–136
    CorKey/CorKit system, 113–119
    DOM IX KG system, 119–121,
        120–121
    high-security strike plates,
        177–179, **178**
    Kaba Gemini system, 121–125,
        122–127
    Medeco cylinders, 126–129, **127**, **128**
    Schlage Primus cylinders, 129–136,
        130–136
high-security strike plates, 177–179, **178**
hinges (*See also* doors and door
    hardware), handing of doors, 83,
    84, 171–172, **172**
Hoffman, Anthony A.J., 121
Hollymade keys, 30, 467
Honda locks, 338–339
Huber keys, 30
Hurd keys, 30–32, 467

Ilco Unican keys and locks, 10, **26**,
    467–469
    depth and space guide, 476–477
    key blanks, 32–36
Ilco Unican 018 Lever-Operated key
    duplicating machine, 293–301
Ilco Unican Corporation, 10, 285, 293,
    306, 314
Ilco Unican Exacta Code key cutter,
    314–317, **315**
Ilco Unican KD80 key coding machine,
    306–314, **306**
Ilco Unican Model .023 key
    duplicating machine,
    285–292, **286**
Illinois key blanks, 32
impressioning plate, **71**
in tumbler locks, 12
in-house locksmiths, 7
Install-A-Lock door reinforcer,
    179–182, **180–183**
    2000 series, 181

Install-A-Lock door reinforcer (*Cont.*):
  original series, 179–181
  Uni-Force door reinforcer,
      181–182, **183**
installation methods, 12
institution lock, 13
instructors of locksmithing, 7–8
insulation on wires, 224
integrated systems (*See* access control
      integrated systems)
interchange, keys, masterkey
      systems, 169
internal construction, 12–13
International Association of Home
      Safety and Security Professionals
      (IAHSSP), 412, 435
Internet advertising, want ads, 2
Internet web sites of interest, 493–494
interviewing for a job, 419–422

J-U-5 replacement hinges, 174–177,
      175, **176**
Jacobson, Jerry L., 361–369
jimmying a lock, 162–163
job search, 414–422
Juncunc keys, depth and
      space guide, 477

Kaba Gemini high-security cylinder
      systems, 121–125, **122–127**
  core cylinders, 125, **127**
  deadbolt locks, 125, **127**
  key-in-knob locks, 124–125, **126**
  padlocks, 125
Keil keys, 469
key blanks, directories, 23–41, 463–472
  barrel keys, 23, **24**
  bit keys, 23
  blank shapes, **29**
  bow of key, 24–26
  choosing the right blank, 23–28
  corrugated keys, 24
  cylinder keys, 24
  directory use, 28–29
  distinctive bow shapes by
      manufacturer, **26**
  flat keys, 24, **25**
  hand-cutting keys, 37
  identification marks on bow, 24–26

key blanks, directories (*Cont.*):
  keyway groove comparison, 26–27,
      27, 38–40
  manufacturer's identification codes,
      25–26, 29, 37
  smoking a key, 40–41
  tubular keys, 27–28, **28**
key coding machines, **72**, **77**, 303–327
  automotive key, typical
      dimensions, **304**
  Borkey 989 Top-Cut key code cutting
      machine, 322–327, **323**
  code charts, 305
  depth knob, 305, **305**
  duplicating keys, 312–313
  Framon DC-300 duplicating code
      machine, 317–322, **317**
  Ilco Unican Exacta Code key cutter,
      314–317, **315**
  Ilco Unican KD80, 306–314, **306**
  maintaining cutters, 313–314
  spacing and depth of cuts, 304
  spacing plates, 304
  theory of code key cutting, 303–305
key duplicating machine, **71**, 273–301
  adjustments, calibrations, 277
  Borkey 954 Rexa 3/CD, 280–282, **281**
  Borkey 986, 276–280, **277**
  deburring a new key, 275
  Framon DBM-1 flat key machine,
      283–285, **283**
  Half-Time key machine, 273–276, **274**
  Ilco Unican 018 Lever-Operated,
      293–301
  Ilco Unican Model .023, 285–292, **286**
  new keys that don't work, 276
  selecting the right machine, 274
  sharpening blades, 276
  troubleshooting, 276
key interchange, 169
key-in-knob lock, 10, 12, **12**, **13**, 54,
      84–86, **85**, **86**
  CorKey/CorKit high-security
      cylinder system, **115**
  exploded views, **95–98**
  installation, 84–86
  Kaba Gemini high-security cylinder,
      124–125, **126**
  parts names/parts numbers, 87–89

key-in-knob lock (*Cont.*):
  servicing, 86, **86**, **89–98**
key types, 10, 14–22
keyway grooves, 19, 26–27, **27**, 38–40
Kwikset keys and locks, 10, **26**, 469
  depth and space guide, 477–478

lawsuits and liability, 426–432
lever locks, 10, 12, **14**
lever tumbler locks, 12, 18, 47–49, **48**
  gates, 48
  masterkeying, 168
  operation, 48–49
  parts, 48, **48**
  picking locks, 157
  servicing tips, 49
  traps, 48
licensing, 413–414
line drop, 257
lock cylinders, 113
lock pick set, **72**
lock picking (*See* picking locks)
lock-picking gun, 157–158
lockset function charts, 457–461
Lockwood keys, 469
loiding a lock, 162
loose-pin butts, 173
Lori Corporation, 121
Lori keys, 469
luggage locks, 10, 18, 40
Lustre Line keys, depth and space
  guide, 478

M.A.G. Eng. & Mfg., Inc., 177
Magnalock electromagnetic locks,
  249–250, **249**, **250**
Magnalock Model 62 (Securitron),
  226–250, **227**
mail box locks, keyways, 39–40
manufacturer brand names, 10
manufacturer's identification codes,
  25–26, 29, 37
manufacturers, suppliers, 487–489
masonry bits for drill, **67**
master keys, 165
Master keys and locks, 10, 25,
  469–470, 478–479
masterkeying, 165–170
  change keys, 165

masterkeying (*Cont.*):
  disc tumbler locks, 168
  key interchange, 169
  lever tumbler locks, 168
  master keys, 165
  multilevel masterkeyed system,
    166, **167**
  pin tumbler locks, 168–170, **170**
  sectional keys, 168, **169**
  skeleton keys, 165
  warded locks, 166
Medeco high-security cylinders,
  126–129, **127**, **128**
  biaxial cylinders, 128–129
Medeco locks, 10
Medeco Security Locks Inc., 21
Merkur keys, Ilco Unican KD80 coding
  machine, 311–312
mobile shops, 5, **6**
monitors, closed circuit TV, 360–361
Moore, Wayne D., 394–397
moped locks, keyways, 40
mortise bit key lock, warded locks, 45
mortise lock, 12, **19**, **20**
  cylinder removal, forced entry, 163
multilevel masterkeyed system,
  166, **167**

National keys, 470
Nelson, Stephen F., 398
noise suppression devices, integrated
  access control systems, 377–378
nontemplate hinges, 172

Ohm's law, 223–224
on-call locksmithing, 7
opening locked vehicles, 353–357,
  355–358
owning your own locksmithing shop,
  5–6

padlocks, 10, **11**, 16
  cutting hasp, forced entry, 163–164
  Kaba Gemini high-security
    cylinder, 125
  warded locks, 44, **45**
pan-and-tilt drives, closed circuit TV,
  361–369
panic exit alarm, 209–213, **212**

parking lot control systems, integrated access control systems, 402

Passive Anti-theft System (PATS) locks, Ford, 342–343

patio door locks, 10, **18**

personal identification number (PIN) systems, integrated access control systems, 400

Personalized Automotive Security System (PASSKey), GM, 346–350

picking locks, 152–159
  disc tumbler locks, 157
  feel method, 156
  lever tumbler locks, 157
  lock-picking gun, 157–158
  pin tumbler locks, 152–156, **153–155**
  rake method, 156–157
  tools, 152
  See also forced entry

picks, **72**

Pierce, Charlie, 370

Pilfergard Model PG-10 emergency exit door, 195–198, **196, 197, 198**

Pilfergard Model PG-20 emergency exit door, 198–200, **199**

pin chambers, pin tumbler locks, 53

pin tray, **73**

pin tumbler cylinder lock, 12

pin tumbler locks, 12, 19, 53–60, **54–60**
  cylinder case, 53
  drilling, forced entry, 163
  impressioning keys, 160–161
  masterkeying, 168–170, **170**
  operation, 55
  parts, 53, **54**
  picking locks, 152–156, **153–155**
  pin chambers, 53
  plug, 53
  rekeying a lock, 56–59, **56–59**
  removing broken keys, 55–56, **56, 57**
  repairs, 55–59
  shear line, 55, **55**
  stack, 53
  top pin replacement, 59, **60**
  tubular key locks, 59–60

pins, warded locks, 45

pivot reinforced hinges, 174

plug:
  disc tumbler locks, 52
  pin tumbler locks, 53

plug followers, 65–66, **67**

plug holder, 66, **67**

plug spinner, **74**

polarity, 222

Precision Products Inc., 273

pricing your services, 424

pushbars, emergency exit doors, 188–189

pushbutton combination locks, 137–149
  installation, 138–146, **138–146**
  lock housing assembly, Simplex 3000, 146–147
  mounting lock to stile, Simplex 3000, 148–150
  reversing lock location, 146, **146**
  Simplex Series 3000, 146–150, **146–150**
  Simplex Unican 1000 Series, 138–146, **138–146**
  template for hole drilling, **139**
  thicker profile doors, installation, 145
  thinner profile doors, installation, 144–145, **145**

rake method, picking locks, 156–157

rekeying a lock, pin tumbler locks, 56–59, **56–59**

removable vs. nonremovable pins for hinges, 172

removing broken keys
  broken-key extractors, 65, **66**
  pin tumbler locks, 55–56, **56, 57**

resistance, 222

resistors, 223

resume writing, 417–419

rim bit key lock, **18**
  warded locks, 45, **45**

rim locks, 12, **19**
  CorKey/CorKit high-security cylinder, **116**

rising butts, 173

Rolfe, Ashley, 188

Russwin keys and locks, 10, 470

safe deposit boxes, 18

Safe keys, 470

safes, change keys, **80**
safety, 224
Sargent keys and locks, 10, 470
scanners, closed circuit TV, 362
scar plates, 101
Schlage keys and locks, 10, 19, **26**, 84, 470
   key blanks, 25
Schlage Lock Company, 84
Schlage Primus high-security cylinders, 129–136, **130–136**
   assembly, 131–133, **131–136**
   key control, 129
screen door locks, keyways, 40
sectional keys, 168, **169**
Securitron Magnalocks, 226–250 **227**
security organizations, 491–492
security systems, designing security products, 8
security systems (*See also* access control integrated systems), 2, **3**
security training programs, 449–452
Segal keys, **26**, 470
Senstat Magnalocks S and C, 242–243
shear line, pin tumbler locks, 55, **55**
shim holder, **74**
shims, **74**
short circuits, 257–258
shoulder of key, 19
side bar locks, 12
side bar wafer locks, 52
Silverman, Lionel, 384–388
simple butts, 173
Simplex Access Controls Corporation, 137
Simplex Series 3000 pushbutton combination locks, 146–150, **146–150**
Simplex Unican 1000 Series pushbutton combination lock, 138–146, **138–146**
skeleton keys, 17, 165
ski locks, 10, 17
Skillman keys, 470
skills required by locksmith, 3
smoking a key, 40–41
split keys, DOM IX KG high-security cylinder, 120–121, **121**
spring-loaded hinges, 174, **174**

sprinkler locks, keyways, 40
stack, pin tumbler locks, 53
standalone card readers, integrated access control systems, 378–384
Star keys, 30–36, 470–471
starting your own business, 422–425
steering wheel locks, keyways, 38–39
stepping motors, closed circuit TV, 362
stop of key, 17
stop plate, warded locks, 45
store-front shops, 5, **6**, 424–425
Strike 3 high-security strike plates, 177–179, **178**
strike plates:
   electric strikes, 251–264, **252**, 260–271
   electromagnetic, 225, **226**
   high-security strike plates, 177–179, **178**
suitcases (*See* luggage locks)
Suneborn, Lars R., 375–378
suppliers, manufacturers, 487–489
surge current, 255
Swiecicki, Michael, 388–394
switches, 220, **221**
symbols used in electrical wiring, 222

Taylor keys, 471–472
teleconferencing with pan-and-tilt drives, closed circuit TV, 369
template for hole drilling, **139**
template hinges, 172
tenant metering systems, integrated access control systems, 402
tension wrenches, **72**, **74**
test for locksmith certification, 412, 435–447
throat cuts of key, 17
time and attendance systems, integrated access control systems, 403
tool box locks, keyways, 40
tools for locksmithing, 61–81
   clip removal tool, 330, **330**, 331, **331**
   lock-picking gun, 157–158
   picking locks, 152
   bezel nut wrench, **77**
   broken-key extractors, 65, **66**
   change keys, **80**
   circular-hole cutter kit, **81**

tools for locksmithing (*Cont.*):
  cordless drills, **65, 66**
  cylinder removal tools, **73**
  dial caliper, **71**
  disc grinder, **67**
  door handle (automotive) clip
    remover, **78**
  door reinforcers, **80**
  drill rigs, **80**
  electric drill, 62–65, **63, 64**
  files, **69**
  GM decoder tool **78**
  hand tools, 61, **62**
  impressioning plate, **71**
  key code machine, **77, 72**
  key duplicating machine, **71**
  list of common tools, 66, 68–70, 76,
    79, 81
  lock pick set, **72**
  masonry bits for drill, **67**
  picks, **72**
  pin tray, **73**
  plug followers, 65–66, **67**
  plug holder, 66, **67**
  plug spinner, **74**
  quality of tools, 61
  shim holder, **74**
  shims, **74**
  tension wrenches, **72, 74**
  torque wrenches **74**
  tubular key decoder, **75**
  tubular key lock pick, **75**
  tubular key lock saw, **75**
  tweezers, **73**
  VATS/PASSKey Analyzer, **78**
  vehicle lock pick, **76**
  wedges, **79**
top pin replacement, pin tumbler
  locks, 59, **60**
torque wrenches, **74**
Toye, Bud, 378–384
training and education, 3–5, 449–452
transformers, 223, 253–254
traps, lever tumbler locks, 48
tubular key, 16–17, 10, 19, **21**, 27–28, **28**
tubular key decoder, **75**
tubular key lock, 10, **18, 21**, 59–60
tubular key lock pick, **75**
tubular key lock saw, **75**

tubular key locks, 10, **18**, 59–60
tumbler cuts of key, 17
tumbler springs, warded locks, 47
tweezers, **73**

Uni-Force door reinforcer, 181–182, **183**

VATS/PASSKey Analyzer, **78**
Vehicle Anti-Theft System (VATS)
  locks, GM, 346–350, **353, 354**
vehicle identification numbers (VIN),
  331, 332
vending machine locks, 12, 19
vestibule locks, 13
video recorders (VCRs), closed circuit
  TV, 361
voltage, 222, 223–224
voltage checking, 256
voltage sources, 254

wafer tumbler locks (*See also* disc
    tumbler locks), 12
ward cuts of key, 17
ward plate, warded locks, 45
warded lock, 12, 43–47, **44–46**
  bit key locks, 45
  deadbolt, 46–47
  dummy plate, 45
  impressioning keys, 159–160
  masterkeying, 166
  mortise bit key lock, 45
  padlocks, 44, **45**
  parts of warded lock, 44–45
  pins, 45
  rim bit key lock, 45, **45**
  servicing tips, 47
  stop plate, 45
  tumbler springs, 47
  ward plate, 45
  wards within a lock, 43–44
wards within a lock, 43–44
wedges, **79**
Weiser keys and locks, 10, **26**, 472, 479
Weslock keys, **26**, 472
wire gauge, 240–242
working for manufacturer/distributor, 7

Yale keys and locks, 10, **26**, 472,
  479–480

ABOUT THE AUTHOR

Bill Phillips is president of the International Association of Home Safety and Security Professionals, and author of nine security related books, including McGraw-Hill's *The Complete Book of Locks and Locksmithing*, 4th Edition. He is also the author of the Lock article in the *World Book Encyclopedia*. His security articles have appeared in *Consumers Digest*, *Crime Beat*, *Home Mechanix* (former Security editor), *Keynotes* (trade journal of the Associated Locksmiths of America), *Locksmith Ledger International* (former contributing editor), *The Los Angeles Times*, *Safe & Vault Technology* (former contributing editor), *Security Dealer*, *Special Report*, and other periodicals.

Bill has worked throughout the United States as a locksmith, safe technician, and alarm systems installer. He's now a security consultant and freelance writer based in Erie, Pennsylvania. He enjoys teaching martial arts and speaking to groups about home, auto and personal security.

ABOUT THE CONTRIBUTORS

Wayne D. Moore is vice president of Engineering for MBS Fire
Technology Inc. in Stockbridge, Georgia; founder and president of the Fire Protection Alliance, a North Reading, Massachusetts, fire protection consulting and engineering firm;
chairman of the NFPA technical committee on Protected
Premises Fire Alarm Systems; editor of the 1993 edition of the
National Fire Alarm Code Handbook; and co-editor of the
national newsletter, *The Moore-Wilson Signaling Report*. He
is a graduate engineer with over 20 years of experience in the
fire detection systems field.

Jerry L. Jacobson, Ph.D. is manager of Corporate Communications for Vicon Industries.

Stephen F. Nelson is manager of Worldwide Building Security, Home and Building Control Division, Honeywell, Inc. in
Minneapolis, Minnesota.

Charlie Pierce is president of L.R.C. Electronics Company
and L.T.C. Training Company in Davenport, Iowa. He is also
the author of many articles on various aspects of CCTV.

Ashely R. Rolfe is group vice president of Newman Tonks,
Inc. in Shepherdsville, Kentucky.

Michael Swiecicki is the national educational accounts
manager for Simplex Time Recorder Company in Garner,
Massachusetts. He has over 20 years of experience in engineering, providing and implementing fire alarm, clock and
program, security and communications systems.

Charles A. Sennewald, CMC, CPP is president of Charles
A. Sennewald & Associates, a security firm in Escondido,

California. He specializes in consulting with corporate management and the legal profession and is the author of several security-related publications. Mr. Sennewald is a former Deputy Sheriff (Los Angeles County), former Director of Security for The Broadway Department Stores (52 major stores in four states), and founder and former president of the International Association of Professional Security Consultants.

Lionel Silverman, PE is vice president of engineered systems for FACT Protective Services Corp. in Tampa, Florida. He has worked in the access control field for over 17 years in the United States and South Africa.

Lars R. Suneborn is National Training Manager for Hirsch Electronics Corporation in Irvine, California.

Frederick D. "Bud" Toye is president of Toye Corporation in Chatsworth, California. He is a member of the ASIS Quarter Century Club.